41.85

Dynamic HTML

Dynamic HTML

Shelley Powers

IDG Books Worldwide, Inc.
An International Data Group Company

Foster City, CA ◆ Chicago, IL ◆ Indianapolis, IN ◆ Southlake, TX

IDG
BOOKS
WORLDWIDE

Dynamic HTML

Published by
IDG Books Worldwide, Inc.
An International Data Group Company
919 E. Hillsdale Blvd., Suite 400
Foster City, CA 94404
www.idgbooks.com (IDG Books Worldwide Web site)

Library of Congress Catalog Card No.: 97-74809

ISBN: 0-7645-8053-1

Printed in the United States of America

10 9 8 7 6 5 4 3 2 1

1B/QY/QR/ZY/FC

Distributed in the United States by IDG Books Worldwide, Inc.
Distributed by Macmillan Canada for Canada; by Transworld Publishers Limited in the United Kingdom; by IDG Norge Books for Norway; by IDG Sweden Books for Sweden; by Woodslane Pty. Ltd. for Australia; by Woodslane Enterprises Ltd. for New Zealand; by Longman Singapore Publishers Ltd. for Singapore, Malaysia, Thailand, and Indonesia; by Simron Pty. Ltd. for South Africa; by Toppan Company Ltd. for Japan; by Distribuidora Cuspide for Argentina; by Livraria Cultura for Brazil; by Ediciencia S.A. for Ecuador; by Addison-Wesley Publishing Company for Korea; by Ediciones ZETA S.C.R. Ltda. for Peru; by WS Computer Publishing Corporation, Inc., for the Philippines; by Unalis Corporation for Taiwan; by Contemporanea de Ediciones for Venezuela; by Computer Book & Magazine Store for Puerto Rico; by Express Computer Distributors for the Caribbean and West Indies. Authorized Sales Agent: Anthony Rudkin Associates for the Middle East and North Africa.

For general information on IDG Books Worldwide's books in the U.S., please call our Consumer Customer Service department at 800-762-2974. For reseller information, including discounts and premium sales, please call our Reseller Customer Service department at 800-434-3422.

For information on where to purchase IDG Books Worldwide's books outside the U.S., please contact our International Sales department at 415-655-3200 or fax 415-655-3295.

For information on foreign language translations, please contact our Foreign & Subsidiary Rights department at 415-655-3021 or fax 415-655-3281.

For sales inquiries and special prices for bulk quantities, please contact our Sales department at 415-655-3200 or write to the address above.

For information on using IDG Books Worldwide's books in the classroom or for ordering examination copies, please contact our Educational Sales department at 800-434-2086 or fax 817-251-8174.

For press review copies, author interviews, or other publicity information, please contact our Public Relations department at 415-655-3000 or fax 415-655-3299.

For authorization to photocopy items for corporate, personal, or educational use, please contact Copyright Clearance Center, 222 Rosewood Drive, Danvers, MA 01923, or fax 508-750-4470.

is a trademark under exclusive license to IDG Books Worldwide, Inc., from International Data Group, Inc.

ABOUT IDG BOOKS WORLDWIDE

Welcome to the world of IDG Books Worldwide.

IDG Books Worldwide, Inc., is a subsidiary of International Data Group, the world's largest publisher of computer-related information and the leading global provider of information services on information technology. IDG was founded more than 25 years ago and now employs more than 8,500 people worldwide. IDG publishes more than 275 computer publications in over 75 countries (see listing below). More than 60 million people read one or more IDG publications each month.

Launched in 1990, IDG Books Worldwide is today the #1 publisher of best-selling computer books in the United States. We are proud to have received eight awards from the Computer Press Association in recognition of editorial excellence and three from *Computer Currents'* First Annual Readers' Choice Awards. Our best-selling ...*For Dummies*® series has more than 30 million copies in print with translations in 30 languages. IDG Books Worldwide, through a joint venture with IDG's Hi-Tech Beijing, became the first U.S. publisher to publish a computer book in the People's Republic of China. In record time, IDG Books Worldwide has become the first choice for millions of readers around the world who want to learn how to better manage their businesses.

Our mission is simple: Every one of our books is designed to bring extra value and skill-building instructions to the reader. Our books are written by experts who understand and care about our readers. The knowledge base of our editorial staff comes from years of experience in publishing, education, and journalism — experience we use to produce books for the '90s. In short, we care about books, so we attract the best people. We devote special attention to details such as audience, interior design, use of icons, and illustrations. And because we use an efficient process of authoring, editing, and desktop publishing our books electronically, we can spend more time ensuring superior content and spend less time on the technicalities of making books.

You can count on our commitment to deliver high-quality books at competitive prices on topics you want to read about. At IDG Books Worldwide, we continue in the IDG tradition of delivering quality for more than 25 years. You'll find no better book on a subject than one from IDG Books Worldwide.

John Kilcullen
CEO
IDG Books Worldwide, Inc.

Steven Berkowitz
President and Publisher
IDG Books Worldwide, Inc.

Eighth Annual Computer Press Awards 1992

Ninth Annual Computer Press Awards 1993

Tenth Annual Computer Press Awards 1994

Eleventh Annual Computer Press Awards 1995

IDG Books Worldwide, Inc., is a subsidiary of International Data Group, the world's largest publisher of computer-related information and the leading global provider of information services on information technology. International Data Group publishes over 275 computer publications in over 75 countries. Sixty million people read one or more International Data Group publications each month. International Data Group's publications include: **ARGENTINA:** Buyer's Guide, Computerworld Argentina, PC World Argentina; **AUSTRALIA:** Australian Macworld, Australian PC World, Australian Reseller News, Computerworld, IT Casebook, Network World, Publish, Webmaster; **AUSTRIA:** Computerwelt Osterreich, Networks Austria, PC Tip Austria; **BANGLADESH:** PC World Bangladesh; **BELARUS:** PC World Belarus; **BELGIUM:** Data News; **BRAZIL:** Annuário de Informática, Computerworld, Connections, Macworld, PC Player, PC World, Publish, Reseller News, Supergamepower; **BULGARIA:** Computerworld Bulgaria, Network World Bulgaria, PC & MacWorld Bulgaria; **CANADA:** CIO Canada, Client/Server World, ComputerWorld Canada, InfoWorld Canada, NetworkWorld Canada, WebWorld; **CHILE:** Computerworld Chile, PC World Chile; **COLOMBIA:** Computerworld Colombia, PC World Colombia; **COSTA RICA:** PC World Centro America; **THE CZECH AND SLOVAK REPUBLICS:** Computerworld Czechoslovakia, Macworld Czech Republic, PC World Czechoslovakia; **DENMARK:** Communications World Danmark, Computerworld Danmark, Macworld Danmark, PC World Danmark, Techworld Denmark; **DOMINICAN REPUBLIC:** PC World Republica Dominicana; **ECUADOR:** PC World Ecuador; **EGYPT:** Computerworld Middle East, PC World Middle East; **EL SALVADOR:** PC World Centro America; **FINLAND:** MikroPC, Tietoverkko, Tietoviikko; **FRANCE:** Distributique, Hebdo, Info PC, Le Monde Informatique, Macworld, Reseaux & Telecoms, WebMaster France; **GERMANY:** Computer Partner, Computerwoche, Computerwoche Extra, Computerwoche FOCUS, Global Online, Macwelt, PC Welt; **GREECE:** Amiga Computing, GamePro Greece, Multimedia World; **GUATEMALA:** PC World Centro America; **HONDURAS:** PC World Centro America; **HONG KONG:** Computerworld Hong Kong, PC World Hong Kong, Publish in Asia; **HUNGARY:** ABCD CD-ROM, Computerworld Szamitastechnika, Internetto online Magazine, PC World Hungary, PC-X Magazin Hungary; **ICELAND:** Tolvuheimur PC World Island; **INDIA:** Information Communications World, Information Systems Computerworld, PC World India, Publish in Asia; **INDONESIA:** InfoKomputer PC World, Komputek Computerworld, Publish in Asia; **IRELAND:** ComputerScope, PC Live!; **ISRAEL:** Macworld Israel, People & Computers/Computerworld; **ITALY:** Computerworld Italia, Macworld Italia, Networking Italia, PC World Italia; **JAPAN:** DTP World, Macworld Japan, Nikkei Personal Computing, OS/2 World Japan, SunWorld Japan, Windows NT World, Windows World Japan; **KENYA:** PC World East African; **KOREA:** Hi-Tech Information, Macworld Korea, PC World Korea; **MACEDONIA:** PC World Macedonia; **MALAYSIA:** Computerworld Malaysia, PC World Malaysia, Publish in Asia; **MALTA:** PC World Malta; **MEXICO:** Computerworld Mexico, PC World Mexico; **MYANMAR:** PC World Myanmar; **NETHERLANDS:** Computer! Totaal, LAN Internetworking Magazine, LAN World Buyers Guide, Macworld Netherlands, Net, WebWereld; **NEW ZEALAND:** Absolute Beginners Guide and Plain & Simple Series, Computer Buyer, Computer Industry Directory, Computerworld New Zealand, MTB, Network World, PC World New Zealand; **NICARAGUA:** PC World Centro America; **NORWAY:** Computerworld Norge, CW Rapport, Datamagasinet, Financial Rapport, Kursguide Norge, Macworld Norge, Multimediaworld Norge, PC World Ekspress Norge, PC World Nettverk, PC World Norge, PC World ProduktGuide Norge; **PAKISTAN:** Computerworld Pakistan; **PANAMA:** PC World Panama; **PEOPLE'S REPUBLIC OF CHINA:** China Computer Users, China Computerworld, China InfoWorld, China Telecom World Weekly, Computer & Communication, Electronic Design China, Electronics Today, Electronics Weekly, Game Software, PC World China, Popular Computer Week, Software Weekly, Software World, Telecom World; **PERU:** Computerworld Peru, PC World Profesional Peru, PC World SoHo Peru; **PHILIPPINES:** Click!, Computerworld Philippines, PC World Philippines, Publish in Asia; **POLAND:** Computerworld Poland, Computerworld Special Report Poland, Cyber, Macworld Poland, Networld Poland, PC World Komputer; **PORTUGAL:** Cerebro/PC World, Computerworld/Correio Informático, Dealer World Portugal, Mac*In/PC*In Portugal, Multimedia World; **PUERTO RICO:** PC World Puerto Rico; **ROMANIA:** Computerworld Romania, PC World Romania, Telecom Romania; **RUSSIA:** Computerworld Russia, Mir PK, Publish, Seti; **SINGAPORE:** Computerworld Singapore, PC World Singapore, Publish in Asia; **SLOVENIA:** Monitor; **SOUTH AFRICA:** Computing SA, Network World SA, Software World SA; **SPAIN:** Communicaciones World España, Computerworld España, Dealer World España, Macworld España, PC World España; **SRI LANKA:** Infolink PC World; **SWEDEN:** CAP&Design, Computer Sweden, Corporate Computing Sweden, Internetworld Sweden, it.branschen, Macworld Sweden, MaxiData Sweden, MikroDatorn, Natverk & Kommunikation, PC World Sweden, PCaktiv, Windows World Sweden; **SWITZERLAND:** Computerworld Schweiz, Macworld Schweiz, PCtip; **TAIWAN:** Computerworld Taiwan, Macworld Taiwan, NEW ViSiON/Publish, PC World Taiwan, Windows World Taiwan; **THAILAND:** Publish in Asia, Thai Computerworld; **TURKEY:** Computerworld Turkiye, Macworld Turkiye, Network World Turkiye, PC World Turkiye; **UKRAINE:** Computerworld Kiev, Multimedia World Ukraine, PC World Ukraine; **UNITED KINGDOM:** Acorn User UK, Amiga Action UK, Amiga Computing UK, Apple Talk UK, Computing, Macworld, Parents and Computers UK, PC Advisor, PC Home, PSX Pro, The WEB; **UNITED STATES:** Cable in the Classroom, CIO Magazine, Computerworld, DOS World, Federal Computer Week, GamePro Magazine, InfoWorld, I-Way, Macworld, Network World, PC Games, PC World, Publish, Video Event, THE WEB Magazine, and WebMaster; online webzines: JavaWorld, NetscapeWorld, and SunWorld Online; **URUGUAY:** InfoWorld Uruguay; **VENEZUELA:** Computerworld Venezuela, PC World Venezuela; and **VIETNAM:** PC World Vietnam. 3/24/97

Credits

ACQUISITIONS EDITOR
John Osborn

DEVELOPMENT EDITOR
Ellen L. Dendy

TECHNICAL EDITORS
Mark McManus
David Medinets

COPY EDITOR
Michael D. Welch

PRODUCTION COORDINATOR
Susan Parini

BOOK DESIGNER
Jim Donohue

GRAPHICS AND PRODUCTION
SPECIALISTS
Mario F. Amador
Shannon Miller
Maureen Moore
Dina F Quan
Elsie Yim

QUALITY CONTROL SPECIALIST
Mick Arellano

PROOFREADER
Mary C. Barnack

INDEXER
Ty Koontz

About the Author

Shelley Powers is a Web application consultant and has authored or contributed to books on Java, HTML, and other Web development languages. Powers has written for *NetscapeWorld* and other Web publications, and is a speaker on Web technology, most recently at the Internet World conference in New York.

As always, to Robert, and the best little cat in the world, Zoe. I also want to dedicate this book to some favorite young people of my acquaintance, my nieces MacKenzie and Alyse, and my nephew Justin.

Preface

DYNAMIC HTML IS THE great new wave of Web page programming. It lets you create engaging, interactive Web pages that require fewer downloads and returns to the server. Unfortunately, this exciting technology has made *cross-browser* Web page creation harder. Because most Web page authors need to create content for both Microsoft's Internet Explorer and Netscape's Navigator, this book takes a cross-browser approach. Using what you learn from this book, you can create interactive, dynamic Web pages that work with both browsers — and you can catch the DHTML wave.

 Because this book focuses on cross-browser compatibility and creating cross-browser effects, it does not cover Microsoft's data binding or DirectAnimation technologies.

Who This Book Is For

If you have experience creating Web page applications and using client-side scripting for one or both of the browsers, *Dynamic HTML* is for you. You don't have to have any experience with dynamic HTML, or with CSS1 (Cascading Style Sheets), the Web-presentation standard associated with dynamic HTML. However, you do need to be familiar with scripting languages and HTML.

How This Book Is Organized

This book is divided into four main parts. The first part presents an overview of CSS1 and the scripting languages used to write dynamic HTML: Microsoft's VBScript and Netscape's JavaScript. The second and third parts cover dynamic HTML as specified by Microsoft and Netscape, respectively. While the companies differ at times in their implementations of dynamic HTML, chapters in these two parts are organized in a similar manner. In other words, the first Microsoft-specific chapter covers many of the same topics and in the same order as the first Netscape chapter. The final part of this book shows you some workaround solutions for creating cross-browser applications, and leads you through the creation of four interactive cross-browser applications.

Part 1: Dynamic HTML Basics

Part I provides an extensive survey of CSS1, and a quick review of VBScript and JavaScript. The review of these languages is provided because the examples in this book were written with one or the other, so you should have at least a basic understanding of both.

Part II: Microsoft's Dynamic HTML

Part II covers Microsoft's implementation of dynamic HTML, including an overview of Microsoft's object model, and the main object model components such as the `window` and `document` objects, and newer ones such as the `style`, `screen`, and `textRange` objects. You'll learn how to use dynamic HTML to move, position, and hide HTML elements, and alter the CSS1 attributes of elements. You'll also learn how to use Microsoft's new visual and transition filters. Part II also covers event handling and shows you how to use dynamic HTML to provide feedback to the Web page reader.

Part III: Netscape's Dynamic HTML

Part III provides a detailed look at Netscape's implementation of dynamic HTML, and is organized similarly to Part III. You'll learn about the Netscape object model, how to work with Netscape's dynamic fonts, and how to create pages that respond to user interaction. Part III also provides a detailed overview of the Netscape `LAYER` element, in addition to JavaScript Accessible Style Sheets (JASS).

Part IV: Creating Cross-Browser Applications

Part IV shows you how to create real-world Web page applications that are compatible with *both* Internet Explorer and Netscape Navigator. You'll learn how to create an interactive presentation that uses absolutely nothing but dynamic HTML and traditional HTML elements — no images, no controls, and no plug-ins. Needless to say, this application downloads very quickly.

You'll also learn how to create objects that work identically in both browsers. You'll see how to create a multipage interactive game for children using these cross-browser objects. Then, the same technology is altered to create a simplified online shopping catalog.

Part IV shows you how to create an interactive document that hides and displays articles on a single page, and maintains communication between multiple pages. After a discussion about Netscape-specific technology, and then Microsoft-specific technology, you'll see how to merge the two technologies into one document.

Appendixes

Appendix A provides Web site URLs that contain valuable information about dynamic HTML, standards, online documentation, examples, technical papers, articles, and other resources. The listing includes URLs for sites at Microsoft, Netscape, and the World Wide Web Consortium. You'll also find the URL listed here for this book's Web page on the IDG Books Worldwide Web site. This site contains any updates to source code based on newer releases of the browsers. My own Web site is also listed, where I will post new dynamic HTML examples.

Appendix B introduces you to the contents and organization of this book's accompanying CD-ROM, which includes copies of Microsoft's Internet Explorer and Netscape's Navigator. Read this appendix to learn how to install these browsers, as well as this book's many sample files.

The Example Code

The examples in this book are meant to provide you with an understanding of dynamic HTML, in particular, how to create cross-browser dynamic HTML pages. Note that the example files have been named in **boldface** type throughout the book for easy identification.

Each chapter in Part II, the Microsoft section, has an equivalent chapter in Part III, the Netscape section, and thus whenever possible I tried to implement the same types of examples, but using browser-specific techniques.

Except for the cross-browser applications in Part IV, most of the example code is simple, and focuses on demonstrating one specific aspect of dynamic HTML. You can copy the examples to see how they work, and then modify them to see what happens. Or you can use the technology in them for your own Web pages. The examples were created without the use of any specialized tools, and you will probably want to work with them directly because many HTML and script-generation tools have not yet been adapted for use with dynamic HTML.

As I said, the cross-browser examples in Part IV are more complex and have multiple files. You should get comfortable with the examples in Parts I, II, and III before working with the Part IV examples. These cross-browser examples use new scripting objects to handle the differences between the browsers. I recommend that you first get comfortable using the cross-browser objects I created for my examples. Then you can extend these cross-browser objects by adding new properties or methods, or by incorporating new events and using them in your own applications (Chapters 13, 14, and 15 describe how to extend the objects).

The example files have been tested with IE 4.0 for Windows 95 and Windows NT 4.0, and with Navigator 4.03 for Windows 95 and NT. If you are using a later version of either browser, the sample files may not always perform as intended. Be aware, as well, that the examples may look a little different from the images in the book because of differences between operating systems, fonts, and so forth. Also, if the technology changes after this book shipped to the printer, new versions of the samples will be posted at the IDG Books Worldwide Web Resource Center site for Web publishing – you can find the URL in Appendix A.

Catch the DHTML Wave

I hope you enjoy this book, and I hope you find it and the examples helpful as you discover and work with this exciting new technology. Good luck and have fun!

Acknowledgments

Thank you to my husband, Robert, for his patient support particularly during the more trying times during the writing and editing of this book, which was based on not just one, but two products going through beta releases. In addition, thanks, Robert, for those neck rubs when I was highly stressed.

The Microsoft Internet Explorer beta team was incredible with their support. They not only responded to every problem report I submitted, they responded to any question I had, many times within minutes of my posted e-mail or newsgroup message. Specifically, thanks to Scott Isaacs for getting me hooked on dynamic HTML in the first place, and Jason Suess and Garth Bruce for their quick responses and for not losing their senses of humor, especially when I lost mine.

Thanks also to the people at Netscape, specifically Jennifer Penuneri, Suzanne Anthony, and Erik Krock, for their assistance while I wrote this book.

Thanks to Ellen L. Dendy, development editor, and Michael D. Welch, copy editor, at IDG Books Worldwide.

Finally, thanks to all those who have read my articles, read my previous books, or visited my Web site and provided encouragement and nice comments that keep me going even during the most difficult "beta" times.

Contents at a Glance

Preface ix

Acknowledgments xiii

Part I   Dynamic HTML Basics

Chapter 1   What Is Dynamic HTML? 3
Chapter 2   Cascading Style Sheets. 15
Chapter 3   JavaScript Review 51
Chapter 4   VBScript Review 75

Part II   Microsoft's Dynamic HTML

Chapter 5   Working with Microsoft's Dynamic HTML
              Object Model 105
Chapter 6   Positioning HTML Elements 151
Chapter 7   Dynamically Changing the Look of HTML
              Elements in Internet Explorer. 179
Chapter 8   Adding Interactive Content to Web Pages 219

Part III   Netscape's Dynamic HTML

Chapter 9   Working with Netscape's Dynamic HTML
              Object Model 245
Chapter 10   Positioning HTML Elements 287
Chapter 11   Dynamically Changing the Look of HTML
              Elements in Netscape Navigator 321
Chapter 12   Adding Interactive Content to Web Pages 351

Part IV   Creating Cross-Browser Applications

Chapter 13   Creating an Interactive Presentation for
              Both Browsers 383
Chapter 14   Creating Interactive Pages for Both Browsers 419
Chapter 15   Creating a Progressive Document for
              Both Browsers 457

              Quick Reference 511

Part V   Appendixes

Appendix A   Web Site URLs 547
Appendix B   What's On the CD-ROM 551

                Index 553
                IDG Books Worldwide, Inc. End-User
                License Agreement 571
                CD-ROM Installation Instructions 576

Contents

Preface ix

Acknowledgments xiii

Part 1　　　　**Dynamic HTML Basics**

Chapter 1　　**What Is Dynamic HTML?** 3
　　　　　　　　Web Page Content Priozr to Dynamic HTML 4
　　　　　　　　　　Static HTML and CGI 4
　　　　　　　　　　Web Page Development Prior to Dynamic HTML 4
　　　　　　　　　　Web Page Authoring 5
　　　　　　　　　　JavaScript 6
　　　　　　　　　　The Object Model 6
　　　　　　　　Enter Dynamic HTML 7
　　　　　　　　　　Cascading Style Sheets 7
　　　　　　　　　　CSS1 Positioning 8
　　　　　　　　　　Exposing Elements to Scripting 9
　　　　　　　　　　New or Enhanced Event Objects 10
　　　　　　　　　　And Then Some 11
　　　　　　　　Why Use Dynamic HTML? 11
　　　　　　　　The Ten-Step Plan 12
　　　　　　　　Summary 14

Chapter 2　　**Cascading Style Sheets** 15
　　　　　　　　Introduction to CSS1 15
　　　　　　　　　　Applying a Simple CSS1 Style Sheet 18
　　　　　　　　CSS1 Structure 19
　　　　　　　　　　Syntactic Conventions 20
　　　　　　　　　　Measurement Units 21
　　　　　　　　　　Color Units 22
　　　　　　　　Applying the Box Properties 23
　　　　　　　　　　The Margin Property 24
　　　　　　　　　　The Padding Property 26
　　　　　　　　　　The Border Property 28
　　　　　　　　Applying Font and Text Properties 31
　　　　　　　　Applying Background Properties 37
　　　　　　　　Designing Lists 40

Using Style Sheets in Web Pages 43
   Linked and Imported Style Sheets 43
   Embedded Style Sheets. 44
   Inline Styles. 45
Combining Style Sheet Rules 45
Summary 48

Chapter 3   **JavaScript Review** **51**
Local and Global Variables and Data Types 51
   Creating and Naming a Variable 52
   Scalar Data Types. 53
   Arrays 55
Looping and Conditional Statements 56
   Conditional Statements 57
   Looping Statements 60
Creating and Calling Functions. 61
Capturing User Events 62
   Event Handlers. 62
   The Event Object 64
   Document- and Window-Level Capturing 66
Working with the Timer 68
Working with Multiple Windows 70
Summary 73

Chapter 4   **VBScript Review** **75**
Local and Global Variables and Data Types 76
   Creating and Naming a Variable 76
   Scalar Data Types. 77
   Arrays 80
Looping and Conditional Statements 81
   Conditional Statements 82
   Looping Statements 84
Creating and Calling Procedures. 86
Capturing User Events 88
   Event Handlers. 88
   The Event Object 92
Working with the Timer 93
Working with Multiple Windows 96
Summary 100

Part II	Microsoft's Dynamic HTML

Chapter 5	**Working with Microsoft's Dynamic HTML Object Model** **105**
	The Microsoft Object Model 106
	Basic HTML Objects: Window and Document 107
	The Window Object 107
	The Document Object 111
	The Location, History, and Navigator Objects 115
	The Style Object 118
	The Screen Object 126
	The TextRange Object 128
	The Inner and Outer HTML and Text Properties 132
	The Event and Selection Objects 135
	HTML Elements 136
	The Collections 140
	The All Collection 141
	The Cells and Rows Collections 143
	The Images Collection 146
	The Frames Collection 147
	The Scripts Collection 148
	StyleSheets and Imports Collections 148
	Summary 149

Chapter 6	**Positioning HTML Elements** **151**
	HTML Positioning: Introduction and Preview 151
	Packaging Elements into Containers 153
	CSS1 Positioning Properties 154
	Absolute Positioning 155
	Relative Positioning 155
	Positioning and Style Sheets 156
	Combining Relative and Absolute Positioning 157
	Clip and Overflow 158
	Visibility 159
	Layering Elements along the Z-Axis 161
	Dynamically Changing Positions of Elements 167
	Animating Elements Using Positioning and Script 171
	The Preview Example Revisited 174
	Summary 176

Chapter 7   **Dynamically Changing the Look of HTML**
Elements in Internet Explorer. **179**
Dynamically Changing Web Pages – A Preview Example . 179
Dynamic Text, Images, and Backgrounds 181
Invisibility versus Display Effects 188
Applying Visual Filters. 193
    The Chroma, Alpha, and Mask Filters. 194
    The Drop Shadow and Shadow Filters 196
    The Flip Vertical and Flip Horizontal Filters. 198
    The Grayscale, Invert, and X-Ray Filters 201
    The Blur and Wave Filters 203
    The Light Filter. 206
Using the Transition Filter. 211
The Preview Example Revisited. 214
Summary 217

Chapter 8   **Adding Interactive Content to Web Pages** **219**
Capturing Mouse Events 219
    Working with Mouse-Click Events 221
    Working with Mouse-Movement Events. 223
    Working with Drag-and-Drop Techniques 224
Capturing Keyboard Events 230
Capturing the Document Load Event 231
Responding to User Interaction. 232
Communicating with the User Using Visual Effects 237
Summary 240

Part III   **Netscape's Dynamic HTML**

Chapter 9   **Working with Netscape's Dynamic HTML**
Object Model **245**
Basic HTML Objects: Window and Document. 246
    The Window Object 246
    The Document Object. 253
The Location, History, and Navigator Objects 257
The Form Objects 260
The Event Object. 264
The Screen Object. 265
The Built-In Arrays. 266
Introducing the New Layer Object 269
    The Layer Object Properties 271
    The Layer Methods. 275
    The Layer Events 276
    The Document Is the Layer Is the Document 280

Console Mode and Signed Scripting 281

    Script Signing. 281

    Console Mode. 282

    Summary 286

Chapter 10   **Positioning HTML Elements** 287

HTML Positioning – Introduction and
Preview Example 287

Packaging Elements into Containers. 289

The CSS Positioning Properties. 290

    Absolute Positioning 290

    Relative Positioning 291

    Positioning and Style Sheets 292

    Combining Absolute and Relative Positioning 292

    Clip and Overflow 294

    Visibility 296

Layering Elements 298

Dynamically Changing Positions of Elements. 304

Creating Animations with Layers 307

Using Positioning to Create Animated Effects. 312

The Preview Example Revisited. 314

Summary 318

Chapter 11   **Dynamically Changing the Look of HTML
Elements in Netscape Navigator** 321

JavaScript Accessible Style Sheets: A Preview Example . . . 321

    Including JASS 322

    JASS Tags, Classes, and IDs 323

    JASS Style Properties. 325

Dynamic Fonts 340

Using Layers to Alter the Appearance of Traditional
HTML Elements 341

Creating Simple Special Effects. 345

The Preview Example Revisited 348

Summary 349

Chapter 12   **Adding Interactive Content to Web Pages** 351

Capturing Mouse Events. 351

    Working with Mouse-Click Events 353

    Working with Mouse-Movement Events. 355

    Working with Drag-and-Drop Techniques 357

Capturing Keyboard Events 365

Capturing the Load Event. 366

Responding to User Interaction. 367

Revealing Hidden Elements 368

Using Transitional Effects to Communicate
with the Reader 374

Summary 379

Part IV   **Creating Cross-Browser Applications**

Chapter 13   **Creating an Interactive Presentation for
Both Browsers** **383**

Creating a Cross-Browser Web Page Object 384

Creating the Base Object 386

Creating the Extended Objects 388

Creating the DHTML Equalizer Objects for IE and Navigator 388

Positioning the Basic Web Page Components 399

Hiding, Displaying, and Clipping Web Page Contents 401

Moving Contents Using CSS Positioning 404

Using Hidden Content to Emulate HTML Change 408

Responding to the Web Page Reader. 412

Summary 416

Chapter 14   **Creating Interactive Pages for Both Browsers** **419**

Different Techniques for Scripting Interactivity 419

Drag and Drop 421

Event Capturing Using the Object Model 425

Creating Interactive Kids' Pages 428

The Introduction Page 429

The Entry Page. 430

The Numbers Page 437

Converting the Kids' Page into an Online Catalog 448

Converting the Introduction and Entry Pages. 448

Converting the Main Page 450

Summary 454

Chapter 15   **Creating a Progressive Document for
Both Browsers** **457**

What Is a Progressive Document?. 458

Picking the Tools 458

Common Elements 459

Style Sheets 459

The Screen-Resolution Object. 460

Cookies. 461

Creating the Navigator-Specific Application. 462

Creating the Layout 462

Activating the Buttons 467

Creating the IE 4.0-Specific Application 481
        Creating the Layout 482
        Activating the Buttons 484
    Combining the Two Approaches to Create a
    Cross-Browser Application 499
        Combining the Layouts 499
        Combining the Code for the TOC and Remember Buttons 500
        Combining the Code for the Menu and Article
            and the Page Buttons. 503
    Summary 509

Part V   Appendixes

Appendix A   Web Site URLs 547

Appendix B   What's On the CD-ROM 551

                Index 553
                IDG Books Worldwide, Inc. End-User
                License Agreement 571
                CD-ROM Installation Instructions 576

Part 1

Dynamic HTML Basics

Chapter 1

What Is Dynamic HTML?

IN THIS CHAPTER

◆ Web page content before dynamic HTML

◆ Aspects of dynamic HTML

◆ Why use dynamic HTML?

◆ Ten steps for creating a dynamic HTML Web page

THE FIRST TIME I heard the term "dynamic HTML" was at an author's workshop I attended at the Microsoft campus in Redmond, Washington. The workshop introduced some of the new features of Internet Explorer 4.0.

I lived in Portland, Oregon, at the time, and had left home at 4:00 a.m. to make it to the workshop on time, so I wasn't all that enthusiastic about the usual hype I expected to hear. After all, we had all heard great claims about technology before, only to find more sizzle than steak.

The first speaker was Adam Bosworth, who started his talk by showing a fairly plain Web page on the overhead projector. Then, with one click on the Web page's title, he changed everything. The contents of the page opened up below it. He continued talking as if nothing out of the ordinary had happened, but I remember leaning forward, pointing at the screen, and saying something to the effect that the Web page contents had changed — *dynamically*. I never did hear what Adam had to say from that point on; all I could do was look at all the technology he was demonstrating.

The funny thing is, the earliest dynamic HTML was fairly primitive, compared to what is possible with the newest releases of Internet Explorer. I still haven't forgotten that first demonstration, though, and I based my last and most complex dynamic HTML (DHTML) example in this book on what I saw in Bosworth's simple little demonstration.

I was blown away, to put it mildly, and to this day, I still get excited about this technology, even after creating tremendous amounts of Web page content that runs in both Internet Explorer 4.0 and Netscape's Navigator 4.0.

So, what is so exciting about Web page contents updating dynamically? That's a big part of what this book is about.

Web Page Content Prior to Dynamic HTML

Before the introduction of dynamic HTML, all dynamic Web content depended on accessing interactive content from the Web server, or using some form of scripting, or both. Using CGI (Common Gateway Interface) and various other server techniques, such as Server Side Includes, Web developers have been able to create an illusion of interactivity between the Web page reader and the Web site.

With the introduction of JavaScript, a new level of interactivity could be added to Web pages, but their contents still remained static and unchanging.

Static HTML and CGI

With static HTML, a reader could only interact with a Web page through forms, and even then, the interaction only occurred when the reader submitted the form and the server sent back a response.

So, what's so bad about interaction from the server? Well, each time the server is accessed, this puts a tiny burden on it. The more a server is accessed, the more it is burdened. For most people, this isn't too much of a problem; their sites are accessed only moderately – about 10,000 "hits" (server accesses) a day. But Webmasters of more popular sites have a keen interest in anything that places less of a burden on the server.

Also, communication between the Web page reader and the server places a burden on the Internet itself. The greater the number of people accessing Web sites, the more the Internet's existing bandwidth is taxed.

Finally, accessing content from a Web server is a slow process, even if you access the site from a T1 line. Most of us do not access content with T1 lines, but instead through modems with highly limited bandwidth capability.

An increasing number of people with home computers use Windows 95, Windows NT, or a Macintosh, so most of them are used to fairly sophisticated interactive applications. Static HTML, CGI, and Server Side Includes seem pretty flat to these people at the best of times, and are highly aggravating at the worst.

Web Page Development Prior to Dynamic HTML

From the perspective of a Web page developer or author, static HTML, CGI, and similar techniques became limiting fairly quickly. My biggest irritation was not being able to layer one HTML element on top of another. For example, I wanted to be able to layer a text block over an image to form a menu. The closest I could come to achieving this was either by placing the text directly below, above, or to the side of the image, or by creating the image with the text embedded directly into it.

So, what's wrong with using different images with different text blocks? The answer lies in the concerns about increased burdens being placed on the already fragile infrastructure that supports the Web and the Internet. Images and other multimedia elements place enormous burdens on the available bandwidth. The ideal solution would be to use a single image, and then change the text based on the Web page, or the content, or even the reader.

A few workarounds existed before the advent of DHTML. Both Internet Explorer (IE) and Navigator released embedded window applications, which are called *plug-ins* by Netscape, and *ActiveX controls* by Microsoft. These helped to increase the animation and interactivity of Web pages considerably. Add to this the use of *Java applets*, and Web pages started to become more and more interactive, animated, and much more interesting to view and work with.

However, some serious limitations are inherent with the use of these multimedia types of objects. First, visitors to the page need to download the plug-in, control, or applet for the contents to operate. Second, anytime they want to access content that requires a plug-in or control, they must stop what they are doing and find the player control, download and install it, and then try accessing the content within the page. If readers judge the content to be lacking, this could actually cause irritation and probably would not encourage them to return to the site.

Another problem is that these techniques require fairly experienced programmers to create the plug-in, control, or applet. Also, one browser's technique does not always work with the other browser. Solutions were offered for some of these incompatibilities, such as a Navigator plug-in that works with ActiveX controls, or vice versa, but this was no guarantee that the control or plug-in would work.

Web Page Authoring

Along with the challenges of adding interactivity to a Web page, Web page authors have also had limited capability to format Web pages. I referred to this in the preceding section when I mentioned that I really missed being able to layer one HTML element on top of another. How about doing something as basic as adding margins to a Web page, or formatting the content into two columns? These tasks seem so trivial, and are features we take for granted with most other applications. But before dynamic HTML, Web page authors had no way to genuinely format their Web pages.

Netscape, IE, and other Web browsers compensated for the lack of HTML formatting by introducing new elements such as the <FONT> or <STRONG> tags so developers could add bold text. Web page authors also resorted to a few tricks to compensate for the lack of formatting power.

One of the more famous formatting tricks involves the one-pixel transparent GIF image created by David Seigal. With this small, transparent GIF, an author could embed blank areas on a Web page with no noticeable additional download time by setting the width and height of the image to any dimension. This GIF can be used to fake margins and scoot elements around on the page. Another approach was to use multiple hard-coded spaces (created using), an approach that wouldn't necessarily work the same way with each browser.

Another workaround was the use of tables. Tables have been used to format columns of data, to ensure spacing around contents, or to add color within a Web page for browsers that supported background colors for columns, rows, or both.

The downside to all these techniques is that they are simply tricks, with no guarantee that the page would appear the same with new versions of the browser or with other browsers.

JavaScript

When releasing version 2.0 of its browser, Netscape, in partnership with Sun, developed and introduced a scripting technique called JavaScript. This was a significant advance in Web page development; this new technique provided Web developers with processing capability that they could embed directly into a Web page, and that would run on the client. No access to the server was necessary.

JavaScript's main purpose was to enable Web developers to add processing to the Web page so the reader could work with the contents of a form before submitting the form to the server. This means that, if information was missing or incomplete in the form, the script could catch this information and notify the Web page reader before the time and effort to submit the form had occurred.

Other uses of JavaScript included Netscape *cookies*, which enabled developers to enter small bits of information on the client's machine, creating some form of persistence between the Web site and the Web reader. Some dynamic Web content was possible when the JavaScript *write* functions were used to dynamically generate HTML once the page was accessed. Once the page was written, however, it was there to stay — aside from some minor changes such as the background color.

In JavaScript 3.0, Netscape exposed the images within a Web page to its object model, which enabled developers to use scripting to actually change which image was showing. A fairly common application of the technology was to use a second image that would act as a highlighter and appear when a reader placed the mouse over the image. Unfortunately, Microsoft did not expose images to its object model, so the code that worked with Navigator did not work with IE. This increased the challenge of trying to create interesting pages that might actually work with both browsers.

The Object Model

I wrote an article in 1996 for an online magazine called *Digital Cats* in which I talked about the differences between a scripting language and an object model. The language is made up of constructs, such as the *for* loop, conditional statements, and assignment to variables. The object model consists of the elements of a Web page that are exposed to the script, and that can be accessed either while a Web page is loading or after the page is loaded.

Netscape and Microsoft do not share a common object model, although they do share many similar elements. Oddly enough, before dynamic HTML, the fact that both companies had different models was not as obvious. But then, with the release of the Navigator 4.0 and IE 4.0 betas, the differences in the object model became obvious. Chapter 5 provides an overview of Microsoft's object model, and Chapter 9 provides one for Navigator's model.

Enter Dynamic HTML

Dynamic HTML is not a single technology that limits developers to performing a specific task – such as dynamically altering a Web page element, for example, or moving an element, or providing style information for a Web page. It consists of all these technologies and more. Furthermore, each of these technologies has its own standards of organization to help the developer community come to a common agreement on Web technology development standards. The following sections introduce each technology, and other chapters in the book cover these technologies in more detail.

Cascading Style Sheets

The Cascading Style Sheet (CSS1) standard is the first released standard that is, in my view, a component of dynamic HTML. It was released by the World Wide Web Consortium (W3C) in 1996.

Style sheets specify formatting characteristics, such as font color, margin, or background image, that can be applied to one page or several pages, or even to one element or a group of elements. You can create style sheets in separate files and link or import them into a Web page. You can also embed style sheets directly into a Web page, or even into the tag of a specific element.

Some rules even exist to determine how style sheets combine, with more specific style sheets taking precedence over more general ones. The following style sheet rule provides a one-inch margin around the Web page, loads the background image and displays it along the left side only, and sets the H1 header in Arial font with a lime green color:

```
<STYLE type="text/css">
  BODY { margin: 1.0in; background-image:
      url(someimage.jpg); background-repeat: repeat-y }
  H1 { color: lime; font-family: Arial}
</STYLE>
```

No more transparent GIFs, no more trying to use the <FONT> tag or HTML tables for formatting. Best of all, both IE and Navigator implement a fairly compatible subset of the style sheet specification.

You can read more about CSS1 in Chapter 2; you will also use the technology throughout this book.

CSS1 Positioning

A paper entitled "Positioning HTML Elements with Cascading Style Sheets" was submitted to the W3C early in 1997. This paper, written by Scott Furman of Netscape Corporation and Scott Isaacs of Microsoft Corporation, details a specification for using the new CSS1 standard to provide positioning of elements anywhere within a Web page, including layering one element over another. Appendix A in this book contains this document's URL.

Finally, I have what I always wanted – the ability to layer text over an image, or one image over another, or anything over anything else! Also, I can place the elements in specific positions anywhere I want on the page.

An added bonus to this specification is that CSS1 style sheet attributes are also accessible by script, which means you can move an element dynamically after the page is loaded. You can also hide an element, or show it, or clip it.

For example, the following code positions the DIV block at 100 pixels from the top-left side of the page margin, and sets it to be invisible. Underneath this DIV block is a scripting block for Navigator that shows the block and moves it 50 pixels to the right. Beneath the Navigator scripting block is another scripting block, for IE, that does the same:

```
<DIV id="test"
  style="position:absolute; left:100; top:100;
      visibility:hidden">
      <H1>Some Content</H1>
  </DIV>
  ...
  <SCRIPT language="javascript1.2">
  ...
  document.test.visibility="inherit";
  document.test.left+=50;
  ...
  </SCRIPT>
  <SCRIPT language="jscript">
  ...
  document.test.visibility="inherit";
  document.test.left+=50;
  ...
</SCRIPT>
```

You can position all elements using absolute or relative positioning, but you can't position all elements dynamically using scripting. It depends on which elements the browser has exposed to their object model. You can read more about positioning elements in Chapter 6 for IE and Chapter 10 for Navigator.

Exposing Elements to Scripting

Microsoft's release of IE 4.0 was a giant step forward because it exposed all HTML elements to scripting. On this basis, any element can trigger events, can be altered dynamically, or can have methods that are invoked in script.

For example, the following script alters the color and font of the H1 element named "header1":

```
document.all.items("header1").style.color="red";
document.all.items("header1").style.fontFamily="Arial";
```

Netscape has not yet exposed all of the CSS1 style attributes for the HTML elements, such as font color or size, to their postloading object model. Navigator, however, does enable you to alter HTML elements with script when a Web page loads, using JavaScript Style Sheets (JSS), as shown in the following example. This code sets all H1 headers to green, bold, and 36-point font size:

```
<STYLE type="text/javascript">
 with (document.tags.H1) {
      color="green";
      fontSize="36pt";
      fontWeight="bold";
      }
</STYLE>
```

In addition to creating JSS, Netscape also created a new HTML element called the LAYER element. This element is a container, which means that it can enclose other HTML elements. It also is exposed to scripting, is capable of being positioned, can be hidden or displayed, and can be accessed by the layers array. Each LAYER has its own document property that behaves in the same manner as the Web page document object, except that the impacted area is the area of the LAYER tag only. You can use this property to dynamically alter the contents of the LAYER tag by using the document write methods to overwrite the existing contents.

Note that with the release of Navigator 4.0, the DIV block and several other HTML elements also have many of these same capabilities.

The W3C has begun an effort to formalize the object model with the DOM (Document Object Model) working group. At the time of this writing, the DOM group had issued a "requirements document" only. Among some of the requirements included was that the model provide developers with the capability to access most HTML elements in script. Once this group issues a recommended specification, I believe that both Navigator and IE will provide scripting support for all HTML elements, although their implementations may differ.

In addition to the DOM working group, ECMA, a European-based standards organization, has just released its recommendation for a standard scripting language, named ECMAScript. I have reviewed the recommendation; it is basically JavaScript 1.1 with some extensions for Unicode and other international support.

You can read more about the elements and their exposure to the models in Chapters 5 and 7 for Internet Explorer, and Chapters 9 and 11 for Navigator. In addition, you can brush up on your scripting with a review of JavaScript/JScript in Chapter 3, and a review of VBScript in Chapter 4.

New or Enhanced Event Objects

Both Microsoft and Netscape created or enhanced its event objects with the 4.0 releases of their browsers. Both browsers offer techniques to trap events for an entire page or a specific element.

For example, the following code uses a scripting block, in IE, to capture all mouse clicks that occur in a Web page, and then moves an element to the location where the click occurred:

```
<SCRIPT language="VBScript" FOR="document" EVENT="onclick">
 Dim newx, newy
 newx = window.event.x
 newy = window.event.y
 document.all.items("test").style.left=newx
 document.all.items("test").style.top=newy
</SCRIPT>
```

The following code does the same task as the previous code, provided the element can be accessed directly and is exposed to CSS1 positioning – for example, a DIV or SPAN element or a LAYER element:

```
<SCRIPT language="javascript1.2">
 document.onclick=handle_click;
 ...
 function handle_click(e) {
      var newx, newy;
      newx = e.x;
      newy = e.y;
      document.test.left=newx;
      document.test.top=newy;
      }
</SCRIPT>
```

A new draft specification for HTML 4.0 was released while I was writing this book. Some of the new attributes defined for all the HTML elements are events that the W3C working group termed *intrinsic* events. With efforts by the HTML and DOM working groups (both mentioned earlier), the 5.0 releases of both IE and Navigator should enable all HTML elements to trigger events.

You can read more about event handling in the scripting review chapters (Chapters 3 and 4), and also in Chapters 6 and 8 for Internet Explorer and Chapters 10 and 12 for Navigator.

And Then Some

Both Netscape Navigator 4.0 and IE 4.0 offer other goodies in addition to the exposure of elements to dynamic change, dynamic positioning, and styles.

Microsoft's Internet Explorer has several windowless, built-in multimedia controls that can influence sprites, handle 2-D drawing, synchronize events, and define paths along which you can animate Web page elements. Microsoft has also exposed a set of interesting properties, which the company calls their filter properties. I don't discuss any ActiveX controls or plug-ins in this book, but I go into some detail about the built-in filters.

As an example of one of the filters, the following code sets the opacity of an image to 50 percent, making it semitransparent to any element or to the background behind it:

```
document.theimg.style.filter="Alpha(opacity=50)";
```

The image remains opaque until the filter is removed or the page is reloaded.

Netscape offers dynamic fonts. This technology provides a way to download fonts from the server if these fonts do not exist on the client machine.

Both browsers offer the capability of opening a browser window full-screen, although with Navigator, the script must be digitally signed in order to remove all "chrome" (the task bar, menu bar, status bar, and so on) from the window. This is also essential in that both browsers offer support for push technology, although I won't get into that in this book. Be aware, though, that most of the interactivity for a *channel* occurs through the use of dynamic HTML.

Why Use Dynamic HTML?

When I stated earlier in the chapter that Netscape's Navigator and Microsoft's Internet Explorer version 4.0 browsers have actually made it more difficult to create cross-browser Web applications with dynamic HTML, your first reaction was probably, "Then why use it?"

The reason for using dynamic HTML is that it provides Web page developers and authors with the ability to create attractive, nicely laid out pages that provide excellent interactivity with the Web page reader. Additionally, it adds interesting animations and effects, all without having to download any images, controls, or multimedia files. With the decrease in both downloads and returns to the server, the burden of Web page access has shifted from the Web page reader to the technology. Unfortunately, a by-product of this extension is that the creation of cross-browser Web pages has become slightly more difficult.

Consider, though, the types of functionality you can now add to a Web page that you didn't have before. At some point, you may have accessed long Web page documents that you had to scroll through considerably. With dynamic HTML, you can now break up a long document into sections, layer the sections, and hide or show them as the reader progresses through the document.

You also may have accessed online magazines that use HTML tables to provide columnar support. HTML tables have a nasty habit of not drawing any of their contents until all the contents of the Web page, including images, are downloaded. As a result, Web page readers are stuck looking at a blank page for an inordinate amount of time, which certainly won't encourage them to hang around and see what's taking so long to download. With dynamic HTML, you can use CSS1 style sheets to position the content and add margins or other touches that make the content more readable. Also, the use of CSS1 doesn't delay the downloading or displaying of content while the page finishes loading.

It's nice to have a page with a hypertext link that changes color or an image that becomes highlighted when a cursor passes over it. Using dynamic HTML, you can easily achieve these effects with little or no extra download time; with static HTML, such effects used to require the addition of controls or extra images.

Instead of having those small, gray message boxes that provide information to the Web page reader, you can completely alter the appearance of the Web page based on the reader's actions. You can place a bold message directly into the page, which is sure to catch your reader's attention. You can change the page colors based on color depth of the reader's video card, or change the font sizes based on the screen resolution. You always knew you could create a great-looking Web page; with dynamic HTML, you can rest assured that your Web page continues to look great, regardless of the client monitor or client operating system.

Dynamic HTML includes the use of CSS1 style sheets, CSS1 positioning, dynamically altering the appearance of HTML elements, and adding special effects. The Internet and the Web require everything that dynamic HTML offers in order to progress from being a novelty to becoming a serious medium for business, pleasure, and education.

Some people may believe, however, that dynamic HTML requires separate Web pages for each browser, or that a site will support one browser over another. I disagree with this completely, and have geared this entire book to dispel this myth.

The Ten-Step Plan

Creating cross-browser dynamic HTML Web pages can be a challenge at times, but if you work through the following steps, you will find the results to be worth the effort.

Follow these ten steps to create a dynamic HTML Web page:

1. Begin by using CSS1 style sheets. This is the area that can have the most impact on the Web page, and it's the most compatible cross-browser tool you can use when creating Web pages for both browsers.

2. After you've added each style sheet rule, test the page with both browsers to catch inconsistencies as they occur.

3. After defining and testing your style sheet, pull it out of your test page and place it in a separate document for use with all your Web pages.

4. For each Web page, decide how much content to place into the page, while still minimizing the amount of scrolling. Layer the content where layering makes sense.

5. As you add each new element, especially when using absolute positioning, test the page with each browser. Again, correct inconsistencies as they occur.

6. Once you've placed the elements into the page, you can add in any non-DHTML scripting the page needs. This type of scripting is likely to be compatible across both browsers, and will probably go into a JavaScript-only scripting block.

7. As you add in each non-DHTML scripting function or block, test them with both browsers.

8. Add in the DHTML-specific scripting that covers CSS1 positioning only, as this DHTML is the most compatible between the two browsers.

9. Again, test the page with each browser after adding each function and each scripting block. Use separate scripting blocks for each browser, if necessary.

10. Finally, add in the more esoteric DHTML elements, such as the use of the IE-specific filter properties or the use of dynamic fonts with Navigator — but only if you can't find alternatives for the missing technology for the other browser.

In the end, it's important to remember that this technology should be fun. Dynamic HTML gives us abilities we never had before; using it should be exciting, helpful, and enlightening. It should never be frustrating or discouraging. If you find you're having a difficult time creating a cross-browser page, then walk away, take a break, and try the technique later, using another approach.

If a certain technique doesn't work for you, find one that does. One way or another, dynamic HTML can definitely work for you.

Summary

This chapter introduced you to dynamic HTML — what it is, what it consists of, and why you should use it.

In this chapter you learned:

♦ Dynamic HTML can provide a whole new level of interaction for your Web page readers.

♦ Dynamic HTML is based on Cascading Style Sheets and CSS1 positioning.

♦ Dynamic HTML also exposes new objects to scripting.

♦ New event models have been added to Navigator 4.0 and IE 4.0.

♦ You can follow the ten-step plan to create your dynamic HTML applications.

Chapters 2, 3, and 4 provide an overview of the technologies you will use in the rest of the book. Chapter 2 begins by providing an overview and examples of Cascading Style Sheets, or CSS1.

Chapter 2

Cascading Style Sheets

IN THIS CHAPTER

◆ Introduction to CSS1

◆ CSS1 structure: style sheets and style sheet rules

◆ Syntactic conventions

◆ Measurement and color units

◆ Applying the box properties to control spacing and borders

◆ Applying font and text properties

◆ Applying background properties

◆ Designing lists

◆ Using style sheets in Web pages

◆ Combining style sheet rules

THIS CHAPTER PROVIDES DISCUSSION and examples intended to help you understand the basics of Cascading Style Sheets (CSS1), the Web-presentation standard associated with dynamic HTML. The chapter covers how CSS1 works, with examples and demonstrations designed to explain various concepts. CSS1 is a very complex subject, so visit the World Wide Web Consortium (W3C) Web page for more detailed information (you can find the W3C URL in Appendix A).

Introduction to CSS1

One of the problems many Web page authors (including myself) have encountered with standard HTML elements is the lack of control over how the tag contents are displayed. For instance, a header can be made larger and bolder than another header using the <H1> and <H2> tags respectively, but the header's font cannot be specified. And while the <P> paragraph tag creates more white space between two sections of text than the break <BR> tag, the exact amount of space cannot be controlled. Also, the appearance of a Web page in any particular browser, such as Netscape's Navigator or Microsoft's Internet Explorer, depends entirely on whether and how the browsers support HTML standards.

Some browser-specific formatting tags, such as <FONT>, provide a way to control font style, size, and color, but because they are not supported by all browsers, they create an incompatibility problem. These formatting tags may actually obscure or garble the appearance of an element when the page is read by a browser that does not support that particular formatting tag. And still, this approach to style definition doesn't enable an author to apply the same formatting to all occurrences of a specific HTML element, or across several areas in a page.

To deal with all of these issues, and more, the World Wide Web Consortium recommended the use of Cascading Style Sheets, or CSS1 (the "1" is for level 1), in December, 1996. Using CSS1, you can create a style definition that applies to every HTML element in a Web page, or multiple Web pages. You can also create styles for a *class* or an *identifier* and then use them for multiple HTML elements. You can also define style sheets and store them in separate documents, and then include them in every Web page to create a consistent look and feel for a Web site. Best of all, CSS1 is a standard that both Netscape and Microsoft have implemented in version 4.0 of Navigator (Netscape) and Internet Explorer (Microsoft). (Microsoft also implemented a subset of the CSS1 standard in version 3.x of its browser.)

Cross-Browser Compatibility

You may think that the only thing you need to do to ensure that a Web page looks exactly the same in both browsers is to use CSS1 style sheets. This isn't true, however. First, several specifications are optional. So while these specifications comply with the CSS1 standard, not all browsers implement them. Also, some Web page elements, such as colors or fonts, can appear drastically different between browsers or operating systems, or even between specific machines. The role of the CSS1 standard is to ensure a *better chance* that pages will appear relatively the same when viewed in different browsers.

CSS1 style sheets provide a great way to dynamically change the appearance of any Web page, while ensuring that those changes work equally well with the two most popular commercial Web browsers. Instead of hunting through several Web pages for each occurrence of a background color or font, changes can be made in one place and in one file, and new styles are automatically applied to every page where the specific style sheet is used.

The following lists identify the style sheet properties of the new CSS1 standard. As you can see, the properties fall into the major groups of font, text, color and background, classification, and box (margin, padding, and border).

CSS1 Style Sheet Properties

Font	Color and Background	Box
font-family	color	margin-top
font-style	background-color	margin-right
font-variant	background-image	margin-bottom
font-weight	background-repeat	margin-left
font-size	background-attachment	margin
	background-position	padding-top
Text	**Classification**	padding-right
word-spacing	display	padding-bottom
letter-spacing	white-space	padding-left
text-decoration	list-style-type	padding
vertical-align	list-style-image	border-top-width
text-transform	list-style-position	border-right-width
text-align	list-style	border-bottom-width
line-height		border-left-width
		border-width
		border-color
		border-style
		border-top
		border-right
		border-bottom
		border-left
		border
		width
		height
		float
		clear

The rest of this chapter gives a more detailed discussion of CSS1, but before we jump into how to implement various style attributes and properties, I'll show you a quick example and then we'll go over the basics of CSS1 structure and syntax.

Applying a Simple CSS1 Style Sheet

The example used in this section is taken from my Web site. It's a fairly complex Web page that shows how to perform a preliminary analysis and design for a fictional Web site. (You'll find this page on the CD-ROM that comes with this book, in a file called **prelim.htm**). I created a simple CSS1 style sheet for the document and combined it with the Web page using an embedded style sheet, naming the resulting file **chap2one.htm**. As you can see from the example shown in Figure 2-1, the document now has a left and right margin, and a white background color. Also, the font of the document changed, as well as the font of the header elements. Finally, some of the paragraphs have a different text layout and background color, and the first line is indented. Listing 2-1 shows the style sheet for this example file.

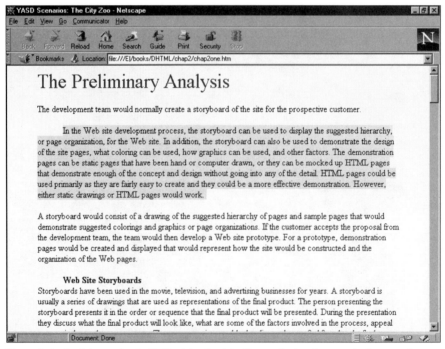

Figure 2-1: Applying a simple CSS1 style sheet to the contents of a sample document

Listing 2-1: Simple demonstration of CSS1 applied to a sample document

```
<STYLE TYPE="text/css">
<!--
  BODY { background-color: white; margin-left: 0.5in;
        margin-right: 0.5in; font-family: Times;
        font-size: 12pt }
  H1 { color: blue; font-size: 28pt;
        font-weight: bolder }
  P { text-indent: 0.5in }
  P.extended { background-color: yellow;
        font-variant: small-caps }
//-->

</STYLE>
```

As stated earlier, these style properties, as well as other similar properties, are covered in more detail in the rest of this chapter. But you can try out CSS1 now by copying the example file **chap2one.htm** (which you can find on the CD-ROM that comes with this book) and changing some of the values — such as the colors or the sizes — and discover what even simple changes can do for the document's appearance.

CSS1 Structure

Now, let's take a look at what goes into a style sheet. A style sheet is delimited by the use of `<STYLE>` and `</STYLE>` tags, and is included in the `<HEAD>` section of the page. Here's an example:

```
<HEAD>
<STYLE TYPE="text/css">
...
</STYLE>
```

Note that the `<STYLE>` tag has an attribute, `TYPE`, that specifies the type of style sheet that's being supplied. In this case, the style sheet is of type `"text/css"` that is the standard for CSS1 styles. Other style sheet implementations have different values for type; for example, Netscape's JavaScript style sheets, covered in Chapter 10, use the value `"text/javascript"`.

Each style sheet rule, defined by a declaration (such as "font-family: arial") and its selector (such as "P"), is listed within the `<STYLE>` and `</STYLE>` tags. The declarations, within curly brackets ({ }), are next to the element, or selector, separated by a space. In the following example, the document margins are set to a half inch on both sides, the background color to white, and the font to Times, with a font size of 12 points in a style declaration for the entire `<BODY>` element:

```
BODY { background-color: white; margin-left: 0.5in;
        margin-right: 0.5in; font-family: Times;
        font-size: 12pt }
```

Note, in the example, the use of the semicolon (;) to separate the style definitions for one style sheet rule. Individual style sheet rules must be separated from other rules by a semicolon. The only exception is when a shorthand rule is used to provide several different values for several different, grouped, styles. Shorthand rules are demonstrated later in this chapter.

Now that you've seen the basic structure of a style sheet and style sheet rule, we'll take a closer look at the syntactic conventions for style sheet properties you will be using to create style sheets, and possible units of color and measurement you will need to provide as values for some of these properties.

Syntactic Conventions

To use the style sheet properties effectively, you need to understand the syntactical notation used for defining them. The syntax for many of the properties in this chapter is taken directly from the CSS1 standard recommended by the W3C. For example, here's the syntax for the margin property:

```
margin-left: <VALUE> | <PERCENTAGE> | auto
```

and the border-left-width property:

```
border-left-width: <VALUE> | thin | medium | thick
```

We'll go over the properties in detail in the following sections, but before that, familiarize yourself with the syntactical conventions catalogued in Table 2-1. For details on other lexical conventions of the CSS1 standard, refer to the Quick Reference section at the end of the book.

TABLE 2-1 CSS1 Syntactic Conventions

Lexical Symbol	Description
<VALUE>	Designates a value appropriate for a property, such as a numeric value for size (for example, "1"), or a keyword value such as color (for example, "red")
<PERCENTAGE>	Indicates a numeric value with a percent sign (%); specifies that the value is a percentage of the associated value of the parent (containing) HTML object
|	Delimits optional choices
[ ]	Elements contained between brackets are grouped together

Lexical Symbol	Description
{#1,#2}	Denotes that the group or option just specified can be repeated from 1 to 2 times
*	Indicates that the group or option is optionally repeated 0 or more times

Measurement Units

Throughout this chapter, you will come across properties that require units of measure for their values. Table 2-2 shows various units that can be used for spacing and sizes.

TABLE 2-2 Units of Measurement

Unit	Measurement
in	inch
cm	centimeter
mm	millimeter
em	height of the current font
ex	height of the letter "x" in the current font
pt	point, which is equivalent to $\frac{1}{72}$ inch
pc	pica, equivalent to 12 points
px	pixels, relative to the canvas resolution

Some CSS1 properties take a literal number, or a percentage as a value. Percentages for width or height are specified as percentage values followed by the percent sign (%), and the resulting values are derived from the value of the parent (enclosing) element. The value of auto means that the size of the element is determined by the browser and is based on the overall size of other elements contained within the parent. So if the parent is the entire document and if the width of the element is set to auto, the browser sets the width of the object to fill in the rest of the available width. When either of these types of values are given, the default unit of measurement is assumed. For example, the default unit of measurement for the document width is pixels.

Color Units

You will also come across properties that require a color value. Table 2-3 shows various ways to indicate color value.

TABLE 2-3 Color Units

Numerical Specification	Description
#rrggbb	Specifies a red, green, blue value in a six-digit hexadecimal form (such as #00dd00)
#rgb	Shorthand for the hexadecimal form in which digits are repeated (such as #fdf, which expands to #ffddff)
rgb(x,x,x)	Where *x* is an integer between 0 and 255 inclusive (such as rgb(0,180,0))
rgb(y%, y%, y%)	Where *y* is a number between 0.0 and 100.0 inclusive (such as rgb(0%, 80%, 0%))

You can also create colors by using a keyword value, such as red, blue, or yellow:

```
P1 { background-color: red; color: yellow }
```

The preceding example sets the background color of all paragraphs in a Web page to red, and changes the color of the text in the paragraphs to yellow. The CSS1 standard has suggested a set of keyword names for the 16 standard VGA colors. These are:

- aqua
- black
- blue
- fuchsia
- gray
- green
- lime
- maroon
- navy
- olive
- purple
- red
- silver
- teal
- white
- yellow

Be forewarned that each browser will also define its own keyword color values — for example, the color "firebrick" may look different in IE than it does in Navigator.

You can also create colors by specifying a red-green-blue (RGB) value. RGB values are color triples, with each value of the triple setting the value of the color component. The RGB range is 0 to 255; setting an RGB value of (0,0,0) generates black, and a value of (255,255,255) generates white. If you wanted to set the background of the Web page to a darker green, for example, and the text to pure, bright red, you would specify the following settings:

```
BODY { background-color: rgb(0,127,0);
       color: rgb(255,0,0) }
```

You can also use percentages with the RGB value, and the colors become a percentage based on the parent element. The following example uses a dark red color for the background of the <EM> tag when it is used with the <H1> tag:

```
H1 { background-color: rgb(255,0,0) }
EM { background-color: rgb(50%,50%,50%) }
...
<H1> This is <EM>Example</EM> Three</H1>
```

Notice in this example that the <EM> element is contained within the header element. As a result, the background-color property percentage is based on the containing HTML element.

Finally, you can also set the color with traditional HTML color formatting, which uses a seven- or four-character field. The first character is the pound sign (#), and the next six or three characters represent the hexadecimal value of the RGB value. This is shown in the following example, which sets the background color of all <H1> headers to yellow, and the text color to pure blue:

```
H1 { background-color: #ffff00 ;
     color: #00f }
```

Note that the color property sets the text color for all occurrences of an element, a specific element, or an element class, while the background-color property sets the background color. These two properties are discussed in more detail later in this chapter.

Applying the Box Properties

Until now, an attempt to control the spacing in a Web page usually meant using a table or a one-pixel transparent GIF file. These aren't bad approaches, but they are awkward. Every time you want to add to or remove content from the page, you also have to add in a new table column or row, or adjust the position of the image.

Also, when you embed images directly into a table, the browser may not display the entire Web page until all the images have been loaded. As a result, your Web page readers may be left staring at a blank page for a considerable length of time.

With CSS1, you now have additional tools, known as the *box properties*, for controlling the space in and around a single page element, and for determining the look of the element's border. The box properties include the following:

◆ *Margin property*: Sets spacing around the element.

◆ *Padding property*: Sets spacing between the border and the contents of the element.

◆ *Border property*: Determines the look of the border surrounding the element.

The Margin Property

As an example of CSS1's control over document spacing, the following code defines a margin of one inch around the entire Web page contents using the margin property:

```
<STYLE TYPE="text/css">
  BODY { margin-left: 1.0in; margin-right: 1.0in;
      Margin-top: 1.0in; margin-bottom: 1.0 }
</STYLE>
```

A simpler approach is to use the margin shorthand property:

```
<STYLE TYPE="text/css">
  BODY {margin: 1.0in }
</STYLE>
```

The latter example sets all margins to one inch. A shorthand property enables you to set all or part of the related properties with one setting. If you wish to set the left and right margins to 30 pixels, and the top and bottom margins to 50 pixels, use the following code:

```
<STYLE TYPE="text/css">
  BODY { margin-left: 30px; margin-right: 30px;
      Margin-top: 50px; margin-bottom: 50px }
</STYLE>
```

Or you could use the following style sheet rule shortcut:

```
<STYLE TYPE="text/css">
  BODY { margin: 50px 30px 50px 30px }
</STYLE>
```

The order of the values for the `margin` shorthand property is clockwise as follows: top, right side, bottom, and then left side. With this property, however, if you specify only two or three values, the missing values are derived from the opposite side. As a result, you can also create the same example using the following rule:

```
<STYLE TYPE="text/css">
 BODY { margin: 50px 30px }
</STYLE>
```

Both the bottom and left margin specifications are missing, but they are pulled from the top and right margin settings respectively. Most CSS1 style sheet properties have a shorthand method. These are listed, along with the more specific rules, in various sections throughout this chapter.

In addition to specifying values directly, you can also supply a percentage:

```
<STYLE TYPE="text/css">
 BODY { margin: 50px 30px 50px 30px }
 P.extended { margin: 15% }
</STYLE>
```

This approach sets the margins of the target HTML element(s) as a percentage of the margins of the enclosing parent object. Figure 2-2 demonstrates this with a simple document that uses the default paragraph settings for the first paragraph, and the extended paragraph settings for the second. To use the new class setting for the second paragraph, the document would use:

```
<P class=extended>
```

An ending paragraph tag, `</P>`, is placed at the end of the paragraph. You can find this example in the file named **css1one.htm**.

Table 2-4 shows the syntax for the `margin` properties.

TABLE 2-4 **Margin Properties**

Property	Values
margin:	[<length> | <percentage> | auto]{1,4}
margin-left:	<value> | <percentage> | auto
margin-right:	<value> | <percentage> | auto
margin-top:	<value> | <percentage> | auto
margin-bottom:	<value> | <percentage> | auto

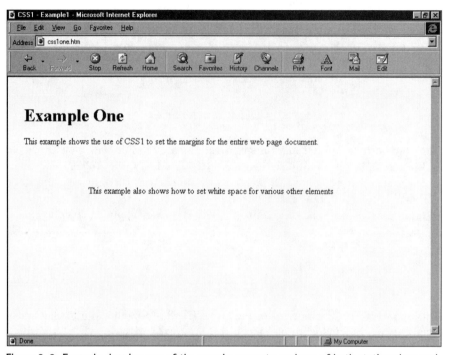

Figure 2-2: Example showing use of the margin property, and use of both static values and percentages

Margin Values Equaling More Than 100 Percent

For the `margin` property, the specified parameter such as value, percentage, or `auto` can be supplied for up to four margin sides. If the specified values total more than 100 percent of the width of the parent (the Web page, for example), Netscape Navigator or Internet Explorer will handle the way the contents wrap (which may or may not result in a desirable presentation). To maintain control of your presentation, make sure that your style property rules, when combined, never exceed the available space.

The Padding Property

The `padding` property can take the same values as the `margin` properties. Instead of creating a margin, however, the browser creates a padding of clear space between the border that surrounds the object and the object itself.

For example, the following style sheet adds a border to the header object, and creates a new class rule for use with the <P> paragraph tag:

```
<STYLE TYPE="text/css">
 BODY {margin: 50px 30px }
 H1 { padding-top: 5% ; border-width: 5px;
      border-style:solid}
 P.extended {margin: 5% ; padding: 2%;
      border-color:green;
      border-width: thick; border-style:groove }
</STYLE>
```

The paragraph class rule surrounds the paragraph with a thick border, pads the contents based on a percentage of the size of the enclosing element, and adds a margin to the entire paragraph. It also specifies a border style. If this border style were not given, and the browser set the border style to none by default, the border would never show.

The style rules are automatically applied to the <BODY> and <H1> tags. Figure 2-3 displays the results of applying this style sheet in IE, and Figure 2-4 displays the results in Navigator. As demonstrated, both the header and one of the paragraphs now have borders, with padding between the border and the element's contents. You can also see the five percent margin for the extended paragraph style. Notice how different the presentation looks within each browser, due mainly to different interpretations of CSS1 styles whenever explicit rules are not given. If the border-style property is removed from the style sheet, the border won't even show in IE. The code for Figures 2-3 and 2-4 can be found in file css1two.htm.

The syntax for the padding properties follows in Table 2-5.

TABLE 2-5 Padding Properties

Property	Values
padding:	[<length>	<percentage>]{1,4}
padding-top:	<length>	<percentage>
padding-left:	<length>	<percentage>
padding-top:	<length>	<percentage>
padding-bottom:	<length>	<percentage>

With either example file, css1one.htm or css1two.htm, try modifying any of the margin, border, or padding-width properties, and see what the modifications can do for the presentation of the document.

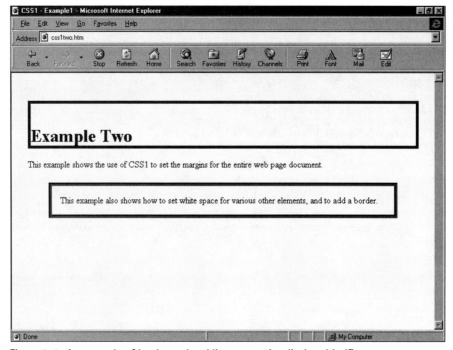

Figure 2-3: An example of border and padding properties displayed in IE

The Border Property

According to the CSS1 standard, each HTML object has a border surrounding it. Normally, this border is not visible, and is set to a fixed value that is defined by the browser; however, several of the properties associated with this border can be changed by using any of the associated `border` properties. These properties can modify the border's visibility, color, and style, as well as width and thickness.

To create a border, properties such as the `border-width` or `color` need a value to make them visible. In the following example, a border has been added to the header tag, `<H1>`, that is five pixels wide on all sides:

```
<STYLE TYPE="text/css">
 BODY {margin: 50px 30px }
 H1 { border-width: 5px; }
</STYLE>
```

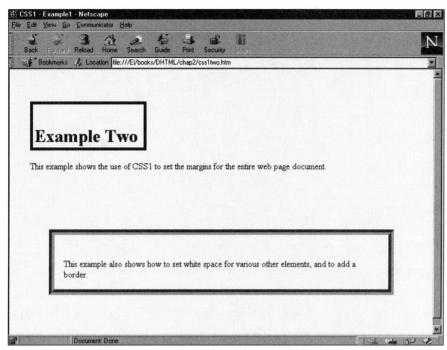

Figure 2-4: An example of border and padding properties displayed in Navigator

The border-width property is a shorthand method of describing the border width for the top, right, bottom, and left sides. As with the margin property, a shorthand property enables you to specify up to four values for the sides, and the browser uses the opposite side to supply any missing values. You could just as easily supply values for each side specifically, using a rule such as:

```
<STYLE TYPE="text/css">
  BODY {margin: 50px 30px }
  H1 { padding-top: 10px ; border-width-top: 5px;
       border-width-bottom: 5px;
       border-width-right: 5px; border-width-left: 5px}
</STYLE>
```

Along with specifying a direct value for the border width, you can also supply a predefined *keyword value*, such as thin, medium, or thick. The individual browser defines the exact values of these keywords. The syntax for the border properties follows in Table 2-6.

TABLE 2-6 Border Properties

Property	Values
border-left-width:	\<value\> | thin | medium | thick
border-right-width:	\<value\> | thin | medium | thick
border-bottom-width:	\<value\> | thin | medium | thick
border-top-width:	\<value\> | thin | medium | thick
border-width:	[\<value\> | thin | medium | thick]{1,4}
border-color:	[\<color\>]{1,4}
border-style:	[none | dotted | dashed | solid | double | groove | ridge | inset | outset]

The border-style property accepts many interesting styles. Each is described in the following table:

The Border Style Values

Value	Description
none	No border is drawn (regardless of the "border-width" value)
dotted	The border is a dotted line drawn on top of the background of the element
dashed	The border is a dashed line drawn on top of the background of the element
solid	The border is a solid line
double	The border is a double line drawn on top of the background of the element; the sum of the two single lines and the space between equals the \<border-width\> value
groove	A 3D groove is drawn in colors based on the \<color\> value
ridge	A 3D ridge is drawn in colors based on the \<color\> value
inset	A 3D inset is drawn in colors based on the \<color\> value
outset	A 3D outset is drawn in colors based on the \<color\> value

Note that browsers may interpret dotted, dashed, double, groove, ridge, inset and outset values as solid.

Applying Font and Text Properties

Both Netscape Navigator 3.0 and Internet Explorer 3.0 support an extended HTML element, <FONT>, that enables the Web developer to change the font of an element. The disadvantage of using this technique is that it has to be applied everywhere the new font is needed, and then, to change the font style for an entire Web site, every occurrence of the tag has to be sought out and changed. This becomes an even more tedious task in Web pages that make use of the font element to create a kind of custom template. For example, the Web page developer may use one font for one type of paragraph, another font for another type of paragraph, another for the headers, and still another to emphasize certain words or phrases. If the font styles have to change (perhaps the fonts need to be a bit larger or smaller), then the developer then has to go through all the documents to make the necessary changes.

CSS1 speeds up Web page development and maintenance – it enables Web page authors to create a single style rule that defines which font is used for each element, either for an entire Web page or for several Web pages. Changing the font style, color, or font family is no more complicated than locating the single instance of the style sheet rule and making one simple change. No longer are font tag specifications scattered throughout the document, and no longer do authors need to hunt through several Web pages to make changes.

The syntax for the font properties available in CSS1 are as given in Table 2-7:

TABLE 2-7 Font Properties

Property	Values
font-family:	[<family-name> | <generic-family>],]* [<family-name> | <generic-family>]
font-style:	normal | italic | oblique
font-size:	<absolute-size> | <relative-size> | length | percentage
font-weight:	normal | bold | lighter | 100 | 200 |300 | 400 | 500 | 600 | 700 | 800 | 900
font-variant:	normal | small-caps

The following example uses a style sheet to apply the font-family, font-style, and font-size properties to the header, H1:

```
<STYLE TYPE="text/css">
 H1 { font-style: italic; font-family: Times;
       font-size: 28pt }
</STYLE>
```

As with other style sheet properties, you can use the following shorthand technique:

```
<STYLE TYPE="text/css">
 H1 { font: italic Times 28pt }
</STYLE>
```

The syntax for the font-family property shows that more than one family name can be specified for a style sheet rule. This enables the browser to choose an alternative font family if the first family in the list is not available. A *specific family name* is Arial or Helvetica, for example; a *generic family* can be one of the following:

- ◆ serif

- ◆ sans serif

- ◆ cursive

- ◆ fantasy

- ◆ monospace

If a font family consists of more than one word, the entire family name is surrounded by quotes:

```
H1 { font-family: "Courier New" }
```

The default value for the font-style property is normal. The style name of oblique may also match fonts that are slanted, inclined, or otherwise defined as having some form of slant.

The absolute sizes listed in the font-size property syntax are an enumerated list of keywords, such as medium or large, that the browser then defines to fit the media — a desktop computer monitor, for example, as opposed to one of the new "palm" computers. The default size fits whatever is defined to be medium.

In addition to applying the font-style, font-family, and font-size properties, the font-weight property can be changed to make it bolder or lighter. The default font-weight is the enumerated value of normal, which is also equivalent to specifying the value `400`. The following style sheet rule sets the font contained within the extended `paragraph` class to bold and italic:

```
P.extended { font-weight: bold; font-style: italic }
```

Also, a font modifier called *variant* can specify whether the font is set to `small-caps` or to `normal` (which is the default), as demonstrated in the following example:

```
<STYLE TYPE="text/css">
  H1 { font-variant: small-caps }
</STYLE>
```

Matching Font Algorithms

How an application displays a particular font has always been problematic when documents are ported between operating systems *and* browsers. The W3C has stated that browsers supporting CSS1 should use a matching algorithm to define exactly which font is used. The CSS1 standard explains this matching algorithm in detail. The algorithm provides a standard for browsers to follow, and although this doesn't guarantee a Web page will look exactly the same in different browsers and operating systems, it means a greater probability exists for the Web page to have the same *presentation effect.*

Figure 2-5 shows a document that makes use of all of these `font` properties. As you can see in this figure, and by opening the example file **css1font.htm**, the `font-family` and `font-size` properties are defined for the body, the `font-weight` property for the header, and the `font-family` and `font-variant` properties for the extended `paragraph` class. To practice using these properties, change the `font` property settings in the sample file, and as you do so, notice how the document's presentation changes.

The style sheet used to create the Web page shown in Figure 2-5 is as follows:

```
<STYLE TYPE="text/css">
  BODY {margin: 50px ; font-size: 12pt;
        font-family: cursive }
  H1 { font-style: Fantasy; font-weight: 200 }
  P.extended {font-size: 10pt ;
        font-variant: small-caps; border-style:solid;
        padding: 5% }
</STYLE>
```

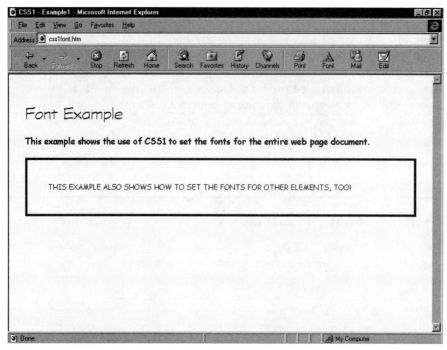

Figure 2-5: Demonstration of the font properties defined by the CSS1 standard

Several CSS1 `text` properties control the layout of text, such as the amount of leading between lines, spacing between characters, and text indentation. The following code provides a demonstration of the various properties you can use to control text layout:

```
<STYLE TYPE="text/css">
 P { text-indent: 0.5in ;
      margin-top: 0.25in;
      font-size: 12pt ;
      text-transform: uppercase ;
      word-spacing: 0.4em; letter-spacing: 0.4em ;
      text-align: center
      font-variant: small-caps}
</STYLE>
```

This style sheet definition applies to all uses of the paragraph HTML element, <P>, within a Web page. The top margin is set to $1/2$ inch, the font is set to 12 pt, and the `font-variant` property is set to `small-caps`. Note that the example uses five new properties: `text-indent`, `text-align`, `letter-spacing`, `word-spacing`, and `text-transform`. These properties are defined as follows:

◆ *Text indent:* Indents the first line of the paragraph by the amount specified.

◆ *Text align:* Determines how the text aligns horizontally, within the element "box."

◆ *Letter spacing:* Adds the specified space between letters.

◆ *Word spacing:* Adds the specified space between words.

◆ *Text transform:* Transforms the text to all uppercase or all lowercase, or capitalizes the first character of each word.

The following code example uses the `text-transform` property to capitalize the first character of each word, and uses letter spacing to stretch the words. Also, a style rule is created for an `<EM>` HTML element that vertically aligns the emphasized text using superscript formatting:

```
P.newstyle { letter-spacing: 0.4em ;
 text-transform: capitalize }
EM.superstyle {vertical-align: super}
```

When these two rules are used together, the emphasized text is placed slightly higher and is slightly smaller than the other text:

```
<P class=newstyle>
This paragraph uses the <EM class=superstyle>newstyle</EM> class with
 the paragraph.It also uses several text-based style settings</P>
```

Other decorative elements can be added to text. The following example places a line above and below the header element when this style sheet rule is used. The `text-decoration` property can have more than one value:

```
H1 < text-decoration: overline underline >
```

The syntax for the `text` properties follows in Table 2-8:

TABLE 2-8 Text Properties

Property	Values
text-indent:	`<length>` | `<percentage>`
text-align:	left | right | center | justify

continued

TABLE **2-8** **Text Properties** *(continued)*

Property	Values
letter-spacing:	<length>
word-spacing:	<length>
text-decoration:	none | [underline || overline || line-through || blink]
text-transform:	capitalize | uppercase | lowercase | none
vertical-align:	baseline | sub | super | top | text-top | middle | bottom | text-bottom | <percentage>

The following table lists the various keyword values for the vertical-align property.

The Keyword Values for the Vertical Align Property

Value	Description
baseline	Align text at the bottom of the HTML element
sub	Align text in the subscript position
super	Align text in the superscript position
top	Align text at the top of the HTML element
text-top	Align text at the top of the parent element's text
text-bottom	Align text at the bottom of the parent element's tex
<percentage>	Numeric value aligning text baseline (bottom) at the point represented by the percentage of the parent element's baseline value

---

The Use of Blink

A note of caution is in order for the `blink` value of the `text-decoration` property. The capability to add blinking text (by using the `<blink>` tag) has been available for quite a while. Unfortunately, it has almost always irritated its viewers. If you must use blinking text in your Web page, use it sparingly, and only to highlight extremely important information. My recommendation is to use an alternative technique to draw attention to important information. This chapter and others present these alternative techniques.

Applying Background Properties

Before CSS1, we had the capability of adding background images and background colors to a Web page. In version 3.0 of Internet Explorer and Navigator, we could add a background color to any cell in a `<TABLE>` element. And in Internet Explorer 3.0, we could to add a background *image* to any table cell. But now, with CSS1, you can go a step further and control the background of *any* HTML element, from a single location. The following example shows how to add a background image for an entire Web page. The style sheet rule names the URL of the image and provides instructions to control the image's placement and repetition:

```
<STYLE TYPE="text/css">
  BODY {background-image: url(largebar.gif);
        Background-repeat: repeat-X;
        background-color: silver}
</STYLE>
```

This rule loads the image named **largebar.gif** if image loading is enabled on the browser; otherwise, it sets the background color to silver. This technique is very similar to the use of style information directly in the `<BODY>` tag (which is a common practice these days), as shown in the following example:

```
<BODY BACKGROUND="largebar.gif" BGCOLOR=#cccccc>
```

The difference between using a style sheet like the one you just saw and putting style information directly in the `<BODY>` tag is this: the style sheet has the additional capability of determining where the background image is attached, whether it is fixed or scrolls when the user scrolls the page, and if and how the image repeats. For instance, with the style sheet just shown, the background image will repeat along the x-axis, which means it will appear across the top of the page. When you look at the style sheet in more detail, you see that it also includes the

Background Repeat property, which controls image repetition. With earlier versions of Internet Explorer and Navigator, the image repeated along the horizontal (*x*) axis and vertical (*y*) axis − depending on the width and height of the image, as compared to the width and height of the Web page. If the image wasn't long enough to fill the Web page, it repeated. This meant that to add a sidebar to a Web page, you needed to create a very, very long image that would not repeat horizontally, regardless of the size of the Web page.

The `background-repeat` property eliminates the need to create long or tall images to prevent repetition. By default, the background image repeats along the horizontal and vertical axis:

```
P1 { background-image: url(bar.jpg);
     background-repeat: repeat-y }
```

The `background-attachment` property controls whether the image scrolls with the Web page as the user scrolls the page, or whether it is fixed to a specific location on the page. For a fixed image, it's best to use an image that has no visual beginning or ending point; for a scrolling image, use an image that has a visual beginning or ending point, such as a logo or a sidebar with text or an image:

```
TABLE { background-image: url(bar.jpg);
        background-attachment: scroll }
```

The `background-position` property controls the initial placement of the image, using these keyword values: `top`, `left`, `right`, `bottom`, and `center`. Percentages as well as absolute values can be used. For example, the following style sheet rule places the background image at the upper-left corner of the HTML element:

```
UL { background-image: url(bar.jpg);
     Background-position: 0% 0%}
```

The syntax for the `background` properties available in CSS1 appears in Table 2-9.

TABLE 2-9 Background Properties

Property	Values
background	[<background-color> || <background-image> || <background-repeat> || <background-attachment> || <background-position]
background-color:	<color>
background-image:	<url> | none

Property	Values
`background-repeat:`	`repeat	repeat-x	repeat-y	no-repeat`
`background-attachment:`	`scroll	fixed`
`background-position:`	`[<percentage>	<length>]{1,2}	[top	center	bottom] || [left	center	right]`

Listing 2-2 shows an example of a CSS1 style sheet using the `background-image` and `color` properties, and Figure 2-6 illustrates the results of applying this style sheet to an HTML document. (Listing 2-2 is in a file called **css1colr.htm**.) The background color fills an imaginary "box" around the elements. Each HTML element is defined within a boxed area, which is normally invisible. Adding a background color or image, or using the `border` property defined earlier in this chapter, makes this *element box* visible. Later in this book, you will see techniques for positioning these element boxes.

Listing 2-2: Style sheet using background-image and color style sheet properties

```
<STYLE TYPE="text/css">
 #bee { background-color: yellow ; color: rgb(0,0,0)}
 #flower { background-color: purple; color: #00cc00 }
 BODY {background-image: url(snow.jpg) ;
       background-color: silver;
       background-attachment: scroll;
       background-position: top center;
       background-repeat: repeat-y }
 H1 { width: 600px; background-image: url(box1.gif);
      background-color: red; ;
      color: white }
 EM { background-color: rgb(50%, 0, 0) }
 TH.imaged { color: red;
             background-image: url(box2.gif) ;
             background-color: yellow;
             width: 4.0in; height: 1.0in; )
</STYLE>
```

Notice also, in the listing, that two of the style rules are assigned to an ID selector rather than a class selector, such as the one used for the table header <TH> element. These two ID-based rules are named "bee" and "flower," and can be applied to more than one HTML element. For practice, open this file and change the different colors and images included with the example to see how even small color changes can affect the appearance of a Web page. You can't hurt the example because it's really ugly to begin with, and it certainly provides an effective demonstration of the color style sheet settings!

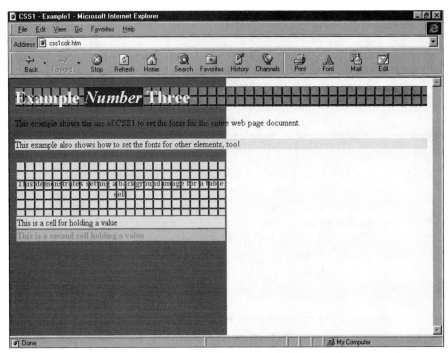

Figure 2-6: Demonstration of the background–image and color style sheet properties

Designing Lists

Some properties are associated with list items. These are `list-style-type`, `list-style-image`, and `list-style-position`, and their associated shorthand property, `list-style`. The following style sheet, for example, defines style rules for an ordered list `<OL>` and an unordered list `<UL>` element:

```
<STYLE TYPE="text/css">
 UL { list-style-type: square;
       list-style-image: url(box1.gif) }
 OL { list-style-type: lower-alpha }
</STYLE>
```

Notice in the example that the `<OL>` rule is set to use lower-alpha characters for each list element, while the `<UL>` rule is set to use an image. If the image cannot be loaded, the code indicates that the `square` list item delimiter should be used instead.

One handy technique to try with lists is to change the background and foreground (text) colors to make the list stand out more. The next example sets the background color of the unordered list to black, with yellow text. Also, the `list-style-position` property is set to `inside`, displaying wrapped text directly under the list delimiter. If the value is set to `outside`, which it is by default, the text would align under the first character of the list item, which is to the right of the delimiter:

```
UL { list-style-position: inside;
  Background-color: black; color: yellow }
```

Table 2-10 provides the syntax for `list` properties.

TABLE 2-10 List Properties

Property	Values
list-style:	\<keyword\> || \<position\> || \<url\>
list-style-type:	disc | circle | square | decimal | lower-roman | upper-roman | lower-alpha | upper-alpha | none
list-style-image:	\<url\> | none
list-style-position:	inside | outside

Listing 2-3 shows a style sheet that uses a combination of `text` and `list` properties in addition to `color`, `background`, `font`, **and** `spacing` properties. While the properties I've described to this point are not the only ones available with CSS1, they are more than enough to give you considerable control over the appearance of a Web page. Figure 2-7 shows how the HTML page looks when some of these properties are applied. The style sheet shown in Listing 2-3 is located in the file named **css1text.htm.** Try changing some of the properties in this file and see what differences the changes can make.

Listing 2-3: CSS1 style sheet using a variety of font, color, text, and list properties

```
<STYLE TYPE="text/css">
 BODY { background: #eeeeee ;
      font-size: 12pt ; font-family: Times;
      margin-left: 1.0in ; margin-right: 0.5in }
 H1 { font-size: 28pt ; color: red ;
      margin-left: -1.0in ;
      text-decoration: overline underline }
 P.subparas { margin-left: 0.5in;
      margin-right: -1.0in ;
      text-align: center ; font-family: "Courier New" ;
      font-size: 10pt ; background-color: white ;
      line-height: 1.2 }
 P { text-indent: 0.5in ;
```

```
         margin-top: 0.25in;
         font-size: 12pt ;
         font-variant: small-caps ;
         word-spacing: 0.4em; letter-spacing: -0.1em }
  P.newstyle { letter-spacing: 0.4em ;
         text-transform: capitalize }
  EM.superstyle {vertical-align: super }
  UL { margin-left: 2.0in; color: #ffff00 ;
         background-color: black
         list-style-type: square ;
         list-style-image: url(box1.gif)}
  OL { margin-left: 1.5in; color: #00ff00 ;
         background-color: #00f;
         list-style-position: outside ;
         list-style-type: lower-alpha;
         font-weight: bold }
</STYLE>
```

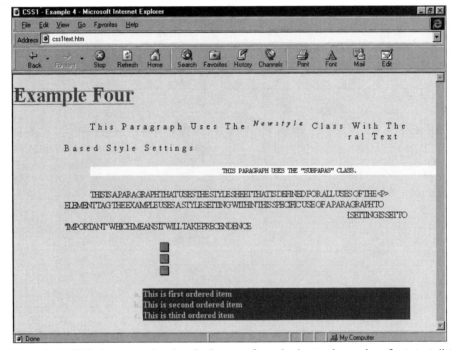

Figure 2-7: HTML document showing the impact of a style sheet using various font, text, list, and color properties

Using Style Sheets in Web Pages

You can include style sheets in Web pages using various techniques. You can create a style sheet file that is *linked* or *imported* into one or more Web pages; you can *embed* a style sheet definition directly into the document, as demonstrated previously in this chapter; or, you can add an *inline* style rule directly to an HTML element.

Linked and Imported Style Sheets

CSS1 style sheets can be created in separate files and then *linked,* or *imported,* directly into one or more Web pages. Both external file approaches are very effective for applying a common look to several Web pages, or to an entire Web site.

To link a style sheet, use the following syntax:

```
<HEAD><TITLE> Some Title </TITLE>
<LINK REL=STYLESHEET TYPE="text/css"
 HREF="style1.css" TITLE="style1">
</HEAD>
```

The linked file contains all the style sheet rules, but does not contain the <STYLE> or </STYLE> tags. Because the file is linked using the STYLESHEET attribute and the "text/css" type, the browser needs no other tags to determine how to process the contents of the file.

When a style sheet is linked into a document, the style sheet rules apply to all the HTML elements, just as if they were created directly in the document. With this technique, you can define and use style sheet rules in several pages. If you change one of the rules, the change is applied to all the Web page documents that contain the linked-in style sheet file. You can link more than one style sheet into the document, with each link providing the style rules for specific HTML elements.

Another approach you can use to incorporate style sheet rules from a separate document is the import method, as shown in the following example:

```
<STYLE TYPE="text/css">
 @import url(basic.css);
</STYLE>
```

According to the W3C, linked style sheets can be chosen by the Web page reader, if the browser provides this option, whereas imported style sheets are automatically integrated into the Web page. Note, however, that some browsers may not implement the imported style sheet, and may automatically merge all linked style sheets.

Embedded Style Sheets

Another approach to style sheets is to embed them directly into the Web page — the procedure used throughout this chapter — as shown in the following example:

```
<STYLE TYPE="text/css">
 BODY { background-color: white }
</STYLE>
```

This approach is most effective if you are adding style sheet information that is pertinent to the specific Web page only.

Another way to use the embedding technique is in combination with a linked style sheet, to extend or override one or more style sheet rules from the linked file.

To view an example of this combination, open the sample file **style1.css**. This style sheet has the following rules defined:

```
BODY { background-color: white ;
 font-size: 12pt ; font-family: Times;
 margin-left: 1.0in ; margin-right: 0.5in ;
 margin-top: 0.5in }

P { text-indent: 0.25in }

H1 { font-size: 28pt ; color: red ;
 margin-top: -.05in ; margin-left: 1.0in }

H2 { color: blue ; margin-top: 0.05in ;
 font-size: 18pt;
 font-family: Arial }
```

If you decide you want to change the color of the <H2> element to purple for one of the pages, and also change the font family for the <H1> header elements, the resulting embedded style sheet definition for this Web page is as follows:

```
<LINK REL=STYLESHEET TYPE="text/css"
 HREF="style1.css" TITLE="style1">
<STYLE TYPE="text/css">
 H1 { font-family: Times }
 H2 { color: purple }
</STYLE>
```

Note that the embedded style sheet definition overrides the color for the <H2> header because it occurs after the linked-in style sheet. All the other style sheet rules for this header still apply. Also, the style sheet rule for the font family for the <H1> header is added to the other style sheet rules from the linked document.

Inline Styles

A final method for incorporating style sheet rules into a Web page is to add them directly to an element. The W3C does not encourage this method; instead, it recommends that Web page authors create new style sheet classes. Both Netscape Navigator and Microsoft Internet Explorer support adding style sheet rules directly to an element, however, and use this method extensively in their own examples.

Continuing on from the previous example, if you wanted to override the `text-indent` property for a specific paragraph and change the color of the font to olive, use the following code in the Web page:

```
<P STYLE=" text-index: 0.0in; color: olive"> Some text...
```

This use of a style sheet applies only to the paragraph that includes the setting.

Combining Style Sheet Rules

Before ending this chapter on style sheets, we'll look at how style sheet rules combine. In the last section, you saw that if you define more than one rule for the property of an element, the last style sheet rule you define is the one that is applied to the element. The exception to this rule occurs when *weights* are applied to an element.

If you set two definitions of a property for an element, the second one you define is the one that applies — *unless* the first one is defined with the *important* weight. Take a look at the following example:

```
H1 { color: red ! important }      // this rule is from a
                                   // linked-in style sheet
H1 { color: blue }                 // this rule is local to
                                   // web page
```

With the use of the `important` weight modifier, any use of the `<H1>` tag results in a red font rather than blue. If the `important` modifier had not been used, the second occurring definition, the one that sets the font to blue, would have been applied.

Also, author style sheet rules take precedence over reader style sheet rules. Again, if a browser enables a reader to choose from several style sheets, the selected style sheet is then designated as the reader's style sheet. If a conflict arises with a style sheet definition that is designated as the Web page author's (for example, a style sheet that is imported or directly embedded into the page), then the author's style sheet takes precedence.

Style sheet rules can also be inherited. Throughout the chapter, several style sheet rules have been applied in the examples. You may have noticed that defining a style sheet rule for one element can impact other elements. For example, such an impact could occur when you define backgrounds, fonts, or margins for the <BODY> element. Unless specifically overridden, these same rules are applied to every other element in the document.

With style inheritance, if a style sheet rule is applied to an element, it is also applied to any other element contained within that element. In the case of the <BODY> element, all other elements are contained within the Web page body, so they *inherit* style sheet rules from the parent. A more subtle example is shown in the following syntax, which defines a rule for the header <H1> element and the emphasis <EM> element:

```
H1 { padding-top: 5% ; border-width: 5px;
  color: red; font-size: 36pt}
EM { color: blue }
```

The <H1> tag is then used for a header, with one word in the header emphasized with the <EM> tag:

```
<H1> This is <em>some</em> header </H1>
```

This results in the <EM> element inheriting properties, including font size, from the <H1> tag, except for where the property is overridden — in this case, the color. The element inherits properties from the *parent* or enclosing element.

These combination rules are controlled by the *cascading order* mechanism, which is the central, most unique characteristic of CSS1. Cascading order determines how styles are combined. For the most part, an element has a basic set of default properties that can be extended or overridden by inheriting properties from a parent element, or by having properties defined explicitly for it. Section 3.2 of the CSS1 W3C recommendation provides a detailed examination of exactly how the cascading order rules are applied.

To provide you with some hands-on experience combining style sheets, we'll look at two separate style sheet documents. Each style sheet is applied to the HTML sample file, **prelim.htm**. The impact of the first style sheet, which is the sample file **style1.css**, is demonstrated in Figure 2-8. This style sheet sets the background of the document to a gray color, sets the code samples in a bright red color, and adds background colors to each of the lists. The paragraphs are indented on the first line, and the backgrounds of the sidebar-like notes are set with an image.

I've applied a second style sheet, the sample file called **style2.css**, to the same HTML document, as shown in Figure 2-9, which changes approximately half the parameters. These changes include the following: the background of the document is set with an image, the background of the sidebars is set to a solid color, some of the text colors have been changed, and text indentation was removed — plus some other small changes. Note, however, the dramatic difference in the appearance of the two documents.

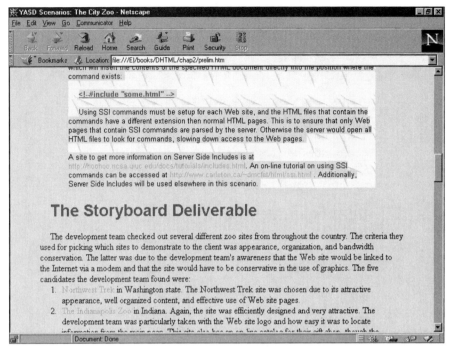

Figure 2-8: The HTML document, prelim.htm, with style1.css applied to it

Try out **style1.css** and **style2.css** with the **prelim.htm** file to see the differences for yourself. Try combining both style sheets within the same Web page to see how the two combine. Or try changing some of the style settings to test how this impacts the presentation.

Not all style sheet properties are inherited, and the W3C CSS1 specification shows which properties are inherited by a contained (child) element, and which properties are not. For example, margins are not inherited by a child element, but the child element is impacted by the margin of the containing (parent) element, because the child element is contained within the parent element. As a general rule, `font` and most `text` properties are inherited, but `spacing`, `border`, and `background` properties are not. Without this limitation on inheritance, it would be virtually impossible to control the appearance of the page. If you applied a border to a `DIV` block, all elements within the block would have their own borders if they inherited the `border` property from their parent element.

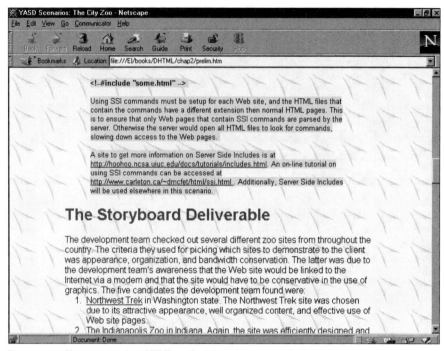

Figure 2-9: Chapter saved as HTML and with style2.css applied to it

Summary

This chapter introduced style sheets and sheet properties and showed you how to put them to work. For more detailed information about CSS1, check the W3C CSS1 recommendation (see Appendix A for the URL); however, this chapter covers all the CSS1 properties you'll need to work with the examples in the rest of this book.

In this chapter you learned:

♦ The spacing of elements on a Web page can be established using the margin and padding style sheet properties.

♦ The font style sheet properties control the appearance of fonts.

♦ Text style sheet properties control how words and text are spaced or indented, or even displayed.

♦ List properties control the appearance of lists, both ordered and unordered.

♦ Style sheets can be imported into a document, linked into a document, and embedded directly into a Web page or into a specific HTML element.

◆ Style sheet rules can be combined to share rules among documents. When conflicts arise, rules that occur first are given priority unless they are overridden.

The next chapter reviews the JavaScript that is used in the examples in the rest of this book. Following that is a chapter on VBScript, for those of you who prefer this scripting language. Note that Microsoft's JScript is exactly the same as JavaScript, except for a different object model, which is discussed in Chapter 5.

Chapter 3

JavaScript Review

IN THIS CHAPTER

◆ Local and global variables and data types

◆ Looping and conditional statements

◆ Creating and calling functions

◆ Capturing user events

◆ Working with the timer

◆ Working with multiple windows

THIS CHAPTER PROVIDES AN overview of the JavaScript techniques used in the rest of this book, and should be especially helpful if you're only familiar with VBScript. Whenever possible, the same examples that appear in this chapter appear again in Chapter 4, using VBScript.

When Netscape released JavaScript, and when Microsoft began to support it in Internet Explorer 3.0, developers noticed inconsistencies between the browsers' object models. For example, Netscape exposed images to its object model with version 3.0 of Navigator, something that Microsoft did not support in version 3.0 of Internet Explorer. As a result, people inundated the JavaScript newsgroup trying to find out why IE's support of JavaScript was broken, or how they could get image scripting to work with IE. To help you sort out the differences between Netscape's and Microsoft's object models, both object models are discussed in detail in Chapters 5 and 9.

Local and Global Variables and Data Types

Variables are used to store information for a specific period of time — either for the life of a program, or until something occurs to change the value. JavaScript variables can be numeric, string, or Boolean values, or null. Also, variables can be created as arrays, holding similar data types but different values, and can contain objects or functions. At this time, JavaScript supports arrays that can hold different data types, but I don't recommend mixing data types. Instead, I recommend that you create an object to hold your different types, and then create arrays of this object.

Creating and Naming a Variable

A variable is created and instantiated with a first value, using either

```
var some_value = "SOME VALUE";
```

or

```
some_value = "SOME VALUE";
```

The use of the `var` keyword is optional, unless you are redeclaring a variable locally that is declared globally. Here's an example:

```
some_value = 0;

Function test_value() {
 var some_value = 1.0;
  ...
}
```

Within the function `test_value`, the variable that is declared with the `var` keyword is local in scope.

Variable names are case sensitive and must begin with a letter or underscore (_). The characters that follow can consist of letters (lower or uppercase), digits, or underscores. The following are all examples of valid and distinct variable declarations:

- ◆ `var Test_Value = 0;`
- ◆ `test_value = "some value";`
- ◆ `_pick_color1 = 33;`
- ◆ `PickColor = true;`

Variables that are declared in a nonfunction-based JavaScript language block are called *global variables*, and are accessible within the Web page document as long as it is not redeclared locally, as shown here:

```
<SCRIPT LANGUAGE="javascript">
 Test_Value = 1;
  ...
 function test () {
      var some_value = 1.0 + Test_Value;
 }
</SCRIPT>
```

Other windows and window frames can access variables that are declared globally, as long as the variable is prefixed with the containing window or frame name. For example, if a frame named `work` contains a global variable named `current_value`, then a second frame can access and set this variable's value using the following:

```
parent.work.current_value = 2;
```

Scalar Data Types

JavaScript variables are not declared with a data type. The data type is implied by the value. The following are acceptable scalar values for JavaScript:

◆ String value such as `"this is a test"` or `'test'` or `"this is a 'test'"`

◆ Numeric values such as 1.0, or –100, or 0xEE, or 2.0E2

◆ Boolean values such as `true` or `false`

Note that plus (+) and minus (–) can be used with numeric values; the values can also be hexadecimal, decimal, or octal, and can contain exponents. String values can also contain special characters that impact the visual appearance of the string. Examples of these special characters are as follows:

```
Test_value = "The backspace character is \b"
Test_value = "The form feed character is \f"
Test_value = "The new line character is \n"
Test_value = "The carriage return character is \r"
Test_value = "The tab character is \t"
Test_value = "The \\backslash escape character"
Test_value = "The \"backslash\" quote combination"
```

The last example uses a backslash (\) as an *escape character* so that the double quote is read as part of the string rather than terminating the string.

JavaScript Is Loosely Typed

JavaScript is loosely typed; you can use different types of variables and values together, and the language converts the values. Consider the following variable, for example, which is defined to hold a string value:

```
var some_value = "test"
```

By assigning a value of the new data type to the original variable, the same example can be used later to hold a different data type:

```
some_value = 1.0
```

You can also convert values based on use. The following example converts the number value into a string for use in an *alert function call*:

```
var some_value = 1.0
...
alert("This is some value " + some_value)
```

You can easily create a new object using JavaScript. An object is nothing more than a variable name and a listing of properties used to define the object. For example, the following JavaScript code creates a constructor function for a new object called "tree," and then creates an instance of the object:

```
function tree (name, type, category, age, health) {
  this.name = name;
  this.type = type;
  this.category = category;
  this.age = age;
  this.health = health;
}
...
sometree = new tree("First","Applet","deciduous",8,true);
```

You can then access the properties and reset them elsewhere in the script, as follows:

```
alert("The tree is " + sometree.name + " and the type is " +
  sometree.type);
```

You can also create and store functions in a variable and then use them later, as shown in the following example:

```
var test_value = new Function ("value","if (value == 1.0) alert('value
  is 1')");
...
// call the function
test_value(1);
```

The function tests to see if the parameter that was passed to it is the value 1 and, if it is, issues a message to that effect.

Arrays

In addition to holding scalar values, variables can also contain an array. Netscape has provided an `array` object, which you can use to create arrays of elements. You can create an array using a couple of different techniques. The first technique creates an array of a specified size, with each element in the array set to a value of `null`:

```
Somearray = new Array(5);
```

This code creates an array called Somearray, which contains five elements, each set to `null`. You can set or access the values in this array using the following:

```
Somearray[0] = 1; // sets element at position 0 to 1
...
var test = Somearray[0]; //sets test to value of '1'
```

You do not have to specify the size of the array. The array expands based on assignment:

```
Somearray = new Array();       //new array, 0 elements
Somearray[49] = 1.23;          //array is now 50 elements,
                               //only 50th element is set
```

In addition to using a numeric index to access an array element, you can also create an array with named elements, and then use the name to access the element:

```
Somearray = new Array();
Somearray["one"] = 1;
```

You'll find this technique especially useful if you want to create an array and access the elements based on a string value, which can be a radio or command button or other element name, as shown in Listing 3-1. To determine which message to display in the alert, the following example uses the name of the form element that triggered the function call.

Listing 3-1: Using names to access individual array elements

```
<SCRIPT LANGUAGE="javascript1.2">

results = new Array("one", "two", "three");
results["one"] = "You pushed button one because...";
results["two"] = "You pushed button two because...";
results["three"] = "You pushed button three because...";
```

```
function echo (somevalue) {

  alert(results[somevalue]);
}
</SCRIPT>
...
<FORM>
<input type=button name="one" value="one"
                            onClick="echo(this.name)">
<input type=button name="two" value="two"
                            onClick="echo(this.name)">
<input type=button name="three" value="three"
                            onClick="echo(this.name)">
</FORM>
```

You can also create an array that is instantiated with values. This type of array is called a *dense array* because it is created with a value for each array element. Also, note from the following example that an array can contain elements of different data types:

```
Somearray = new Array("one", 1.0, true);
```

Finally, you can add a defined property to an array using the `prototype` property. This adds the property to each instantiation of an object. The following example adds the `prototype` property `description` to all array variables:

```
Array.prototype.description=null; //set to no value

results = new Array("one", 1.0, true);
results.description = "This is the results array";
...
alert(results.description);         //print the description
```

Adding a `description` property to an array is a handy technique for embedding online help information that can be displayed based on some type of action. I cover this technique in greater detail in Chapter 12.

Looping and Conditional Statements

JavaScript provides several different types of programming statements. Previous examples in this chapter used the simplest type, which is the assignment statement:

```
var some_var = 1.0;    // set variable to value
```

Along with assignment statements, several conditional and looping statements are also available in JavaScript. If you want to include several statements on one line, separate each statement with a semicolon (;), as the following code demonstrates:

```
some_var = 1.0; that_var = some_var + 1;
```

Though it is not required, you should end all JavaScript statements with a semicolon.

Conditional Statements

In a conditional statement, an expression is evaluated and then, based on the results, one section of code is executed over another. The most common form of a conditional statement is the if...then...else statement, which was the only one available before the release of Navigator 4.0. Now, Navigator 4.0 provides you with access to the switch statement.

IF...THEN...ELSE AND CONDITIONAL EXPRESSIONS AND OPERATORS

Conditional statements are dependent on an expression that can be evaluated as *true* or *false*. For example, the following statement tests a variable using equality to see if it is equal to a given constant:

```
if (some_var == "three")
  alert("The value is three");
else
  alert ("The value is not three");
```

More than one value can be tested, if each one is tested in a separate expression:

```
if (some_var == "three")
  alert ("The value is three");
else if (some_var == "two")
  alert ("The value is two");
else
  alert ("The value is not two or three");
```

Beginning with JavaScript 1.2 (the version of JavaScript released with Navigator 4.0), the test for equality or inequality between two variables, or a variable and a constant, is no longer automatically converted between data types. The next example shows how this situation was handled prior to JavaScript 1.2. Note that the following expression is successfully evaluated and returns a value of true:

```
var some_var = 3;

if (some_var == "3"); // compare numeric and string
```

Now, with JavaScript 1.2, attempting to perform an equality operation between a numeric value and a string value results in the expression evaluating to `false`, regardless of what the values are. In order to test two values for equality (or inequality), you need to convert one value to the other value's data type. For example, the following code converts the number value to a string:

```
var some_var = 3;

if (string(some_var) == "3") //convert number to string
```

The following example converts the string value to a number:

```
var some_var = 3;

if (some_var == ("3"-0)) // compare string to number
```

Table 3-1 lists the operators you can use in an expression.

TABLE 3-1 Operators for Use in an Expression

Operator	Syntax
Equality operator	`if (some_var == 3) // true if some_var is 3`
Inequality operator	`if (some_var != 3) // true if some_var is not 3`
Greater than operator	`if (some_var > 3) // true if some_var is 4 or more`
Greater than or equal	`if (some_var >= 3) // true if some_var is 3 or up`
Less than operator	`(some_var < 3) // true if some_var 2 or less`
Less than or equal	`if (some_var <= 3) // true if some_var is 3 or less`

In addition to evaluating one expression in a conditional statement, you can also evaluate several expressions and combine the results using Boolean operators, as shown in the following example:

```
if ((some_var == 3) && ((other_var == "three") ||
      (other_var == "two")))
 // if some_var is 3 and other_var is either
 //    "three" or "two"
```

The symbol to use for a Boolean "and" value is `&&`, and the symbol to use for a Boolean "or" value is `||`.

THE SWITCH STATEMENT

The `switch` statement was added to JavaScript in version 1.2. This type of statement enables you to test specifically for several values or ranges of values, without having to use chained `if...then...` statements.

The code in Listing 3-2, for example, tests to see which button the user pressed. Based on the value passed to the `switch` statement, a different message appears.

Listing 3-2: The use of a `switch` statement to test which button was pressed and to output appropriate message (JavaScript 1.2)

```
<HEAD>
<SCRIPT language="javascript1.2">
<!--
function echo (somevalue) {

  switch(somevalue) {
        case "one" :
                alert("You pressed button one");
                break;
        case "two" :
                alert("You pressed button two");
                break;
        default:
                alert("Well you pressed something!");
        }
}
//-->
</SCRIPT>
</HEAD>
<BODY>
<FORM>
<input type=button name="one" value="one"
        onClick="echo(this.name)">
<input type=button name="two" value="two"
        onClick="echo(this.name)">
<input type=button name="three" value="three"
        onClick="echo(this.name)">
</FORM>
</BODY>
```

If the `break` statement wasn't used, the program would continue processing the next statement within the `switch` statement. If the user had pressed button one and the `break` statement had not been provided, the user would have seen all three alert messages. The `break` statement prevents this situation by forcing the program execution to continue with the next statement, after the `switch` statement.

Notice the use of "javascript1.2" in the `<SCRIPT>` tag. The `switch` statement, in addition to the `break` statement, is only available with JavaScript version 1.2. Using the version when specifying the scripting language prevents this block of code from being processed by a browser version that cannot handle the statements.

Looping Statements

Repeatedly executing a set of statements based on an expression is called *looping*. The types of looping statements implemented in JavaScript are the `for` statement, the `while` statement, and the `do...while` statement.

The `for` loop iterates through its contained statements a set number of times. The following example loops through an array and concatenates the values into a single string:

```
var some_string = ""
For (var i=0; i < some_array.length; i++) {
  some_string= some_string + some_array[i];
  alert("string to date is " + some_string);
}
```

The `for` statement contains an expression that initializes a value, a conditional expression that tests to see whether the statement should continue, and an expression to increment the test value.

Another type of looping statement is the `while` statement. Instead of having a loop iterate through contained statements a fixed number of times, the statements contained within a `while` statement are processed until an expression evaluates to *false*. The following example demonstrates the same functionality as the `for` statement, except that the code manages the values that are evaluated in the conditional expression:

```
var i = 0;
var some_string = "";
while (i < some_array.length) {
  some_string= some_string + some_array[i];
  alert("string to date is " + some_string);
  i++;
}
```

A new looping statement was added with JavaScript 1.2: the `do...while` statement. This looping statement is executed until a condition is met. The difference between the `do...while` and the `while` statements is that, with the former, the conditional expression is evaluated after the contained statements are processed, rather than before. This ensures that the statements are executed at least once:

```
var i = 0;
var some_string = "";
do {
  some_string= some_string + some_array[i];
  alert("string to date is " + some_string);
  i++;
} while (i < some_array.length)
```

As you can imagine, you need to use the `do...while` statement carefully, and make sure that the enclosed JavaScript can be safely executed at least once. In the preceding example, if the array had no values, the string would have been set to "undefined," because the first array element has not been created.

Creating and Calling Functions

Functions in JavaScript are usually created in the `<HEAD>` section of a Web page. This is primarily so that the function's code is parsed and available before any call is made to it from anywhere in the rest of the page.

A function consists of the function keyword, followed by the function name, and then followed by zero or more arguments enclosed in parentheses. The body of the function is enclosed in brackets:

```
Function return_larger(arg1, arg2) {
  if (arg1 < arg2)
        return arg2;
  else
        return arg1;
}
```

The preceding example demonstrates a function that returns a value. The code tests to see which of the arguments passed to the function is larger; the value of the larger argument is then returned. The function can be called as follows:

```
var result = return_larger(some_var, 50);
```

If the variable `some_var` contained the value of 40, the function would return the value of 50, which is the larger value. If the variable contained 60, this would be the value returned.

Functions do not have to return values unless you want them to. Also, you don't need to provide all the parameters when calling a function, as long as the function is intelligent enough to test for the existence of a value before attempting to process it. Listing 3-3 demonstrates this operation with a function that can take zero, one, or two parameters and process them accordingly.

Listing 3-3: Example of a function that can take zero, one, or two parameters

```
<HEAD>
<SCRIPT language="javascript1.2">
<!--
function echo (somevalue, othervalue) {
  if (!somevalue)
        alert("no value is provided");
  else if (othervalue)
        alert(somevalue + othervalue);
```

```
    else
          alert(somevalue);
}
//-->
</SCRIPT>
</HEAD>
<BODY>
<FORM>
<input type=button name="one" value="one"
       onClick="echo()">
<input type=button name="two" value="two"
       onClick="echo('one')">
<input type=button name="three" value="three"
       onClick="echo(true, 'one')">
</FORM>
</BODY>
```

Capturing User Events

JavaScript was mainly created to enable users to interact with a Web page without having to go back to the Web server. With this goal in mind, the capability to capture events such as mouse movements and button clicks is essential.

With the introduction of JavaScript 1.2, Netscape added the event object, and included a feature that lets you capture events at the *window* or *document* level. But let's start at the beginning. The first thing you need to understand about event capturing is how to create an event handler.

Event Handlers

To capture an event, an *event handler* is created for that particular event, and for the object that receives the event. For example, to capture the event that occurs when a user clicks a button, you can either use the onClick event with the button and call a function, or process the event directly in the object. Following is an example of processing the event from a function:

```
<SCRIPT language="javascript">

function clicked_button(button_name) {

  alert("You clicked " + button_name);
}
</SCRIPT>
...
<INPUT type=button name="some_name"
       onClick="clicked_button(this.name)">
```

The function for this event is small; it's nothing more than an alert message showing the name of the button pressed. This could just as easily be processed directly in the object:

```
<INPUT type=button name="some_name"
       onClick="alert('You clicked ' + this.name)">
```

Table 3-2 provides a list of events and *some* of the objects that can generate the event. For a complete listing of objects, check the *JavaScript Guide* provided by Netscape. The URL for the guide is listed in this book's Appendix A.

TABLE 3-2 List of JavaScript Events

Event Handler	Triggered By	Object
onabort	Stop loading image	Image
onblur	Object losing focus	Radio Button, Button, Window, Submit
onchange	Object value changed	Select, Text, Textarea, Fileupload
onclick	Object is clicked	Button, Checkbox, Link, Radio Button
onerror	Scripting error	Image, Window
onfocus	Object gets focus	Radio Button, Button, Window, Submit
onload	When object is loaded	Window, Image
onmouseout	When mouse leaves	Area, Link
onmouseover	When mouse is over	Area, Link
onreset	Form is reset	Form
onselect	User selects text	Text, Textarea
onsubmit	User submits form	Form
onunload	Exit document	Window
ondragdrop	User drops object on window	Window
onkeydown	User presses key	Document, Image, Link, Textarea
onkeyup	User releases key	Document, Image, Link, Textarea
onmousedown	User presses mouse button	Button, Document, Link

continued

TABLE 3-2 List of JavaScript Events *(continued)*

Event Handler	Triggered By	Object
onmousemove	User moves mouse	Occurs only with event capturing
onmouseout	Cursor moves out of object	Area, Layer, Link
onmouseover	Cursor moves over object	Area, Layer, Link
onmouseup	User releases mouse button	Button, Link, Document
onmove	User moves window or frame	Window, Frame
onresize	User resizes window or frame	Window, Frame

The Event Object

Netscape added a new object to its object model called the event object. This object contains information about the event, such as the X and Y coordinates of the position (in the layer, page, and screen) where the event occurred; usually, some sort of mouse event; the URL, if the event is the drag-drop event; the presence of modifiers such as the Alt or Shift keys; and which mouse button the user pressed, if any. The event object also has information about which type of event it is.

The JavaScript in Listing 3-4, for example, captures the mousedown event for the document, and calls a function named click. This function prints out the X and Y coordinates of the event using the layerX and layerY properties. The function also prints out which mouse button triggered the event, and checks to see if the user pressed one of the traditional key modifiers (the Shift, Control, or Alt key). The click event is also captured for the button on the page, and the type of event is printed out.

Listing 3-4: JavaScript code that accesses and prints out the event object properties

```
<HEAD>
<SCRIPT language="javascript1.2">
<!--
function click(e) {
  alert("Click occurred at X:" + e.layerX + " and at Y:" + e.layerY);
  alert("Click occurred with mouse button: " + e.which);

  if (e.modifiers & Event.ALT_MASK)
      alert(" and you held down the ALT key");
  else if (e.modifiers & Event.SHIFT_MASK)
      alert(" and you held down the SHIFT key");
  else if (e.modifiers & Event.CONTROL_MASK)
```

```
      alert(" and you held down the CONTROL key");
  else
      alert("you did not hold down any other key");

}

document.onmousedown=click;

//-->
</SCRIPT>
</HEAD>
<BODY>
<FORM name="test">
<INPUT type=button name="button1" value="button1"
  onClick="alert('received event ' + event.type)">
</FORM>
</BODY>
```

Table 3-3 defines the available properties of the event object.

TABLE 3-3 Event Object Properties

Property	Description
type	Type of event
layerX	Object width during resize, or horizontal position relative to the layer and expressed in pixels
layerY	Object height during resize, or vertical position relative to the layer and expressed in pixels
pageX	Pixel value of horizontal position relative to the page
pageY	Pixel value of vertical position relative to the page
screenX	Pixel value of horizontal position relative to the screen
screenY	Pixel value of vertical position relative to the screen
which	Number of mouse button pressed or ASCII value of pressed key
modifiers	Used to check for presence of modifier keys (for use with ALT_MASK, CONTROL_MASK, SHIFT_MASK, or META_MASK)
data	Array of strings with the URLs of dropped objects

You'll note that I use the `event` object extensively throughout this book. If you have not had much exposure to this object, try out the example code in Listing 3-4, contained in file **event.htm** located on the CD-ROM. Try changing the code to capture different events, and examine the `event` object properties after the event.

Document- and Window-Level Capturing

Along with adding the `event` object, Netscape also extended JavaScript 1.2 to include capturing events at the document or window level that would normally go to other objects, or that have not been associated with an object in earlier versions of JavaScript. You then associate a function as the event handler for the object, and at that time determine if you want the code to pass the event on to its original target, if any.

The JavaScript in Listing 3-5, for example, captures both the `click` and the `mouseup` events for the `window` object, using the `captureEvents` method. The `document` object also captures the `click` event. The `captureEvents` method has been added to both the `window` and the `document` objects. Event handlers are then added and set to the appropriate function:

♦ `click` for the window click event

♦ `document_click` for the document click event

♦ `mouse_up` for the window mouse up event

The `mouse_up` event handler function returns a value of `true` as its last statement. This result does not cancel the `mouse_up` event, which forms one part of the window click event. Returning a value of `false` prevents this window click event from firing.

Listing 3-5: Adding event capturing for click and mouseup events for window and document objects

```
<HEAD>
<SCRIPT language="javascript1.2">
<!--
turn = 0;
// turn on or off event capturing,
// based on turn
function mouse_up (e) {
  alert("Mouse up event: X is " + e.layerX + "
        and Y is " + e.layerY)
  if (turn == 0) {
        end_capture();
        turn = 1;
        }
  else {
```

```
        start_capture();
        turn = 0;
        }
 return true;
}

// window click event
function click(e) {
 alert("Window click event");
 var ret = routeEvent(e);
 return ret;
}

// start event capturing
function start_capture() {
 window.captureEvents(Event.CLICK | Event.MOUSEUP);
 document.captureEvents(Event.CLICK);

}

// document click event
// also route event to button 1
function document_click(e) {
 alert("document click event");
 window.document.forms[0].elements[0].handleEvent(e)
}

// stop event capturing
function end_capture() {
 window.releaseEvents(Event.CLICK | Event.MOUSEUP);
 document.releaseEvents(Event.CLICK);
}

// assign event handlers
window.onclick=click
document.onclick=document_click
window.onmouseup=mouse_up

//-->
</SCRIPT>
</HEAD>
<BODY onLoad="start_capture()">
<H1> This is a test document</H1>
<FORM name="testform">
<input type=button name="one" value="one"
 onClick="alert('button1');start_capture()">
<input type=button name="two" value="two"
 onClick="alert('button2');start_capture()">
<input type=button name="three" value="three"
 onClick="alert('button3');start_capture()">
</FORM>
</BODY>
```

Each event handler function prints out a message that may or may not include information about the event. Also, the click object event handler function calls the RouteEvent method, to route the event to other objects that may also be capturing it. This routes the window click event to the document click event handler. The document event handler function uses the HandleEvent method to pass the event to the first button in the form in the Web page, regardless of which button actually was pressed.

The way this works probably sounds confusing, but it becomes much clearer when you try out the example yourself; you can do this by accessing the file **capture.htm**.

Capturing events is an integral part of several examples in other chapters in this book. Take a little time now to try out this code, and try changing the event handling to see what happens. Here's a hint: Try changing the return value of the mouseup event handler, mouse_up, to false. This should cancel any other event handling.

Working with the Timer

If you are adding animations or presentations to your Web page, you may need to use the setTimeout or the setInterval functions. These functions create a timer and associate it with a function or an expression. At the end of the specified time, the function is processed or the expression is evaluated. The setTimeout function only calls the associated function once. An example of setTimeout with an expression is shown in the following code, which sets the background color to red after five seconds:

```
TimerID = setTimeout("document.bgColor='#ff0000'", 5000);
```

With JavaScript 1.2 and Navigator 4.0, the new function setInterval calls the same function repeatedly. For example, the JavaScript in Listing 3-6 creates a function called change_image, which changes a displayed image every ten seconds until the user clicks the button labeled "Stop Timer." At this point, the timer is cleared with the clearInterval function.

Listing 3-6: Creating a timer interval that changes the displayed image every five seconds

```
<HEAD>
<SCRIPT language="javascript1.2">
<!--

image_number = 1;

function end_timer() {
  alert("end_timer");
  clearInterval(timerID);
}
```

```
function start_timer() {
 timerID = setInterval("change_image()", 5000);
}

// based on image number, change displayed image
function change_image() {
 switch (image_number) {
 case 1:
       document.images[0].src = "two.gif"
       image_number = 2;
       break;
 case 2:
       document.images[0].src = "three.gif";
       image_number = 3;
       break;
 case 3:
       document.images[0].src = "four.gif";
       image_number = 4;
       break;
 default:
       document.images[0].src = "one.gif";
       image_number = 1;
       }
}
//-->
</SCRIPT>

</HEAD>
<BODY onLoad="start_timer()">
<H1> This is a test document</H1>
<p>
<img src="one.gif" name="testimage">
<p>
<FORM>
<INPUT type=button value="Stop Timer"
       onClick="end_timer()">
</FORM>
</BODY>
```

Figure 3-1 displays the document just after it is loaded. The image displayed is the first in the series — the word "one."

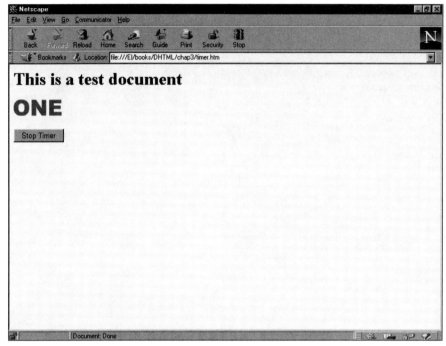

Figure 3-1: The timer just after test file, timer.htm, is loaded

The next image is the word "two," the third is the word "three," and the fourth is the word "four," as shown in Figure 3-2. Clicking the button at any time stops the figures from cycling. You can test this for yourself by accessing the file **timer.htm**.

Working with Multiple Windows

The code to open a new browser window, and to maintain communication between the parent and child windows, is relatively simple if default behavior is used. The following code loads an existing HTML document into a new window, and then links the two through a property called the `opener` property. One function creates a window with all properties set to the default values. Another function closes the new window's parent window (the window that opened the new window) via the `opener` window property:

```
<SCRIPT language="javascript1.2">
<!--

new_window = null

function start_window() {
```

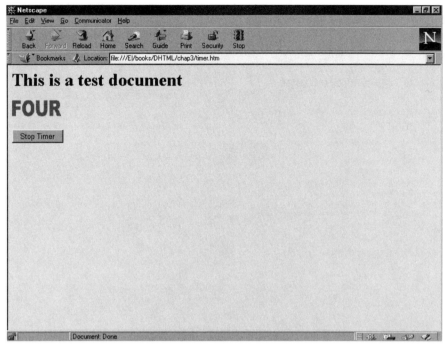

Figure 3-2: The timer after the timer event has occurred several times and the image has been changed

```
 new_window = open("timer.htm", "newWindow");
}
function close_window() {
 new_window.opener.close();
}

//-->
</SCRIPT>
```

When a function creates a new window, some of the window properties the function specifies may require that the JavaScript be *signed*. (This can make creating a new browser window more complicated.) When users access the script via a Web page, they receive information about who created the script, and are given an option to decline to run the script. The concept of signed scripts, including examples, is covered in Chapter 10.

Table 3-4 lists the window properties you can specify when opening a new window, values you can use to set the property, and whether it's required that the script be signed. When the valid values specify something like "[yes|no] [0|1]," this indicates that either a "yes" or "1" value means *true*, and a "no" or "0" value means *false*. For a full description of these properties, check the *JavaScript Guide* at the URL provided in this book's Appendix A.

TABLE 3-4 Window Object Properties

Property	Valid Values	Requires Signed Script
alwaysLowered	[yes|no] [0|1]	yes
alwaysRaised	[yes|no] [0|1]	yes
hotkeys	[yes|no] [0|1]	no
innerWidth	pixels	yes if window smaller than 100 × 100
innerHeight	pixels	yes if window smaller than 100 × 100
outerWidth	pixels	yes if window smaller than 100 × 100
outerHeight	pixels	yes if window smaller than 100 × 100
dependent	[yes|no] [0|1]	no
screenX	pixels	yes if window placed offscreen
screenY	pixels	yes if window placed offscreen
titlebar	[yes|no] [0|1]	yes if set to *false* ('no' or 0)
z-lock	[yes|no] [0|1]	yes
location	[yes|no] [0|1]	no
directories	[yes|no] [0|1]	no
status	[yes|no] [0|1]	no
menubar	[yes|no] [0|1]	no
scrollbars	[yes|no] [0|1]	no
resizable	[yes|no] [0|1]	no
toolbar	[yes|no] [0|1]	no

What About JScript?

Microsoft has its own version of JavaScript, which it calls JScript. Except for a few enhancements, such as supporting the IE object model, JScript is equivalent to JavaScript. In fact, any time you use the JavaScript language with IE, you are actually using JScript, not JavaScript. With JScript, you use the following tag in your Web page:

`<SCRIPT LANGUAGE="JScript">`

Remember, however, that JScript is basically JavaScript with support for the IE object model.

Summary

This chapter provided an overview of JavaScript, and should help you understand the JavaScript examples throughout this book. I've introduced basic techniques and provided a translation tool for those who have coded only in VBScript.

In this chapter you learned:

♦ How to use variables to store values, either locally within a function or globally throughout all functions.

♦ Variables can consist of different data types, but the typing occurs when you assign a value to a variable.

♦ You can create arrays to hold different data types, or even to hold entire JavaScript objects.

♦ JavaScript is loosely typed; you can assign a value of any data type to a variable, and the variable adjusts for the type — except when two variables, or a value and a variable, are being compared.

♦ You can use a combination of conditional statements, such as the `if...then...else` or the `switch` statements.

♦ JavaScript 1.2 provides several looping style statements, such as the `while`, `for`, or `do...while` statements.

♦ Functions can be legally called with zero or more of the arguments, and can return a result or not.

♦ You can capture events using traditional methods (such as using the `onClick` event handler in a link), or you can enable event capturing for a `window` or `document` object.

◆ Beginning with Navigator 4.0 and JavaScript 1.2, a new object called the `event` object can provide information about the event.

◆ You can create timer events with the `setTimeout` function, in which case the function or expression is processed once, or with the `setInterval` function, which persistently calls the same function or evaluates the same expression.

◆ A window can open a new browser window and maintain communication with it.

The next chapter provides a similar overview of VBScript, a language supported by IE. Many good examples of dynamic HTML written in VBScript are available at the Microsoft Web site, as well as other Web sites, so it's a good idea to become familiar with how this scripting language compares to JavaScript.

Chapter 4

VBScript Review

IN THIS CHAPTER

- ◆ Local and global variables and data types
- ◆ Looping and conditional statements
- ◆ Creating and calling procedures
- ◆ Capturing user events
- ◆ Working with the timer
- ◆ Working with multiple windows

THIS CHAPTER REVIEWS THE VBScript techniques that I use in the rest of the book. Because both Navigator and Internet Explorer support JavaScript, many Web developers commonly use JavaScript rather than VBScript. However, it's still important to know how to read and work with VBScript because Microsoft and other resource sites use VBScript, in addition to JavaScript, in their examples.

You will get more out of this chapter if you have worked with VBScript before, but even if you have worked only with JavaScript you shouldn't have any problems understanding the concepts and converting them to scripting terms familiar to you.

The Object Model

As I stated in the introduction to Chapter 3, writing script code for both Netscape's Navigator and Microsoft's Internet Explorer will probably always be different because each company has its own object model. An object model defines the objects, events, methods, and properties that are accessed within script, and has nothing to do with the scripting language itself. For example, when Netscape released Navigator 3.0, they exposed images to their object model, but Microsoft did not do the same. With IE 4.0, Microsoft has exposed every HTML element to their model, something that Netscape has not yet fully implemented. However, both companies use JavaScript, and the scripting language is virtually identical. The point to remember is that the *scripting language* and the *object model* are two different things. I provide a description of the Microsoft object model in Chapter 5.

Local and Global Variables and Data Types

Variables store information either for a specific time period, until something occurs to change the value, or for the life of a program. Variables hold values of several different data types, but in VBScript, each variable is of a fundamental data type called `Variant`. Variables can also be created as arrays.

Creating and Naming a Variable

You can create a VBScript variable using the `Dim`, `Public`, or `Private` statement. Variables declared with `Dim` are given scope according to their context (that is, where they are created). If you create the variable within a procedure, it is valid only within the procedure and is referred to as a *procedural-level* variable. However, if you declare the variable at *script level*, outside any procedure but within a scripting block, it is available globally. For example, if the following line of code occurred at script level, the variable would be local to the script block that it was created in and available to all procedures within that block:

```
Dim some_value:REM avail to all procs in block
```

The `Public` statement declares variables at script level that are available for all procedures in all script blocks. This means the variable is available for an entire Web page:

```
Public some_value    :REM available to all VBScript
```

The `Private` statement declares a script-level variable that is available only within the script block in which it is declared:

```
Private some_value    :REM available to all procs in block
```

Variable names are not case sensitive and must begin with an alphabetic character. They cannot contain a period (.) and must be unique within the scope of their use. Also, variables must not be longer than 255 characters. The following lines of code are each examples of valid and distinct variable declarations:

```
Dim Test_Value
Private pick_color1
Public Other_variable-that-is-created-Once1
```

You might want to restrict the lengths of your names. Long names, such as Other_variable-that-is-created-Once1, can make your code hard to read, and write.

VBScript does not require that a variable be explicitly created. Assigning a value to the variable within the script sets the value *and* creates it, if it hasn't been created yet. However, this can be a problem for those times when you didn't intend to create a new variable but instead accidentally mistyped the name of the variable you wanted to reference. To prevent this problem, you can set a flag that forces you to create each variable, the Option Explicit flag. After using this flag, if you access a variable that has not been explicitly created, you will get an error.

Script-level Dim variables in one frame or window can be accessible in another. As an example, one frame, named "workFrame," may contain the following script:

```
<SCRIPT language="vbscript">

Public test
test = 23.00

</SCRIPT>
```

Another frame can then access and print this value:

```
<SCRIPT Language="VBScript">
<!--
 Dim mX, mY

 Sub getvalue
      Dim test
      Test = parent.workFrame.test
      MsgBox(test)
 End Sub
//-->
</SCRIPT>
```

Remember to specify parent when accessing another frame. Notice that this example uses several variations of case when referring to the variable test. This is perfectly legal, though rather confusing to read. You should consider using the same case whenever you work with VBScript variables.

Scalar Data Types

VBScript variables are not declared with a data type. The data type is implied by the value. Acceptable scalar, or single, values can be found in Table 4-1.

TABLE 4-1 Acceptable VBScript Variable Scalar Values

Scalar Type	Example Value
String	Values such as "this is a test" or 'test' or "this is a 'test'"
Byte	Range 1 to 255
Integer	Range of –32,768 to 32,767
Currency	Range of –922,337,203,685,477.5808 to 922,337,203,685,477.5807
Long	Range of –2,147,483,648 to 2,147,483,647
Single	Single-precision floating-point number such as 1.45 or 1.2E2 (range of –3.402823E38 to –1.401298E45 for negative numbers and 1.401298E-45 to 3.402823E38 for positive)
Double	Double-precision floating-point number (range of 1.791.79769313486232E308 to –4.94065645841247E–324 for negative numbers and 4.94065645841247E–324 to 1.797.69313486232E308 for positive)
Date, Time	Represent a value from 1/1/100 to 12/31/9999 (for dates)
Object	Can contain an object
Boolean	True or False

Note that with numeric values, plus (+) and minus (–) can be used. Exponents can also be used (such as "3.45E4").

In addition, a literal date must be surrounded with pound signs (#), as the following code demonstrates:

```
some_var = #12/31/1999#
```

VBScript variables are always of one data type, the Variant data type. However, the context of the variable's use determines how it is handled. The following line of code provides an example:

```
Dim some_value = "test"
```

This line of code creates a variable with the variant type of string. You can later use it to hold a different data type by using assignment, as shown in Listing 4-1. Notice from the code that, although the variable can be converted to a different type, an explicit conversion function, CStr, must be used when the value is used in an operation, such as addition with another value.

Listing 4-1: Applying implicit and explicit conversions of a variable in VBScript

```
<HEAD>
<SCRIPT language="vbscript">
<!--

Dim some_string
some_string = "this is a test"
Sub run_test
 document.testform.test.value = some_string
 some_string = 1.0
 MsgBox("the value is " + Cstr(some_string))
End Sub

//-->
</SCRIPT>
</HEAD>
<BODY >
 <H1> This is a test document</H1>
<form name=testform>
<INPUT type=button value="Run Test" onClick="run_test()">
<INPUT type=text name=test>
</BODY>
```

Concatenating the value for the message without using the explicit conversion results in an error.

You can also assign a variable the value Null, which indicates that the variable has no assigned value. Using the variable in a control statement, a Null value returns the value of False. The function IsNull returns a Boolean value and tests for a Null value.

To indicate that a variable has not been initialized, you can also assign a value of Empty. The function IsEmpty returns a Boolean value and can test for an uninitialized variable or one that has been explicitly set to Empty. You can create a variable to hold an object, such as a Web page form or form element, but you need to assign the object to the variable using the Set command. The code in Listing 4-2 creates a variable and initializes it to Nothing, equivalent to an object-based Null value. The object is then set to hold a text field from a form.

Listing 4-2: Assigning a Web page element to a variable using VBScript

```
<HEAD>
<SCRIPT language="vbscript">
<!--

REM create object variable
Dim some_object
Set some_object = Nothing
Dim some_string
some_string = "this is a test"
```

```
' procedure to assign object to variable
Sub run_test()
 Set some_object = document.testform.test
 some_object.value = some_string
End Sub

//-->
</SCRIPT>
</HEAD>
<BODY >
<H1> This is a test document</H1>
<form name=testform>
<INPUT type=button value="Run Test"
 onClick="run_test()">
<INPUT type=text name=test>
</BODY>
```

Arrays

In addition to holding scalar or single values, a variable can also contain an array
of values. You can create an array using a couple of different techniques. The first
technique creates an array of a specific size with each element in the array set to
an empty string (" ") for a string array or a value of 0 for a numeric array.
Remember that these are base values that are literally determined at the time of
assignment to a member, as shown in the following code:

```
Dim Somearray(5)

Somearray(0) = "test":REM string value
Somearray(1) = 1.0    :REM numeric value
```

As shown in the code, the array can hold different data types. Within a procedure, the array can actually be redimensioned to be a different size. When this
occurs, the existing data in the array can be maintained or can be wiped out based
on the use of the Preserve keyword:

```
ReDim Somearray(6)    :REM does not preserve data
ReDim Preserve Somearray(6) :REM preserves data
```

A *dynamic array* is created with no initial size, and then can be redimensioned
within a procedure:

```
Dim some_array()
...
Sub some_procedure
 ReDim some_array(5)
```

The array can be redimensioned as much as necessary; the language handles all memory allocation. You can also create an array that is instantiated with values. Note from the following example that an array can contain elements of different data types:

```
Dim some_array
some_array = Array("test", 1.0, "again", 3.5E8)
MsgBox(" the value of the last element is " +
  Cstr(some_array(3)))
```

This code results in a message box displaying the value 350000000.

Multiple-dimension arrays can be created easily – just list a second upper limit for a second dimension on the array, as follows:

```
Dim some_array(3,3)    :REM 3 x 3 array
some_array(0,1) = 1.0
some_array(1,0) = 2.0
some_array(3,3) = 3.0
```

A couple of functions are very helpful with arrays. The first is the IsArray function, which takes a variable as its argument and returns a Boolean value of False if the variable is not an array, or True if it is. The Erase function resets the values of a fixed array (one that is declared with an initial size) to the appropriate empty string or zero value, or to Nothing if the element had been assigned an object. For a dynamic array (one not declared with an initial size), Erase releases the memory associated with the array. To use the array again, it needs to be redimensioned with ReDim. Finally, the Ubound function returns the subscript of the uppermost element. Considering that the lower boundary of an array is zero (0), the upper-bound value is the length of the array minus 1:

```
Dim some_array(5)             :REM five elements
Lnth = Ubound(some_array)     :REM will be set to 4
```

Next in line for review are looping and conditional statements.

Looping and Conditional Statements

Previous examples in this chapter have shown the assignment statement:

```
some_var = 1.0:REM assigning value to a variable
```

In addition to assignment statements, VBScript has several conditional and looping statements available. If you want to have several statements on a line, separate each one with a colon (:), as shown in the following example:

```
some_var = 3 : other_var = some_var + 1 :REM comment
```

Conditional Statements

A conditional statement is one in which an expression is evaluated and, based on the expression results, one section of code is executed rather than another. The most common form of a conditional statement is the `If...Then...Else` statement. The `Select Case` statement can also be used to control which code is processed.

IF...THEN...ELSE AND CONDITIONAL EXPRESSIONS AND OPERATORS

Conditional statements are dependent on an expression that can be evaluated as true or false. For example, the following statement tests a variable using equality to determine if it is equal to a constant:

```
If some_var = "three" Then
 alert("The value is three")
Else
 alert("The value is not three")
End If
```

More than one value can be tested if each value is tested in a separate expression:

```
If some_var = "three" Then
 MsgBox "The value is three"
ElseIf some_var = "two" Then
 MsgBox "The value is two"
Else
 MsgBox "The value is not two or three"
End If
```

The variables, or a variable and a constant, can be of different data types, and the language handles the conversion to the best of its ability:

```
some_var = "1"

If some_var > 1 Then :REM compare numeric and string
```

Operators that can be used in an expression appear in Table 4-2.

Table 4-2 Operators

Operator Name	Operator	Example of Use
Equality operator	=	If some_var = 3 Then : REM true if some_var is 3
Inequality operator	<>	If some_var <> 3 Then : REM true if some_var is not 3
Greater than operator	>	If some_var > 3 Then : REM true if some_var is 4 or more
Greater than or equal	>=	If some_var >= 3 Then : REM true if some_var is 3 or up
Less than operator	<	If some_var < 3 Then : REM true if some_var 2 or less
Less than or equal	<=	If some_var <= 3 Then : REM true if some_var is 3 or less

In addition to evaluating one expression in a conditional statement, you can evaluate and combine the results of several expressions using Boolean operators:

```
If some_var = 3 And (other_var = "three" Or other_var = "two") Then
  REM if some_var is 3 and other_var is either
  REM   "three" or "two"
```

The keyword to use for a Boolean *and* value is And, and the keyword to use for a Boolean *or* value is Or.

THE SWITCH STATEMENT

The Select Case statement provides a way to test for several different expressions and follow a separate path for each. You provide a value or variable in the main Select statement. This variable or value is then used in the expression for each specific Case statement.

As an example, the code in Listing 4-3 tests to see which button was pressed. Based on the value passed to the Select Case statement, a different message is displayed.

Listing 4-3: The use of a Select Case statement in VBScript code to test which button was pressed and to produce an appropriate message

```
<HEAD>
<SCRIPT language="VBScript">
```

```
<!--
Sub echo (somevalue)

  Select Case somevalue
        Case "one"
                MsgBox "You pressed button one"
        Case "two"
                MsgBox "You pressed button two"
        Case Else
                MsgBox "Well you pressed something!"
  End Select
End Sub
//-->
</SCRIPT>
</HEAD>
<BODY>
<FORM>
<input type=button name="one" value="one"
        onClick="echo 'one'">
<input type=button name="two" value="two"
        onClick="echo 'two'">
<input type=button name="three" value="three"
        onClick="echo 'three'">
</FORM>
</BODY>
```

The VBScript in Listing 4-3 tests for equality for the Select Case statement. However, the expression could use some other comparison operator, as demonstrated in the following code:

```
Select Case some_var
  Case Is < 3
        MsgBox "Value is less than 3"
  Case Is < 10
        MsgBox "Value is less than or equal to 10"
  Case Else
        MsgBox "Value is greater than 10"
End Select
```

Looping Statements

Executing a set of statements over and over again based on some expression is the basis of looping. The looping statements most commonly used in VBScript are the Do...Loop, For...Next, and For Each...Next statements.

The For...Next loop iterates through its contained statements a set number of times. The following example loops through an array and concatenates the values into a single string:

```
Dim some_string
some_string = ""
```

```
For I = 0 To 9 Step 1
  some_string= some_string + some_array(I)
  MsgBox("string to date is " + some_string)
Next
```

The For...Next statement contains a beginning value, an end value, and an optional step value (by default the step is set to 1) that determine how the test value is incremented. If the step value is set to 2, the test variable is incremented by 2 each time the For statement is tested.

Instead of the For...Next loop, you can use the For Each...Next loop for processing elements of an array or a *collection* (a grouping of like objects). As an example, the following code iterates through the same array that was processed in the preceding example:

```
For Each some_item In some_array
  some_string= some_string + some_item
  MsgBox("string to date is " + some_string)
Next
```

The variable some_item is set to the next array element with each pass through the loop. The For Each...Next statement is used to iterate through the built-in collections for a Web page. Existing collections such as Images hold a reference to all the images in a Web page; other collections, such as the All collection holds a reference to every element in a Web page. A listing of the collections that Microsoft implemented with its scripting model is provided in Chapter 5.

Another type of looping statement is Do...Loop. Instead of iterating through a set of statements a fixed number of times, the statements contained within the loop are processed until the test expression for the loop evaluates to False. For example, the following code performs the same functionality as the For...Next statement, except the code manages the values evaluated in the conditional expression:

```
Dim some_string
some_string = "
Dim lnth
lnth = UBound(some_array)
I = 0
Do While I <= lnth
  some_string= some_string + some_array(I)
  MsgBox("string to date is " + some_string)
  I=I+1
Loop
```

A second approach to take with the Do...Loop statement is to use the Until option instead of the While option. When you use the Do...Loop statement, the loop executes until a condition is met, which is the opposite of what happens when you use While. With While, the loop executes while a condition is met. Another option you can use with Do...Loop is to place the conditional test at the end of the looping block rather than at the beginning. This approach is different from the one

I just mentioned in that the conditional expression is evaluated after the contained statements are processed rather than before. This ensures that the statements are executed at least once, as shown in the following code sample:

```
I = 0
Dim some_string
some_string = ""
Dim lnth
lnth = Ubound(some_array)
Do
  some_string= some_string + some_array(I)
  MsgBox("string to date is " + some_string)
  I=I+1
Loop Until(I = lnth)
```

As you can imagine, you need to use this type of looping statement carefully, and make sure that enclosed VBScript can safely execute at least once. In the previous example, if the array had no values, the string would have been set to "undefined" because the first array element has not been defined. The next section covers how procedures are handled in VBScript.

Creating and Calling Procedures

Procedures in VBScript can be *functions*, which return a value, or *subroutines*, which don't return a value. Each type of procedure has its own keyword.

A function consists of the Function keyword followed by the function name and then followed by zero or more arguments contained within enclosing parentheses. The function is terminated with End Function, as demonstrated here:

```
Function return_larger(arg1, arg2)
  If arg1 < arg2 Then
        return_larger = arg2
  Else
        return_larger = arg1
  End If
End Function
```

The code tests to see which argument passed to the function is larger and returns this value. The function can be called as:

```
result = return_larger(some_var, 50)
```

If the variable some_var contained the value of 40, the function would return the value of 50, which is the larger value. If the variable contained 60, this is the value returned.

Subroutines do not have to return values. In addition, the number of arguments defined for the procedure must match the number of arguments passed to it.

VBScript doesn't allow procedure overloading. However, Listing 4-4 demonstrates a technique that can work around this limitation by passing the `Null` value in the position of the missing argument.

Listing 4-4: Example of a workaround for missing parameter values

```
<HEAD>
<SCRIPT language="VBScript">
<!--

Sub echo (somevalue, othervalue)
 If (IsNull(somevalue) And IsNull(othervalue)) Then
       MsgBox "no value is provided"
 ElseIf IsNull(somevalue) Then
       MsgBox othervalue
 ElseIf IsNull(othervalue) Then
       MsgBox somevalue
 Else
       somevalue = Cstr(somevalue) + othervalue
       MsgBox somevalue
 End If
End Sub
//-->
</SCRIPT>

</HEAD>
<BODY>
<FORM>
<input type=button name="one" value="one"
       onClick="echo Null, Null">
<input type=button name="two" value="two"
       onClick="echo 'one', Null">
<input type=button name="three" value="three"
       onClick="echo 1, 'one'">
</FORM>
</BODY>
```

Arguments for subroutines and functions can be passed by reference using the `ByRef` keyword. This keyword passes the address of the variable rather than the value, and any changes to the variable within the procedure impact the variable outside of the procedure. Arguments can also be passed using `ByVal`. When you use `ByVal`, a change made to the variable in the procedure does not change it in the calling code. This is an argument default behavior.

Also, you do not specify the parentheses when calling a procedure (as several of the code examples in this section demonstrated) if you are not capturing the return result for a function. In fact, using parentheses with a `Sub` procedure or a function without intercepting its return value generates a VBScript error.

This concludes the discussion on the statement-specific aspects of VBScript. The next section covers the language's event handling capability.

Capturing User Events

With Internet Explorer 4.0, Microsoft has extended its object model so that every HTML element is an object that can trigger an event. Because of this, virtually every area of a Web page can respond to user events. Understanding how to capture events such as mouse movements and button clicks is essential to creating Web pages that provide users with feedback.

Event Handlers

To capture an event, an event handler is created for the event and the object that receives the event. For example, to capture the event that occurs when a user clicks a button, you can use the onClick event with the button and call a function, or process the event directly in the object. An example of the former technique is:

```
<SCRIPT language="VBScript">

Sub clicked_button(button_name)
 MsgBox "You clicked " + button_name
End Sub

</SCRIPT>
...
<INPUT type=button name="some_name"
       onClick="clicked_button some_name">
```

The function for this event is small, nothing more than a message displaying the name of the button that is pressed. This could just as easily have been processed directly in the object:

```
<INPUT type=button name="some_name"
       onClick="MsgBox 'some_name'">
```

VBScript can capture an event using the syntax object_onEvent. For example, an event handler could have trapped the click event for a button as shown in the following code:

```
Sub some_name_onclick
' some code
```

Table 4-3 has a list of events and the event handlers that are used throughout the rest of this book. A complete description of the events and event handlers can be found at the Microsoft Web site, the URL of which can be found in this book's Appendix A.

TABLE 4-3 VBScript Events

Event Handler	Triggered By	EventHandler
`onAbort`	image loading is aborted, usually by reader pressing Stop button	`object_onabort()`
`onbeforeunload`	immediately before page unloads	`window_onbeforeunload`
`onBlur`	object losing focus	`object_onblur()`
`onBounce`	object reaches side (marquee)	`object_onbounce()`
`onChange`	object value has changed	`object_onchange()`
`onClick`	object is clicked	`object_onclick()`
`onDblClick`	object is double-clicked	`object_ondblclick()`
`onDragStart`	selected object is dragged	`object_ondragstart()`
`onError`	image loading error	`object_onerror()`
`onFinish`	object loop is complete (marquee)	`object_onfinish()`
`onFocus`	object gets focus	`object_onfocus()`
`onHelp`	user presses F1 or help key	`object_onhelp()`
`onKeyDown`	user presses any key	`object_onkeydown()`
`onKeyPress`	user presses a key	`object_onkeypress()`
`onKeyUp`	user releases a key	`object_onkeyup()`
`onLoad`	object is loaded	`object_onload()`
`onMouseDown`	user presses mouse button	`object_onmousedown()`
`onMouseMove`	user moves mouse	`object_onmousemove()`
`onMouseOut`	when cursor leaves element	`object_onmouseout()`
`onMouseOver`	when cursor is over element	`object_onmouseover()`
`onMouseUp`	user releases mouse button	`object_onmouseup()`
`onReadyStateChange`	ready state for object changes	`object_onreadystate change()`
`onReset`	form is reset	`object_onreset()`
`onRowEnter`	current row has changed	`object_onrowenter()`

continued

Table 4-3 VBScript Events *(continued)*

Event Handler	Triggered By	EventHandler
onRowExit	current row is changing	object_onrowexit()
onScroll	scroll box has changed	object_onscroll()
onSelect	user selects text	object_onselect()
onStart	loop starts (marquee)	object_onstart()
onSubmit	user submits form	object_onsubmit()
onUnload	exit frame or window	object_onunload()

Beginning with Internet Explorer 4.0, Microsoft added HTML elements to their object model. This exposure of HTML elements to the model lets you dynamically alter an element's presentation style, position the element, or even replace the element. For example, the code in Listing 4-5 captures the onMouseOver and onMouseOut events for the header, and the onClick event for the two paragraphs and body element. Moving the cursor over the header changes the color, and clicking the first paragraph turns off the paragraph's display. Clicking the second paragraph turns on the display for the first paragraph, and changes the font color to green. Clicking the document body turns on the display for the first paragraph, and sets the font variant style property to small-caps. It also sets the font color to black.

Listing 4-5: Capturing events for several HTML elements using VBScript

```
<HEAD>
<SCRIPT language="vbscript">
<!--

Sub header_onmouseover
  header.style.color="red"
End Sub

Sub header_onmouseout
  header.style.color="black"
End Sub

Sub paragraph1_onclick
  paragraph1.style.display="none"
  window.event.cancelbubble=true
End Sub
```

```
Sub paragraph2_onclick
 paragraph1.style.display=""
 paragraph1.style.color="green"
 paragraph1.style.fontVariant="normal"
 window.event.cancelbubble=true
End Sub

Sub thebody_onclick
 paragraph1.style.display=""
 paragraph1.style.color="black"
 paragraph1.style.fontVariant="small-caps"
End Sub

//-->
</SCRIPT>
</HEAD>
<BODY id=thebody>
<H1 id="header"> This is a test document</H1>
<p id=paragraph1>
The main reason for the creation of client-side scripting was to
 provide some means for the user to interact with a web page without
 having to go back to the web server each time. Based on this,
 trapping events such as mouse movements and button clicks is
 essential.
</p>
<p id=paragraph2>
With Internet Explorer 4.0, Microsoft has extended their object
 model to include every HTML element as an object that can trigger
 an event. Due to this, virtually every area of a web page can now
 respond to user events.
</p>
</BODY>
```

Notice from the example code that a property cancelbubble is set to true for the window.event object. This setting prevents the event from bubbling up the event hierarchy, and is discussed in more detail in the next section. Without this precaution, the body click event handler, in addition to the paragraph event handler, would process the onclick event. Try this yourself by accessing the sample file **vbevent.htm**. Figure 4-1 shows the example after it is first brought up and then after clicking anywhere on the document page except over the paragraphs.

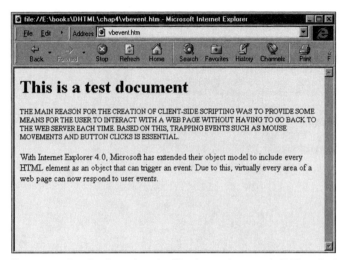

Figure 4-1: Result of running the file vbevent.htm, and clicking the body

The Event Object

Microsoft also created a new object, in Internet Explorer 4.0, called the Event object. The Event object controls event processing, as was demonstrated in the last section, and also contains some information specific to the event, such as the x and y coordinate values of the event.

To access or change the event properties, use syntax such as the following:

```
window.event.cancelbubble
```

Changing the event properties within the event handler can impact the behavior resulting from the event. For example, you can capture the event for the pressing of a key, and alter the property `keyCode`. Doing this alters the character sent to the object receiving the event.

Table 4-4 lists the available properties of the Event object.

TABLE 4-4 Event Object Properties

Property	Description
keyCode	Integer that represents the ASCII code of the key — can be read or modified
fromElement	Element being moved with the `mouseout` or `mouseover` events — read only

---

Property	Description
toElement	Element being moved to with the mouseout or mouseover events — read-only
CancelBubble	When set to true, prevents event from bubbling up the object event hierarchy — read or write
x	Horizontal position of cursor — read-only
y	Vertical position of the mouse — read-only
clientX	Horizontal position of cursor relative to client area
clientY	Vertical position of cursor relative to client area
shiftKey	Set to true if Shift key is held; otherwise set to false — read-only
ctrlKey	Set to true if the Ctrl key is held; otherwise set to false — read-only
altKey	Set to true if the Alt key is held; otherwise set to false — read-only
button	The button currently pressed, if applicable
returnValue	Overrides normal return value from event — can read or write

Microsoft's event capturing is used extensively in the examples in the rest of the book and I hope this review provided a useful introduction. Animated effects can also be created using the Timer, which is discussed in the next section.

Working with the Timer

You might need to make use of the setTimeout or setInterval functions when working with animations or presentations. These functions create a timer and associate it with a function or an expression. At the end of the specified time, the function is processed or the expression is evaluated. The setTimeout function only calls the associated function once, and the setInterval function evaluates the expression repeatedly until the interval is cleared. For example, the following use of setTimeout sets the background color to red after five seconds:

```
TimerID = setTimeout("document.bgColor='#ff0000'", 5000, "vbscript")
```

To continue the process, refresh the timer operation after each iteration of the function or expression. As an example, the VBScript in Listing 4-6 creates a function called change_image that changes a displayed image every three seconds. The timer operation is started in a procedure called start_timer, which also creates a timer to change the Web page's background color. The latter timer operation, however, does not repeat.

Listing 4-6: Creating a timer that changes the displayed image every three seconds using VBScript

```
<HEAD>
<SCRIPT language="VBScript">
<!--

Dim image_number
image_number = 1

Sub start_timer
  timerID = window.setTimeout("change_image()", _
       5000, "vbscript")
  timerID2 = _
       window.setTimeout("document.bgColor='yellow'",_
       3000, "vbscript")
End Sub

Sub change_image
  Select case image_number
  Case 1
       document.images(0).src = "two.gif"
       image_number = 2
  Case 2
       document.images(0).src = "three.gif"
       image_number = 3
  Case 3
       document.images(0).src = "four.gif"
       image_number = 4
  Case Else
       document.images(0).src = "one.gif"
       image_number = 1
  End Select
  timerID = window.setTimeout("change_image()",_
       3000, "vbscript")
End Sub

//-->
</SCRIPT>
</HEAD>
<BODY onLoad="start_timer()" language="vbscript">
<H1> This is a test document</H1>
<p>
<img src="one.gif" name="testimage" width=150 height=30>
</BODY>
```

Figure 4-2 shows the document just after it is loaded. The image displayed is the word "one." The next image is the word "two," the third is the word "three," and the fourth is, what else but the word "four," as displayed in Figure 4-3. You can test this for yourself by accessing the file **vbtimer.htm**.

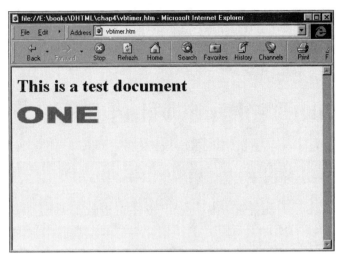

Figure 4-2: The timer, just after the test file, vbtimer.htm, is loaded

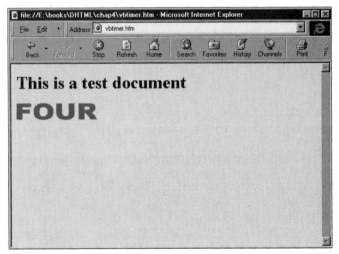

Figure 4-3: The timer, after the timer event has occurred several times and the image has been changed

You can also use the `setInterval` function instead of `setTimeout`. In this case, you wouldn't call the `setTimeout` function for each iteration; you would use the `setInterval` function just once, and then associate some event with clearing the interval using `clearInterval`.

The timer is essential for creating animation effects, or altering the contents of a Web page after a specified period of time has elapsed. The next section discusses opening new browser windows and also covers the new modal dialog technique introduced in IE 4.0.

Working with Multiple Windows

The code to open a new browser window and maintain communication between the parent and child windows is actually relatively simple if it uses default functionality. The following code loads an existing HTML document into a new window, and then links the two through a property called the Opener property. One function creates a window with all properties set to the default values. Another function closes the new window's parent window (the window that opened the new window) via the Opener window property:

```
<SCRIPT language="vbscript">
<!--

Dim new_window
Sub start_window
  Set new_window = window.open("vbtimer.htm",
"NewWindow", _
  "directories=no, menubar=yes, width=300, height=300")
End Sub

Sub close_window
  new_window.opener.close()
//-->
</SCRIPT>
```

The first parameter of the method is the URL of the file that will be loaded into the window. If you want to dynamically create content in the new window, you can provide an empty string for this parameter. The second parameter is optional and specifies a name for the new window. The third parameter is also optional and is a string of window properties.

Another approach to opening a separate window is the ShowModalDialog method, which creates a modal dialog window. A modal dialog captures the application focus and all the events for the application until the dialog box is closed. The ShowModalDialog method returns a result of type Variant, which you can assign to a variable and use to refer to the window. Table 4-5 provides a listing of features that can be set when creating a new window using open. Table 4-6 provides the listing of features that can be set when using showModalDialog.

TABLE 4-5 Window Object Properties

Property	Allowable Values
fullscreen	[yes|no] [0|1]
channelmode	[yes|no] [0|1]
location	[yes|no] [0|1]
directories	[yes|no] [0|1]
status	[yes|no] [0|1]
menubar	[yes|no] [0|1]
scrollbars	[yes|no] [0|1]
resizable	[yes|no] [0|1]
toolbar	[yes|no] [0|1]
width	number of pixels
height	number of pixels
top	number of pixels
left	number of pixels

TABLE 4-6 Modal Dialog Properties

Property	Valid Values
dialogWidth	dialogWidth:number
dialogHeight	dialogHeight:number
dialogTop	dialogTop:number
dialogLeft	dialogLeft:number
center	center:[yes|no] [0|1]
font	font:CSS1 value
font-family	font-family:CSS1 value

continued

TABLE **4-6 Modal Dialog Properties** *(continued)*

Property	Valid Values
font-style	font-style:CSS1 value
font-weight	font-weight:CSS1 value
font-style	font-style:CSS1 value
font-variant	font-variant:CSS1 value
border	border:[thick | thin]
help	help: [yes|no] [0|1]
minimize	minimize: [yes|no] [0|1]
maximize	maximize: [yes|no] [0|1]

Listing 4-7 shows the code for an HTML page that contains two buttons. Pressing the button labeled "open" uses the Open method to create a new browser window. Pressing the second button, labeled "show dialog," opens a separate browser window using the ShowModalDialog method. The code for the listing can also be found in the file named **openex.htm**. This functionality is used elsewhere in examples throughout this book, so you might want to take some time to try out the example and change the properties to understand the impact of each change.

Listing 4-7: Window.open and window.showModalDialog functions

```
<HEAD>
<SCRIPT language="VBScript">
<!--

Dim new_window
Sub start_window
  window.open "vbtimer.htm", "New Window", _
  "directories=no, menubar=yes, width=300, height=300" + _
  "borderSize=thick, border=thin"
End Sub

Sub start_dialog
  Dim ret_value
  ret_value = window.showModalDialog("diag.htm", _
  "dialog", "font-family:Cursive, border:thick, help:yes")
  MsgBox(ret_value)
End Sub

//-->
```

```
</SCRIPT>
</HEAD>
<BODY>
<INPUT type=button value="open" onClick="start_window()">
<INPUT type=button value="show dialog" onClick="start_dialog()">
</BODY>
```

Figure 4-4 demonstrates the dialog window that is opened with the ShowModalDialog method, and Listing 4-8 contains the code for the dialog window. Also, you can view the dialog window contents in the file **diag.htm**. Note, from this example, that a value is returned to the window that used the showModalDialog function when a value is assigned to the ReturnValue property. If the dialog window file **diag.htm** was not opened from another Web page and with the use of ShowModalDialog, assigning a value to ReturnValue will cause an error. Try opening the modal dialog window by pressing the "show" button in the **openex.htm** application, and type anything into the text box that receives the focus when the window is first opened. Then click the button to close the window. A message box in the parent window displays the value you typed.

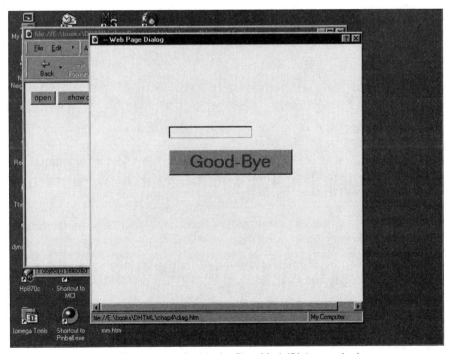

Figure 4-4: The modal dialog, created with the ShowModalDialog method

Listing 4-8: Modal dialog page demonstrating setting returnValue, and the new BUTTON tag

```
<HEAD>
<SCRIPT language="VBScript">
<!--
Sub document_onload
  document.test.value = "test"
End Sub
Sub close_window
  window.returnValue = document.all.test.value
  window.close()
End Sub
</SCRIPT>
<BODY style="margin: 1.5in">
<INPUT type=text name="test">
<p>
<BUTTON onclick="close_window()">
<H1 style="color:red">Good-Bye</H1>
</BUTTON>
</BODY>
```

Notice from Listing 4-8 that the button that closes the window uses the new BUTTON element, which is included in the HTML 4.0 draft at the time this was written. This element is a container object that allows you to enclose any HTML element, which IE then displays as a button.

Summary

This chapter has been a review of VBScript, with emphasis on the examples used throughout this book. It has not been extensive, nor is it meant to be a tutorial in the use of VBScript. It is meant to be an introduction to VBScript techniques, as well as a translating tool for those who have only coded in JavaScript.

In this chapter you learned:

- ◆ You can use variables to store values either locally within a function, or globally throughout all functions.

- ◆ Variables can be of different data types, but the typing occurs when a value is assigned to a variable.

- ◆ Arrays can be created to hold different data types, or even to hold entire VBScript objects.

- ◆ You can use a combination of conditional statements such as the If...Then or the Select Case statements.

- ◆ VBScript provides several looping style statements such as the Do...Loop, For...Next, and For Each...Next statements.

◆ Events can be captured using traditional methods, such as by using the `onclick` event handler in a link, or by naming the event handler with the object name followed by the appropriate syntax for the event.

◆ Beginning with Internet Explorer 4.0, the new Event object can provide information about an event.

◆ Timer events can be created with the `setTimeout` function, which processes the expression or function call when the timer triggers, and the `setInterval` function, which evaluates an expression until the interval is cleared.

◆ A *window* can open a new browser window and maintain communication with it. Windows can be opened as a distinct browser window or as modal dialogs.

The next section of the book contains a detailed look at Microsoft Internet Explorer-specific dynamic HTML. This begins with Chapter 5, which provides an overview of Microsoft's Internet Explorer object model.

Part II

Microsoft's Dynamic HTML

Chapter 5

Working with Microsoft's Dynamic HTML Object Model

IN THIS CHAPTER

◆ Microsoft's object model

◆ Basic HTML objects: window and document

◆ The location, history, and navigator objects

◆ The style object

◆ The screen object

◆ The TextRange object

◆ The body object

◆ The inner and outer HTML properties

◆ The event and selection objects

◆ HTML elements

◆ The collections

THIS CHAPTER CONTAINS AN overview of Microsoft's object model, including the properties and methods for each object. The chapter begins with a big-picture look at the Microsoft object model. The differences between an object model and a scripting language have caused confusion for Web developers working with both Netscape's Navigator and Microsoft's Internet Explorer. For example, in Internet Explorer version 3.01, Microsoft supported the language extensions for JavaScript 1.1 but did not support Netscape's object model extensions, including the image object (so code that included these extensions would not work with IE 3.01). It is essential to understand the differences between a scripting language and an object model when developing applications intended to work on more than one type of browser.

The Microsoft Object Model

Microsoft's approach to dynamic HTML makes use of several different objects, many of them new. The basic objects, such as `window` and `document`, form the foundation of the object model. Additionally, with Internet Explorer 4.0, several new objects have been specifically added to enable dynamic HTML, such as the `event` and `style` objects, as well as several new collections, such as `images` and `scripts`. Figure 5-1 illustrates the hierarchy of Microsoft's object model.

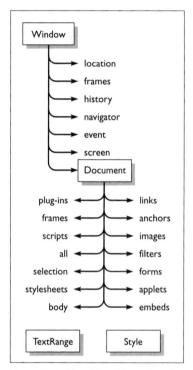

Figure 5-1: The object hierarchy of Microsoft's object model

As you'll learn in the next section, and sections to follow, the `document` object owns many objects, and is, in turn, owned by the `window` object.

Note that the other basic objects are the form and input elements, such as `text` and `button`, but because these aren't necessarily directly associated with dynamic HTML, they won't be discussed in detail.

Basic HTML Objects: Window and Document

The most fundamental object in the model, the `window` object, obtains data regarding the current state of the window. It also accesses the window's document and events, as well as important browser-specific information.

The `document` object obtains information about the document, and uses it to analyze and change HTML text and elements within the document, and to process events. Both of these objects are covered in more detail in this section.

The Window Object

A window can be a separate browser window, or it can be a specific frame within a FRAMESET. Every object in Microsoft's object model is owned by the `window` object. Because of this, the keyword `window` is usually left off when referring to an object. For example, the following code demonstrates two ways to set the `SRC` attribute of two image objects, one using the `window` reference, the other not:

```
document.images(0).src = "some.gif"
window.document.images(0).src = "some.gif"
```

The properties of the `window` object are listed in Table 5-1. All the properties that specify a measurement are in units of pixels.

TABLE 5-1 Window Properties

Property	Description
client	Browser
closed	Boolean value indicating whether the reference window is closed
defaultStatus	Message that is displayed, by default, in the status bar
dialogArguments	Variable or array of variables passed to the dialog
dialogHeight	Height of dialog
dialogWidth	Width of dialog
dialogTop	Window top
dialogLeft	Window left

continued

TABLE 5-1 **Window Properties** *(continued)*

Property	Description
document	document object
event	event object
history	history object
length	When used with the frames collection, the number of frames (read-only)
location	location object
navigator	navigator object
name	Name of window if one has been assigned; set to a value when a new browser window is opened using open and the name is specified, or when a frame and a name is given in the FRAMESET (read-only)
offscreenBuffering	Specifies whether to use the offscreen buffer
opener	Reference to the window that opened the current window
parent	If a window is a frame, returns FRAMESET window (read-only)
returnValue	Used with modal dialog windows; set this value to return the value to the calling routine
self	Current window (read-only)
status	Message displayed in the status bar
top	Top-most ancestor window (read-only)

Table 5-2 lists the methods available for the window object, including any parameters.

Table 5-2 Window Object Methods

Method	Functionality	Parameters
alert	Displays alert message	message
blur	Loses focus and triggers onBlur	
clearTimeout	Cancels an existing timer	timer id
clearInterval	Cancels an existing interval timer	timer id
close	Closes a window	
confirm	Displays confirmation message	message
execScript	Executes script	script, language (such as JScript)
focus	gets focus and triggers onFocus	
navigate	Sets the URL (VBScript only)	URL
open	Opens a new browser window	URL, title, attributes, replace
prompt	Displays prompt message and input field	message, default
setTimeout	Creates a timer that evaluates an expression	expr, time, language
setInterval	Creates an interval timer that evaluates an expression	expr, time
scroll	Turns scroll bar on or off	'yes'	'no'
showHelp	Shows a help file	URL, arguments
showModalDialog	Opens a modal dialog	URL, title, attributes

Next, take a look at Listing 5-1, which demonstrates the window object and some of its methods. This example, which can be found in file **opentst.htm**, has three buttons. Pressing the first button opens a new browser window, pressing the second closes it, and pressing the third displays the message "Window has never been opened" in the status bar. Additionally, the status and defaultStatus properties are set and reset during the example.

VBScript or JavaScript/JScript?

The examples in this chapter, and in other IE-specific chapters, use both VBScript and JScript. (Most of you probably know this, but just to clarify: Microsoft refers to its form of JavaScript as "JScript." So when "JavaScript" is used in this book, I'm referring to both JavaScript and JScript.)

Different reasons exist for choosing JScript or VBScript for a given application. Usually, when I'm creating a new object, or if I need JavaScript-specific functions or array capabilities, I use JScript. I also use JScript when creating a cross-browser application. When I want to use Windows-specific technology, I use VBScript.

Most of the time, it really doesn't matter which language you use. However, I try to use both languages often enough to keep my scripting skills up to speed. (The only drawback I find to working with both languages is that I keep using the semi-colon (;) with VBScript, and forget to use it with JScript.)

Note that JavaScript is used most predominately in the last part of this book because it is the most commonly used language.

Listing 5-1: Opening and closing a new window, and getting the window's open status

```
<HEAD>
<SCRIPT language="javascript">
<!--

new_window = null;
function start_window() {
  new_window = window.open("blank.htm","NewWindow",
  "directories=no, menubar=yes, width=300, height=300" +
  "borderSize=thick, border=thin" +
  "defaultStatus='Window is open'");
}

function close_window() {
 if (new_window==null)
   status="no window to close";
 else {
   new_window.close();
   new_window = null;
   defaultStatus = "Window is closed";
 }
}

function test_window() {
 if (new_window == null)
   status="Window has never been opened or is closed";
 else
```

```
        status="Window is currently open";
}

//-->
</SCRIPT>
</HEAD>
<BODY onLoad="status='Window is closed'">
<INPUT type=button value="open"
        onClick="start_window()">
<INPUT type=button value="close"
        onClick="close_window()">
<INPUT type=button value="Test Window"
        onClick="test_window()">
</BODY>
```

If you use the `window.open` method to open a window and assign its result to a variable (as shown in Listing 5-1), you can use the `closed` property of that object reference to test whether that window is still open, as shown in the following code:

```
if (new_window.closed)
  status = "The window is closed";
```

This is only effective, though, if you know whether the variable has been instantiated. If the variable `new_window` has not been instantiated, a scripting error will result.

The Document Object

If the `window` object *owns* everything, the `document` object *controls* most of it. You access most elements of an HTML page through the `document` object. This object is the part of the window that contains the Web page users will see onscreen, so it's important to be able to programmatically access the elements of the page through the `document` object.

The properties of the `document` object are listed in Table 5-3.

TABLE 5-3 Document Object Properties

Property	Description
alinkColor	Color of the active links within the document
activeElement	Element that currently has focus (read-only)
bgColor	Background color of the object
cookie	Information that can be persistently stored on the client machine

continued

TABLE 5-3 Document Object Properties *(continued)*

Property	Description
domain	Domain suffix, to enable pages to share code, though server host name may differ (read-only)
fgColor	Color of foreground text
linkColor	Color of the links within the document
lastModified	Date and time the Web page was last modified (read-only)
location	location object
parentWindow	Window that owns document
referrer	URL of previous location (read-only)
readyState	Status of object being loaded with values of: complete(4), interactive(3), loading(2), uninitialized(1) (read-only)
title	Title of document
URL	URL of document (read-only)
vlinkColor	Color of the unvisited links within the document

The document object methods used in the example and other methods are listed in Table 5-4, along with any parameters.

TABLE 5-4 Document Object Methods

Method	Functionality	Parameters
close	Closes the document and displays contents	
blur	Removes focus from document	
open	Opens document for write methods	mimeType
clear	Clears document	
createElement	Creates element of type IMG or OPTION	tag of element
write	Writes HTML to document	HTML expression

continued

Method	Functionality	Parameters
writeln	Writes HTML/carriage return to document	HTML expression
execCommand	Runs command over range	cmd, value, UI flag
elementFromPoint	Returns element at position	x,y
queryCommandEnabled	Is command enabled	command
queryCommandText	String associated with command	command
queryCommandSupported	Specifies whether command is on/off	command
queryCommandState	Returns true, false, null — current state	command
queryCommandIndeterm	Specifies whether command is indeterminate	command
queryCommandValue	Value of current command	

Note that the execCommand method and the query methods use *command identifiers* to execute a command on a specific object. These same commands are also supported for the new TextRange object, and are discussed later in this chapter.

I'll now show you some of these document object properties and methods in an example that uses the cookie property. As you probably know, a *cookie* is a small bit of persistent information that is stored on the client machine. Because changes made by dynamic HTML are essentially "erased" every time a page reloads, maintaining state information can be very important. Using Netscape-style cookies extensively, this example shows how to maintain state information by setting and retrieving a cookie and also how to write out information about a Web page directly on the page using the writeln method (see Listing 5-2). This example can be found in the file called **doctest.htm**.

Listing 5-2: A demonstration of document properties and methods

```
<HEAD>
<title>test</title>

<SCRIPT language="javascript">
```

```
function set_cookie() {

    var cookieDate = new Date();
    cookieDate.setTime (cookieDate.getTime() +
            (1000 * 60 * 60 * 24));
    var content = document.forms[0].elements[2].value;
    document.cookie = "test_cookie=" + escape (content) +
        "; expires=" + cookieDate.toGMTString();
    document.forms[0].elements[2].value = "";
    }

function get_cookie() {
 var content = document.cookie;
 var loc = content.indexOf("=");
 var results = content.substring(loc + 1,
        content.length);
 results = unescape(results)
 document.forms[0].elements[2].value = results;
}

</SCRIPT>
</HEAD>
<BODY>
<FORM>
<INPUT type=button value="Set Cookie"
        onClick="set_cookie()">
<INPUT type=button value="Get Cookie"
        onClick="get_cookie()">
<INPUT type=text name="cookie_text">
<p>
<h2>Document Information: </H2>
<SCRIPT language="VBScript">
<!--

document.writeln("This file was created " +
        CStr(document.fileCreatedDate) + "<br>")
document.writeln("Document was last updated at " +
        CStr(document.lastModified) + "<br>")
document.writeln("Document size is " +
        CStr(document.fileSize) + " bytes<br>")

//-->
</SCRIPT>
</BODY>
```

As you can see from the example code, a Netscape cookie contains a "name-value" pair and an expiration date. The cookie is then stored by reference to the Web page location, which means that a cookie set from one location is not accessible from a Web page at another location. Also, notice the use of the escape and unescape functions. These functions translate the string into content that can be successfully transferred using HTTP, which is used for setting and retrieving the cookies. Figure 5-2 shows what this page looks like in IE 4.0.

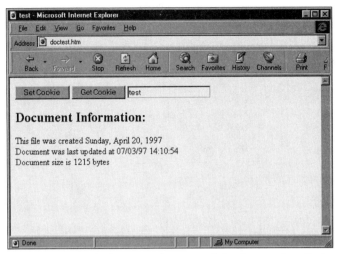

Figure 5-2: Example demonstrating some of the document methods

Now that you're familiar with the `window` and `document` objects, we will move on to a handful of other objects that will help you create compelling Web pages.

The Location, History, and Navigator Objects

As you'll learn in this section, the `location`, `history`, and `navigator` objects enable you to add functionality helpful to both you and anyone visiting your site. The `location` object contains information about the URL currently loaded. The `history` object contains information about which URLs have been visited, and in what order. The `navigator` object maintains information about which browser and version is accessing the page. Table 5-5 shows the properties of each of these objects.

Note that, in the final section of this book, the `navigator` object is used in complex examples that work in both Navigator and Internet Explorer.

TABLE 5-5 Location, History, and Navigator Object Properties

Object	Property	Description
location	hash	The string minus the pound sign (#) with a named anchor tag
location	host	Host name concatenated with port, if any
location	hostname	Host name of the Web page
location	href	URL that is the target of the link
location	pathname	Relative path of the Web page
location	port	Port number, if any
location	protocol	Type of protocol used to access the page, such as HTTP:
location	search	Form data or query string
history	length	Number of URLs currently maintained in history
navigator	appName	Name of the browser
navigator	appVersion	Version of the browser
navigator	codeName	Code name of the browser
navigator	cookieEnabled	Specifies whether cookies are enabled
navigator	plugins	Collection; plug-ins loaded for the browser
navigator	mimeTypes	Collection; MIME types defined for the browser
navigator	userAgent	User agent header sent with HTTP protocol

The methods for the navigator, history, and location objects are listed in Table 5-6, along with any parameters.

These properties and methods can help you test for both the application and version of the browser loading your Web page, which is really important when you are scripting objects unique to a specific browser and browser version. The code in Listing 5-3, which can be found as file **lochist.htm**, tests to see if the client is running Internet Explorer 4.0. If the program is running, the background color is set to yellow. If not, the background is set to aqua. Additionally, the example prints out information about the location object and history object.

TABLE 5-6 Navigator, History, and Location Object Methods

Method	Functionality	Parameters
navigator.javaEnabled	Call to determine if Java is enabled	
navigator.taintEnabled	Call to determine if data tainting is enabled; returns false for IE 4.0 as data tainting is not enabled	
history.back	Loads previous URL	
history.forward	Loads next URL	
history.go	Loads specific URL	location delta | URL
location.reload	Refreshes current document	
location.replace	Replaces current document, including history list	URL
location.assign	Sets current location to given URL	URL

Listing 5-3: Script to check for browser version, change background color if browser is IE 4.0, and print out location and history information

```
<HEAD>
<title>test</title>

<SCRIPT language="javascript">
<!--
window.isIE4 = ((parseInt(navigator.appVersion.substring(0,1)) >= 4)
 && (navigator.appVersion.indexOf("MSIE"))>0)

//-->
</SCRIPT>
</HEAD>
<BODY bgcolor="aqua"
  onLoad="if (window.isIE4) document.bgColor='yellow'">
<h2 id=test>Location/History Information: </H2>

<SCRIPT language="javascript">
<!--

document.writeln("host is " + location.host + "<br>")
document.writeln("hostname is " + location.hostname +    "<br>")
document.writeln("pathname is " + location.pathname +    "<br>")
document.writeln("protocol is " + location.protocol +    "<br>")
```

```
document.writeln("length is " + history.length + "<br>")
//-->
</SCRIPT>

</BODY>
```

Note that the write and writeln methods are used in a script block after all the other page contents. This prevents the methods from overwriting all the other Web page content. To see a full demonstration of the differences in the objects' properties, open the page (lochist.htm) as a file in more than one browser and then compare this to how it opens from a Web server.

The Style Object

In IE 4.0, Microsoft exposed all of the standard HTML elements to their object model. This means that you can modify the properties of an element, such as an <H1> header, programmatically. In this section, however, I want to discuss only one of these properties, style, which is also an object in its own right.

The style object is used to modify the CSS1 attributes for any HTML element. As an example of this, the script in Listing 5-4, file **elemsty.htm**, creates a Web page that displays content based on what happens when a parent element is clicked. You probably recognize this type of behavior from presentation software such as Microsoft's PowerPoint, which progressively displays parts of the displayed page, based on user input.

Listing 5-4: A presentation-style Web page, with content displayed based on user input

```
<HEAD>
<title>test</title>
<STYLE text="text/css">
 H1 { margin-left: 0.25in; color: navy;
      font-size: 24pt }
 H2 { margin-left: 0.5in; color: red;
      font-size: 18pt }
 P { margin-left: 0.75in; margin-right: 1.5in;
      color; blue;
      font-size: 12pt }
</STYLE>

<SCRIPT language="javascript1">
<!--

function clicked_element(){
    var child = document.all[event.srcElement.child]
    if (child!=null)
        child.style.display = child.style.display ==
                    "none" ? "" : "none"
 }
```

```
//-->
</SCRIPT>

</HEAD>
<BODY onclick="clicked_element()">
<H1 child=test> Dynamically replacing HTML</H1>
<h2 id=test child=content style="display:none"> This is
        second header</h2>
<p id=content style="display:none"> This is the content that you see
  if you click on both of the headers. This is similar in style to
  presentation software, in which the content unfolds based on the
  presenter's actions</p>
</BODY>
```

When the Web page is first opened, as demonstrated in Figure 5-3, only the top-most header is shown. However, when you click this header and then click the second one, contents previously hidden are displayed, as shown in Figure 5-4. Also, in this example, clicking a header hides the associated content if it is already visible.

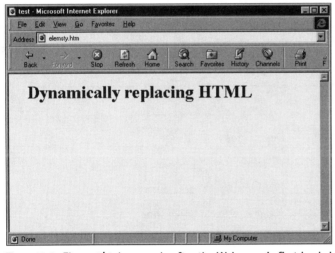

Figure 5-3: Element/style example after the Web page is first loaded

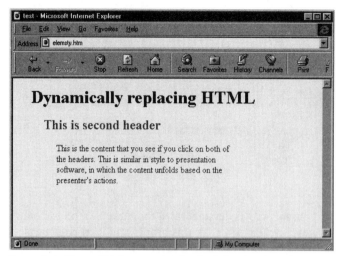

Figure 5-4: Element/style example after both headers have been clicked

As you can see in this example, modification of CSS1 attributes for an HTML element occurs through the style object. These attributes have been converted to properties that can be set, dynamically, from script. Table 5-7 lists each of the style object properties along with a brief description.

TABLE 5-7 **Style Object Properties**

Property	Description
background	Shortcut method for setting background properties
backgroundColor	Color of element background
backgroundImage	Image of element background
backgroundRepeat	Indicates how the background image repeats
backgroundAttachment	Indicates how the background image is attached
backgroundPosition	Position where the background image is attached
backgroundPositionX	Left position for the background image
backgroundPositionY	Top position for the background image
border	Shortcut method for setting border properties
borderBottom	Shortcut method for setting border bottom properties

continued

Property	Description
`borderTop`	Shortcut method for setting border top properties
`borderRight`	Shortcut method for setting right border properties
`borderLeft`	Shortcut method for setting left border properties
`borderStyle`	Shortcut method for setting border style
`borderTopColor`	Top border color
`borderRightColor`	Right border color
`borderBottomColor`	Bottom border color
`borderLeftColor`	Left border color
`borderTopWidth`	Width of top border
`borderRightWidth`	Width of right border
`borderLeftWidth`	Width of left border
`borderBottomWidth`	Width of bottom border
`borderBottomStyle`	Style of bottom border
`borderTopStyle`	Style of top border
`borderLeftStyle`	Style of left border
`borderRightStyle`	Style of right border
`clear`	Vertical space for text alignment around an image
`clip`	Clipping dimensions for element
`color`	Color of text
`cssText`	Persisted representation of style rule, which is the style sheet set for the individual element explicitly within the tag for the element
`cursor`	Sets type of mouse cursor when over element
`display`	Whether the item is displayed or not
`filter`	Any filters applied to element
`font`	Shortcut method for setting font properties
`fontSize`	Size of font

continued

TABLE 5-7 Style Object Properties *(continued)*

Property	Description
fontStyle	Style of font
fontVariant	Font variant
fontWeight	Weight of font
fontFamily	Font family
height	Height in absolute units or percentages
left	Left location of element including units
letterSpacing	Spacing between letters
lineHeight	Distance between the baselines of two adjacent lines
listStyleType	Type of style for list element
listStyleImage	Image used with list elements
listStylePosition	Indicates how the list marker is drawn
margin	Shortcut method for setting margins
marginLeft	Left margin of element
marginRight	Right margin of element
marginTop	Top margin of element
marginBottom	Bottom margin of element
overflow	Indicates how content overflow is handled
paddingTop	White space between contents and top border
paddingRight	White space between contents and right border
paddingBottom	White space between contents and bottom border
paddingLeft	White space between contents and left border
pageBreakBefore	Page break before element
pageBreakAfter	Page break after element
pixelHeight	Height of element in pixels
pixelWidth	Width of element in pixels

continued

Property	Description
pixelLeft	Location of the left side of the element in pixels
pixelTop	Location of the top side of the element in pixels
position	Type of positioning used with the element
posLeft	Location of the left side of the element in style-based units
posTop	Location of the top of the element in style-based units
posHeight	Height of the element in style-based units
posWidth	Width of the element in style-based units
styleFloat	Specifies whether the image floats left or right
textAlign	Horizontal alignment of text
textDecoration	Decoration applied to text, such as underlining
textDecorationBlink	Specifies whether text blinks
textDecorationUnderline	Specifies whether text is underlined
textDecorationOverline	Specifies whether text is overlined
textDecorationLineThrough	Specifies whether a line is drawn through text
textIndent	Indentation of text for the first line
textTransform	Transformation of text, such as all caps
top	Top position of the element
verticalAlign	Vertical alignment of text
visibility	Specifies whether the element is visible, or visibility is inherited
width	Length in absolute units or percentages
zIndex	Z-index of the element; indicates how elements layer

Now take a look at the file **styletst.htm,** which contains the contents of one of the pages from my Web site. It's a good example of how styles can be changed dynamically using the style object. The file includes the onClick, onMouseOver, and onMouseOut events for several of the HTML elements. Depending on which item receives the event, a style setting is changed for one or more elements. This example has the following dynamic features:

◆ A `mouseOver` event, in which the main header, "The Implementation Alternative," changes to red, and when the mouse leaves the element (the `mouseOut` event), the color is set to navy:

```
<h1 onMouseOver="this.style.color='red'"
    onMouseOut="this.style.color='navy'">
    The Implementation Alternatives</h1>
```

◆ An `onClick` event, in which "Alternatives" makes visible its hidden subordinate listing:

```
<h3 onClick="listitem1.style.display=listitem1.style.display
    == 'none' ? '' : 'none'">
    Alternatives -
    <span style="color: red;font-weight: 400;
        font-size: 10pt">click me</span></H3>
<OL id=listitem1 style="display:none">
...
</OL>
```

Notice the words "click me" have a different font than the rest of the header. Also notice that because the `<OL>` element is hidden, the list of items it contains, by default, inherit their visibility property from their parent element and are also not displayed until the header is clicked.

◆ A `mouseOver` event, in which the heading "Alternative 1" changes the style of the paragraph below it to a cursive font and a green background color (as seen in Figure 5-5). When the mouse leaves the header area (the `mouseOut` event), the paragraph is returned to normal:

```
<h2 onMouseOver="alt1.style.backgroundColor='lime';
    alt1.style.fontFamily='Cursive'"
    onMouseOut="alt1.style.backgroundColor='white';
    alt1.style.fontFamily='Arial'">
Alternative 1 - Linux, mSQL, and Java Applets
        created by Visual J++</h2>
<P id=alt1>
...
</P>
```

◆ A `mouseOver` event, in which "What is Linux?" pops up an element next to it that reads "Beats the Heck out of Me," as seen in Figure 5-6:

```
<SPAN onMouseOver="whoknows.style.display=''";
        onMouseOut="whoknows.style.display='none'"
        style="font-weight: 700; font-size: 14pt">
What is Linux?</span>
<SPAN id=whoknows
    style="color:red;font-style:italic;
    font-family:cursive;font-weight:200;display:none">
Beats the Heck out of Me!</SPAN>
```

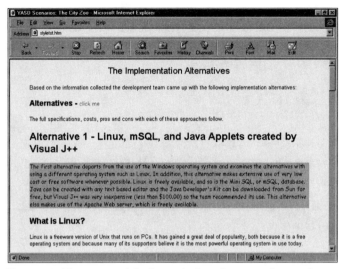

Figure 5-5: The paragraph is changed when the mouse is over the preceding header

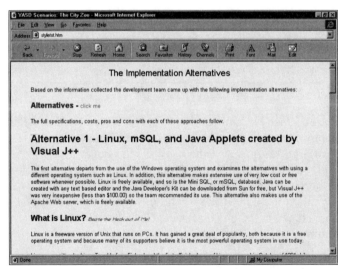

Figure 5-6: When the mouse is over the "What is Linux?" heading, a phrase pops up

Instead of using a regular header such as <H3>, I emulated a header by using the same font and weight, and then used the <SPAN> element to change the style setting inline. I didn't include a page break because I think it ruins the effect. If you have some time and want to have a little fun, try your own HTML event trapping and style setting with the rest of the Web page document using this example as a template.

The Screen Object

The screen object provides information about the screen settings, including color depth and horizontal and vertical resolutions. This object provides a way to test the screen settings of the client accessing the Web page. This object's properties are listed in Table 5-8.

TABLE 5-8 Screen Object Properties

Property	Description
bufferDepth	Enables buffering for bitmaps
colorDepth	Represents the BPI (bits per inch) of the current screen color settings; a value of 8 is equivalent to 256-color mode
updateInterval	Timing that determines how long between updates of window
width	Horizontal pixel settings
height	Vertical pixel settings

Take a look at Listing 5-5, which has a function, change_doc, that is called when the page is loaded. This function tests the color depth and resolution of the screen and changes the image to high-resolution if the color depth is over 8 (256-color mode). If the screen is in 256-color mode or less, the page loads a low-resolution gray image. Also, if the horizontal resolution is greater than or equal to 800, the page loads a larger image than it would if the resolution were less than 800. The background color is also changed based on color depth. The example can be found in the file named **visual.htm**.

Listing 5-5: Web page containing script to test the properties of the visual object and load the appropriate image

```
<HEAD>
<title>test</title>
<SCRIPT language="vbscript">
<!--
Sub change_doc
```

```
    Dim filename
    If screen.colordepth > 8 Then
        filename = filename + "haysthi"
        document.bgColor = "#ffdd33"
    Else
        document.bgColor = "yellow"
        filename = filename + "haystlw"
    End If
    If screen.width >= 800 Then
        filename = filename + "1.JPG"
    Else
        filename = filename + "2.JPG"
    End If

    document.images(0).src = filename
End Sub
//-->
</SCRIPT>

</HEAD>
<BODY onLoad="change_doc">
<H1> Dynamically altering HTML</H1>
<img src="blank.gif" id="someimage">
</BODY>
```

The preceding technique loads a lower-resolution image that remains on the page rather than acting as a placeholder. Try this yourself with your current screen settings, and then change the settings to a higher or lower color depth and resolution, and run the example again. Figure 5-7 shows the file when it is run with a screen setting of 800 × 600 and a 16-bit (high color) color depth setting.

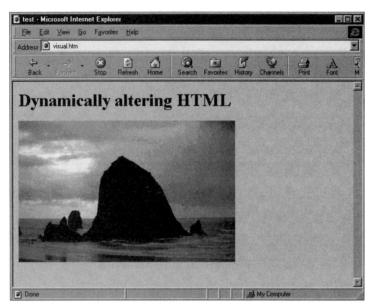

Figure 5-7: The file, opened with a display set at 800 × 600 and a 16-bit color depth

The TextRange Object

With the `TextRange` object, you can search for a specific word or group of words within the Web page, or within an element in the page. If the words can be found, they can be replaced with other text, or with one or more HTML elements. In addition, the `Scroll Window` method can be used to scroll the window to the coordinates of the text, creating your own inline search technique. Or you can change the text of an element in order to provide feedback to the Web page reader.

You create a `TextRange` object by calling a function, `createTextRange`, for any HTML element that has text associated with it. This includes the `BODY`, `BUTTON`, or `TEXTAREA` elements. You can also create a `TextRange` object using the `createRange` function on the `document.selection` object, as shown in the following code:

```
var tmp = document.selection;
var tmptxtobj = tmp.createRange();
```

This code creates a `TextRange` object from the selected text within the Web page. Once the range is created, several methods can be used to insert or replace HTML elements contained within the `TextRange` object.

The properties for the TextRange object are:

- htmlText — HTML source as an HTML fragment
- text — actual text from selection

Listing 5-6, which is in the file called **txtrng.htm**, demonstrates JavaScript that traps a clicked event for the document, creates a TextRange object, and then moves the point of this object to where the click occurred using the moveToPoint method. Then, an execCommand function call with the command identifier BOLD is issued. If you click a word within this Web page, it is set to a bold font.

Listing 5-6: Using JavaScript and the TextRange object to change the format of the clicked word

```
<HTML>
<HEAD>
<SCRIPT FOR=document EVENT=onclick language="javascript">
<!--
 x = event.x;
 y = event.y;
 thebody = document.body.createTextRange();
 thebody.moveToPoint(x,y);
 thebody.expand("word");
 thebody.execCommand("BOLD");
//-->
</SCRIPT>

</HEAD>
<BODY>
The first alternative departs from the use of the Windows operating
 system and examines the alternatives with using a different
 operating system such as Linux. In addition, this alternative makes
 extensive use of very low-cost or free software whenever possible.
 Linux is freely available, and so is the Mini SQL, or mSQL,
 database. Java can be created with any text-based editor and the
 Java Developer's Kit can be downloaded from Sun for free, but
 Visual J++ was very inexpensive (less than $100.00) so the team
 recommended its use. This alternative also makes use of the Apache
 Web server, which is freely available.
</BODY>
</HTML>
```

Figure 5-8 shows the Web page after several words have been clicked, and their font has been set to bold.

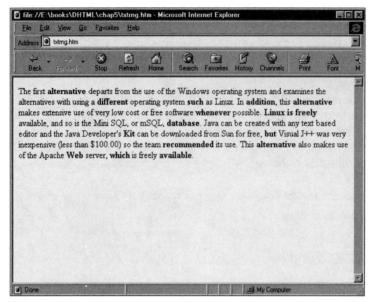

Figure 5-8: Example page demonstrating the new TextRange object

Notice from Listing 5-6 that a couple of methods are used with the `TextRange` object. Table 5-9 has a list of methods valid for this object, along with any parameters.

TABLE 5-9 **TextRange Object Methods**

Method	Functionality	Parameters
collapse	Creates empty range at the beginning/end of range	true/false
compareEndPoints	Compares endpoints between two `TextRange` objects	numeric comparison
duplicate	Duplicates range	
execCommand	Runs command over range	cmd, value, UI flag
expand	Expands the range to include a component	component
findText	Searches for text within the range	text string

continued

Method	Functionality	Parameters
getBookmark	Creates a bookmark, which is an opaque string and is used to return to a previous text range	
inRange	Specifies whether the given range is within the current range	range to compare
isEqual	Specifies whether the given range is equal to the range	range to compare
move	Moves the range over the text	unit to move, number
moveEnd	Adjusts the size of the range at the end	unit to size, number
moveStart	Adjusts the size of the range at the beginning	unit to size, number
moveToBookmark	Moves to the bookmark	
moveToElementText	Moves to the text range encompassed within the element	element
moveToPoint	Moves to the point within TextRange	x,y
parentElement	Parent of the element	
pasteHTML	Pastes HTML into the current range	HTML string
queryCommandEnabled	Is command enabled	command
queryCommandText	String associated with the command	command
queryCommandSupported	Specifies whether the command is on/off	command
queryCommandState	Returns true, false, null; current state	command
queryCommandIndeterm	Specifies whether the command is indeterminate	command
queryCommandValue	Value of the current command	
scrollIntoView	Specifies whether to go to beginning of the range	true/false

continued

TABLE 5-9 TextRange Object Methods *(continued)*

Method	Functionality	Parameters
select	Actively selects the range	
setEndPoint	Sets endpoint on the TextRange element based on another TextRange	elementtype, range

The Inner and Outer HTML and Text Properties

The TextRange object is not the only technique used to replace Web page contents. You can also use four new properties to work with element text and HTML content: the innerHTML, outerHTML, innerText, and outerText properties. In addition, two new methods, insertAdjacentHTML and insertAdjacentText, enable you to insert HTML and text respectively.

The innerHTML and outerHTML properties work with the HTML that falls between the start and end tags of the element. The difference between the two is that innerHTML replaces the content between the tags of the element, and the outerHTML property replaces the start and end tags of the element as well as the element contents. The property takes any valid (and it must be valid or an error results) HTML string, including any element tags.

The innerText and outerText properties replace the text-based, not HTML-based, content. Again, the innerText property replaces the text contained within the existing element's start and end tags; the outerText property replaces the text contained within the enclosing tags. The property takes any string.

When one of these properties is used, the string is immediately parsed, and any embedded HTML is processed.

As a fun example of using these very handy properties, I created an electronic version of an old favorite – tic-tac-toe. This version builds a playing board using an HTML table and sets the class of each table cell (delimited by the <TD> and </TD> tags) to a class named val. This class sets the background color of the cell to yellow. However, the most important aspect of the class is its name, as you will soon see. The key to the game is the use of innerHTML to replace the contents of the cell the Web page reader clicks. The code for the game is shown in Listing 5-7 and the corresponding file is called **tictac.htm**.

Listing 5-7: Web page of the tic-tac-toe game, using the innerHTML property

```
<HEAD>
<title>X marks the spot</title>
<STYLE type="text/css">
 body { margin: 0.5in; background-color: white }
 TD.val { background-color: yellow;
             width: 30; height:35; text-align:center }
 TD.noval { background-color: lime;
             width: 30; height: 35; text-align: center }
 DIV.game { margin-top: 0.5in; margin-left: 1.5in }
</STYLE>
<SCRIPT language="javascript">
<!--
var figname = "o.gif"
function make_play() {
    // get clicked location and drop image
    var obj=window.event.srcElement;
    if (obj.className != 'val')
        return

    obj.className = 'noval';
    figname = figname == "x.gif" ? "o.gif" : "x.gif";
    var thefigname = "<IMG src='" + figname + "'>";
    obj.innerHTML = thefigname;
}
//-->
</SCRIPT>

</HEAD>
<BODY onClick="make_play()">
<H1 id=header> Dynamic HTML tic-tac-toe</H1>
<p>
Now, I hope you know how to play this game...it's as old as time.
 Player 1 is 'X' and Player 2 is 'O'. The first player to get three
 boxes in a row, diagonally, horizontally, or vertically wins. If no
 player gets three boxes in a row, the game is a draw.
<DIV class=game>
<table border=5 cellpadding=0 cellspacing=5>
<tr><td id="one" class=val> </td><td id="two" class=val> </td>
 <td id="three"class=val> </td></tr>
<tr><td id="four" class=val> </td><td id="five" class=val> </td>
 <td id="six" class=val> </td></tr>
<tr><td id="seven" class=val> </td><td id="eight" class=val> </td>
 <td id="nine" class=val> </td></tr>
</table>
</DIV>
</BODY>
```

When the reader clicks the table cell, the function make_play is called. The srcElement property of the event object is accessed and its class name is checked. If it is equal to the game board table cell class, val, which represents a cell that hasn't been played yet, a string containing the HTML to embed a figure (either X or O depending on whose turn it is) is assigned to the `innerHTML` property of the table cell. To make sure the cell isn't played again, its class is changed to the `noval` class, which also changes the background color of the table cell. Figure 5-9 shows the Web page after X has won.

Figure 5-9: Tic-tac-toe game after X has won; demonstrates use of HTML replacement

Instead of replacing an entire element, you can also use the `insertAdjacentHTML` and `insertAdjacentText` methods to insert content into the element. For example, the following code inserts HTML into the Web page, and positions it just before the given element:

```
document.all.test.insertAdjacentHTML("BeforeBegin", "<img
   src='someimage.gif'>");
```

This statement inserts the image into the Web page just before the element named `test`. Positioning values for the insertion are: `BeforeBegin`, `AfterBegin`, `BeforeEnd`, and `AfterEnd`.

Most HTML elements have the properties and methods described in this section. Combining these with the `srcElement` property of the `event` object can make for some interesting interactive content possibilities, such as capturing the reader's mouse events and altering the Web contents based on these events.

The Event and Selection Objects

The final objects of the Microsoft object model I will discuss are the event and selection objects. The event object maintains information about the most recent event, such as which keys are pressed or the location of a clicked event. The selection object has information about the currently selected HTML element. Table 5-10 lists the properties for the event object.

TABLE 5-10 Event Properties

Property	Description
altKey	Specifies whether the Alt key is pressed during an event
button	Button pressed to generate an event
cancelBubble	Prevents the current event from passing to other objects in the hierarchy
clientX	Left position of the event within client units
clientY	Top position of the event within client units
ctrlKey	Specifies whether the Ctrl key is pressed during an event
fromElement	Element being moved with the mouseOver and mouseOut events
keyCode	ASCII value of the key currently pressed
offsetX	Left position of the element relative to a container element
offsetY	Top position of the element relative to a container element
returnValue	Return value of an event
shiftKey	Specifies whether the Shift key is pressed during an event
srcElement	Element within which an event originated
srcFilter	Filter that caused the event
toElement	Target element for the mouseOver and mouseOut events
type	Type of event
x	Horizontal position where the event occurred
y	Vertical position where the event occurred

An example in Chapter 4 uses the new event object, in addition to listing event handlers. You might want to review this chapter for information on this object.

The selection object has just a single property:

◆ selection.type — type of selection such as control, text selection, or table element

A selection object is created whenever the select method is used for a TextRange element, or whenever the Web page reader selects a block of text within a Web page. To work with a selection, use the following methods:

◆ clear — clears the selection

◆ createRange — creates a TextRange object of the selection

◆ empty — clears the selection and sets the item to null

The following code shows how to use this object to capture a reader's selection and clear it:

```
<SCRIPT language="jscript" FOR="document"
        EVENT="onmouseup">
 selection.clear();
</SCRIPT>
```

This script removes whatever the reader has selected on the page whenever the mouseUp event occurs.

This concludes the discussion on objects. Next to be covered are HTML elements, and how they differ in IE 4.0.

HTML Elements

Microsoft exposed HTML elements to its object model beginning with IE 4.0. In addition, Microsoft also added new HTML elements to reflect the HTML 4.0 draft specification under consideration at the time this was written.

The elements that are currently accessible from script are listed in Table 5-11. Elements related to HTML 4.0 are delimited with an asterisk.

TABLE 5-11   HTML Elements Exposed to Scripting

Element	Purpose	Element	Purpose
A	anchor tag	ADDRESS	address block
APPLET	Java applet	AREA	client-side image map hot spot
B	bold text	BASE	document's base URL
*BASEFONT	base font	BGSOUND	background sound
BIG	bigger font	BLOCKQUOTE	text quotation
BODY	body tag	BR	line break
*BUTTON	container for HTML rendered as button	CAPTION	table caption
CENTER	centers content	CITE	renders text in italic
CODE	code sample	COL	table column
*COLGROUP	group of columns	COMMENT	HTML comment
DD	definition list definition	DFN	defining term
DIR	directory list	DIV	HTML block-level container
DL	definition list	DT	definition term in definition list
EM	emphasis	EMBED	embedded document
*FIELDSET	groups form elements	FONT	defining font
FORM	HTML form	FRAME	individual frame
FRAMESET	defines frames		
H1...H6	headers	HEAD	document head section
HR	horizontal rule	HTML	HTML document tag
I	italic font	*IFRAME	inline floating frame
IMG	image	INPUT	form input control
KBD	fixed-width font	*LABEL	label for a control
*LEGEND	FIELDSET caption	LI	list item

continued

TABLE 5-11 HTML Elements Exposed to Scripting *(continued)*

Element	Purpose	Element	Purpose
LINK	link	LISTING	fixed-width type
MAP	client-side image map hot spots	MARQUEE	scrolling text
MENU	individual block elements	META	meta tag
*NEXTID	text editing software for unique IDs	OBJECT	page object
OL	ordered list	OPTION	select list option
P	paragraph	PLAINTEXT	fixed-width type
PRE	fixed-width type	S	strike-through type
SAMP	code sample	SCRIPT	scripting block
SELECT	select box	SMALL	relatively smaller font
SPAN	inline text container	STRIKE	strike-through type
STRONG	text in bold	STYLE	style sheet tag
SUB	subscript type	SUP	superscript type
TABLE	HTML table	TBODY	table body
TD	table cell	TEXTAREA	text control
TFOOT	table foot	TH	table column header
THEAD	table head	TITLE	document title
TR	table row	TT	teletype text in fixed-width type
U	underline text	UL	unordered list
VAR	small fixed-width font	XMP	example text in fixed-width type

You can access each of the preceding elements with a given name or identifier, or via the `all` collection discussed in the section on collections. Additionally, applicable CSS1 style sheet settings for those elements that are visible can be set using the `style` object property discussed in the preceding section.

In addition to style sheet settings, several properties can be read and/or modified and several methods can be called, although each property and method is not applicable to all elements. This list is fairly large and can be found in the "Quick Reference" section of this book.

The properties and methods for HTML elements are used throughout the book. But right now, let's look at an example that implements the marquee element. The marquee element scrolls any text contained within the <MARQUEE> begin and end tags. You can control the type of control that occurs within the element using scripting, as seen in the following example, **banner.htm**, shown in Listing 5-8. As the Web page reader moves his or her mouse over any of three headers, the scrolling is stopped, the text contained within the marquee is changed, and the scrolling is started again.

Listing 5-8: Using the marquee element and scripting to control content of the marquee element

```
<HTML>
<HEAD>
<STYLE type="text/css">
 MARQUEE { color: firebrick; font-size: 18pt;
             font-weight:bold;
             font-family: Cursive }
 BODY { background-color: ivory; margin: 0.5in }
 H1 { color: forestgreen }
</STYLE>
<SCRIPT language="javascript">
function change_text(indx) {
 document.all.marq.stop();
 if (indx == 0)
      document.all.marq.innerText=
      "This is our top of the line Product";
 else if (indx == 1)
      document.all.marq.innerText=
      "This is our good quality Product";
 else
      document.all.marq.innerText=
      "This product is cheap, cheap, cheap";
 document.all.marq.start();
}
</SCRIPT>
</HEAD>
<BODY>
<marquee id="marq" behavior="alternate" scrollDelay=0>
We want you to Buy!
</marquee>
<p>
<H1 onmouseover="change_text(0)"
onmouseout="document.all.marq.innerText='We want you to Buy!'">
Product A</H1>
<H1 onmouseover="change_text(1)"
onmouseout="document.all.marq.innerText='We want you to Buy!'">
```

```
Product B</H1>
<H1 onmouseover="change_text(2)"
onmouseout="document.all.marq.innerText='We want you to Buy!'">
Product C</H1>

</BODY>
</HTML>
```

 Note that the marquee element started out as an IE-only object but has been mentioned in the draft HTML 4.0 specification as a new HTML element.

This example uses the `innerText` property (discussed earlier in the chapter), which replaces the contents of the marquee without altering the control. I could also have replaced the marquee control by setting the `outerHTML` property to another HTML element, such as an image, as shown here:

```
document.all.marq.outerHTML =
  "<img id='marq' src='x.gif'>";
```

To get a better idea of how this element works, access the sample file, change the properties for the element and check out the results for yourself.

You can find a complete and up-to-date listing of the HTML elements at the Microsoft Web site, at the URL given in Appendix A.

The Collections

A *collection* is a VBScript term, and it represents an array of like values. Although it's a VBScript term, the actual arrays/collections are also accessible using JScript. Several predefined collections for HTML elements are available, and this section details each type.

Many of the collections, such as `forms`, reference elements that existed before IE 4.0, and before dynamic HTML, and they won't be covered in this section. Some collections have changed based on new features associated with IE 4.0 and some were created specifically to implement dynamic HTML techniques. Among the ones created specifically for dynamic HTML are the `all` collection, which contains a reference to all elements within a Web page, and the `filters` collection, which holds the multimedia filters defined for a specific element. Chapter 7 has an in-depth exploration of the new filter properties.

Style sheets have two collections: the `imports` collection, containing references to all imported style sheets, and the `styleSheets` collection, which maintains references to all style sheets for a page. Additionally, you can access all table elements with the `cells` and `rows` collections, and access images with the `images` collection.

Collections can be created dynamically by naming more than one element with the same name. For example, the following code creates a collection of link elements identified by the value of `"somename"`:

```
<A name="link1" id="somename">Link 1</a>
<A name="link2" id="somename">Link 2</a>
<A name="link3" id="somename">Link 3</a>
```

To access and build a string containing the names of all the members of the collection `"somename"`, use the following code:

```
Set someelements = somename
For Each someelem In someelements
  somenames = someelem.name
  If Not IsNull(somenames) Then
        allnames = allnames + somenames + " "
  End If
Next
MsgBox(allnames)
```

Collections are essential tools of Microsoft's implementation of dynamic HTML, and are discussed in the following sections.

The All Collection

The `all` collection is pretty much what it sounds like — a listing of all elements within a specific HTML document. Use this collection if you need to iterate through all the elements of a page for a specific reason.

With the `all` collection, you can use two methods to access the elements within a Web page. The first is the `tags` method, which enables you to access all elements of a certain tag type. The cross-browser scripting objects created in Chapter 13 and used throughout Chapters 13, 14, and 15, use the `tags` method to access all `DIV` elements within a Web page. The other method is the `item` method. You can use this method to access a specific element, either by location within the page or by ID.

As an example of this collection and its methods, Listing 5-9, all.htm, demonstrates scripting that accesses each element on a page using the `all` collection and generates an HTML string containing the `tagName` properties for each HTML element in the page. This is then written out using the `innerHTML` property, discussed in an earlier section.

Using JavaScript and VBScript Together

Listing 5-9 demonstrates that Microsoft's Internet Explorer can process JavaScript, JScript, and VBScript. Additionally, a global variable set in one language is also accessible in the others, and a function defined in one language can be called in any of the others.

Listing 5-9: Accessing each element on a Web page and printing out its tagName property

```
<HEAD>
<title>test</title>
<SCRIPT language="VBscript">
<!--

Dim allnames
Sub element_loop
 Dim somename
 allnames = ""
 Dim ct
 ct = 0
 Dim thegroup
 Set thegroup = document.all
 For i = 0 To thegroup.length-1
        somename = thegroup(i).tagName
        If Not IsNull(somename) Then
                ct = ct + 1
                if ct < 5 Then
                        allnames = allnames +
                        somename + "   "
                else
                        allnames = allnames + somename + "<br>"
                        ct = 0
                end if
        End If
 Next

 write_results
End Sub

//-->
</SCRIPT>

<SCRIPT language="javascript">

function write_results() {
 document.all.results.innerHTML=allnames
}
</SCRIPT>
</HEAD>
```

```
<BODY onclick="element_loop()">
<H1 child=test name="header1"> I am Header One</H1>
<h2 id=test name="header2">
I am header two</h2>
<p name="para1"> I am paragraph 1</P>
<img src="x.gif" name="X">
<OL name="list">
<LI name="item1">This is the first item</LI>
<LI name="item2">This is the second</LI>
</OL>
<FORM name="someform">
<INPUT type=button name="button1" value="I am button1">
</FORM>

<DIV>
And the Results are:
</DIV>
<DIV id="results">
</DIV>

</BODY>
```

As you can see from the listing, `tagName` is one property that all of the HTML elements share. With the use of the `all` collection, as with the other collections, you should always test a specific property to see if it exists or is set before using it in some way. Otherwise, an error will occur. Also, as with other arrays, notice that the `all` collection has a length property that contains the number of elements within the page.

In this example, try adding and removing HTML elements to see what happens when you run the script.

The Cells and Rows Collections

Two collections with some interesting application possibilities are the `cells` and the `rows` collections. The `cells` collection is an array that references all cells within a table row, whether those cells use the `<TH>` table column header tag or the `<TD>` table column data tag. The `rows` collection has an array with all the rows contained within a specific table.

One use for this technology is to do something to a table row or cell based on some user activity. Listing 5-10, file **cellloop.htm**, has a table with each cell set to a background color of lime, green, red, or blue. Users push a button to signify that they have accomplished a specific task, and the appropriate cell's background color, font color, and font family are changed to show that the task is accomplished.

Listing 5-10: Accessing both the rows and the cells of a table using their associated collections

```
<HEAD>
<title>test</title>
```

```
<SCRIPT language="VBScript">
<!--

Sub element_loop
  Set myrows = ani_table.rows

  ' for each row
  For Each somerow In myrows
   Set mycols = somerow.cells
   tstvalue = 1

    ' for each column, check background color
    For Each somecol In mycols
       If somecol.style.backgroundColor = "red" Then
              tstvalue=0
              somecol.style.backgroundColor = "maroon"
       ElseIf somecol.style.backgroundColor = "blue" Then
              tstvalue=0
              somecol.style.backgroundColor = "navy"
       ElseIf somecol.style.backgroundColor = "lime" Then
              tstvalue=0
              somecol.style.backgroundColor = "green"
       ElseIf somecol.style.backgroundColor = "white" Then
              tstvalue=0
              somecol.style.backgroundColor = "black"
       End If
       ' if target color found, change font and exit loop
       If tstvalue = 0 Then
              somecol.style.color="white"
              somecol.style.fontFamily="Cursive"
              Exit For
       End If
    Next
     ' if no other values to change exit outer loop
    If tstvalue = 0 Then
       Exit For
    End If
  Next
End Sub

//-->
</SCRIPT>
</HEAD>
<body>

<center>
<INPUT type=button value="Push Me as you complete each task"
 onClick="element_loop()">
</center>

<p>
<table ID="ani_table" cols=4 border=3 cellspacing=5 align=center>
<tr>
<td width=125 align=center
```

```
  style="background-color: lime"> Task One </td>
<td width=125 align=center
  style="background-color: white"> Task Two </td>
<td width=125 align=center
  style="background-color: blue"> Task Three </td>
<td width=125 align=center
  style="background-color: red"> Task Four </td>
</tr>
<tr>
<td width=125 align=center
  style="background-color: white"> Task Five </td>
<td width=125 align=center
  style="background-color: blue"> Task Six </td>
<td width=125 align=center
  style="background-color: red"> Task Seven </td>
<td width=125 align=center
  style="background-color: lime"> Task Eight </td>
</tr>
<tr>
<td width=125 align=center
  style="background-color: blue"> Task Nine </td>
<td width=125 align=center
  style="background-color: red"> Task Ten </td>
<td width=125 align=center
  style="background-color: lime"> Task Eleven </td>
<td width=125 align=center
  style="background-color: white"> Task Twelve </td>
</tr>

</BODY>
```

As the Web page reader pushes the button, each element in the table is tested to see whether the element is still showing the "uncompleted task" color. If it is, it is set to its complementary "task completed" color. Figure 5-10 shows the Web page after the user has clicked the button several times.

Using the Rows and Cells Collections with Data Binding

I don't cover Microsoft's data binding techniques in this book because the technique is unique to IE, and this is a cross-browser book. However, data binding is a technique that lets you bind a data value from an ODBC-based table to an HTML element, such as a table cell. When the page is accessed, a set of the data that matches a defined query is copied from the database on the server and cached in a file on the client. The data is then displayed with the HTML element it is bound to. Using the rows and cells collections, you can alter the properties of the cell displays based on the data values to provide an effective display.

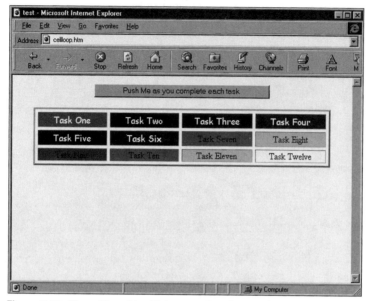

Figure 5-10: The cellloop.htm Web page after the user has clicked the button several times

The Images Collection

The images collection is an array that contains a reference to every image within a Web page. This can be useful for something such as an online animation. An animation can be created using the images collection by loading several images into a Web page, setting all but one to invisible, and then changing the one visible image element based on a timer or other operation. Additionally, images can be cached in a JavaScript array. The images are then loaded into the page but not displayed. For example, the following code creates an image array:

```
<SCRIPT language="javascript">

myimages = new Array(4)
myimages[0] = new Image()
myimages[0].src = "menua.jpg"
myimages[1] = new Image()
myimages[1].src = "menub.jpg"
myimages[2] = new Image()
myimages[2].src = "menuc.jpg"
myimages[3] = new Image()
myimages[3].src = "menud.jpg"

</SCRIPT>
```

Then, the actual displayed image can be changed to reflect the next stage of animation, similar to the following:

```
ct = 1
function element_loop() {
 document.images[0].src = myimages[ct].src
 ct = ct + 1
 if (ct > 3)
      ct=0
}
```

The Frames Collection

The frames collection retrieves a collection of all window objects defined by a given document or defined by a document associated with the given window.
You can use either of two different types of frames collections, depending upon how frames are defined within the Web page. If documents use the FRAMESET element (and thus, do *not* include the <BODY> tag) to define its frames, the collection contains one window for each FRAME element in the document. If documents use the IFRAME element (and thus, *do* include the <BODY> tag) to define its frames, the collection contains one window for each IFRAME element in the document.

The frames collection is really a collection of windows, and only window-based properties, events, and methods can be used with this collection. Listing 5-11 shows a simple example that accesses an inframe object by using the frames collection.

Listing 5-11: Accessing a single inframe window using the frames collection

```
<HTML>
<HEAD>
<SCRIPT language="vbscript">
Sub doc
 MsgBox(window.frames(0).location)
End Sub
</SCRIPT>
</HEAD>
<BODY onload="doc()">

<IFRAME src="all.htm"></IFRAME>
</BODY>
</HTML>
```

This simple code creates an inframe object, sets the source to **all.htm** (discussed earlier in this chapter), and then accesses the frame when the page loads. The location of the inframe source is printed out in a message box.

This collection contains only window objects and does not provide access to the corresponding FRAME and IFRAME elements. To access these elements, use the all collection (discussed earlier) for the document containing the elements.

The Scripts Collection

The scripts collection maintains a reference to every script block within a page (a script block is delimited by enclosing <SCRIPT> and </SCRIPT> tags). The scripts collection is rather intriguing. Taking the previous example, I can actually print out the script itself rather than the location of the inframe object with one simple change of code:

```
MsgBox(document.scripts(0).text)
```

What can you do with the scripts collection? You can access any one of the scripts within a Web page as an individual script object and also access any of its properties or methods. If you want to run a sample site, or display the script that creates an effect, display the script text as a small window.

StyleSheets and Imports Collections

The styleSheets collection contains a reference to all style sheets within a Web page, while the imports collection contains all style sheets included within a Web page through the use of the CSS1 import attribute.

Once you access a specific style sheet, you can add an entirely new style sheet with the addImport method, or add new style sheet rules with the addRule method. As an example, I borrowed a couple of files from Chapter 2. First, the document **prelim2.htm** contains some lengthy text that I want to format, so I link in a style sheet named **style1.css**. I trap the onClick event for the Web page and switch style sheets and styles based on a global number variable that acts as a switch. Listing 5-12 contains the style sheet linking and scripting section for the document. You can find this example, **prelim2.htm**, on the CD-ROM.

Listing 5-12: StyleSheets setting and script from prelim2.htm, demonstrating accessing and altering style sheet information

```
<LINK REL=STYLESHEET TYPE="text/css"
 HREF="style1.css" TITLE="style1">
<SCRIPT type="jscript">
 num = 1;
</SCRIPT>
```

```
<SCRIPT type="jscript" FOR=document EVENT=onclick>
 if (num == 1) {
        document.styleSheets(0).href="style2.css";
        document.styleSheets(0).addRule("BODY", "background-
        color:ivory");
        num = 2;
        }
 else {
        document.styleSheets(0).href="style1.css";
        num = 1;
        }
</SCRIPT>
```

Note that, in the code, I link in a style sheet named **style1.css** as the document is loaded. Also, I use two scripting blocks, one to set the original value of the global variable, num, and the other to process the specific event. Clicking on the page the first time accesses the page's style sheet using the styleSheets collection and sets the style sheet to another one named **style2.css**. Another click sets the style sheet back to the original, except this time, I also use the addRule method to add a rule that sets the background color of the document to ivory.

Try the example yourself by accessing **prelim2.htm**. Also, try changing its appearance by adding in new rules, or altering the linked-in style sheets.

Using these collections and methods, you can alter the presentation of your Web pages based on the readers' actions, and even store their preferences in Netscape cookies for use each time they log on to your site. Or you can create three different style sheets — one for morning, one for afternoon, and one for evening — by testing the time of day and loading the appropriate set of styles to match the time. Or you can change the style sheet based on the colordepth value you get from the screen object, discussed earlier in this chapter. Or you can adjust the size of the font based on the screen resolution. There really is no limit to what you can do with the styleSheets collection and object.

Summary

This chapter provided an overview, with examples, of the major components of Microsoft's dynamic HTML.

In this chapter you learned how to:

♦ Access properties and methods for the window object.

♦ Open multiple browser windows.

♦ Work with the document object, including how to use it to reference most other objects in the object model.

- ◆ Use Netscape-style cookies to maintain small bits of persistent information on the client machine.

- ◆ Use the `navigator` object to determine browser and version.

- ◆ Change the `style` properties of any HTML element.

- ◆ Use the `screen` object to determine which image and colors to use in the Web page.

- ◆ Use the `TextRange` object to dynamically locate and replace or modify text-based HTML elements.

- ◆ Use the inner and outer HTML and text properties to access and alter element content.

- ◆ Access properties of all page elements using the `all` collection and to check element properties.

- ◆ Access table rows and cells using their respective collections and change properties of the cells based on user input.

- ◆ Create an image cache and use the cache with the new `images` collection.

- ◆ Access frame information with the `frames` collection.

- ◆ Print out the contents of a `<SCRIPT>` block.

- ◆ Access style sheets using the `styleSheets` collection.

- ◆ Dynamically change the style sheet used with a page.

- ◆ Dynamically add style sheet rules to style sheets.

The next chapter covers how to move, layer, and animate HTML elements using the positioning techniques supported by Internet Explorer. The chapter also explores how to display and hide elements, in addition to positioning them.

Positioning HTML Elements

IN THIS CHAPTER

- ◆ HTML positioning: introduction and preview
- ◆ Packaging elements into containers
- ◆ CSS1 positioning properties
- ◆ Layering elements along the z-axis
- ◆ Dynamically changing positions of elements
- ◆ Animating elements using positioning and script

THIS CHAPTER EXPLORES HOW to take advantage of new positioning attributes offered in Internet Explorer 4.0. These new capabilities let you position elements absolutely on a page, layer elements along the z-axis, and script dynamic changes in element positions. This chapter covers these topics in detail, also providing illustrative examples.

HTML Positioning: Introduction and Preview

We've all seen, and probably used, various techniques to work around the lack of HTML positioning tags. One popular technique, created by David Siegel, a well-known Web page designer and author, is to use a transparent one-pixel GIF image for spacing. The use of HTML tables to control text layout is another very popular positioning workaround. The problem with these workarounds is that they don't give the designer absolute control over where the elements end up on a Web page because of the many differences between browsers, browser releases, and browser platforms.

Now, using Cascading Style Sheets (covered in detail in Chapter 2) and HTML positioning, you no longer have to rely on these positioning tricks. In addition, not only can you statically position elements, but you can also dynamically position them from JavaScript, VBScript, or any other scripting language.

Both Netscape and Microsoft participated in writing a CSS1 positioning proposal for the W3C (World Wide Web Consortium). At the time version 4.0 of the browsers were introduced, this proposal was still in draft format, but both companies have implemented positioning with version 4.0 of their browsers. To read about Netscape's implementation of positioning, see Chapter 10. To read more about the W3C proposal, check out the corresponding URL located in Appendix A.

To provide you with a quick experience of CSS1 positioning, I created an example that demonstrates both static and dynamic positioning techniques for Microsoft's IE 4.0. You can check out the example by opening the **quickpos.htm** sample file (available on the CD-ROM) and pressing the Cycle Images button. Doing so triggers the script that moves the number images around the page. You can control image movement using a timer and moving the image to a new position with each timer event. If you continue to press the button, the images eventually cycle around the page, returning to their original positions, ready to begin the path cycle around the page again.

The listing for this example, and the positioning techniques that are used, are shown at the end of this chapter. Figure 6-1 shows the page when it is first opened within IE 4.0, and Figure 6-2 shows the page after you press the Cycle Images button two times.

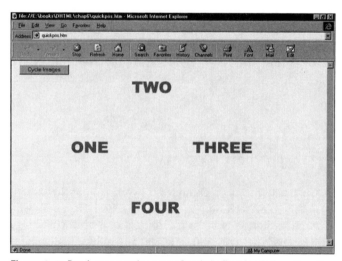

Figure 6-1: Preview example page after it is first loaded; notice the positioning of the images

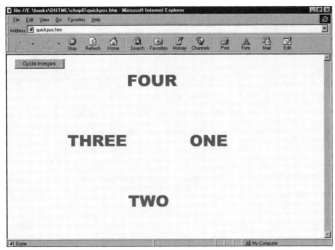

Figure 6-2: Preview example page after clicking the Cycle Images button twice; notice the difference in the image positions

The techniques used for this example, and others, are explained and demonstrated in more detail in the rest of this chapter.

Packaging Elements into Containers

Before I jump into how to position elements on a Web page, I'll first demonstrate how you can group them within containers, because you may need to position groups of elements rather than individual ones. Some elements have a natural grouping container, such as table rows and cells used by the HTML table element. For example, in the following code, the position of the table is 50 pixels from the top of the Web page and 50 pixels from the left. Because the table cells are naturally contained within the table, all the items contained within the table are positioned according to the table's position information:

```
<HEAD>
<STYLE type="text/css">
#block1 {position: absolute; top: 50px;
        left: 50px; width: 300px}
</STYLE>
</HEAD>
<body>
<TABLE id=block1>
<tr><td>
Some text field: <INPUT type=text>
<p>
```

```
<INPUT type=button value="push me">
</td></tr>
</table>
</body>
```

To group other elements within containers, though, you need to use an external agent. Elements can be grouped and positioned using the <DIV> and </DIV> or the <SPAN> and </SPAN> tags. <DIV> and <SPAN> were introduced to CSS1 as neutral style tags, meant only to *apply* styles to an element or groups of elements. Anything contained within the <DIV> or <SPAN> tags is treated as one group, and positioning applies to each of the elements, relative to each other. The difference between <DIV> and <SPAN> is that <DIV> is a block-level element, so it may contain paragraphs, headings, tables, and even other divisions. <DIV> is ideal for creating containers within a Web page, such as notes, paragraphs, and captions. <SPAN> is a text-level element, so it may be used midstream in a sentence to apply a style, functioning like the <B> and <I> tags.

CSS1 Positioning Properties

With just a handful of properties in Internet Explorer 4.0, you can place elements anywhere on a Web page by specifying an "x" and "y" value for the "left" and "top" corner of the element, or you can position elements relatively, according to the element's place in an HTML document.

You can also make elements visible or hidden, and set properties for how they are clipped when they exceed their specified boundaries. Table 6-1 lists the available properties for positioning elements in Internet Explorer 4.0.

TABLE 6-1 Positioning Properties

Property	Values
position	absolute | relative | static
left	<length> | <percentage> | auto
top	<length> | <percentage> | auto
width	<length> | <percentage> | auto
height	<length> | <percentage> | auto
clip	<shape> | auto

continued

Property	Values
overflow	none | clip | scroll
z-index	auto | <integer>
visibility	inherit | visible | hidden

Absolute Positioning

Absolute positioning is the capability of placing an object, either an HTML element or control, anywhere on a Web page by setting the left-top corner of the element to specific x and y values, respectively. To place an element absolutely on a Web page, specify the top-left corner of the rectangular space occupied by the element using the top and left properties.

For example, in the following code, the text located with the enclosing <DIV> and </DIV> tags is positioned 250 pixels from the top and 200 pixels from the left of the Web page container (the default container for Web pages; the <BODY> element, for instance, flows within the default container).

```
<DIV
   style="background-color: red; position: absolute; top: 250px;
   left: 200px">
This is the beginning of a block of text that should start 250
   pixels from the top and 200 pixels from the left. The rectangle
   that is used to enclose this text will extend all the way to the
   right margin of the Web page, and the height will be long enough to
   enclose the text, and no more.
</DIV>
```

This code creates a rectangle with a red background, with its top-left corner at 250, 200, extending all the way to the right margin. The height of the rectangle should accommodate the text. Absolute positioning places an element according to left and top properties regardless of the location of other Web page elements. If more than one element is set to the same location, they are placed on top of one another, stacking up in the display in the order they appear in the HTML document.

Relative Positioning

Another type of positioning is *relative* positioning. Relative positioning means the HTML object is positioned relative to its original position as it occurs naturally within the HTML flow. This includes any line breaks that may occur within the object. As an example, the following code places the image included within the text block to the left of the starting point of the block, and overlaps the text at the end:

```
<DIV style="position: absolute; top: 30px; left: 30px; width=200px">
This is another block of text, but one that also includes an <img
 src="three.gif"
 style="position: relative; left: 20px"> image.
</DIV>
```

Figure 6-3 shows a relatively positioned image within an absolute container. Note from the figure that the image overlaps the text that follows. If the image had been positioned within the natural flow of the HTML document using relative positioning, and if the left property weren't set, it would not have overlapped the text.

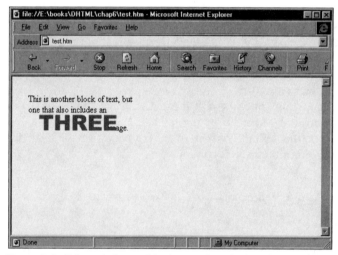

Figure 6-3: Using relative positioning to alter the location of an image relative to where it would occur naturally within the HTML document

Positioning and Style Sheets

Along with defining positioning styles directly in the element, positioning can be defined using style sheets, as the following code demonstrates:

```
<HEAD>
<STYLE type="text/css">
#block1 {position: absolute; top: 30px; left: 30px; width: 200px}
#image1 {position: relative; left: 20px }
</STYLE>
</HEAD>
<body>
<DIV id=block1>
This is another block of text, but one that also includes
an <img src="three.gif" id=image1> image.
```

```
</DIV>
</body>
```

Using the style sheet in this example results in the exact same presentation shown in Figure 6-3, which was created by embedding the style information directly into the HTML element.

Combining Relative and Absolute Positioning

Listing 6-1 demonstrates how relative and absolute containers combine by using two separate <DIV> blocks, each containing an image and some text describing the image. The first block is positioned relative to the HTML document, meaning that it is positioned relative to the margins set for the Web page body. The second block is positioned using absolute positioning, and ignores any other page elements.

Listing 6-1: Positioning multiple HTML elements using <DIV> tags as containers

```
<HEAD>
<STYLE type="text/css">
BODY { margin-left: 0.25in; margin-top: 0.5in }
#block1 {position: relative; top: 50px;
        left: 20px; width: 300px;
        background-color: lemonchiffon }
#block2 {position: absolute; top: 50px;
        left: 400px; width: 300px;
        background-color: lightcoral}
</STYLE>
</HEAD>
<body>
<DIV id=block1>
<img src="flourite3tn.JPG">
<strong>Fluorite</strong><p>
Fluorite is a member of the <em>halides</em>. Fluorite can come in
  various colors, and is a fairly common mineral. I collected this
  piece because of its unusual coloration, which the photograph
  demonstrates. This sample is one of my largest, being 4 inches
  across.
This makes it a 'hand' sample, and it comes from the Denton Mine,
  Hardin County, Illinois.
</DIV>
<DIV id=block2>
<img src="apophyllite2tn.JPG">
<strong>Apophyllite</strong><p>
Apophyllite is a member of the <em>Phyllosilicate</em> class. It is
  a colorless crystal, yet has a grayish cast. The sample is
  associated with Stilbite, which is not visible in the existing
  photograph. This sample is from Poone(Pune), India. This crystal
  can be differentiated from other clear crystals by its relative
  weight, it is a light stone, and a distinctly greasy feeling.
</DIV>
</body>
```

The example displays the two blocks side by side, as shown in Figure 6-4. Also note that the relative positioning of the first block sets the block slightly more to the right and much lower than if it were absolutely positioned because the body margins are also applied to the block. In addition, the background colors of both blocks have been set to make the positioning rectangle more obvious. You can try this example yourself by opening the sample file named **twoblcks.htm** (on the CD-ROM).

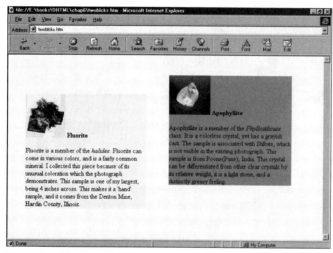

Figure 6-4: Using the <DIV> tag to create two separate containers, one absolute and the other relative

Clip and Overflow

The clip property determines the shape of the clipping region. At this time, the clipping region is specified in the CSS1 positioning draft as a shape, and only works with absolute positioning. Microsoft currently implements this property as a "rectangle," with four properties representing the clipping rectangle's left, top, right, and bottom properties.

Following is the syntax for the values available using the clip property:

```
clip: <shape> | auto
<shape>: rect (<top><right><bottom><left>)
top: <length> | auto
right: <length> | auto
bottom: <length> | auto
left: <length> | auto
length: a plus or minus sign, followed by a number, followed by a
  size specifier
```

For example, the following code sets the clipping region for a <DIV> block:

```
var rectstring = "rect(" + top + "," + right + "," + bottom + "," +
  left + ")";
document.all.somediv.style.clip = rectstring;
```

You don't have to specify all the parameters when building the clipping rectangle. A value of auto sets the parameter to the existing clipping region value. In the previous example, setting the *top* and *bottom* parameters to auto and changing only the right and left values clips the block along the horizontal axis only.

Each element has a semirectangular area that surrounds it and includes, by default, the content for the element. The rectangular area for a paragraph can have a jagged right edge, but the rectangular area for a <DIV> block can have a smooth right edge.

If you use the width and height properties to specify a size for this area that is too small for the content, the content that extends beyond the rectangle is considered the element's overflow. The overflow property determines what is done with this overflow content. Applicable values are none, which is the default, hidden, clip, and scroll. The value of none means that no clipping is performed and the contents will extend beyond the boundaries. A value of scroll displays either a horizontal or vertical scroll bar for the element. A value of clip clips the element, hiding the excess content so that it fits into the rectangle.

When used with the scroll property, the value of hidden actually hides the overflow, creating a clipping effect.

Visibility

The visibility property specifies whether the element is visible or is hidden. The possible values for this property are:

- ◆ hidden — the element is not visible but still takes up the same space it normally would if the element were visible

- ◆ visible — the element is visible

- ◆ inherit — the default value; the element inherits its visibility property from the enclosing parent item

Note from the properties that, even though an element is set to be invisible, a space to hold the object is still reserved within the HTML document. As an example, the following code sets the image to be invisible within the <DIV> block:

```
<HEAD>
<STYLE type="text/css">
#block1 {position: absolute; top: 30px; left: 30px; width: 200px}
#image1 {position: relative; left: -20px; visibility: hidden }
</STYLE>
</HEAD>
```

```
<body>
<DIV id=block1>
This is another block of text, but one that also includes
an <img src="three.gif" id=image1>
image.
</DIV>
</body>
```

As shown in Figure 6-5, the text of the `<DIV>` block displays as it normally would if the image were present. However, because no image is displayed, a gap is left in the contents.

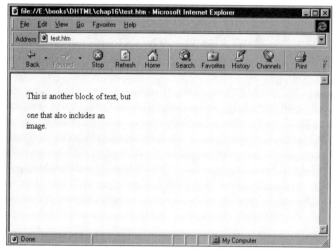

Figure 6-5: Setting the visibility of an image to be hidden; notice that the image "space" is still provided

By default, if an enclosing element is invisible, the child element is also invisible. Setting the visibility of the `<DIV>` block to `hidden`, as the following code demonstrates, hides both the text and the image. This occurs because the enclosed *child* element, the image, inherits its `visibility` property from the parent element:

```
<HEAD>
<STYLE type="text/css">
#block1 {position: absolute; top: 30px;
       visibility: hidden; left: 30px; width: 200px}
#image1 {position: relative; left: -20px; }
</STYLE>
</HEAD>
<body>
<DIV id=block1>
This is another block of text, but one that also includes
an <img src="three.gif" id=image1>
```

```
image.
</DIV>
</body>
```

Chapter 7 further discusses the `visibility` property and compares it to another similar CSS1 property, the `display` property.

Layering Elements along the Z-Axis

Positioning also enables you to layer objects along the z-axis. You can layer one or more objects by setting their absolute positions so that they are placed one on top of the other in a stack. The objects lower in the stack are not visible unless those above them have a transparent background, such as a GIF image, or are an HTML element, such as a header.

At my Web site I have four images on every page that act as a menu bar. To take advantage of image caching, I use the same four images for each menu bar on all of my Web pages. The images are downloaded when the first page is downloaded, and from that time on, unless the Web page reader has turned off caching, the images are accessed from the client machine rather than through the Internet.

What changes from page to page is the text associated with the image, and the URL of the document that is loaded when the image is clicked. Prior to IE 4.0, the text for the menu bar was located directly below each image, as shown in Figure 6-6. I never cared for this look but no other approach worked, and I definitely did not want to provide all new images for each Web page and have the Web page reader download four new images with each page he or she accessed.

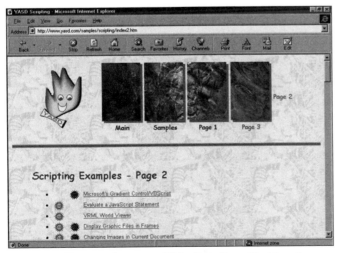

Figure 6-6: The menu bar on my Web site before object layering was possible

With absolute positioning, it is now possible to place the text of the link directly on the image, suggesting that the menu bar images have been modified explicitly for each page, even though all the pages are using the same set of images. This approach takes advantage of image caching and yet provides a more customized look. It is also a simple matter of changing the images for the menu bar each month: I just save the new images as the image name used in all the menu bars.

To convert the old menu bar into one that uses style sheets with positioning information, the first step was to define style sheets for the page background and each of the images:

```
BODY { background-image: url(snow.jpg) }
image { width: 100; height: 150 }
#logo { position: absolute; top: 20px; left: 50px;
      width: 102px }
#image1 { position: absolute; top: 20px; left: 180px}
#image2 { position: absolute; top: 20px; left: 290px}
#image3 { position: absolute; top: 20px; left: 400px}
#image4 { position: absolute; top: 20px; left: 510px}
```

Next, I defined style sheets for each of the menu text bars. I decided to use the <h2> header tag for the titles and added a style sheet for this also, to set the font family, size, and color:

```
h2 { font-family: Cursive; font-size: 12pt;
      font-weight: 400; color: white }
#title1 { position: absolute; top: 20px; left: 185px;
      height: 20px }
#title2 { position: absolute; top: 20px; left: 295px;
      height: 20px }
#title3 { position: absolute; top: 20px; left: 405px;
      height: 20px }
#title4 { position: absolute; top: 20px; left: 515px;
      height: 20px }
```

Next, I placed the images and the titles on the page, using <DIV> blocks for the titles:

```
<body>
<!-- Set menu titles -->
<DIV id=title1>
<h2>Services</h2>
</DIV>
<DIV id=title2>
<h2>Sites</h2>
</DIV>
<DIV id=title3>
<h2>Scribbles</h2>
</DIV>
<DIV id=title4>
<h2>Samples</h2>
</DIV>
```

```
<!-- Set menu images-->
<img src="yasd.gif" id=logo>
<a href="http://www.yasd.com/services">
 <img src="menua.jpg" border=0 id=image1></a>
<a href="http://www.yasd.com/sites">
 <img src="menub.jpg" border=0 id=image2></a>
<a href="http://www.yasd.com/scribbles">
 <img src="menuc.jpg" border=0 id=image3></a>
<a href="http://www.yasd.com/samples">
 <img src="menud.jpg" border=0 id=image4></a>

</body>
```

After creating the last section of the Web page, I loaded it into the browser. Instead of seeing the expected results, text layered on images, all I saw where the images. So what happened to the titles?

Elements are layered in the order in which they occur in the HTML document, with those occurring first placed at the bottom of the stack, and those occurring later placed above. Because I embedded the images after I inserted the text, the images are placed on top of the text, hiding them, as demonstrated in Figure 6-7.

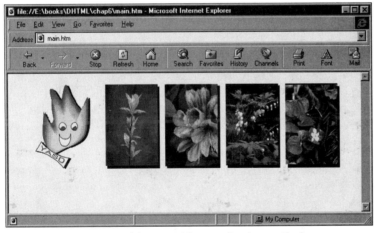

Figure 6-7: Image menu with menu titles not showing on the images

To fix the disappearing text problem, I could have moved the text of the titles so that they occurred *after* the images, but instead I decided to use the z-index positioning property. The z-index property is a numeric property that determines the order in which to stack objects. Objects with smaller z-index values are placed further down in the stack than objects with larger z-index values. In other words, an object with a z-index of 2 is placed above one with a z-index of 1.

To fix the hidden-text problem, I modified the images and gave them a z-index value of 1, and gave the title styles a z-index of 2. When I reloaded the page, the titles displayed above the images as originally planned.

When I tested my example, I tried moving my cursor over the image and noticed that the cursor changed from an active link cursor to the regular text cursor when it was over the titles. Because the titles partially overlay the images, the hypertext link connection for the images did not work when the mouse was over the text. To correct this problem, I also added the hypertext link to the titles as well as the images, as demonstrated in the following code:

```
<!-- Set menu titles -->
<DIV id=title1>
<h2><a href="http://www.yasd.com/services">Services</a></h2>
</DIV>
<DIV id=title2>
<h2><a href="http://www.yasd.com/sites">Sites</a></h2>
</DIV>
<DIV id=title3>
<h2><a href="http://www.yasd.com/scribbles">Scribbles</a></h2>
</DIV>
<DIV id=title4>
<h2><a href="http://www.yasd.com/samples">Samples</a></h2>
</DIV>
```

Unfortunately, this addition triggered the visited and unvisited link colors within my browser. I wanted to control the text colors that appeared on the images so I could be sure they would always appear nicely against their backgrounds. So I added style sheet rules for the links in order to set the visited and unvisited link colors to white. I also removed the default underline text decoration from the link. Because I only wanted this style to apply to the <H2> headers (my image titles), I set a contextual style for the link styles so they would only affect all hypertext links embedded within <H2> headers, as follows:

```
h2 A { text-decoration: none; color: white }
h2 A:link { color-white }
h2 A:visited { color: white }
```

After applying these changes and reloading the page, I saw that the image titles displayed in the appropriate location, white, and with no underlines, as shown in Figure 6-8.

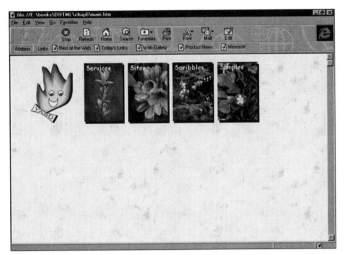

Figure 6-8: Image menus with menu titles showing appropriately on the images

My problems were not yet over, however. I also noticed that when the cursor passed over the portion of the header titles for each menu image that did not contain text, the hypertext link was again lost. To correct this mistake, I set the width and height of the link text to one pixel in the style sheet, as shown in the following code:

```
#title1 { position: absolute; top: 20px; left: 185px;
          z-index: 2; height: 1px; width: 1px }
```

By default the text overlaps the underlying rectangle if the width is not set to be large enough. Setting the width to one pixel means that the text displays appropriately, but the width of the headers does not extend beyond the displayed text. Now, with this approach, the entire image and text headers are active hypertext links, and my new image menu bar is complete.

To make effective use of the image bar, I packaged the title and image style sheets into a separate CSS1 style sheet file, **menu.css** (you'll find this sample file on the CD-ROM), and linked it into every one of the Web pages. Then, for each page, I inserted the image and text HTML with the links and text appropriate to the page. Listing 6-2 shows the use of the new menu bar with my main Web page, and Listing 6-3 shows how the menu bar would be modified for my JavaScript samples page.

Listing 6-2: My main Web page with the menu bar set to main page menu hierarchy

```
<HEAD>
<LINK REL=STYLESHEET TYPE="text/css"
 HREF="menu.css">
</HEAD>
<body>
```

```
<!-- Set menu titles -->
<DIV id=title1>
<h2><a href="http://www.yasd.com/services">Services</a></h2>
</DIV>
<DIV id=title2>
<h2><a href="http://www.yasd.com/sites">Sites</a></h2>
</DIV>
<DIV id=title3>
<h2><a href="http://www.yasd.com/scribbles">Scribbles</a></h2>
</DIV>
<DIV id=title4>
<h2><a href="http://www.yasd.com/samples">Samples</a></h2>
</DIV>

<!-- Set menu images-->
<img src="yasd.gif" id=logo>
<a href="http://www.yasd.com/services">
 <img src="menua.jpg" border=0 id=image1></a>
<a href="http://www.yasd.com/sites">
 <img src="menub.jpg" border=0 id=image2></a>
<a href="http://www.yasd.com/scribbles">
 <img src="menuc.jpg" border=0 id=image3></a>
<a href="http://www.yasd.com/samples">
 <img src="menud.jpg" border=0 id=image4></a>

</body>
```

Listing 6-3: The same menu bar style sheet and layering, with different URL targets and titles

```
<HEAD>
<LINK REL=STYLESHEET TYPE="text/css"
 HREF="menu.css">
</HEAD>
<body>
<!-- Set menu images-->
<img src="yasd.gif" id=logo>
<a href="http://www.yasd.com">
 <img src="menua.jpg" border=0 id=image1></a>
<a href="http://www.yasd.com/samples">
 <img src="menub.jpg" border=0 id=image2></a>
<a href="http://www.yasd.com/scripting">
 <img src="menuc.jpg" border=0 id=image3></a>
<img src="menud.jpg" border=0 id=image4>

<!-- Set menu titles -->
<DIV id=title1>
<h2><a href="http://www.yasd.com">Main</a></h2>
</DIV>
<DIV id=title2>
<h2><a href="http://www.yasd.com/samples">Samples</a></h2>
</DIV>
<DIV id=title3>
```

```
<h2><a
 href="http://www.yasd.com/samples/scripting">Scripting</a></h2>
</DIV>
<DIV id=title4>
<h2>JavaScript</h2>
</DIV>
</body>
```

You can try these out yourself – the main Web page can be found in **main.htm** and the JavaScript samples page can be found in **javascrpt.htm**. The CSS1 style sheet file is **menu.css**. You'll find these sample files on the CD-ROM. More complex uses of layering are provided in the chapters in this book's last section.

Dynamically Changing Positions of Elements

So far, we have explored ways to position elements statically on a Web page, meaning that the elements are positioned once when the page loads, and do not move during the presentation. But with just a little scripting, we can turn these static elements into dynamic ones.

With a few changes to the code in Listing 6-1, we can change the positions of the blocks using a couple of different techniques. The first approach is to dynamically change the positions of the blocks by switching their assigned style sheets. The following code shows how this is done. First, two style sheets are defined, both using absolute positioning, and both placed side by side:

```
<STYLE type="text/css">
DIV.firstblock {position: absolute; top: 50px;
      left: 20px; width: 300px;
      background-color: lemonchiffon }
DIV.secondblock {position: absolute; top: 50px;
      left: 350px; width: 300px;
      background-color: lightcoral}
</STYLE>
```

Each `<DIV>` block contains an image and associated text and is assigned one of the style sheets using the following syntax:

```
<DIV id=block1 class=firstblock>
<DIV id=block2 class=secondblock>
```

A button is added to the second `<DIV>` block. Pressing this button triggers the script that switches the style sheets of the two blocks:

```
<INPUT type=button name="transfer"
 value="Switch blocks">
```

Finally, VBScript is used to test which style sheet the first <DIV> block is using, and then switches the style sheets between the two blocks:

```
<SCRIPT language="vbscript">
Sub transfer_onClick
  If block1.className = "firstblock" Then
        block1.className = "secondblock"
        block2.className = "firstblock"
  Else
        block1.className = "firstblock"
        block2.className = "secondblock"
  End If
End Sub
</SCRIPT>
```

As shown in Figure 6-9, when the page is first opened, each block is positioned according to the style sheet assigned to the <DIV> block. Pressing the Switch blocks button switches the style sheets of the block, and moves the contents accordingly, as shown in Figure 6-10. You can try this yourself by accessing the sample file on the CD-ROM named **dynablck.htm**.

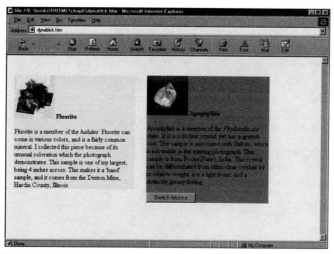

Figure 6-9: Two <DIV> blocks positioned side by side, after dynablck.htm is first opened

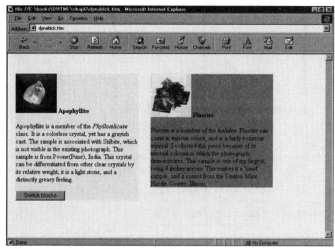

Figure 6-10: After pressing the button labeled Switch blocks once,
the style sheets of the two <DIV> blocks are switched

A second way to dynamically reposition HTML elements is to directly change
the top and left position properties of the style object. Applying this approach
to the previous example, the VBScript code would look as follows:

```
<SCRIPT language="vbscript">
Sub transfer_onClick
  If block1.style.posLeft = 20 Then
        block1.style.posLeft = 350
        block2.style.posLeft = 20
  Else
        block1.style.posLeft = 20
        block2.style.posLeft = 350
  End If
End Sub
</SCRIPT>
```

This approach only changes the position of the two <DIV> blocks rather than
changing the style sheets associated with them. The advantage to this method is
that they retain all other style sheet settings. Open the sample files **dynablck.htm**
and **dynblck2.htm** on the CD-ROM and compare the two approaches.

Table 6-2 lists the position properties that you can access via scripting.

TABLE 6-2 Positioning Properties

Property	Description
left	Left position of the object including positioning units.
height	Height of the object including positioning units.
invisible	Determines if the object is visible. Applicable values are "hidden," "visible," and "inherit."
overflow	Determines how content overflow is handled. Applicable values are "none," "clip," "hidden," and "scroll."
pixelLeft	Left position of the object in pixels.
pixelTop	Top position of the object in pixels.
pixelWidth	Width of the object in pixels.
pixelHeight	Height of the object in pixels.
position	Type of positioning, whether "absolute" or "relative."
posTop	Top position of the object in floating point. A new value can be assigned without using size units because it is converted to the type of size unit originally assigned to the object.
posLeft	Left position of the object in floating point. As with the posTop property, changing this value automatically converts the numeric value to the size unit originally specified for the object.
posWidth	Width of the object in floating point.
posHeight	Height of the object in floating point.
top	Top position of the object including positioning units.
width	Width of the object including positioning units.
zIndex	Determines how the object is layered in respect to other objects.

The top, left, width, and height properties are strings, and include the type of units as well as the number. For numeric values, you'll want to use the pixel- or pos- properties.

Animating Elements Using Positioning and Script

In the previous sections you had a chance to position elements both statically and dynamically, and along *x*, *y*, and *z* axes. This section looks at how all of these techniques can be used together to add an opening animation effect to the menu bar.

The script for this animation effect pulls in the menu images from the sides of the Web page just after it is loaded, and positions the images next to one another at the exact same time, and the position in which they will remain until the page is changed. You have to see this for yourself to truly appreciate the impact of this transitioning effect. You can find the listing in the **maintrns.htm** sample file on the CD-ROM. The best aspect of this effect is that it places no additional burden on either the server or the Internet, and results in no increased download times.

The same style sheets created in the previous menu bar are used in this example. The main page has also been modified in several ways to implement this effect. First, to make things a bit simpler, the linked style sheet is now embedded in the Web page to make it easier to work with while testing changes. Secondly, it now has eight new arrays — four for the *x* path points, and four for the *y* path points. Finally, an onLoad event procedure sets the path targets, starts the path movement timer, and sets the images to visible. This in turn calls another function that starts the menu items moving. The complete Web page code can be seen in Listing 6-4.

Listing 6-4: The maintrns.htm example file using synchronized path objects for an animated menu bar

```
<HEAD>
<STYLE TYPE="text/css">
 BODY { background-image: url(snow.jpg) }
 image { width: 100; height: 150; visibility:hidden }
 h2 { font-family: Cursive; font-size: 12pt;
       font-weight: 400; color: white }
 h2 A { text-decoration: none; color: white }
 h2 A:link { color-white }
 h2 A:visited { color: white }
 #logo { position: absolute; top: 20px; left: 50px;
             width: 102px }
 #image1 { position: absolute; top: 20px; left: 180px;
             z-index: 1 }
 #image2 { position: absolute; top: 20px; left: 290px;
             z-index: 1 }
 #image3 { position: absolute; top: 20px; left: 400px;
             z-index: 1 }
 #image4 { position: absolute; top: 20px; left: 510px;
             z-index: 1 }
 #title1 { position: absolute; top: 20px; left: 185px;
             z-index: 2; height: 20px; width: 1px }
 #title2 { position: absolute; top: 20px; left: 295px;
             z-index: 2; height: 20px; width: 1px  }
```

```
#title3 { position: absolute; top: 20px; left: 405px;
          z-index: 2; height: 20px; width: 1px  }
#title4 { position: absolute; top: 20px; left: 515px;
          z-index: 2; height: 20px; width: 1px  }
</STYLE>
<SCRIPT language="javascript">
currentTick = 0;

TimingObjectsX = new Array(4);
TimingObjectsY = new Array(4);
TimingObjectsX[0] = new Array(-100,50,75,120,150,180);
TimingObjectsY[0] = new Array(400,350,220,150,100,20);

TimingObjectsX[1] = new Array(290,290,290,290,290,290);
TimingObjectsY[1] = new Array(600,500,400,300,200,20);

TimingObjectsX[2] = new Array(600,580,530,480,430,400);
TimingObjectsY[2] = new Array(600,500,400,300,200,20);

TimingObjectsX[3] = new Array(900,800,750,620,550,510);
TimingObjectsY[3] = new Array(400,350,220,150,100,20);

// start path movement timer
// display images
function StartObjects() {
  image1.style.visibility="inherit";
  image2.style.visibility="inherit";
  image3.style.visibility="inherit";
  image4.style.visibility="inherit";
  setTimeout("MoveObjects()", 200);
}

// move images to next coordinate in path
function MoveObjects() {
  document.all.image1.style.posLeft =
      TimingObjectsX[0][currentTick];
  document.all.image1.style.posTop =
      TimingObjectsY[0][currentTick];
  document.all.image2.style.posLeft =
      TimingObjectsX[1][currentTick];
  document.all.image2.style.posTop =
      TimingObjectsY[1][currentTick];
  document.all.image3.style.posLeft =
      TimingObjectsX[2][currentTick];
  document.all.image3.style.posTop =
      TimingObjectsY[2][currentTick];
  document.all.image4.style.posLeft =
      TimingObjectsX[3][currentTick];
  document.all.image4.style.posTop =
      TimingObjectsY[3][currentTick];
  currentTick++;
  if (currentTick < 6)
      setTimeout("MoveObjects()", 200);
}
```

```
</SCRIPT>
</HEAD>
<BODY onLoad="StartObjects()">
<!-- Set menu titles -->
<DIV id=title1>
<h2><a href="http://www.yasd.com/services">Services</a></h2>
</DIV>
<DIV id=title2>
<h2><a href="http://www.yasd.com/sites">Sites</a></h2>
</DIV>
<DIV id=title3>
<h2><a href="http://www.yasd.com/scribbles">Scribbles</a></h2>
</DIV>
<DIV id=title4>
<h2><a href="http://www.yasd.com/samples">Samples</a></h2>
</DIV>

<!-- Set menu images-->
<img src="yasd.gif" id=logo style="visibility:inherit">
<a href="http://www.yasd.com/services"><img src="menua.jpg" border=0
 id=image1></a>
<a href="http://www.yasd.com/sites"><img src="menub.jpg" border=0
 id=image2></a>
<a href="http://www.yasd.com/scribbles"><img src="menuc.jpg"
 border=0 id=image3></a>
<a href="http://www.yasd.com/samples"><img src="menud.jpg" border=0
 id=image4></a>

</body>
```

Rather than set the font color to white, I could have set it to another color, and the titles would be visible while the images are downloading. With this approach, if Web page readers don't want to wait for the images to load, they can click one of the text-based links. Also, I could have placed text in the background stating that images are loading, and then set their visibility to `hidden` after the images are loaded.

Moving Objects Using an Array Rather than the Path Control

Why did I not use the Path Control that Microsoft provides, instead of the arrays? The Path Control is unique to Microsoft, which means that Netscape has nothing equivalent. Also, Netscape doesn't provide anything that I couldn't implement using script, as demonstrated in this chapter's examples, although the control is easier to use and the movement is a bit smoother. By not relying on Microsoft- or Netscape-specific controls, it will be easier to implement dynamic HTML techniques that are viewable by both Navigator and IE.

The Preview Example Revisited

Now that we've covered the basics of HTML positioning and seen how to script changes in these positions, let's take a deeper look at the preview example, from the beginning of the chapter, to see how it ticks.

In this example (see Listing 6-5), an embedded style sheet sets the absolute positions of four images and a button on a Web page. Eight path arrays, two for each image path, (one holding the x coordinates, the other the y coordinates) form a circular path in the middle of the Web page. When the button is pressed, a timer is started and the objects move along the coordinates in the assigned arrays for that particular run. For practice, try changing the timer to a value of 400 or 50 instead of 200 to see the how this setting changes the demonstration. Also, try changing the style sheet position property for the images from absolute to relative, and see what happens to the page layout.

Listing 6-5: The preview example illustrating dynamic absolute positioning

```
<HEAD>
<STYLE type="text/css">
<!--
    #container1 { position: absolute; top: 200px;
        left: 150px}
    #container2 { position: absolute; top: 50px;
        left: 300px}
    #container3 { position: absolute; top: 200px;
        left: 450px}
    #container4 { position: absolute; top: 350px;
        left: 300px}
    #container5 { position: absolute; top: 10px;
        left: 20px}
-->
</STYLE>

<SCRIPT LANGUAGE="JavaScript">

var TimingObjectsX
var TimingObjectsY
var object_order = new Array(4)
var currentTick = 0
var current_cycle = 3

TimingObjectsX = new Array(4)
TimingObjectsY = new Array(4)
TimingObjectsX[0] = new
  Array(150,165,180,195,210,225,240,255,270,285,300)
TimingObjectsY[0] = new
  Array(200,185,170,155,140,125,110,95,80,65,50)

TimingObjectsX[1] = new
  Array(300,315,330,345,360,375,390,405,420,435,450)
```

```
TimingObjectsY[1] = new
 Array(50,65,80,95,110,125,140,155,170,185,200)

TimingObjectsX[2] = new
 Array(450,435,420,405,390,375,360,345,330,315,300)
TimingObjectsY[2] = new
 Array(200,215,230,245,260,275,290,305,320,335,350)

TimingObjectsX[3] = new
 Array(300,285,270,255,240,225,210,195,180,165,150)
TimingObjectsY[3] = new
 Array(350,335,320,305,290,275,260,245,230,215,200)


function cycle() {
 current_cycle++;
 if (current_cycle == 1) {
      object_order[0] = 1;
      object_order[1] = 2;
      object_order[2] = 3;
      object_order[3] = 0;
      }
 else if (current_cycle == 2) {
      object_order[0] = 2;
      object_order[1] = 3;
      object_order[2] = 0;
      object_order[3] = 1;
      }
 else if (current_cycle == 3) {
      object_order[0] = 3;
      object_order[1] = 0;
      object_order[2] = 1;
      object_order[3] = 2;
      }
 else {
      for (i = 0; i < 4; i++)
           object_order[i] = i;
      current_cycle = 0;
      }
 setTimeout("MoveObjects()", 200)
}

function MoveObjects() {
 var first = object_order[0];
 var second = object_order[1];
 var third = object_order[2];
 var fourth = object_order[3];
 document.all.container1.style.posLeft=
      TimingObjectsX[first][currentTick];
 document.all.container1.style.posTop=
      TimingObjectsY[first][currentTick];

 document.all.container2.style.left=
      TimingObjectsX[second][currentTick];
```

```
document.all.container2.style.top=
    TimingObjectsY[second][currentTick];

document.all.container3.style.left=
    TimingObjectsX[third][currentTick];
document.all.container3.style.top=
    TimingObjectsY[third][currentTick];

document.all.container4.style.left=
    TimingObjectsX[fourth][currentTick];
document.all.container4.style.top=
    TimingObjectsY[fourth][currentTick];

currentTick++
if (currentTick < 11)
    setTimeout("MoveObjects()", 200)
else
    currentTick = 0;
}

</SCRIPT>


</HEAD>
<BODY>
<img src="one.gif" id=container1 width=90 height=29 >
<img src="two.gif" id=container2 width=97 height=30 >
<img src="three.gif" width=145 height=28 id=container3>
<img src="four.gif" id=container4 width=119 height=29 >
<input type=button value="Cycle Images" onClick="cycle()"
 id=container5>
</BODY>
```

Summary

In this chapter you had a chance to work with some of the new HTML positioning capabilities Microsoft has provided in Internet Explorer 4.0. Appendix A has several URLs leading to more information on HTML positioning.

In this chapter you learned how to:

◆ Group multiple HTML elements into a package with the <DIV> tags to facilitate the positioning of groups.

◆ Use absolute positioning to have complete control over where an object is placed.

◆ Use relative positioning to control the placement of an object while still maintaining traditional HTML flow.

- Use layering techniques, such as the z-index property, to control placement of objects.

- Use script to dynamically change the positions of HTML objects.

- Use absolute positioning, layers, dynamic HTML, and path arrays to create animated effects.

The next chapter looks at how to dynamically change CSS1 attributes to alter the appearance of HTML elements after a page loads. We'll also look at the new filters and transitions properties built into Internet Explorer 4.0.

Chapter 7

Dynamically Changing the Look of HTML Elements in Internet Explorer

IN THIS CHAPTER

- ◆ Dynamic text, images, and backgrounds
- ◆ Hiding and revealing elements
- ◆ Applying visual filters
- ◆ Creating transitions with the transition filter

MICROSOFT HAS EXPOSED CSS1 `style` attributes to the company's scripting object model with Internet Explorer 4.0. This means that an element's style settings can be accessed and altered, dynamically, after the page is displayed. Several new features to Internet Explorer 4.0 enable the altering of text and images, as well as other HTML elements. In this chapter, you'll get a look at a property that lets you hide and reveal objects on the fly, and learn how to assign transition effects to elements using the transition filter.

The chapter also covers new multimedia filters in Internet Explorer 4.0 that let you create incredible special visual effects with no additional download times and no unnecessary burden to the Web server. Special filters let you add drop shadows, convert elements to grayscale, splash your Web pages with interesting lighting effects, and flip objects horizontally or vertically.

In the concluding section, we'll combine all of the new techniques discussed in this chapter to create a transitional effect that literally lights up your page.

Dynamically Changing Web Pages — A Preview Example

Internet Explorer 4.0 presents very few limits to what you can do with style sheets and script. To have a little fun and to introduce you to some of the technologies you'll learn about in the rest of the chapter, I've created a preview example that demonstrates some of the dynamic changes you can apply to perfectly ordinary HTML elements. The listing for this example appears at the end of this chapter.

Take a look at the example by opening the **quickchg.htm** sample file on the CD-ROM. As you can see, this page was formatted using CSS1 style properties, and has several HTML elements, including a couple of <DIV> blocks, a header <H1> block, a paragraph, and an image, as shown in Figure 7-1. As you move your cursor over each of the elements, its style changes. The first <DIV> block gains a shadow and the header font changes color, the second <DIV> block acquires a motion blur and the image gets turned upside down, and finally, the third section, the paragraph, just disappears, as shown in Figure 7-2.

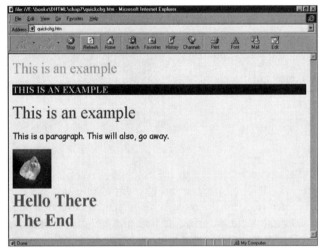

Figure 7-1: The preview example just after the page is opened

The example page demonstrates the techniques further discussed in this chapter such as changing fonts and images, applying style changes to any HTML element, and using the new multimedia style filters. You can begin experimenting with these styles yourself by changing various style settings in **quickchg.htm**.

Notice, in Figure 7-2, the effect of combining several visual filters with the last header. I particularly like the strong 3D effect this creates.

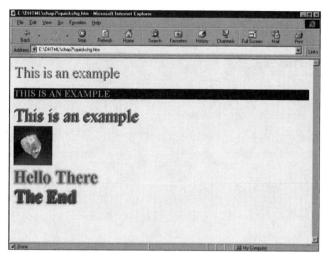

Figure 7-2: The preview example after moving the mouse over the entire page

Dynamic Text, Images, and Backgrounds

Most Web pages consist of mainly text, a background, and some images. This section shows you how to add dynamic flair to these very basic elements. But before we begin scripting, take a look at Table 7-1, which shows how the background, font, and text properties can be referred to in script. As you can see, they are slightly different than how styles are first assigned in style sheets:

TABLE 7-1 CSS1 Background, Font, and Text Properties

Basic Element	Property
Background	`background`
	`backgroundAttachment`
	`backgroundColor`
	`backgroundImage`
	`backgroundPosition`

continued

TABLE 7-1 CSS1 Background, Font, and Text Properties *(continued)*

Basic Element	Property
Background	backgroundPositionX
	backgroundPositionY
	backgroundRepeat
Font	font
	fontFamily
	fontSize
	fontStyle
	fontVariant
	fontWeight
Text	letterSpacing
	lineHeight
	textAlign
	textDecoration
	textDecorationBlink
	textDecorationLineThrough
	textDecorationNone
	textDecorationOverline
	textDecorationUnderline
	textIndent
	textTransform

Now that you've seen how to refer to an element's background, color, and font family, I'll show you how you can use VBScript to change the values on a mouse-click event. As you can see in the following example, the styles of a specific paragraph, indicated by an identifier named para1, change to a black background, yellow text, and a cursive font when it detects a mouseover event:

```
Sub para1_onmouseover
  para1.style.backgroundColor="black"
```

```
para1.style.color="yellow"
para1.style.fontFamily="Cursive"
End Sub
```

The following code makes other background, text, and font changes to the paragraph, this time triggered when the user's cursor leaves the region (a mouseout event):

```
Sub para1_onmouseout
  para1.style.backgroundColor="white"
  para1.style.color="black"
  para1.style.fontFamily="Times"
End Sub
```

Note that the preceding code example assumes that the original style for the paragraph uses a white background, black text, and the font family of Times.

This kind of rollover effect can have a dramatic effect within a Web page. Figure 7-3 shows three paragraphs in a Web page. As demonstrated, the second paragraph does not especially stand out, until you move your cursor over the page. Then, as shown in Figure 7-4, the second paragraph literally leaps off the page and definitely grabs your attention. Check this out for yourself by opening the **textchg.htm** sample file.

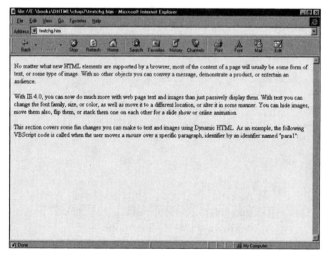

Figure 7-3: Three paragraphs embedded in a Web page; notice that none of the three particularly stands out

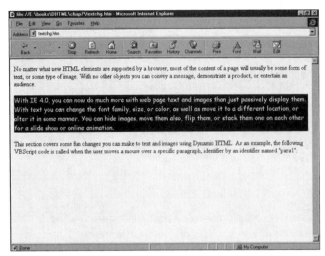

Figure 7-4: The same three paragraphs, but note how the second paragraph stands out with just a little change in the background color, font color, and font family

Images don't have as many properties as text, but you can create some interesting effects with them. You can use images as background for any HTML element, position them anywhere on a page, or size them any way you want. For example, the following code sets the background of the header to an image, and makes additional changes to the text alignment and color, when the page loads:

```
Sub Window_onload
  heading1.style.width=400
  heading1.style.textAlign="center"
  heading1.style.fontSize="40pt"
  heading1.style.backgroundImage="apophyllite2tn.JPG"
  heading1.style.backgroundRepeat="repeat-x"
  heading1.style.color="gold"
End Sub
```

The image repeats along the X or horizontal access, and completely covers the background of the header. This effect can have a very dramatic impact on the presentation of your page, with very little cost in terms of download time.

Okay, time for a little fun. Listing 7-1 demonstrates how to add an image to a header's background. This is nice, but not so fun. However, it also demonstrates some other changes you can apply to an image, including a variation of the famous "moving button" gag popular with Windows. This button moves whenever the cursor approaches it.

Listing 7-1: Adding images to the background of elements, and creating an image button that moves to avoid being clicked

```
<!DOCTYPE HTML PUBLIC "-//W3C//DTD W3 HTML 3.2//EN">
<HTML>
<HEAD>
<TITLE>Image Change</TITLE>
<SCRIPT language="vbscript">
<!--
Dim maxsize
Dim minsize
Dim adjustor
maxsize=600
minsize=100
adjustor=100

Sub Window_onload
  heading1.style.width=400
  heading1.style.textAlign="center"
  heading1.style.fontSize="40pt"
  heading1.style.color="gold"
  heading1.style.backgroundImage="url(apophyllite2tn.JPG)"
End Sub

Sub image1_onmouseover
  image1.style.borderWidth=10
  image1.style.borderColor="gold"
  If image1.style.posLeft > maxsize Then
       adjustor=-100
  ElseIf Image1.style.posLeft < minsize Then
       adjustor=100
  End If
  image1.style.posLeft = image1.style.posLeft+adjustor
End Sub
'-->
</SCRIPT>

</HEAD>
<BODY>
<P>
<H1 id="heading1"> Working with Text and Images</H1>
<p>
With IE 4.0, you can now do much more with web page text and images
  than just passively display them. With text you can change the font
  family, size, or color, as well as move it to a different location,
  or alter it in some manner. You can hide images, move them also,
  flip them, or stack them one on each other for a slide show or
  online animation.
</P>
<h2>Click on the image to see the most important change you can
  make!<h2>
<img src="apophyllite2tn.JPG" id=image1 width=100
  style="position:relative" border=0>
```

```
</BODY>
</HTML>
```

As you can probably tell from the code, it's pretty hard to click something that is always moving. You can try out my variation of the moving button by opening the file **imagechg.htm** on the CD-ROM.

The example in Listing 7-2 gives you a chance to play with backgrounds. The page in this listing, which you can find in the sample file named **elemchg.htm**, captures the onclick event anywhere within the Web page document and changes the background color of the element that received the event. Open **elemchg.htm** to see some interesting results.

Listing 7-2: Capturing all click events and setting the background color of the clicked object to "darkcoral"

```
<!DOCTYPE HTML PUBLIC "-//W3C//DTD W3 HTML 3.2//EN">
<HTML>
<HEAD><TITLE>Element Change</TITLE>
<SCRIPT language="vbscript">
<!--
Sub Document_onclick
  Dim clickedobjectobject
  Set clickedobject = window.event.srcElement
  clickedobject.style.backgroundColor = "red"
End Sub
'-->
</SCRIPT>
</HEAD>
<BODY>
<H1 id=HEAD1
style="background-image: url(apophyllite2tn.JPG); background-color:
  yellow; color: black">
Working with Traditional HTML elements</H1>
<P id=para1 style="background-color: lime; color:red">
You can now apply changes to all traditional HTML elements, such as
  changing font, modifying the background, adding a border, moving
  the element, or other effects. As an example, With IE 3.0 you could
  add a background image to a table, but, as was demonstrated in the
  previous section, you can now add an image to a header, a
  paragraph, or any other HTML element.
<strong id=strong1>You can also change the background color</strong>
  of elements as well as their fonts, and you can do all of this
  based on events.
</P>
<OL id=ordlist
  style="background-color: pink; color: silver">
<LI id=tete>This is the first list item</LI>
<LI>This is the second list item</LI>
<LI style="background-color: white; color: red">
  This is the third list item</LI>
<LI>This is the fourth list item</LI>
</OL>
```

```
<A id=link1 href="http://somelink.com">
 This is some link</a>
<ADDRESS id=addr1
 style="background-color: blue; color: yellow">
This is at the bottom of the document
</ADDRESS>
</BODY>
</HTML>
```

This example demonstrates how elements inherit properties from their containing parent, unless specifically overridden. As you can see, the background color for the `<strong>` tag contents is set to the same background as the enclosing paragraph. Clicking the paragraph containing the tag sets the background color for both. However, clicking the `<strong>` tag itself only changes the background color of the text contained within the tag, as shown in Figure 7-5. The items in the ordered list, defined with the `<OL>`, inherit their background color from their parent, except for the case in which the one list item has its own background color.

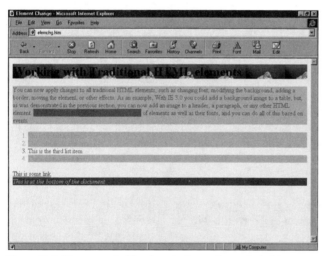

Figure 7–5: The example file elemchg.htm after only bold text contained within the paragraph is clicked

This example uses the `srcElement` property of the window `event` object to access the element that receives the event, and then changes the background color of the element. Other properties that could have been changed are any of the font/text properties (identified in the previous section) as well as the position of the element, any background image, and whether a border is shown around the element, and if so, its color and thickness.

Using the Tagname Property to Access Element Properties

Not all properties can be set for all elements, but you can access the type of element with the `tagname` property. The following example provides a message box listing the type of element that received the element:

```
someobject = window.event.srcElement
MsgBox(someobject.tagname)
```

If the object that received the event was defined with an `<H1>` tag, the message box would display "H1" as the contents. Once you know what type of element received the event, you can then determine which property to change.

Invisibility versus Display Effects

You can use two techniques to specify whether an object is displayed, and if so, whether it continues to take up space within the page. Preventing the display of an object, including any space usage in the page, is controlled by the `display` property. The `visibility` property can make an object invisible, but it still continues to use page space.

An example of the `display` property in use can be seen in Figure 7-6, which shows a Web page with three paragraphs. The `display` property is set to `none` for the second paragraph, using the following code:

```
<P id=para1 style="display:none">
```

If the `visibility` property had been used, the page would have looked like Figure 7-7. Note the large space between the two paragraphs. This is the amount of space that the second paragraph takes, regardless of its visibility. Setting this property for the paragraph uses the following code:

```
<P id=para1 style="visibility:hidden">
```

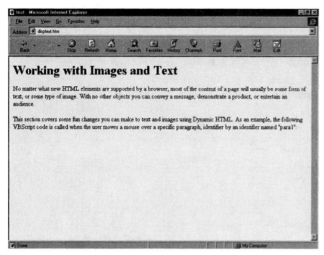

Figure 7-6: An example of a Web page with one paragraph set so
it does not display; the page looks like it contains only two paragraphs

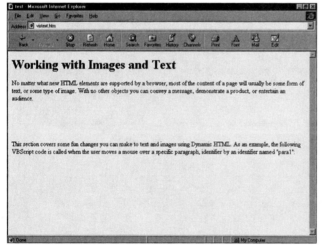

Figure 7-7: A Web page with one paragraph set to be invisible;
the page has a large gap between the two displayed paragraphs

You can check out the differences that occur when these two properties are used. The sample file **disptext.htm** contains three paragraphs, with the second paragraph set so it doesn't display. When the header is clicked, the display for the second paragraph is turned on through the use of a function, as shown in Listing 7-3.

Listing 7-3: Using the display property to hide and show a paragraph

```
<HTML>
<HEAD><TITLE>test</TITLE>
<SCRIPT language="javascript">
<!--
function clicked_header() {
    para1.style.display = para1.style.display == "none" ? "" : "none"
}
//-->
</SCRIPT>

</HEAD>
<BODY>
<P>
<H1 id=head1 onclick="clicked_header()">Working with Images and
  Text</H1>
No matter what new HTML elements are supported by a browser, most of
  the content of a page will usually be some form of text, or some
  type of image.
</P>
<P id=para1 style="display:none">
With IE 4.0, you can now do much more with web page text and images
  than just passively display them. With text you can change the font
  family, size, or color, as well as move it to a different location,
  or alter it in some manner. You can hide images, move them also,
  flip them, or stack them one on each other for a slide show or
  online animation.
</P>
<p>
This section covers some fun changes you can make to text and images
  using dynamic HTML. As an example, the following VBScript code is
  called when the user moves a mouse over a specific paragraph,
  identifier by an identifier named "para1":
</P>
</BODY>
</HTML>
```

This example tests the value of the property, and sets it to an empty string ("") if the property is set to none; if the property isn't equal to none, it is then set to none. To redisplay an HTML element, set the property to an empty string.

A similar file, **vistext.htm** (on the CD-ROM), uses this same technique to set the visibility property of the second paragraph, as shown in Listing 7-4.

Listing 7-4: Using the visibility property to hide and show the paragraph

```
<HTML>
<HEAD><TITLE>test</TITLE>
<SCRIPT language="javascript">
<!--
function clicked_header() {
   para1.style.visibility = para1.style.visibility == "hidden" ?
 "inherit" : "hidden"
}
//-->
</SCRIPT>

</HEAD>
<BODY>
<P>
<H1 id=head1 onclick="clicked_header()">Working with Images and
 Text</H1>
No matter what new HTML elements are supported by a browser, most of
 the content of a page will usually be some form of text, or some
 type of image.
</P>
<P id=para1 style="visibility:hidden">
With IE 4.0, you can now do much more with web page text and images
 than just passively display them. With text you can change the font
 family, size, or color, as well as move it to a different location,
 or alter it in some manner. You can hide images, move them also,
 flip them, or stack them one on each other for a slide show or
 online animation.
</P>
<p>
This section covers some fun changes you can make to text and images
 using dynamic HTML. As an example, the following VBScript code is
 called when the user moves a mouse over a specific paragraph,
 identifier by an identifier named "para1":
</P>
</BODY>
</HTML>
```

This example tests the value of the property, setting it to visible if the property is hidden, and to hidden if the property is visible. A third value for this property is inherit, which means that the property is inherited from any parent element.

When do you use one property over the other? As demonstrated, use the display property when you want to remove all reference to an element or group of elements from a Web page, including the space it or they would normally take. Use the visibility property if you want to maintain the space for an object, or if you don't care whether the space is maintained. A good example of this choice is shown in Listing 7-5, demonstrating a page that creates a slide show effect by using the visibility property. Images are placed on a page in the exact same position. As the button is pushed, the currently visible image is set to invisible and the next image in the "stack" is set to be visible. A counter is used to determine which image is displayed. The images in this page are from my "Photos with an Attitude" collection and you will see why if you access the sample file **badatt.htm**.

Listing 7-5: The "Photos with an Attitude" example page demonstrating an effective use of the visibility property

```
<!DOCTYPE HTML PUBLIC "-//W3C//DTD W3 HTML 3.2//EN">
<HTML>
<HEAD>
<STYLE type="text/css">
 img { position: absolute; top: 100px; left: 100px;
             width: 200px; height: 204px;
             border-width: 10px; border-color: ivory;
             visibility:hidden }
 BODY { background-color: salmon }
 #button { position: absolute; top: 160px; left: 360px;
             border-width: 5px; border-color: ivory;
             background-color: lightcoral; color: white;
             font-family: Cursive; font-weight: 300; font-size:
 14pt }
</STYLE>
<SCRIPT language="vbscript">
<!--
Dim currentimage
currentimage = 0
Dim theimages

Sub window_onload
  Set theimages = document.images
  theimages.item(0).style.visibility="visible"
End Sub

Sub changeimg_onclick
  theimages.item(currentimage).style.visibility="hidden"
  currentimage = currentimage + 1
  If currentimage > 7 Then
        currentimage = 0
  End If
  theimages.item(currentimage).style.visibility="visible"
End Sub
'-->
</SCRIPT>
</HEAD>
<BODY>
<img src="badattr.jpg">
<img src="badatt2r.jpg">
<img src="badatt3r.jpg">
<img src="badatt4r.jpg">
<img src="badatt5r.jpg">
<img src="badatt6r.jpg">
<img src="badatt7r.jpg">
<img src="badatt8r.jpg">
```

```
<input type=button name="changeimg" value="Change Image" id=button>

</BODY>
</HTML>
```

Listing 7-5 also demonstrates the use of the `images` collection, which Chapter 5 presented in more detail. The effect could also have been created by switching out the z-order value associated with each element to place images higher up in the stack.

Chartreuse Button, Anyone?

The example in Listing 7-5 demonstrates the changes you can make to ordinary input controls such as the button. The example also changes the border, background color, font color, as well as font family and size of the button. If you are a little tired of that traditional plain, gray button, try changing some of the CSS1 attributes. Remember, though, to not get so carried away that people have no idea that what they are looking at *is* a button.

Applying Visual Filters

Microsoft provides built-in filter properties that can be used to control the appearance of HTML elements. In this section, I discuss the visual filter properties. Each filter has a set of parameters used to control how it is applied. Among the filter effects are as follows:

- chroma
- drop shadow
- flip
- grayscale
- invert
- light
- mask
- blur
- opacity
- shadow
- glow
- wave
- x-ray

A `filter` object can be applied to one and only one visual object, but more than one effect can be applied to the same object. To attach a filter to an object, you assign it to the filter property of the object, as follows:

```
image1.style.filter="Gray()";
```

Creating more than one filter effect for the same object is actually quite simple. The following code creates blur, glow, and drop shadow filter effects and applies them all to the same object:

```
div3.style.filter= _
"dropshadow(color=#880000, offX=2, offY=2, add=true)+_
" blur(add=true, direction=38,strength=5)" + _
" glow(color=#FFFF00, strength=5)"
```

When specific parameters of a filter are accessed, an array reference is used to ensure that the appropriate change is made to the appropriate filter. This change occurs even if only one effect is defined for the filter object. In the previous example, both the drop shadow and the glow filter effects have a color parameter. To change the color property for the glow effect if you are using VBScript, use the following:

```
div3.filters(2).color=RGB(0,255,0)
```

If you are using JScript, use the following:

```
div3.filters[2].color=RGB(0,255,0);
```

You can assign one of the filters to a variable so you can work with the filter without having to reference the object:

```
var tmp = div3.filters[2];
tmp.ChangeColor(0,0,0,255,1);
```

To remove an existing filter, just set the filter to an empty string:

```
Image1.style.filter = ""
```

The rest of this section discusses the individual visual filter effects, and provides samples and demonstrations of each.

The Chroma, Alpha, and Mask Filters

This section covers three filters that provide transparency effects. The chroma filter effect alters a visual object by setting a specified color to be transparent for the object. The alpha filter effect sets the amount of transparency for an object. The mask filter effect creates a transparent mask from nontransparent pixels. The syntax for the chroma, alpha, and mask filters follows:

```
{FILTER: Chroma(Color=color)}
{FILTER: Alpha(Opacity=opacity, FinishOpacity=finishopacity,
 Style=style, StartX=startX, startY=startY, FinishX=finishX,
 finishY=finishY)"}
{FILTER: Mask(Color=color)}
```

The only parameter for the chroma and mask visual filters is:

color — Hexadecimal color value using a format of #RRGGBB to be set to transparent for the object for chroma, or to paint transparent pixels for the mask effect. According to Microsoft documentation, the chroma filter's effect does not work well with compressed or dithered images, such as JPEG images, nor does it work well with anti-aliased images.

The alpha visual filter has six parameters, as listed in Table 7-2.

TABLE 7-2 Alpha Filter Parameters

Parameter	Description
opacity	The percentage of transparency applied to the object
finishopacity	The percentage of transparency applied to the object at the finish
style	The style of transparency; allowable values are 0 (uniform), 1 (linear), 2 (radial), and 3 (rectangular)
startX	Starting x coordinate where the gradient transparency begins
startY	Starting y coordinate where the gradient transparency begins
finishX	Finishing x coordinate
finishY	Finishing y coordinate

As an example, Listing 7-6 provides a Web page that uses the chroma and alpha effects. Note from the code that, when the page is loaded, an image is set to 50 percent transparency and is placed on top of three headers. Clicking the top image in the page switches the transparent color to black if it is currently white, and to white if it is currently black. The example shown in Listing 7-6 can be found on the CD-ROM in the sample file **chromkey.htm**.

Listing 7-6: Using the chroma and alpha visual filter effects

```
<HTML>
<HEAD><TITLE>Chromakey Effect</TITLE>
<STYLE type="text/css">
  BODY { background-color: lightblue }
</STYLE>
<SCRIPT language="vbscript">
<!--
Dim currentcolor
currentcolor = 1
```

```
Sub image1_onclick
  image1.style.filter = ""
  If currentcolor = 1 Then
        image1.style.filter="chroma(color=#000000, enabled=1)"
        currentcolor = 0
  Else
        image1.style.filter="chroma(color=#FFFFFF, enabled=1)"
        currentcolor = 1
  End If
End Sub
'-->
</SCRIPT>
</HEAD>
<BODY onload="image2.style.filter='alpha(opacity=50)'">
<img src="bar.gif" width=422 height=76 id=image1 hspace=20
 vspace=20>
<p>
<DIV style="margin: 1.0in">
<H1>This is the header</H1>
<img src="rhodie.jpg" width=250 height=190 id=image2
 style="position: absolute; top: 205px; left: 70px">
<H1 style="color: red">This is a second header</H1>
<H1 style="color: yellow">This is a third header</H1>
</DIV>

</BODY>
</HTML>
```

The Drop Shadow and Shadow Filters

The drop shadow filter effect creates a silhouette of an object that is offset from the original, creating a drop shadow effect. This filter enables you to specify a color and size for the shadow. The shadow effect is a simpler filter, enabling you to specify the color and direction of the shadow only.

The syntax for the drop shadow and shadow filters follows:

```
{FILTER: Shadow(Color=color, Direction=direction)}
{FILTER: DropShadow(Color=color, OffX=offX, offY=offY,
 Positive=positive)}
```

The parameters for the drop shadow visual filter are shown in Table 7-3.

TABLE 7-3 Drop Shadow Parameters

Parameters	Description
Color	The color of the drop shadow, a hexadecimal color value using a format of #RRGGBB
OffX	The horizontal pixel width of the shadow, with positive values placing the shadow to the right, negative values placing it to the left
OffY	The vertical pixel width of the shadow, with negative values moving the shadow up, positive values moving it down
Positive	A value of 0 (false) creates a shadow for any nontransparent pixel of the object; a positive value (true) creates a shadow for any transparent pixel

The parameters of the shadow visual filter are shown in Table 7-4.

TABLE 7-4 Shadow Parameters

Parameter	Description
Color	The color of the shadow, a hexidecimal color value using a format of #RRGGBB
Direction	A numeric value representing the direction of the shadow — values from 0 to 315 degrees are acceptable, in increments of 45 degrees. A value of 0 sets the shadow from the top, 90 sets the shadow to the right, 180 to the bottom, and 270 to the left.

The sample file **shadow.htm** on the CD-ROM is a simple demonstration of the use of the drop shadow and shadow effects for two different headers, respectively. Listing 7-7 contains the example. In the first, the drop shadow effect is set dynamically when the page loads. In the second, the shadow filter effect is initially created by the inclusion of the filter setting within the header's `style` setting.

Listing 7-7: Applying the drop shadow and shadow filters to two headers

```
<!DOCTYPE HTML PUBLIC "-//W3C//DTD W3 HTML 3.2//EN">
<HTML>
<HEAD>
<STYLE type="text/css">
```

```
BODY { background-color: firebrick }
</STYLE>
</HEAD>
<BODY
onload="head1.style.filter='dropshadow(color=#EEEEEE, offX=3,
 offY=3, add=true)'">
<DIV id=head1 style="width:100%">
<H1>This is an example of drop shadows</H1></DIV>

<DIV id=head2 style="width:100%;
 filter:shadow(color=#FFFF33,direction=135)">
<H1 style="color: blue">
This is an example of drop shadows</H1></DIV>

</BODY>
</HTML>
```

Change the offset values to see for yourself what a difference this setting can make. Also, try some different colors, and switch the direction of the shadows with the use of negative and positive offset values, or change the direction number for the shadow effect.

The Flip Vertical and Flip Horizontal Filters

The flip-horizontally and flip-vertically filter effects flip an object along the horizontal or vertical planes using the following simple syntax:

```
{FILTER: FlipH}
{FILTER: FlipV}
```

As an example of how to use these filters with an image, the file **fliptest.htm** displays an image and a single button. When the page is first loaded, as shown in Figure 7-8, the button displays "Flip Horizontally," and the image is displayed normally. Clicking the button sets the image filter property to `FlipH`, flipping the image horizontally, and changes the button caption to "Flip Vertically." Clicking the button again sets the image filter property to `FlipV`, flipping the image vertically, and changes the button caption to "Return to Normal," as shown in Figure 7-9. These effects continue to cycle as long as the page is loaded. The code to create this page is shown in Listing 7-8.

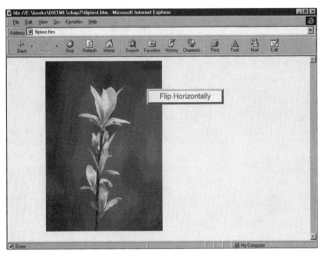

Figure 7-8: The fliptest.htm example when the page is first loaded

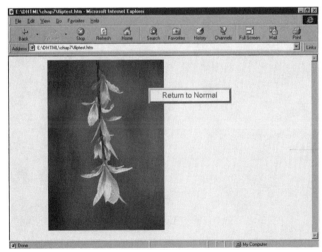

Figure 7-9: The fliptest.htm example after the button has been clicked a couple of times and the flip-vertically filter effect is applied to the image

Listing 7-8: Applying the flip-horizontally and flip-vertically visual filter effects to an image

```
<!DOCTYPE HTML PUBLIC "-//W3C//DTD W3 HTML 3.2//EN">
<HTML>
```

```
<HEAD>
<STYLE type="text/css">
 img { position: absolute; top: 10px; left: 100px;
            width: 300px; height: 424px;
            border-width: 10px; border-color: khaki }
 BODY { background-color: cornsilk }
 #button { position: absolute; top: 80px; left: 360px;
            border-width: 5px; border-color: khaki;
            background-color: ivory; color: forestgreen;
            font-family: Arial; font-weight: 300; font-size: 14pt
 }
</STYLE>
<SCRIPT language="JavaScript">
<!--
function ClickedButton(button_type) {
 if (button_type == "Flip Horizontally") {
        image1.style.filter = "FlipH()";
        changeimg.value = "Flip Vertically"
        }
 else if (button_type == "Flip Vertically") {
        image1.style.filter = "FlipV()";
        changeimg.value = "Return to Normal"
        }
 else {
        image1.style.filter = ""
        changeimg.value = "Flip Horizontally"
        }
}
//-->
</SCRIPT>

</HEAD>
<BODY>
<img src="leaves1.jpg" id=image1>
<input type=button name="changeimg" value="Flip Horizontally"
 id=button
 onClick="ClickedButton(this.value)">

</BODY>
</HTML>
```

Positioning HTML Elements

As Figures 7-8 and 7-9 demonstrate, IE 4.0 does not require you to position input controls, images, or even text in separate nonoverlapping regions on a page. Experiment a bit with the design and try overlapping some of the HTML elements for an interesting effect.

The Grayscale, Invert, and X-Ray Filters

The grayscale visual filter effect removes all colors from an object, reducing it to grays. The invert filter reverses the hue, saturation, and brightness of an object, providing a "negative" effect. The x-ray filter removes most of an object's depth and reduces it to black and white, creating an x-ray effect.

None of these visual filters has parameters — they have only the class identifier parameters that are used to create the effect, as shown in the following syntax:

```
{FILTER: Gray}
{FILTER: Invert}
{FILTER: Xray}
```

I was curious as to how these filters worked with images and text, so I created an example that applies each of the three filters to an image, a control, and a header, enclosed within a <DIV> block. You can find this example on the CD-ROM in the file **graytest.htm**.

Listing 7-9 contains just the style sheet settings and <DIV> block HTML for the page. The code containing the ClickedButton function, referenced by the <DIV> block, is created in the next listing, Listing 7-10.

Listing 7-9: The style sheet setting and <DIV> block for the example page

```
<STYLE type="text/css">
  BODY    { background-color: lightcoral }
  H1      { color: maroon; width: 200px; height: 30px;
            font-size: 24pt; font-family: Cursive }
  img     { position: absolute; top: 100px; left: 50px;
              width: 250px; height: 190px;
              border-width: 10px; border-color: honeydew }
  #button { border-width: 5px; border-color: firebrick;
              position: absolute; top: 170px; left: 370px;
              background-color: honeydew; color: maroon;
              font-family: Arial; font-weight: 300;
              font-size: 14pt }
  DIV     { position: absolute; top: 50px; width: 100%; height: 100%
  }
</STYLE>
...
<BODY>
<DIV id=block1>
<H1 style="margin-left: 0.5in">This is an example header</H1>
<p>
<img src="rhodie.jpg">
<p>
<input type=button name="changeimg"
  value="Apply GrayScale" id=button
  onClick="ClickedButton(this.value)">
</DIV>
```

When the user presses the button, the effect as well as the button label is changed to reflect what filter effect is being demonstrated next, as shown in Listing 7-10.

Listing 7-10: A script to alter the visual filter effect and modify button text

```
<SCRIPT language="JavaScript">
<!--
function ClickedButton(button_type) {
 block1.style.filter=null
  if (button_type == "Apply GrayScale") {
        block1.style.filter = "Gray()";
        changeimg.value = "Apply Invert"
        }
  else if (button_type == "Apply Invert") {
        block1.style.filter = "Invert()";
        changeimg.value = "Apply XRay"
        }
  else if (button_type == "Apply XRay") {
        block1.style.filter = "Xray()";
        changeimg.value = "Return to Normal"
        }
  else
        changeimg.value = "Apply GrayScale"
}
'-->
</SCRIPT>
```

When the page is first loaded, it looks similar to Figure 7-10. However, applying the different filters creates amazing effects on the objects contained within the <DIV> block. For example, Figure 7-11 shows all three of the contained visual objects with the invert visual filter applied.

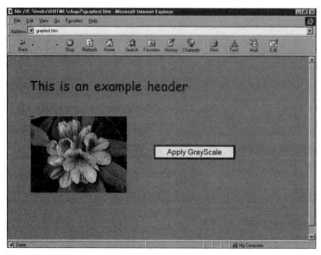

Figure 7-10: The grayscale, x-ray, and invert sample file after first loading

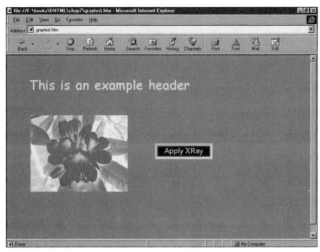

Figure 7-11: The example file after the invert filter has been applied; all the colors of the visual objects have been set to their "negative" value

Try the example file yourself, and make sure to use some of the other images supplied on this book's CD-ROM, or use your own images. If you do change the image, make sure you reset the width and height in the style sheet.

The Blur and Wave Filters

The blur effect provides a blurred shadow to an image, implying movement. The wave filter warps the object by transforming it with a wave-like effect. The syntax for the blur and wave filters follows:

```
{FILTER: Blur(Add=add, Direction=direction, Strength=strength)}
{FILTER: Wave(Add=add, Freq=freq, LightStrength=lightstrength,
 Phase=phase, Strength=strength)}
```

The blur filter has three parameters, listed in Table 7-5.

TABLE 7-5 Blur Parameters

Parameter	Description
Add	Specifies whether to add the original image to the effect; a value of zero (0) is false, and any positive value is true

continued

TABLE 7-5 Blur Parameters *(continued)*

Parameter	Description
Direction	Direction of effect
Strength	Strength of effect

Table 7-6 lists the five parameters for the wave visual filter.

TABLE 7-6 Wave Parameters

Parameter	Description
Add	Specifies whether to add the original image to the effect; a value of zero (0) is false, and any positive value is true
Freq	Number of waves in the effect
Light	Strength of the wave, from 0 to 100
Phase	Offset for the start of the sine wave effect, with values from 0 to 100; a value of 50 is equal to 180 degrees, and 100 is equal to 360 degrees
Strength	Strength of the effect

These two filters can apply some very interesting effects, particularly to fonts. For example, the sample file **testmove.htm**, given in Listing 7-11, applies each of these filters to different headers when the cursor is moved over each filter.

Listing 7-11: The contents of the testmove.htm file with examples of the blur and wave visual filters

```
<!DOCTYPE HTML PUBLIC "-//W3C//DTD W3 HTML 3.2//EN">
<HTML>
<HEAD><TITLE>Blur and Wave</TITLE>
<STYLE type="text/css">
 BODY { background-color: white }
</STYLE>
<SCRIPT LANGUAGE="VBScript">
<!--
Sub div1_onmouseover
 div1.style.filter="Blur(Add=0, Direction=315,Strength=20)"
```

```
End Sub

Sub head1_onmouseover
 head1.style.filter=
 "Wave(Add=1,Freq=1,LightStrength=50,Phase=0,Strength=6)"
End Sub

Sub div2_onmouseover
 div2.style.filter = "Wave(Add=0,Freq=5,lightStrength=20,
 Phase=0,Strength=12)"
End Sub
'-->
</SCRIPT>
</HEAD>
<BODY>

<DIV id=div1
  style="width:100%; font-size: 36pt; color: orange">
This is an example
</DIV>
<DIV id=head1 style="width: 100%">
<H1 style="color: forestgreen; font-size: 48pt">
This is an example
</H1>
</DIV>
<DIV id=div2
  style="width: 100%; font-family: Cursive; font-size: 48pt; font-
 weight: 800; color: red">
This is an example
</DIV>
<DIV id=head2 style="width:
 100%;filter:Blur(Add=1,Direction=135,strength=5)">
<H1 style="width: 100%; color: blue; font-size: 36pt">
This is an example
</H1>
</DIV>
</BODY>
</HTML>
```

Notice in Figure 7-12 what happens when the original image is not added when the blur effect is used. The impact on the wave effect is also readily apparent from Figure 7-12.

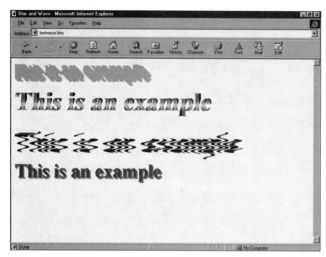

Figure 7-12: The impact of two different tests of the drop shadow
visual filter effect

Try the example yourself, but change values for the filters. For example, add the
original image, or change the direction and strengths associated with each of the filters. Particularly note the nice effect you can create by using the wave filter, with a
highlight setting and a frequency set to 1, as shown with the second header.

The Light Filter

The final visual filter I will talk about is the light filter, because it is the most complex. This effect alters visual objects by creating pinpoint, cone, or ambient lights
that "shine" directly or indirectly on the objects. You create a light object using the
following syntax:

```
{FILTER: Light}
```

and then you use one or more of several methods to set the light object properties.
The methods and values for the light visual filter are shown in Table 7-7 along
with the possible parameters each method accepts.

TABLE 7-7 **Light Visual Filter Effect Methods and Parameters**

Method	Result	Parameters
addAmbient	Adds all-over light effect	R, G, B, strength — the first three parameters are a value of from 0–255 and are used to define the color, and strength is the intensity of the effect
addCone	Adds a cone of light	x1, y1, z1, x2, y2, R, G, B, strength, spread — the first coordinates are the light source coordinates, the second coordinates are the target, the RGB parameters are the red-green-blue values respectively, the strength is the intensity, and the spread determines how small a circle or ellipse the cone is
addPoint	Adds a point light source	x, y, z, R, G, B, strength — the first three parameters are the coordinates of the light source, the RGB parameters are the red-green-blue values respectively, and the strength is the intensity of the effect
changeColor	For light source, changes color	light, R, G, B, absolute — light is the number associated with the light effect (you can use more than one), the RGB parameters are the red-green-blue values respectively, and a false value for absolute adds the value to the existing color, true sets the color of the light to the new value explicitly

continued

TABLE 7-7 Light Visual Filter Effect Methods and Parameters *(continued)*

Method	Result	Parameters
ChangeStrength	For light source effect, changes strength	light, strength, absolute — light is the number associated with the light effect (you can use more than one), the strength is the new strength values, and a false value for absolute adds the value to the existing strength, true sets the strength of the light to the new value explicitly
Clear	Deletes all lights associated with the filter	
MoveLight	Moves light source effect	light, x, y, z, absolute — light is the number associated with the light effect (you can use more than one), the XYZ values are the new coordinate system for the light, and a false value for absolute sets the coordinate system to relative, true to absolute

The light visual filter is probably the toughest of the filters to work with. You will need to control not only the target of the effect, but the density, color, spread, and source among other things. An example of how to use this filter is provided on the CD-ROM in the sample file litetest.htm.

In this example, a <DIV> block is created to enclose three elements: an image, some text, and a button:

```
<DIV id=block1>
<H1 style="margin-left: 0.5in">This is an example header</H1>
<p>
<img src="rhodie.jpg">
<p>
<input type=button name="changeimg" value="Apply Red Ambient Light"
  id=button
  onClick="ClickedButton(this.value)">
</DIV>
```

A light filter is applied to the <DIV> block when the button, contained in the block, is pressed.

The first button-click casts bright red ambient light, as shown in the following code:

```
if (button_type == "Apply Red Ambient Light") {
  block1.style.filter="light";
  var light = block1.filters[0];
  light.addAmbient(255,0,0,100);
  changeimg.value = "Change to Blue"
  }
```

As you can see, to achieve this effect, the light filter is added to the style setting for the block. Then the filter is accessed from the filters array, and the addAmbient method is added to the filter. The color for the method is set to red. Additionally, the button text is changed to invite the user to click it for the next filter effect, Change to Blue.

Clicking Change to Blue changes the ambient light to blue, and changes the button text to "Apply PinPoint Lights," as shown in the following code:

```
else if (button_type == "Change to Blue") {
  var light = block1.filters[0];
  light.ChangeColor(0,0,0,255,1);
  changeimg.value = "Apply PinPoint Lights"
  }
```

Note that I did not issue a clear method call because I wanted to apply the color change to the existing light object.

Clicking Apply PinPoint Lights applies several pinpoint lights on the page by issuing several AddPoint method calls:

```
else if (button_type == "Apply PinPoint Lights") {
  var light = block1.filters[0];
  light.clear()
  light.addPoint(50,50,50,255,0,0,400)
  light.addPoint(150,100,150,0,255,0,400)
  light.addPoint(200,150,50,0,0,255,400)
  light.addPoint(250,200,150,255,255,0,400)
  light.addPoint(300,250,50,0,255,255,400)
  light.addPoint(350,300,150,255,0,255,400)
  light.addPoint(400,250,150,0,255,255,400)
  light.addPoint(200,150,150,255,0,255,400)
  light.addPoint(150,100,50,255,255,0,400)
  changeimg.value = "Apply Cone Lights"
  }
```

Note that in this effect, the light object is cleared first. You may also wonder, "Why call the addPoint method only ten times?" The reason is that only ten filter effects can be used with one visual filter at a time.

The pinpoint lights are shown in Figure 7-13. This lighting scheme can create gradient, almost metallic effects, which opens up some interesting design possibilities.

Figure 7-13: The litetest.htm example file with the pinpoint l
ighting effect applied

By clicking the Apply Cone Lights button, the final special lighting effect is applied in the form of cone lighting using the addCone method, as follows:

```
else if (button_type == "Apply Cone Lights") {
 var light = block1.filters[0];
 light.clear()
 light.addCone(200,10,50,50,50,255,0,0,400,15)
 light.addCone(150,10,50,150,100,0,255,0,400,20)
 light.addCone(100,10,50,250,150,0,0,255,400,10)
 light.addCone(50,10,50,200,200,255,255,0,400,25)
 light.addCone(400,600,50,250,150,0,255,255,400,10)
 light.addCone(450,500,50,300,250,255,0,255,400,20)
 light.addCone(400,300,50,250,200,0,255,255,400,25)
 light.addCone(400,50,150,250,150,0,255,255,400,40)
 light.addCone(450,100,150,400,350,255,0,255,400,40)
 light.addCone(750,50,150,450,300,0,255,255,400,25)
 changeimg.value = "Normal Image"
}
```

The cone lighting effect is much more drastic than the pinpoint lighting, as shown in Figure 7-14. Note that the light does not tend to diffuse at the edges, but instead has fairly strong borders.

To become more familiar with the light visual filter effect, I strongly recommend that you open **litetest.htm** and try changing each of the light sources. For the ambient light, try changing the colors and strength. For the pinpoint and cone lights, change the targets, the z-axis value, the spread, and the strength to see how they impact the presentation.

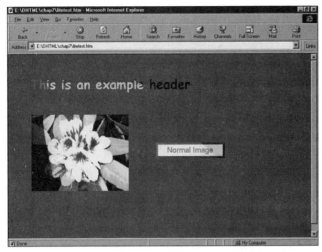

Figure 7-14: Applying the cone lighting filter effect to several HTML elements

Using the Transition Filter

In addition to the new visual filter, you can also use the transition filter, which adds transitional effects to text or visual objects.

The three methods to use with the transition filter are as follows:

- `revealTrans` — Applies defined effects, described later in this section

- `Apply` — Stops painting and enables changes, such as a new transition effect or the altering of an image or text

- `Play` — Plays the transition from the time of the last `Apply` method

Transitions can be applied to components within a page, or to an entire page. For example, **trans.htm** contains two identical images and a text block, all of which are contained within one `<DIV>` block. The block is positioned using absolute positioning and the `revealTrans` filter is applied to the block, with effect "1" (Box In) applied.

The `onclick` event for the document is captured and a function called `Clicked` is created as an event handler. This function hides the second text block (which contains the name of the transition currently being demonstrated), and hides the image currently being displayed.

The `Apply` method is called on the image that had been hidden, the transition effect is changed, and then the transition is replayed. The image is then set to be visible. The function cycles through all of the transitions, and then starts over when the last transition number is reached. Listing 7-12 contains the code from the example page.

Listing 7-12: Using the transition filter

```html
<HTML>
<HEAD>
<STYLE type="text/css">
 img { position:absolute; top:0; left: 0; width: 300px; height:
 424px;
              border-width: 10px; border-color: khaki }
 #text1 { position: absolute; top: 25; left: 25; z-index: 5;
      width: 250; height: 375; font-family: Cursive; color: yellow;
      font-size: 12pt }
 #image { position: absolute; top: 10px; left: 100px; width: 300;
 height: 424}
 BODY { background-color: forestgreen }
</STYLE>
<SCRIPT language="JavaScript">
<!--
transeffect = 0;
theeffects = new Array(24);
theeffects[0] = "Box In";
theeffects[1] = "Box Out";
theeffects[2] = "Circle In";
theeffects[3] = "Circle Out";
theeffects[4] = "Wipe Up";
theeffects[5] = "Wipe Down";
theeffects[6] = "Wipe Right";
theeffects[7] = "Wipe Left";
theeffects[8] = "Vertical Blinds";
theeffects[9] = "Horizontal Blinds";
theeffects[10] = "Checkerboard Across";
theeffects[11] = "Checkerboard Down";
theeffects[12] = "Random Dissolve";
theeffects[13] = "Split vertical in";
theeffects[14] = "Split vertical out";
theeffects[15] = "Split horizontal in";
theeffects[16] = "Split horizontal out";
theeffects[17] = "Stripes left down";
theeffects[18] = "Stripes left up";
theeffects[19] = "Stripes right down";
theeffects[20] = "Stripes right up";
theeffects[21] = "Random bars horizontal";
theeffects[22] = "Random bars vertical";
theeffects[23] = "Random";

current_image = "image1";
function Clicked() {
 var the_image, the_other;
 text2.style.visiblity="hidden";
 if (image1.style.visibility=="inherit") {
      the_image = image2;
```

```
                the_other = image1;
                }
        else {
                the_image = image1;
                the_other = image2;
                }
        the_other.style.visibility="hidden";
        the_image.filters.item(0).Apply();
        the_image.filters.item(0).Transition = transeffect;
        the_image.filters.item(0).Play(2.0);
        the_image.style.visibility="inherit";
        text2.innerText=theeffects[transeffect];
        transeffect++;
        if (transeffect == 24)
                transeffect = 0;
        text2.style.visibility="visible";
}
//-->
</SCRIPT>

</HEAD>
<BODY onclick="Clicked()">
<DIV id=image>
<DIV id=text1>
The transition property can add interesting
effects such as dissolve, scatter, fade in, and others.
</DIV>
<img src="leaves1.jpg" id="image1"
style="visibility:hidden;
 FILTER:revealTrans(Duration=3.0,Transition=1)">
<img src="leaves1.jpg" id="image2"
style="visibility:hidden;
 FILTER:revealTrans(Duration=3.0,Transition=1)">
</DIV>
<DIV id=text2 style="position:absolute; left: 450; top: 300; color:
 yellow; font-size: 14pt; font-family: Cursive">
 
</DIV>
</BODY>
</HTML>
```

If two alternating images weren't used, the transition effect would not work properly. As the name of the filter implies, transitions are applied to create the effect of one element transitioning into another, which means you need at least two elements. Instead of using a duplicate of the image, I could also have used a different image or block of text and applied the transitioning effect between the two elements. I could also have kept the alternating blocks opaque during the transition.

See Chapter 15 for an example of a transition filter applied to multiple images.

To apply transitional effects to an entire page, use the <META> tag. To apply the effect when the page is entered, use the following syntax:

```
<META http-equiv="Page-Enter"
CONTENT="RevealTrans(Duration=4.0,Transition=3)">
```

This uses the Circle In transitional effect, with a duration of four seconds, when the Web page is entered. To apply the effect when the page is exited, use the following syntax:

```
<META http-equiv="Page-Exit"
CONTENT="RevealTrans(Duration=2.0,Transition=20)">
```

This code uses the Stripes right up transition, with a duration of two seconds, when the page is exited. At the time this was written, only one or the other of the effects was supported for a page.

To try this effect yourself, test it out with the sample file called **transmeta.htm**, which uses a page opening transition. My preference is to use only the page enter transitions in my own pages because I have control over how the page is presented, how the transition type looks with my content, and how long I need for the transition to complete. I dislike applying effects to others Web pages using the Page Exit transition because I would be, in effect, altering their Web page presentation.

The Preview Example Revisited

In the beginning of this chapter, you saw a preview example of a page that used CSS1 style properties, and had <DIV> blocks, a header <H1> block, a paragraph, and an image. When a reader moves his or her cursor over each element, its style changes as follows:

- First <DIV> block: acquires a shadow
- Header font: changes color
- Second <DIV> block: acquires a motion blur
- Image: turns upside down
- Paragraph: disappears

Listing 7-13 shows the code for this example.

Listing 7-13: A demonstration of some of the filter and other effects that can be applied to traditional HTML elements

```
<!DOCTYPE HTML PUBLIC "-//W3C//DTD W3 HTML 3.2//EN">
<HTML>
<HEAD>
<STYLE type="text/css">
 BODY { background-color: white }
</STYLE>
<SCRIPT LANGUAGE="VBScript">
<!--
Sub div1_onmouseover
  div1.style.filter="dropshadow(color=&H880000, offX=2, offY=2,
  add=true)"
End Sub

Sub header1_onmouseover
  header1.style.color="silver"
End Sub

Sub div2_onmouseover
  div2.style.filter="blur(add=true, direction=38,strength=5)"
End Sub

Sub image1_onmouseover
  image1.style.filter = nothing
  image1.style.filter="flipv"
End sub

Sub para1_onmouseover
  para1.style.display="none"
End Sub

Sub div3_onmouseover
  div3.style.filter= _
  "dropshadow(color=&H880000, offX=2, offY=2, add=true)" + _
  " blur(add=true, direction=38,strength=5)" + _
  " glow(color=&HFFFF00, strength=5)"
End Sub

Sub div4_onmouseover
  div4.style.filter="glow(color=&H00FF00, strength=5)"
End Sub
'-->
</SCRIPT>
</HEAD>
<BODY>

<DIV id=div1
  style="position: relative; width:100%; font-size: 28pt; color:
  orange">
```

```
This is an example
</DIV>
<H1 id=header1
  style="font-variant: small-caps; background-color: black; color:
 yellow">
This is an example
</H1>
<DIV id=div2
  style="position: relative; width:100%; font-size: 32pt; color:
  firebrick">
This is an example
</DIV>
<p id=para1 style="font-family: cursive; font-size: 16pt">
This is a paragraph. This will also, go away.
</P>
<img src="apophyllite2tn.JPG" width=100 id=image1>
<DIV id=div4
  style="position: relative; width:100%; font-weight: bold; font-
  size: 32pt; color: forestgreen">
Hello There
</DIV>
<DIV id=div3
  style="position: relative; width:100%; font-weight: bold; font-
  size: 32pt; color: red">
The End
</DIV>
</BODY>
</HTML>
```

As you can see from the preceding example, some of the effects are achieved by using CSS1 style properties, others by using the new visual filters that you learned about in this chapter. The CSS1 style properties are assigned directly, and the filters are assigned by using the specific filter function.

In this example, several visual filter effects are combined with the last header, to create a strong 3D effect. Instead of using images for a menu, you can use a text-based menu to provide highlighting of a menu item when the cursor is over the item. This approach enables a strong visual effect without the additional burden of long download times for images.

This discussion of the preview example, along with its listing, concludes the chapter on accessing and altering an element's style settings after a page is displayed.

Summary

This chapter provided an extensive overview of several techniques that you can use to alter the appearance of HTML elements.

In this chapter you learned how to:

◆ Use dynamic HTML to change and apply styles, such as font color, family, background, border, and position

◆ Use the `display` property to remove an element or group of elements from a page

◆ Use the `visibility` property to hide and reveal objects

◆ Use the visual filters, alpha, chroma, drop shadow, flip vertical, flip horizontal, grayscale, x-ray, invert, blur, and wave

◆ Use the visual light filter to set and change light objects on a Web page

◆ Use the transition filter for a page component and an entire page

Chapter 8 applies the dynamic HTML features discussed in this and the previous two chapters to build interactive Web pages, in which the user's interaction with your pages determines the presentation of those pages.

Chapter 8

Adding Interactive Content to Web Pages

IN THIS CHAPTER

- ◆ Capturing mouse events
- ◆ Capturing keyboard events
- ◆ Capturing the document load event
- ◆ Responding to user interaction
- ◆ Using visual effects to communicate with the user

To IMPLEMENT DYNAMIC HTML successfully, you need to know how to use the technology to make Web pages interactive. This chapter provides an overview of techniques you can use to give feedback to Web page visitors. The event capturing supported by Microsoft is covered, and you'll see how to capture mouse movements as well as keyboard activity. The chapter also provides examples that redefine HTML component behavior based on user actions.

If you have not had a chance to work with the Microsoft event object before, you'll want to take the time to read Chapter 4 for an overview of the event object and Microsoft's event handling.

Capturing Mouse Events

Several events are triggered by each use of the mouse. These events can be categorized into movement-based events, such as mouseover or mouseout, or mouse-click events, such as mousedown, click, and dblclick.

Some of the events are actually made up of several other events, such as the dblclick event, which triggers the following event sequence, and the associated event handlers for each event:

1. mousedown — onmousedown
2. mouseup — onmouseup
3. click — onclick

219

4. mouseup — onmouseup

5. dblclick — ondblclick

The following code shows the dblclick event at work:

```
<HTML>
<HEAD><TITLE> </TITLE>
<SCRIPT language="vbscript">
Dim events
events=""
Sub header1_onclick
 events = events + " click"
End Sub
Sub header1_onmousedown
 events = events + " mousedown"
End Sub
Sub header1_onmouseup
 events = events + " mouseup"
End Sub
Sub header1_ondblclick
 events = events + " doubleclick"
End Sub
Sub header2_onclick
 MsgBox(events)
End Sub
</SCRIPT>
</HEAD>
<BODY>
<H1 id="header1">test</H1>
<H1 id="header2">howmany</h1>
</BODY>
```

Information about the event can be accessed from the event object, including the properties shown in Table 8-1.

TABLE 8-1 Event Properties

Property	Description
altKey	Specifies whether the Alt key is pressed
button	Mouse button that causes the event, or is pressed during the event; a value of 1 means the left button is pressed, 2 indicates the right button, and 4 indicates the middle button
cancelBubble	Specifies whether to cancel event bubbling within the element hierarchy

continued

Property	Description
clientX	Horizontal position of the event in the window's client area
clientY	Vertical position of the event in the window's client area
ctrlKey	Specifies whether the Ctrl key is pressed
fromElement	Element being moved with the onmouseover and onmouseout event
keyCode	If a keyboard event, indicates the ASCII number of the key being pressed
offsetX	Horizontal position of the event relative to the parent element
offsetY	Vertical position of the event relative to the parent element
returnValue	If set to false, cancels the default behavior for the event
srcElement	Element that receives the event
srcFilter	Filter that receives the event
shiftKey	Specifies whether the Shift key is pressed
toElement	Target element of the onmouseover and onmouseout event
y	Vertical position of the event relative to the coordinate system
x	Horizontal position of the event relative to the coordinate system

You can access the preceding parameters by accessing the event object within the script. A little later in this section, you'll find a drag-and-drop example that uses these parameters.

Working with Mouse-Click Events

This section shows you an example of the click event as it applies to events that occur when the mouse is clicked. The following mouse-click actions can trigger the click event (many of which are used in this chapter and in the last section of this book):

◆ Clicking with the left mouse button

◆ Clicking a hypertext link

◆ Clicking an item from a combo or list box to select it

Do note that while the `click` event is described under the section about mouse events, it can also be triggered by the following keyboard events: selecting an item in a combo or list box by using the arrow keys and then pressing the Enter key, pressing the Enter key or spacebar if the button, radio button, or checkbox has focus, or pressing any command button.

In addition to the preceding events, other events can also trigger the `click` event. Information on these events can be found in the client software development kit (SDK), downloadable from Microsoft's Web site (see Appendix A for the URL).

With IE 4.0 you can access the `click` event for any HTML element. To capture this event for a Web page document, you can create the following subroutine:

```
<SCRIPT language="VBScript">
<!--
Sub document_onclick
 Dim object_name, object_type
 object_name = window.event.srcElement.id
 object_type = window.event.srcElement.tagName
 MsgBox("object name is " + object_name + _
       " object_type is " + object_type)
End Sub
//-->
</SCRIPT>
```

The preceding code displays the object's identifier, if any, and displays the object's type, both accessible via the `srcElement` property of the `event` object. Any HTML element on the page triggers this subroutine. To add a name to each element, you can use code such as the following:

```
<BODY id=thebody style="background-color: white; margin: 0.5in">
<H1 id=header1>Demonstration of what can receive a clicked
 event</H1>
<P id=para1>A header can, and a paragraph can. So can an image.</p>
<img src="bigclda.gif" id=image1
 STYLE="height:92;width=162">
<P id=para2> So can the Web page body, and you can name it, too!</p>
<UL>
<LI id=list1>A list item can</LI>
<LI id=list2>So can I</LI>
</UL>
</BODY>
```

Notice that even the `<BODY>` tag of the page contains an ID assignment. You can also name any object on a page in addition to capturing events for it. Try this out for yourself by accessing the example file **clkevnt.htm** (on the CD-ROM). Explore the options by adding other HTML element types, extending the code to make the object invisible, or changing its background color.

Other events can be triggered indirectly by clicking with the mouse. An example is the blur event, which is triggered when another control or element on the page gets focus. In addition, the focus event is triggered when an element or control receives the focus, and the change event is triggered when Web page readers change their selection of an item, say, for example, from a list.

Working with Mouse-Movement Events

Button clicks aren't the only mouse events you can capture. You can also capture mouse movement and where that movement occurs. As stated earlier, the movement-based events are mouseover, mouseout, mouseenter, and mousemove.

Two application possibilities for these events come to mind. The first is to alter an HTML element when the cursor is over it, a kind of rollover effect. Based on this possibility, you can highlight important text or images by changing the background color, image, or text color while the cursor is over it.

The example file on the CD-ROM, **buttons.htm**, contains three button images when the page is first displayed. Moving the cursor over an image adds a highlighting effect to it. Moving the cursor away from an image sets its appearance back to its original state.

When you view the page, it looks like it has only three images, but it really has six. Each image has an attached style sheet that sets the positioning to absolute, and the top property to 50 pixels. Three of the images use a second style sheet, which hides them when the page loads. This style is shown in the following code:

```
<STYLE text="text/css">
    img         { position: absolute; top: 50px;
            width: 150; height:150 }
    img.imgover { visibility: hidden }
</STYLE>
```

The first three images are embedded into the page at equal distances to each other, and the mouseover event is trapped for them. Script creates the highlighted effect by displaying a second, associated image. This is accomplished by setting the highlighted image's visibility property to visible:

```
<img src="button1.gif" style="left: 50px"
 onmouseover="one.style.visibility='visible'">
<img src="button2.gif" style="left: 225px" id=img2
 onmouseover="two.style.visibility='visible'">
<img src="button3.gif" style="left: 400px" id=img3
 onmouseover="three.style.visibility='visible'">
```

The next three images are placed on the page in the exact same position as their associated, nonhighlighted images. The second set of images is set to be invisible when the mouseout event is triggered:

```
<img src="button1o.gif" class=imgover id=one
  style="left: 50px"
  onmouseout="this.style.visibility='hidden'">
<img src="button2o.gif" class=imgover id=two
  style="left: 225px"
  onmouseout="this.style.visibility='hidden'">
<img src="button3o.gif" class=imgover id=three
  style="left: 400px"
onmouseout="this.style.visibility='hidden'">
```

The mouseover event is trapped for the original images because the associated highlighted images are not visible, and cannot accept events. However, the mouseout event is trapped for the highlighted images because they appear, when they are visible, on top of the other nonhighlighted images and receive all events at that point. In other words, when the highlighted red button (the first button) is invisible, its nonhighlighted, associated button receives the trapped mouseover event, causing the highlighted button to be displayed. The cursor is still over the location of the two stacked images at this time. When it moves out of this location, the mouseout event is triggered for the highlighted red button, which is then hidden, and the nonhighlighted button begins to receive events again.

Working with Drag-and-Drop Techniques

With the release of Internet Explorer 4.0, Microsoft also provided an example, titled "Alien Head," that demonstrated a drag-and-drop technique using their version of dynamic HTML, a demonstration that I appreciated very much. I used this technique with extensions of my own to create a fun little drag-and-drop Web page that enabled Web page readers to express their artistic natures by creating their own forest scenes. You can find the example on the CD-ROM in the file called **drgdrp.htm**, which you might want to investigate before reading about how to create the page.

When the page opens, the elements are displayed in no apparent order, as shown in Figure 8-1. Click any of the elements with the left mouse button and move the mouse with the button still pressed. You'll notice that the element moves with the mouse. When the element is in the position you want, just let go of the mouse button.

A fun extension to this page enables you to move an object along the z-axis, which means you can place one image in front of another. First, choose an object that you want to move, then pick it up and drag it. When the object you are dragging is over another object, press the Shift key; doing so places the selected object *behind* the object it is over. Press the Ctrl key to place the selected object *over* any underlying object. You may find that adjusting the z-axis of the underlying object can actually slow the image object movement. Figure 8-2 shows the same Web page after I have positioned the elements one way, and Figure 8-3 displays a second arrangement.

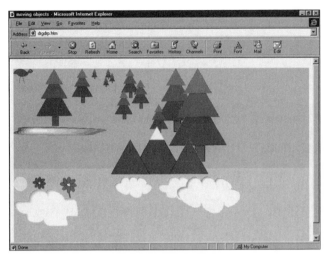

Figure 8-1: The drag-and-drop forest scene demonstration after the page is loaded

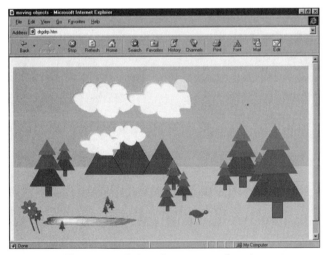

Figure 8-2: The drag-and-drop forest scene after elements are moved into one display

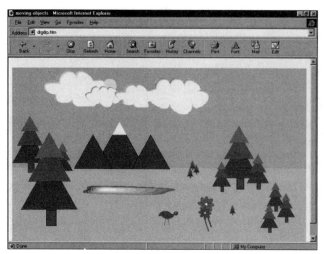

Figure 8-3: The drag-and-drop forest scene after elements are
moved into a second display

To make this page, I first created style sheet definitions for the page "sky" and
"ground," as shown next:

```
<STYLE type="text/css">
  img {position: absolute; z-index: 1 }
  #drawsurface { background-color: skyblue;
                 position:relative; top: 10px;
                 width:100%;height:100%}
  #ground { background-color: lightgreen; left:0;
            position:absolute; top: 50%;
            width:100%; height:50%; z-index= -10}
</STYLE>
```

The drawing surface must be set to 100 percent of the width of the page for the
display to work accurately. Not only is this important visually, it also determines
the position of an image as it is being moved. A script block is started and, when
the page first loads, a small subroutine is called that gets the overall size of the
drawing surface as it is displayed in the browser:

```
<SCRIPT language="vbscript">

Dim surface
Dim surface_left
Dim surface_top
Dim imageobj
set imageobj = Nothing

' set global values
Sub window_onload
```

```
    Set surface = document.all.drawsurface
    surface_left = surface.offsetLeft
    surface_top = surface.offsetTop
End Sub
```

In addition to setting drawing surface variables, the code sets a variable called imageobj to Nothing, to show that no image has been selected yet.

The next functions are shown in Listing 8-1. In the first function, the mousedown event for the document is trapped, and if the left button is pressed and the target of the event is an image, the imageobj variable is set to this image. The next function traps the mouseup event for the document and clears the image object variable.

Listing 8-1: The movement-trapping script function (of the drag-and-drop example) that determines the new position of the dragged element

```
' start capture by
' trapping which element has received click
function document_onmousedown(button, shift, x, y)
    if (button = 1) then
        set imageobj = window.event.srcElement
    end if
End function

function document_onmouseup(button, shift, x, y)
    if (button = 1) then
        set imageobj = Nothing
    end if
End function
```

In the next subroutine, the tagname attribute of the moved object is checked to make sure an image is being moved. Then, a new horizontal coordinate is created by subtracting the width of the image (divided by 2), and then subtracting the width of the drawing surface from the current horizontal position of the movement (the x value passed to the event function). If the result is less than 0 or greater than the drawing surface width, the new horizontal position is set to 0. This means that the image does not move further left than the drawing surface's left edge, and the image wraps to the left if it exceeds the right margin of the surface. The same techniques are applied to the vertical position, except that the *height* of the drawing surface and image are used, instead of the width:

```
' capture mouse movement and move object
' if control key or shift are pressed, set
' z-index value accordingly to move image in stack
function document_onmousemove(button, shift, x,y)
dim objleft, objtop
    if (button = 1) Then
        if imageobj.tagname="IMG" then

        ' new X location is point of click -
        ' left edge of drawing surface and
```

```
' set to middle of object
    objleft=x -
        surface_left - (imageobj.offsetWidth/2)

' if object has exceeded either border,
' set to 0
if objleft<0 then objleft=0
if objleft > surface.offsetWidth then objleft = 0
imageobj.style.pixelLeft= objleft

' new Y location is point of click -
' top edge of drawing surface and
' set to middle of object
objtop=y - surface_top -(imageobj.offsetHeight/2)

' if object has exceeded either border,
' set to 0
if objtop<0 then objtop=0
if objtop > 430 then objtop = 0
imageobj.style.pixelTop= objtop

 ' prevent event from bubbling up
 ' element hierarchy
window.event.returnValue = false
window.event.cancelBubble = true

' if press control, place image on top
if shift = 2 then
    imageobj.style.z-index=imageobj.style.z-index + 1
    if imageobj.style.z-index > 2 then
            imageobj.style.z-index=2

' if press shift, move image to bottom
elseif shift = 1 then
    imageobj.style.z-index=imageobj.style.z-index - 1
    if imageobj.style.z-index < 0 then
            imageobj.style.z-index=0
    end if
  end if
 end if
end function
```

The cancelBubble property of the event is set to true to prevent the event from moving through the hierarchy of elements that may be placed in proximity to each other. This ensures that only one image receives the dragging event at a time. Setting the returnValue property also ensures smooth movement of the object.

The script at the end of the function checks to see if the Web page reader is pressing the Shift or Ctrl key while the movement is occurring. If so, the z-index property of the image is adjusted accordingly.

All that's left to this example is the ground and drawing surfaces, and all of the images. Listing 8-2 contains the complete section of the document body. Notice

that all of the elements added to the page are contained within the drawing surface
<DIV> block.

Listing 8-2: The body of the drag-and-drop example, containing the references to all the images for the example

```
<BODY>
<!-- add in drawing surface - contain all images
     to be moved -->
<DIV id=drawsurface align=center>

<!-- add ground, no other contents -->
<DIV id=ground>
</DIV>

<!-- add images to use for drawing -->
<img src="bird.gif"
 STYLE="TOP:0;LEFT:0;width:54;height:36">
<img src="medtree.gif"
 STYLE="TOP:0;LEFT:60;height:143;width:91">
<img src="smltree.gif"
 STYLE="TOP:0;LEFT:150;height:86;width:54">
<img src="tnytree.gif"
 STYLE="TOP:0;LEFT:200;height:26;width:17">
<img src="smlgroup.gif"
 STYLE="TOP:0;LEFT:230;height:46;width:32">
<img src="medgroup.gif"
 STYLE="TOP:0;LEFT:260;height:127;width:90">
<img src="othgroup.gif"
 STYLE="TOP:0;LEFT:350;height:165;width:144">
<img src="bigtree.gif"
 STYLE="TOP:0;LEFT:400;height:233;width:148">
<img src="lake.gif"
 STYLE="TOP:145;LEFT:0;height:22;width:242">
<img src="hills.gif"
 STYLE="TOP:145;LEFT:250;height:119;width=251">
<img src="sun.gif"
 STYLE="TOP:270;LEFT:0;height:35;width:35">
<img src="flower1.gif"
 STYLE="TOP:270;LEFT:50;height:62;width:34">
<img src="flower2.gif"
 STYLE="TOP:270;LEFT:120;height:77;width:42">
<img src="smlclda.gif"
 STYLE="TOP:270;LEFT:260;height:53;width:95">
<img src="smlcldb.gif"
 STYLE="TOP:270;LEFT:370;height:59;width=106">
<img src="bigclda.gif"
 STYLE="TOP:270;LEFT:420;height:92;width=162">
<img src="bigcldb.gif"
 STYLE="TOP:300;LEFT:0;height:92;width=165">

</DIV>
</BODY>
```

All the images could have been placed on top of each other, dispensing with the style positioning definitions, but then the reader could not see what they had to work with before they started dragging elements all over the place. Plus, if this page is downloaded, the reader sees changes occurring to the page, which shows the reader why the page is taking so much time to download.

Capturing Keyboard Events

As the drag-and-drop example in the previous section demonstrated, you can capture information from the keyboard, such as whether the Shift key is pressed when an event occurs. Keyboard activity can also trigger events explicitly. Events that are triggered by some form of keyboard activity are the help, keydown, keypress, and keyup events.

The help event is triggered when the Web page reader hits the F1 key, or whatever key is defined as the help key. Pressing any of the noncontrol keys triggers the other events. The keydown and keyup events can pass a parameter that provides information about whether the Alt, Shift, or Ctrl key is also pressed at the time the other key is pressed. Both of these events and the keypress event have a return value equal to the ASCII integer that represents the pressed key. This ASCII integer can be modified before the event is passed on the browser. The key that is pressed is passed in with the event object as the keyCode property.

I created a very simple little application that could be handy if, like me, you can never remember the ASCII values of individual keys. The application captures the keypress event and displays the ASCII value, found in the keyCode property of the event object. The complete code for this little utility is shown in Listing 8-3, and the utility itself can be found on the CD-ROM in the file **fndascii.htm**.

Listing 8-3: The Find ASCII key utility, used to find the ASCII value of the key pressed

```
<HTML>
<HEAD><TITLE>Finding the ASCII value</TITLE>
</HEAD>
<BODY style="background-color: azure; color: firebrick; margin:
  0.5in">
<H1>ASCII Code Finder</H1>
Press any key and if there is an equivalent ASCII value for the key,
  it will be displayed here:
<p>
<INPUT type=text name="conversion">

<SCRIPT language="vbscript">

Sub document_onkeypress
  conversion.value = window.event.keyCode
  window.event.returnValue=0
End Sub
</SCRIPT>
</BODY>
```

You may notice that I set the `returnValue` property of the `event` object to 0 at the end of my subroutine. Doing so overrides the keystroke value and ensures that even if the text field has the focus, only the ASCII value shows and not the output of the keystroke.

Capturing the Document Load Event

Usually, most of the events that you trap are related to either the keyboard or to the mouse. However, you can trap other events to provide feedback to the Web page reader. For example, you can trap and process the document `load` event for at least one of your Web pages. An excellent use for this event is to trap the document `load` event and display an image-based menu bar, or other content that requires the page to load entirely before the reader interacts with it.

Listing 8-4 demonstrates a Web page with three images contained within a `<DIV>` block that is not displayed until the entire page displays. What does show while the page is loading is a message of "Please wait while images are downloading . . ."

Listing 8-4: Trapping the document load event for the Web page

```
<HTML>
<HEAD><TITLE>onload example</TITLE>
</HEAD>
<BODY>
<DIV id=download style="position: absolute; top=20 left=20">
<h1>Please wait while images are downloading...</h1>
</DIV>
<div id=thumbnails top=20 left=20 style="display:none">
<img src="twinstn.JPG" width=99 height=86 hspace=5 id=image1>
<img src="apophylliteltn.JPG" width=101 height=99 hspace=5>
<img src="fluorite3tn.JPG" width=100 height=108 hspace=5>
</div>

<SCRIPT language="vbscript">

Sub window_onload
  download.style.display="none"
  thumbnails.style.display=""
End Sub

</SCRIPT>
</BODY>
```

Use this approach anytime you want to hide page contents until some event is reached. For example, you could use it while the reader is waiting for the images or the page to finish loading.

You can also capture errors using the error event. Or you can track the progress of a page-loading by capturing the individual load events for the images within the page and displaying the progress. You can also capture the reader's use of the scroll bar to change the display contents, or perhaps to better track the reader's location on the page.

Responding to User Interaction

As we saw briefly in the example at the end of the previous section, one very important reason to capture events is to provide feedback to the Web page reader. Before dynamic HTML came along, most Web pages provided feedback as a message displayed either in the browser's status bar or in an alert box. Starting around 1996, code could be used to change images when the reader had his or her cursor over a menu bar. Or, as in Navigator 3.x, a page could load automatically if the reader's mouse was over a hypertext link.

These techniques were a start in providing feedback, but were still pretty primitive when compared with the feedback techniques of such applications as Microsoft Word or Visual C++. However, with IE version 4.0, you can do so much more.

For example, I know that most Web page authors and developers would like to provide some form of their own "tips window" – an area displayed when the user places their cursor over an item to provide information about that item. IE 3.0 has a little tips window that pops up when the mouse is over an image. The window displays whatever text is contained in the Alt property for that particular image.

Using dynamic HTML, you can provide your own tips for any HTML element. With CSS1 attributes you create blocks of text, highlighted in some manner and placed anywhere on the Web page. The blocks would not initially display, so the invisible or display property is used to hide the block. If you use the invisible property, the blocks must be displayed in some manner that does not leave gaps when they are not displayed. Then, based on keyboard or mouse movement, or some other factor, display the appropriate text box to match the Web page reader's actions.

For example, Figure 8-4 shows a Web page containing a form with several fields. As the mouse cursor passes over a field, or as the field gets the focus, and if a help message is associated with the field, the tips window displays prominently below the form, as shown in Figure 8-5. This is no ordinary "small and hard to read" tips window. This is a large and "no way will you make any mistake with this form" window.

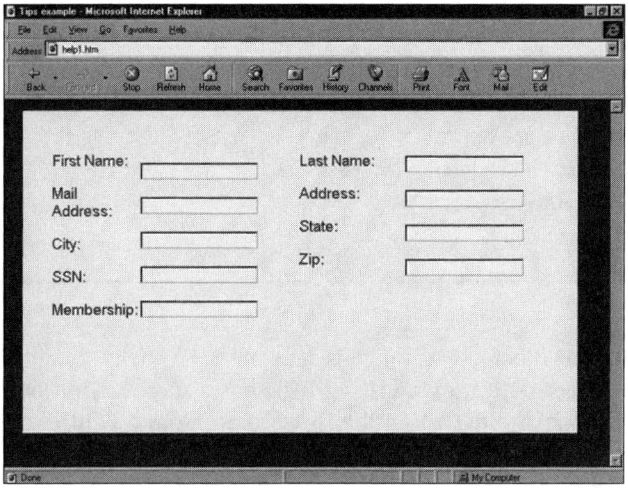

Figure 8-4: The interactive form after the page is first loaded

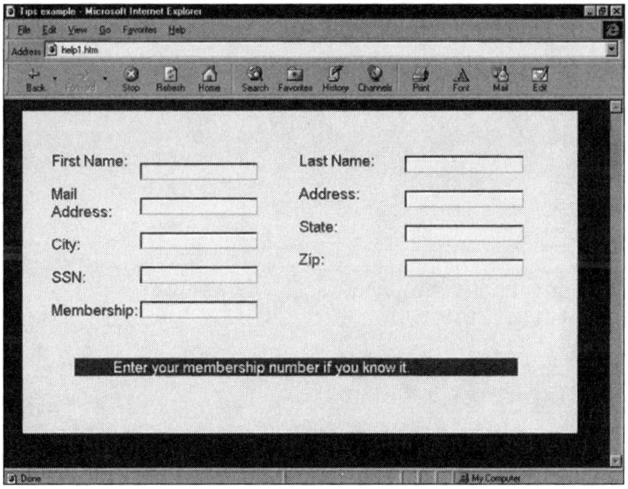

Figure 8-5: The interactive form with a help message for the field displayed

Visibility versus Display

Remember, you can hide elements until an event triggers their visibility. You can use the visibility property if you want the hidden elements to keep their places in the layouts, leaving gaps where they will appear. You can use the display property if you want the Web page to display the Web page contents without reserved areas for the hidden elements.

The first thing you create for this form example is, as usual with many dynamic HTML examples, the style sheet definitions. Listing 8-5 shows these definitions, which are used to create the background, align the form columns, and control the appearance of the help message block.

Listing 8-5: Style sheet definitions for providing built-in help for a form using dynamic HTML

```
<STYLE type="text/css">
BODY { background-color: indigo; color: firebrick;
            font-family: arial; font-size: 14pt }
    #formOuterBlock { background-color: ivory;
            color: firebrick;
            position: absolute; width: 94%; height: 94%;
            top: 3%; left: 3%;  }
    #formInnerBlock { position: absolute; top: 4%;
            width: 92%;
            height: 92%; left: 4% }
    #firstcolumn  { position: absolute; top: 15%;
            left: 8%; width: 15%;
            height: 60% }
    #secondcolumn { position: absolute; left: 23%;
            top: 18%; width: 20%;
            height: 60% }
    #thirdcolumn  { position: absolute; left: 50%;
            top: 15%; width: 15%;
            height: 60% }
    #fourthcolumn { position: absolute; left: 68%;
            top: 16%; width: 20%;
            height: 60%}
    DIV.message { position: absolute; left: 12%;
            width: 75%; top: 75%;
            background-color: firebrick; color: white;
            margin-left: 0.5in; margin-right: 0.5in  }
</STYLE>
```

After the style sheet, insert the Web page body, which contains the form and background definitions, as well as the different help messages. Listing 8-6 contains the form definitions, including the events being trapped for the mouse and focus events. Note that each input field of type "text" that has help associated with it captures both mouse and keyboard events using handlers such as the onmouseover, onmouseout, onfocus, and onblur events.

Listing 8-6: The form definition for the dynamic HTML example, providing mouse-based online help

```
<DIV id=formOuterBlock> </DIV>
<FORM name="personform">

<DIV id=firstcolumn>
First Name: <p>
Mail Address: <p>
City: <p>
SSN: <p>
Membership:<p>
</DIV>

<DIV id=secondcolumn>
<INPUT type=text name="firstname"
 onmouseover="message1.style.visibility='visible'"
 onmouseout="message1.style.visibility='hidden'"
 onfocus="message1.style.visibility='visible'"
 onblur="message1.style.visibility='hidden'"><p>
<INPUT type=text rows=10 cols=20 name="street1"
 onmouseover="message3.style.visibility='visible'"
 onmouseout="message3.style.visibility='hidden'"
 onfocus="message3.style.visibility='visible'"
 onblur="message3.style.visibility='hidden'"><p>
<INPUT type=text name="city"><p>
<INPUT type=text name="SSN"><p>
<INPUT type=text name="member"
 onmouseover="message6.style.visibility='visible'"
 onmouseout="message6.style.visibility='hidden'"
 onfocus="message6.style.visibility='visible'"
 onblur="message6.style.visibility='hidden'"><p>
</DIV>

<DIV id=thirdcolumn>
Last Name: <p>
Address:<p>
State: <p>
Zip: <p>
</DIV>

<DIV id=fourthcolumn>
<INPUT type=text name="lastname"><p>
<INPUT type=text name="street2"
 onmouseover="message4.style.visibility='visible'"
 onmouseout="message4.style.visibility='hidden'"
 onfocus="message4.style.visibility='visible'"
 onblur="message4.style.visibility='hidden'"><p>
<INPUT type=text name="state"><p>
<INPUT tyep=text name="zip"
```

```
onmouseover="message5.style.visibility='visible'"
onmouseout="message5.style.visibility='hidden'"
onfocus="message5.style.visibility='visible'"
onblur="message5.style.visibility='hidden'"><p>
</DIV>
```

Finally, the messages are created, but they are not displayed when the page loads – they are only displayed based on user movements. Listing 8-7 shows the rest of the Web page.

Listing 8-7: The hidden messages for the online form example

```
<DIV class=message id=message1 style="visibility:hidden">
Enter the first name you would like to use with your mail.
</DIV>
<DIV class=message id=message2 style="visibility:hidden">
Enter the Last name you would like to use with your mail.
</DIV>
<DIV class=message id=message3 style="visibility:hidden">
Enter your mailing address.
</DIV>
<DIV class=message id=message4 style="visibility:hidden">
Enter your street address if this differs from your mailing address.
</DIV>
<DIV class=message id=message5 style="visibility:hidden">
Enter the 9 character extended zip if you have it. Otherwise use
 your 5 digit zip code.
</DIV>
<DIV class=message id=message6 style="visibility:hidden">
Enter your membership number if you know it.
</DIV>
</DIV>
</FORM>
```

One for All, and All for One — with Style Sheets

In the example that shows you how to display help for the Web page reader based on mouse and keyboard movements, the `visibility` property was set for each individual message, rather than being set just once in the style sheet. Why is that? When one or more elements share a style sheet definition, making a change to the style sheet for one element propagates this same change to all elements. So in the example, if I made one element visible, all would be visible and the one that is on the top of the stack is the only message that displays. The rule of thumb is to apply style sheet settings that change dynamically, and for only one element at a time, either in a separate style sheet definition or directly in the element using an inline style.

Aligning the columns is actually a lot tougher than providing bold and noticeable help, as you can see for yourself by opening the sample file on the CD-ROM, **help1.htm**. The chapters in the last section of this book, as well as the next section in this chapter, contain other examples of how to provide feedback to the Web page reader.

Communicating with the User Using Visual Effects

Now let's look at an example that applies some of the techniques discussed in this chapter to provide some interesting feedback. Open **message.htm** on the CD-ROM and press the h or H key. As you can see, pressing either of these keys causes a message associated with the keystroke to "pop up."

This effect is achieved by setting the `visibility` property of the message area from `hidden` (its `onload` setting) to `visible` in response to the keyboard event. And when a message is displayed, a visual filter is applied to all the contents of the page.

The first part of the file is the style sheet setting and is shown in Listing 8-8.

Listing 8-8: The example file message.htm uses visual effects to create a noticeable message for the Web page reader; this listing contains the style sheet settings

```
<HEAD>
<STYLE type="text/css">
BODY { background-color: honeydew; margin: 0.25in }
DIV.message1 { position: absolute; color: white;
       top: 25%; left: 25%; width: 400px; height: 120px;
       background-color: firebrick;
       z-index: 2; visibility: hidden;
       font-family: Cursive }
DIV.message2 { position: absolute; color: white;
       top: 25%; left: 25%; width: 400px; height: 120px;
       background-color: indigo; color: aqua;
       z-index: 2; visibility: hidden;
       font-family: Cursive }
</STYLE>
</HEAD>
```

Again, notice that the `visibility` property of both message blocks is set to `hidden`.

The next section of the file contains the actual contents that show on the page. The first two blocks contain the messages, as shown in Listing 8-9. The first message is displayed when the Web page reader hits the H key. The second message displays when the reader hits the h key. In addition, moving the mouse over the first image highlights the first paragraph by changing the color of the text. The same holds true with the second image and the second paragraph.

Listing 8-9: The document contents that are viewable in normal mode in the example file message.htm

```
<body>
<DIV class=message1 id=messagebox1>
<p style="width: 80%; margin: 20px">
This could be any one of several different types of error, warning,
 or information messages. Make sure to give your Web page readers a
 way back to the regular page. For instance, to return from this
 message you....
</P>
</DIV>
<DIV class=message2 id=messagebox2>
<p style="width: 80%; margin: 20px; background-color: indigo">
This message was displayed because you, fair reader, pressed the 'h'
 key. Hit the Enter key to return to normal.
</P>
</DIV>

<DIV id=wholedoc style="width: 100%; height: 100%">
<H1 style="text-align: center; font-family: Cursive">
Some Crystals from the Collection
</H1>
<CENTER>
<img src="fluorite3tn.JPG" hspace=10 id=pict1
 onmouseover="para1.style.color='red'"
 onmouseout="para1.style.color='black'">
<strong>Flourite</strong>
<img src="apophyllite2tn.JPG" hspace=10 id=pict2
 onmouseover="para2.style.color='red'"
 onmouseout="para2.style.color='black'">
<strong>Apophyllite</strong>
</CENTER>
<p id=para1>
<strong>Fluorite</strong>: Fluorite is a member of the
 <em>halides</em>.
Fluorite can come in various colors, and is a fairly common mineral.
 I collected this piece because of its unusual coloration which the
 photograph demonstrates. This sample is one of my largest, being 4
 inches across. This makes it a 'hand' sample, and it comes from the
 Denton Mine, Hardin County, Illinois. Normally, I only collect what
 are known as <em>thumbnail</em> crystals, crystals about the size
 of your thumb, naturally. I also prefer to collect samples that are
 still attached to a matrix, or background material. I took this
 photograph by placing the sample on a non-glare piece of glass, and
 shining a photographer's lamp directly on the background just
 behind the sample. This is reflected off the white background, and
 shines through the sample.
</P>
<p id=para2>
<strong>Apophyllite</strong>
Apophyllite is a member of the <em>Phyllosilicate</em> class. It is
 a colorless crystal, yet has a grayish cast. The sample is
 associated with Stilbite, which is not visible in the existing
```

```
photograph. This sample is from Poone(Pune), India. This crystal
can be differentiated from other clear crystals by its relative
weight, it is a light stone, and a distinctly greasy feeling.
</P>
</DIV>
```

The mouseover and mouseout events are captured for the images in order to apply the highlighting effect to their associated paragraphs.

Lastly, the scripting to control the appearance of the messages is created. Pressing the H key brings up the contents of one of the messages, and pressing the h key brings up the contents of the second. Hitting Enter returns the page back to normal. Listing 8-10 shows how message display is controlled.

Listing 8-10: The script that controls the display of the messages in the example file message.htm

```
<SCRIPT language="vbscript">
<!--
Dim current_status
current_status = 0
Sub document_onkeypress
  If window.event.keyCode = 13 AND _
        current_status = 1 Then
        wholedoc.style.filter=""
        messagebox1.style.visibility="hidden"
        messagebox2.style.visibility="hidden"
        current_status = 0
  ElseIf window.event.keyCode = 72 Then
        wholedoc.style.filter="Alpha(opacity=25)"
        messagebox1.style.visibility="visible"
        current_status = 1
  ElseIf window.event.keyCode = 104 Then
        wholedoc.style.filter="Alpha(opacity=25)"
        messagebox2.style.visibility="visible"
        current_status=1
  End If
End Sub
'-->
</SCRIPT>
```

Using this approach, I can guarantee that Web page readers will get your message. It's very effective in displaying very important messages that require the Web page reader's immediate attention, as shown in Figure 8-6. Nothing is subtle about this approach and it should guarantee immediate response. Just make sure your reader knows how to return to "normal" after you display a message using the filter message technique.

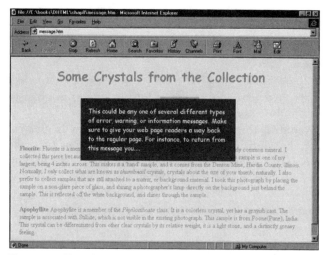

Figure 8-6: The Web page with an error message simulation displayed across the page

Match Visual Displays with Audio Output

The example in Figure 8-6 is an effective way to provide *visual* feedback to the reader. For visually impaired readers, you should also provide an audio message equivalent to the visual one. For example, you could also play a sound file with the same recorded message.

Summary

This chapter covered some of the techniques you can use to capture events and provide feedback to Web page readers.

In this chapter you learned how to:

♦ Capture mouse-click events

♦ Capture mouse-movement events

♦ Use the mouse to create drag-and-drop effects

♦ Capture keyboard events

♦ Determine if the Ctrl, Shift, or Alt keys are pressed during an event

♦ Use dynamic HTML to provide feedback to the user

◆ Capture indirect events such as the `load` event

◆ Create a user feedback technique guaranteed to get your Web page reader's attention

This is the last chapter covering the Microsoft-specific dynamic HTML techniques. The next section of this book covers Netscape-specific dynamic HTML techniques, with the next chapter covering the Netscape-specific object model.

Part III

Netscape's Dynamic HTML

Chapter 9

Working with Netscape's Dynamic HTML Object Model

IN THIS CHAPTER

◆ Basic HTML objects: `window` and `document`

◆ The `location`, `history`, and `navigator` objects

◆ The `form`, `event`, and `screen` objects

◆ The built-in arrays

◆ Introducing the `LAYER` tag

◆ Console mode and signed scripting

THIS CHAPTER PROVIDES AN overview of Netscape's object model, including properties, methods, and events that make up the basic components of Netscape's dynamic HTML. Netscape and Microsoft support many of the same basic objects, such as the `window` and `document` objects, and both companies promise to adhere to the W3C CSS1 standard. However, as you will discover in this chapter, Netscape's object model is noticeably different from Microsoft's.

Like Microsoft's object model, the `window` and `document` objects are the two most basic components of Netscape's object model. However, *unlike* the Microsoft object model, Netscape's model includes a unique `layer` object that lets you partition a Web page into layers, and then move, hide, or show the layers. The layer object, which is discussed near the end of this chapter, is a key component of Netscape's object model. First, I'll show you the `window` and `document` objects and how they can be used with Navigator.

Basic HTML Objects: Window and Document

In this section you'll see how to work with the `window` and `document` objects as they apply to Netscape's object model. In the Netscape object model, the `window` object owns the `document` object, just as it owns everything else in the object model (except for the `navigator` object). The `document` object in turn owns all other objects except for the `location` and `history` objects.

The Window Object

As I just stated, the `window` object owns most objects in the object model. When referring to them in script, you don't normally need to precede any of the objects with the `window` specifier. Either example in the following code runs without errors:

```
document.forms[0].elements[1].value = "test";
window.document.forms[0].elements[1].value = "test";
```

All objects owned directly by the `window` object, such as `document`, `history`, and `location`, are considered properties of the `window` object. Table 9-1 lists additional properties, their descriptions, and whether they can only be modified within signed script (a topic discussed later in this chapter). If a property requires script signing, using it in an unsigned script will nullify its functionality.

TABLE 9-1 **Window Properties**

Window Property	Description
`closed`	Boolean; indicates whether the window is open or not
`innerHeight`	Height of window contents; signed script only if the dimensions are less than 100 × 100
`innerWidth`	Width of window contents; signed script only if the dimensions are less than 100 × 100
`locationbar.visible`	Hide or show the location bar; signed script only
`menubar.visible`	Hide or show the menu bar; signed script only
`outerHeight`	Height of the window's outer boundary; signed script only if the dimensions are less than 100 × 100

continued

Window Property	Description
outerWidth	Width of the window's outer boundary; signed script only if the dimensions are less than 100 × 100
pageXOffset	Current *x*-position of viewed page; read-only
pageYOffset	Current *y*-position of viewed page; read-only
personalbar.visible	Hide or show the personal bar; signed script only
scrollbars.visible	Hide or show scroll bars; signed script only
statusbar.visible	Hide or show the status bar; signed script only
toolbar.visible	Hide or show the toolbar; signed script only
status	Message displayed in the status bar
defaultStatus	Message displayed, by default, in the status bar
name	Name of the window if a name has been assigned; set to a value when a new browser window is opened via the open method with a name specified, or through a frame with a name given in the FRAMESET; read-only
self	Current window; read-only
length	The number of frames when used with the frames collection; read-only
top	Top-most ancestor window; read-only
parent	If a frame, returns FRAMESET window; read-only
opener	Reference to the window that opened the current window
window	Refers to the current window, equivalent to self
frames	Array of frames contained within FRAMESET for the window

Listing 9-1 demonstrates how to work with the window properties. This example has three buttons. Pressing the first button opens a new browser window and pressing the second closes it. Pressing the third button checks the status of the new window by testing whether the new window variable is still null (has not been set), and then the code uses the closed property to check whether the window is closed or not. The example also sets and resets the status and defaultStatus properties. You can find the example on the CD-ROM in the sample file named **nsopntst.htm**.

Listing 9-1: Window properties at work

```
<HEAD>
<SCRIPT language="javascript">
<!--

new_window = null
function start_window() {
  new_window = window.open("blank.htm", "NewWindow",
  "outerWidth=300, outerHeight=300, left=0, top=0",
  defaultStatus="Window is open")
}

function close_window() {
 if (new_window == null)
    status="no window to close"
 else {
   new_window.close()
   defaultStatus = "Window is closed"
 }
}

function test_window() {
 if (new_window != null)
      if (new_window.closed)
            defaultStatus = "New Window is closed"
      else
            defaultStatus = "New Window is open"
 else
      defaultStatus = "Window is not open"
}
//-->
</SCRIPT>
</HEAD>
<BODY onLoad="status='Window is closed'">
<FORM>
<INPUT type=button value="open" onClick="start_window()">
<INPUT type=button value="close" onClick="close_window()">
<INPUT type=button value="test" onClick="test_window()">
</FORM>
</BODY>
```

Compare Listing 9-1 with the similar example, Listing 5-1, in Chapter 5. Note that the main differences between these two examples are the attributes used to create the new window and the fact that INPUT items for a Navigator page must be enclosed within a form. Table 9-2 lists the attributes that can be specified when a new browser window is opened.

Note that some of the attributes for the window `open` method require that the JavaScript be *signed*. JavaScript applet signing is discussed in more detail later in this chapter. If the script is not signed, the property will not work or will not work correctly. For example, the `alwaysRaised` property will not force the window to remain on top in an unsigned script.

TABLE 9-2 **Window Attributes**

Attribute	Allowable Values	Purpose
innerHeight	Numeric	Dimension of content height; dimensions of less than 100 × 100 require signed script
innerWidth	Numeric	Dimension of content width; dimensions of less than 100 × 100 require signed script
outerHeight	Numeric	Outside height of the window; dimensions of less than 100 × 100 require signed script
outerWidth	Numeric	Outside width of the window; dimensions of less than 100 × 100 require signed script
alwaysRaised	yes,no (1,0)	Window remains as the top-most window; signed script and is platform-dependent
alwaysLowered	yes,no (1,0)	Window remains as the bottom-most window; signed script and is platform-dependent
dependent	yes,no (1,0)	Creates a dependent child; will not show on the Windows task bar
hotkeys	yes,no (1,0)	Disables hot keys for window with no menu bar except for security and quit keys
screenX	Numeric	Distance the new window is placed from the left edge of the screen
screenY	Numeric	Distance the new window is placed from the top of the screen
titlebar	yes,no (1,0)	Hides the title bar; signed script

continued

TABLE 9-2 **Window Attributes** *(continued)*

Attribute	Allowable Values	Purpose
z-lock	yes,no (1,0)	Window does not move above other windows when activated; signed script and platform-dependent
toolbar	yes,no (1,0)	Specifies whether the window has a toolbar
location	yes,no (1,0)	Specifies whether the window has a location bar
directories	yes,no (1,0)	Specifies whether the window has a personal bar
status	yes,no (1,0)	Specifies whether the window has a status bar
menubar	yes, no (1,0)	Specifies whether the window has a menu bar
scrollbars	yes,no (1,0)	Specifies whether the window has scroll bars
resizeable	yes,no (1,0)	Specifies whether the window is resizeable
type	fullWindow	Specifies whether the window is open to cover the screen fully

Listing 9-1 also demonstrates a couple of window object methods. I've listed all of the methods, their functionality, and their parameters (if any) in Table 9-3.

TABLE 9-3 **Window Object Methods**

Method	Functionality	Parameters
alert	Displays an alert dialog with the message	Message
blur	Removes focus from the window/frame	
clearTimeout	Removes the time-out	
close	Closes the window	
confirm	Displays a confirmation message	Message

continued

Method	Functionality	Parameters
eval	Evaluates a JavaScript string in the context of the object	JavaScript string
focus	Sets focus to window	
open	Opens a new browser window	Strings containing an HTML content file, if any, name of the window, and attribute lists
prompt	Displays a prompt message	Message, default
scroll	Scrolls the window	X value, y value
setTimeout	Creates a time-out for the window that will call a specified function or evaluate a specified expression	Expressions, time
toString	Converts the object into a string	
valueOf	Primitive value of the object (if one exists), or object itself	
back	Returns to the previous URL in the history list	
enableExternalCapture	Enables the frames window to capture events in other pages; signed script only	
disableExternalCapture	Disables event capturing	
find	Finds the specified string in the page	String, case-sensitive, backward-search
forward	Moves to the next URL in the history list	
home	Moves to the page designated as the home page	
moveBy	Moves the window by amount specified	Horizontal, vertical
moveTo	Moves the window to the specified coordinates	X-position, y-position

continued

TABLE 9-3 Window Object Methods *(continued)*

Method	Functionality	Parameters
resizeBy	Resizes the window by moving the lower-right corner	Horizontal, vertical
resizeTo	Resizes the window to the specified dimensions	Width, height
scrollBy	Scrolls the viewing area by the given amount	Horizontal, vertical
scrollTo	Scrolls the viewing area to specific coordinates	X-position, y-position
stop	Stops the current document from downloading	

I have found that the stop method can be particularly helpful if a problem occurs during a page load process and the page has a large amount of content. Web page readers appreciate knowing what's going on when a page loads.

In addition to the methods available for the window object, several methods are shared by both the window and document objects. These methods are listed in Table 9-4.

TABLE 9-4 Window and Document Shared Methods

Method	Functionality	Parameters
captureEvents	Capture events of specified type	Event type
clearInterval	Release interval timer	
handleEvent	Invokes the handler for the event	Event
print	Prints the window or frame contents	

continued

Method	Functionality	Parameters
releaseEvents	Releases all event capturing for type	Event type
routeEvent	Passes the event along the hierarchy	Event
toString	Converts object and arrays to literals, including a listing of all properties	

When something is described as shareable, it means that the method can be used with either the document or the window itself. Also, most objects in the Netscape object model share some of these methods such as the toString and valueOf methods. Other properties and methods unique to the document object are covered in the next section.

The Document Object

The window object owns everything while the document object controls most of it. Most elements of an HTML page are accessed through the document. If you take into account that the document is the part of the window that contains the Web page displayed onscreen, you should understand why page elements are accessed through the document object. The properties of the document object are listed in Table 9-5.

TABLE 9-5 Document Object Properties

Document Object Property	Attribute
alinkColor	Color of the active links within the document
linkColor	Color of the links within the document
vlinkColor	Color of the unvisited links within the document
title	Title of the document
bgColor	Background color of the object
cookie	Information that can be persistently stored on the client machine

continued

TABLE 9-5 Document Object Properties *(continued)*

Document Object Property	Attribute
lastModified	Date and time the Web page was last modified (read-only)
referrer	URL of the previous location (read-only)
fgColor	Color of the foreground text
URL	URL of the document (read-only)
domain	Domain of the server

Note that you can trap information about the URL that a person was visiting just before coming to your Web site. You could store this information in a cookie and provide an option in all of your Web pages to return the reader to the previous site from any of your Web pages — a thoughtful and impressive gesture.

In addition to the scalar properties, the document object also has reference to several built-in arrays, such as the images or links arrays. These are discussed in detail later in this chapter.

A downside to dynamic HTML is that when the Web page reader reloads the page, whatever state the page was in is lost, and the display returns to its original (loading) state. You can address this problem by implementing cookies. *Cookies* are small bits of persistent information stored on the client machine. The code in Listing 9-2, **nsdoc.htm**, has an example of setting and retrieving a cookie, and prints out several different properties to the Web page using the document Writeln method.

Listing 9-2: Setting and getting a Netscape cookie and printing out several document properties

```
<HEAD>
<title>test</title>

<SCRIPT language="javascript">
<!--
function set_cookie() {

    var cookieDate = new Date();
    cookieDate.setTime (cookieDate.getTime() +
        (1000 * 60 * 60 * 24));
    var content = document.forms[0].elements[2].value;
    document.cookie = "test_cookie=" + escape (content) +
        "; expires=" + cookieDate.toGMTString();
```

```
    document.forms[0].elements[2].value = "";
    }

function get_cookie() {
 var content = document.cookie;
 var loc = content.indexOf("=");
 var results = content.substring(loc + 1, content.length);
 results = unescape(results);
 document.forms[0].elements[2].value = results;
}
//-->
</SCRIPT>

</HEAD>
<BODY>
<FORM>
<INPUT type=button value="Set Cookie"
 onClick="set_cookie()">
<INPUT type=button value="Get Cookie"
 onClick="get_cookie()">
<INPUT type=text name="cookie_text">
</FORM>
<p>
<h2 id=test>Document Information: </H2>
<SCRIPT language="JavaScript1.2">
<!--
document.writeln("Document was last updated at " +
 document.lastModified + "<br>");
document.writeln("Document domain is " + document.domain) + "<br>";
document.writeln("Document background color is " + document.bgColor
 + "<br>");
document.writeln("Document text color is " + document.fgColor);
//-->
</SCRIPT>
</BODY>
```

The cookie in Listing 9-2 is named `test_cookie`, and expires 24 hours from the time it is set. Figure 9-1 shows what the page looks like after it loads. Try setting the cookie to a specific value in the example file on the CD-ROM, **nsdoc.htm**, closing and reopening Navigator, and then retrieving the cookie.

Check out Chapter 15, which includes an example of what is called a *progressive document* — a document (or set of documents) that remembers where the reader was the last time he or she accessed the document and resets the display accordingly. This example also uses Netscape-style cookies extensively.

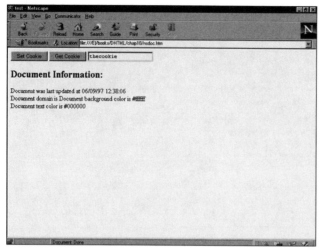

Figure 9-1: Printing out document properties and setting and retrieving a Netscape cookie

What Is a Cookie and What is OPS?

One of the online magazines came out with an article that declared, "Open Profiling Standard is replacing the Netscape Cookie." Well, this just isn't so. A cookie enables the Web page developer to store a bit of information on the client machine. A browser can then access this bit of information at a later time.

OPS is a way of establishing a personal profile that a company can access on the client machine. The company can then customize the Web page to fit the Web page reader's interest and preferences. This personal profile is under the complete control of the reader, and only information that the reader permits to be read is read. The FAQ (frequently asked questions) on OPS (maintained on Netscape's Web site) specifically states that OPS is not the same thing as a Netscape cookie.

Table 9-4, found in the discussion on the `window` object, lists several `document` object methods that are shared with the `window` object. Other methods for the `document` object follow in Table 9-6.

TABLE 9-6 Document Object Methods

Method	Functionality	Parameters
GetSelection	Returns a string with the current selection	
close	Closes the document and displays the contents	
open	Opens the document for write methods	mimeType
write	Writes HTML to the document	HTML expression
writeln	Writes HTML/carriage return to the document	HTML expression
eval	Evaluates a JavaScript string in the document context	string
toString	Converts a document to string format	
valueOf	Primitive value of the object, if it exists, or the object itself	

The Location, History, and Navigator Objects

Now, let's take a look at the location, history and navigator objects, which are defined as follows:

- ◆ *location object:* Contains information about the currently loaded URL.

- ◆ *history object:* Contains information about which URLs have been visited, and in what order.

- ◆ *navigator object:* Maintains information about which browser and version is accessing the page.

One major difference between Internet Explorer and Netscape Navigator is that in Navigator, the window object owns the location object, but in IE, the document object owns it.

Table 9-7 lists the properties of each of the location, history, and navigator objects.

TABLE 9-7 Location, History, and Navigator Object Properties

Property	Description
location.hash	With a NAME attribute, it is the string minus the pound sign (#)
location.host	Host name concatenated with the port, if any
location.hostname	Host name of the Web page
location.href	URL that is the target of a link
location.pathname	Relative path of the Web page
location.port	Port number, if any
location.protocol	Protocol used to access the Web page, such as "http:"
location.search	Form data or query string
history.length	Number of URLs currently maintained in the history
history.current	URL of the current Web page
history.next	Next URL in the history list
history.previous	Previous URL in the history list
navigator.language	Two-letter code representing the browser's language
navigator.platform	Platform of the browser
navigator.appName	Name of the browser
navigator.appVersion	Version of the browser
navigator.appCodeName	Code name of the browser
navigator.plugins	Array of plug-ins installed on the client
navigator.mimeTypes	Arrays of MIME types supported by the client
navigator.userAgent	User-agent header

Using these objects, the code in Listing 9-3, **nsloc.htm**, tests to see if the client is running Navigator 4.0 and, if it is, sets the background color to yellow. If not, the background is set to aqua. In addition, the example prints out information about the location and history objects.

Listing 9-3: This code runs a test to discern which browser is attempting to open the page, and the code also displays history and location properties

```
<HEAD>
<title>test</title>

<SCRIPT language="javascript">
<!--
if (navigator.appName == "Netscape")
 window.isNS4 =
        ((parseInt(navigator.appVersion.substring(0,1))
             >= 4))
//-->
</SCRIPT>
</HEAD>

<BODY bgcolor="aqua"
  onLoad="if (window.isNS4) document.bgColor='yellow'">
<h2 id=test>Location/History Information: </H2>

<SCRIPT language="javascript">
<!--

document.writeln("host is " + location.host + "<br>")
document.writeln("hostname is " + location.hostname +
 "<br>")
document.writeln("pathname is " + location.pathname +
 "<br>")
document.writeln("protocol is " + location.protocol +
 "<br>")
document.writeln("length is " + history.length + "<br>")
//-->
</SCRIPT>

</BODY>
```

To get a good understanding of the differences in the objects' properties, access the page from more than one browser. Also, compare how the page changes when you open it as a file from the CD-ROM (or your local hard drive), and when it's opened from a Web server.

The methods for the navigator, history, and location objects are listed in Table 9-8.

TABLE 9-8 Location, History, and Navigator Object Methods

Method	Functionality	Parameters
location|history.back	Previous URL in the history list	
location|history.go	Go to a specific object in the history list	Object index
location|history|navigator .eval	Evaluate JavaScript in the context of the object	JavaScript string
location|history|navigator .toString	Convert the object to a string	
location|history|navigator .valueOf	Primitive value of the object, if it exists, or the object itself	
location|history.forward	Next object in the history list	
navigator.javaEnabled	Whether Java is enabled	
navigator.taint	Enabled	Whether data tainting is enabled

Note that if more than one object has the same function, the objects are separated by a vertical bar (|).

The Form Objects

One way JavaScript was first used was to let readers "interact" with an HTML form. The form object is a nonvisual object that acts as a container for several different input objects, and which is submitted as a whole if the reader presses a Submit button or invokes a Submit method. The input objects that are owned by the form object are listed in Table 9-9.

TABLE 9-9 Input Objects Owned by the Form Object

Input Object	Description
Button	Standard button
Checkbox	Checkbox that the reader can click to check or uncheck
FileUpload	Special input text component that accesses a file name for uploading
Hidden	Hidden component, commonly used for containing nondisplay values
Password	Password field that does not display the password as entered
Radio	Radio button, representing exclusive or choices (only one choice)
Reset	Resets the form (puts form components back to loading state)
Select	A select list is a control that lists several different options for the reader to pick from
Submit	A special type of button that submits the form to the server
Text	Text field
Textarea	Multiple column, row text field

 Because this book is not a definitive guide to JavaScript, I won't cover these controls in detail aside from how they apply to dynamic HTML.

Listing 9-4, which you can find as the file **nsforms.htm** on the CD-ROM, shows how you can manipulate forms in various ways using layers in dynamic HTML. This Web page has two forms, one for information about the reader and one for information about the reader's company. The first form appears when the page is loaded. The second form does not show until the reader presses the button to switch the form pages. I enclosed each form within LAYER tags, and created a third layer that contains a message set to display only when the second form submission button is pressed.

Listing 9-4: Multiple form example

```
<HEAD>
<SCRIPT language="javascript1.2">
<!--
```

```
side = 1;
function switch_forms() {
 // just in case, hide the message layer
 document.layers["message"].visibility="hide";
 if (side == 1) {
       document.layers["one"].visibility="hide";
       document.layers["two"].visibility="show";
       side = 2;
       }
 else {
       document.layers["two"].visibility="hide";
       document.layers["one"].visibility="show";
       side = 1;
       }
}
function submit_form() {
 document.layers[0].visibility="hide";
 document.layers[1].visibility="hide";
 document.layers[2].visibility="show";
}
//-->
</SCRIPT>
</HEAD>
<BODY>
<H2>Press the button to display the second part of the form</H2>
<form>
<input type=button value="Switch Form Pages"
 onclick="switch_forms()">
<input type=button value="Submit Information"
 onclick="submit_form()">
</form>
<p>
<LAYER id=one left=30 top=100 width=300 height=150
 bgColor="skyblue">
<h2>Please enter information about yourself:</h2>
<form name="firstform">
<table>
<tr><td>
Enter Name:
</td><td><input type="text" name="readername"></td>
<tr><td>
Address:
</td><td><input type="text" name="address"></td>
<tr><td>
Phone:
</td><td><input type="text" name="phone"></td></tr></table>
</form>
</layer>
<layer id=two left=30 top=100 width=300 height=150
 bgColor="yellow" visibility="hide">
<h2>Please enter information about your company:</h2>
<form name="secondform">
<table>
```

```
<tr><td>
Company Name:
</td><td><input type="text" name="coname"></td>
<tr><td>
Company Address:
</td><td><input type="text" name="coaddress"></td>
<tr><td>
Company Phone:
</td><td><input type="text" name="cophone"></td></tr></table>
</form>
</layer>
<layer name="message" left=30 top=100 width=300 height=150
 bgColor="aqua" visibility="hide">
<h1 align=center>Your information has been submitted</h1>
</layer>
</BODY>
```

Notice that when the forms are switched, the message layer is automatically hidden, just in case the Web page reader switches the forms after the form is submitted. Hiding an already hidden layer costs nothing. Although layers are discussed in more detail later in this chapter, I want to mention a couple of important items from this example. First, each layer contains its own separate `document` object. Because of this, the input controls within each layer must be contained within a separate form. This means that one form is needed for the buttons outside the layer, and one form is needed for the input controls within each layer. Figure 9-2 shows the page after the button used to switch the forms has been pressed, and the second form is displayed.

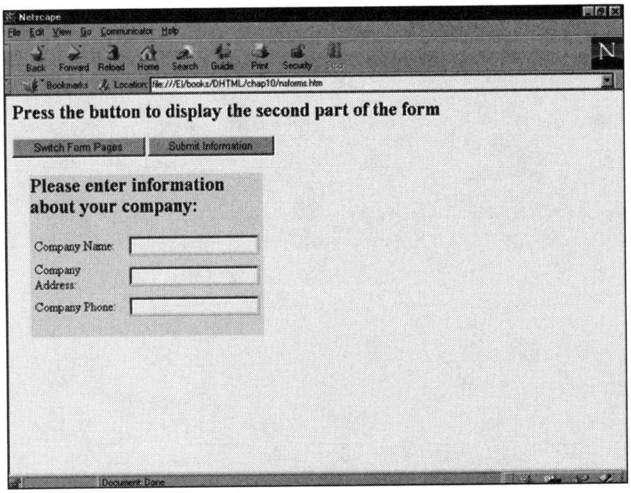

Figure 9-2: The second form (previously hidden) in a layer is displayed when the reader presses the button to switch forms

When the Submit Information button is pressed, all it does is expose the layer that says the form has been submitted. If this were a real-life example of multiple forms, the form submission process would also combine the information from both of the layer forms (probably into separate hidden fields of the form that are outside of layers), and would then submit the form with the contained information. Accessing information from one of the layer forms is similar to the following code:

```
var name = document.layers["one"].
  document.forms["firstform"].elements[0].value;
```

More information on the document-to-layer-to-document relationship appears later in this chapter, in the section on layers. For now, try the example yourself by accessing the file **nsforms.htm** on the CD-ROM.

The Event Object

The event object is passed to event handlers and contains information about an event, such as which mouse button was pressed and where it occurred. The event object is therefore an essential tool for creating interactive applications. In this section I'll give you only a brief rundown of the object, which was discussed in Chapter 3 and will be used extensively in Chapter 13.

You have two ways to access the event object. The first is to provide an event handler using the following code, which captures the window resize event:

```
window.onresize=resize_window;
...
function resize_window(e) {
// where e is the event object
```

Another approach is to pass the event object in a direct function call, as demonstrated in the following code:

```
<input type="button" value="press me"
  onclick="call_function(Event)">
...
call_function(e) {
```

The preceding code accesses the event object properties directly in the inline event handler, as shown next:

```
<input type="button" name="test" value="press me"
  onclick="alert(Event.target)">
```

This code is equivalent to applying the toString function to the button object and printing it out, because the target property is the object that receives the event. The output would look similar to the following:

```
<input type="button" name="test" value="press me"
  onclick='alert(Event.target);'>
```

Each event has a specific set of event object properties. For instance, the target property should be set for all events that are received via some object (as demonstrated in the previous code), and the width and height properties should be set for the resize event. Appendix A contains the URL for the documentation page at the Netscape site that details what event sets which properties.

The Screen Object

Netscape has also provided a new object, the screen object, that provides information about the screen settings, including color depth and screen width and height. This object's properties are listed in Table 9-10.

TABLE 9-10 Screen Object Properties

Screen Object Property	Description
colorDepth	Represents the BPI (bits per inch) of the current screen color settings; a value of 8 is equivalent to 256-color mode
availHeight	Height of the screen in pixels minus features such as task bars
availWidth	Width of the screen in pixels minus features such as task bars
width	Width of the screen in pixels
height	Height of the screen in pixels
pixelDepth	Bits per pixel of the display

This object can be used very effectively to test the screen settings of the client that is accessing your Web page. As an example of the screen object, I created the page in Listing 9-5, **screen.htm**, which uses JavaScript. The script tests the color depth and resolution of the screen, and changes the image to a high-resolution image if the color depth is over 8 (256-color mode). If the screen is in 256-color mode or less, the code tells the page to load a low-resolution gray image. Also, if the horizontal resolution is greater than or equal to 800, the page loads a larger image than it would if the resolution was less than 800. The background color is also changed based on color depth.

Listing 9-5: Testing the properties of the screen object and loading the appropriate image

```
<HEAD>
<title>test</title>
</HEAD>
<BODY>
<SCRIPT language="javascript1.2">
<!--
    var filename
    if (screen.colorDepth > 8) {
        filename = "haysthi";
        document.bgColor = "#ffdd33";
    }
    else {
        document.bgColor = "yellow";
        filename = "haystlw";
    }
    if (screen.width >= 800)
        filename = filename + "1.JPG";
    else
        filename = filename + "2.JPG";
    filename = filename + "'>";

    // write out document
    document.writeln("<H1> Dynamically altering HTML</H1>");
    document.writeln("<img src='" + filename);
    document.close();
//-->
</SCRIPT>

</BODY>
```

With this approach, images, fonts, and other Web page elements can be tailored to the size and capability of the monitor accessing the page. Doing so ensures that you are providing Web page readers with the best possible page content.

Try out the example file **screen.htm** on the CD-ROM. Start with your current screen settings and then change the settings to a higher or lower color depth and resolution and run the example again.

The Built-In Arrays

Previous releases of Navigator have included arrays containing objects such as all the forms within the page, or all the elements within a specific form, and/or all the document images. But now, with the release of Navigator 4.0, the list of array-based objects has grown to include the layers array.

Table 9-11 provides a current list of all array-based objects, their contents, and the object to which they belong.

TABLE 9-11 Array-Based Objects

Array Element	Contents	Owning Object
Anchors	Entries for all hypertext links within a page	document
Applets	Entries for all Java applets within a page	document
Arguments	Arguments passed to a function	The specific function
Elements	Form elements	The specific form
Embeds	All Web page objects inserted using the EMBED tag	document
Forms	All forms within a page	document
Frames	Frames	window and frame objects
History	URLs visited and that are available when the Web page reader presses the Go menu item	window
Images	All images within a page	document
Layers	All layers relative to the document or any containing layer within a Web page	document and layer objects
Links	All area and link objects within a Web page	document
MimeTypes	All MIME types supported on the client	navigator
Options	All options for a select object	The select object
Plugins	All plug-ins installed on the client	navigator

An individual array element can be accessed either by its name, if one has been assigned, or by an array index representing the element's location within the page. In other words, an index of 3 would access the fourth element in the page.

As an example of how to access an array element by its array index, I created the following code listing, Listing 9-6, that you can find on the CD-ROM as **marquee.htm**. This listing demonstrates a moving image show, and uses the images array to move images from one location to another on the page, creating an effect similar to a movie theater marquee. The page begins with ten images, all fairly dark. When the page is loaded, a timer rotates through each of the displayed images and highlights one of the darker images at a time, creating the marquee effect.

Listing 9-6: Movie marquee effect created with setInterval and the images array

```
<HEAD>
<title>test</title>
<script language="javascript1.1">
<!--

ball_number = 9;
highlight_ball = new Image(26,26);
lowlight_ball = new Image(26,26);
highlight_ball.src = "ball2.gif";
lowlight_ball.src = "ball1.gif";

function start_marquee() {
  document.images[ball_number].src = lowlight_ball.src;
  if (ball_number < 9)
      ball_number++;
  else
      ball_number=0;
  document.images[ball_number].src=highlight_ball.src;
}

//-->
</SCRIPT>

</HEAD>
<BODY onload="setInterval('start_marquee()',160)">
<H1>Moving Marquee Demonstration</H1>
<img src="ball1.gif" width=26 height=26 hspace=10>
<img src="ball1.gif" width=26 height=26 hspace=10>
<img src="ball1.gif" width=26 height=26 hspace=10>
<img src="ball1.gif" width=26 height=26 hspace=10>
<img src="ball1.gif" width=26 height=26 hspace=10>
<img src="ball1.gif" width=26 height=26 hspace=10>
<img src="ball1.gif" width=26 height=26 hspace=10>
<img src="ball1.gif" width=26 height=26 hspace=10>
<img src="ball1.gif" width=26 height=26 hspace=10>
<img src="ball1.gif" width=26 height=26 hspace=10>
</BODY>
```

Note in Listing 9-6 that each image is returned to its "normal" state after the high-lighted image moves on. Also, both the darker and lighter images are *cached* in the page by the new Image notation in the script block. Caching prevents the page from accessing the images from the Web server each time they are changed. You can use this technique to animate a progress bar or a different style of animated marquee.

Along with accessing an array element by its index number (as seen in the previous example), you can use the element's name, if it has one. The following code shows how to access a named image using this technique:

```
document.images["image1"].src="someimage.gif";
...
<img src="otherimage.gif" name="image1">
```

Accessing arrays by names rather than numbers makes adding elements to a Web page at a later time a simpler procedure, as index numbers change when new elements are added.

Introducing the New Layer Object

The real key to Netscape's dynamic HTML is the layer object. This new object gives you the capability to partition a Web page into layers, and then move, hide, or show the layers as you want.

There are actually two layer objects. The first is known as a *positioned* or *out-of-flow* layer, and is created with LAYER and /LAYER tags. The second is the *inflow* layer, which follows the natural flow of the document when positioning its contents and which is created using the ILAYER and /ILAYER tags. The rest of this section focuses on the positioned layer because it's used in the majority of this book. However, I created a short example demonstrating the differences between the two layer objects.

The code in Listing 9-7, which is the example file called **difflayr.htm** on the CD-ROM, shows four layers, two inflow and two positioned layers. Note from Figure 9-3 that the second inflow layer flows naturally after the first, positioned all the way to the left and below the first header. Inflow layers are not influenced by the positioned layer elements, which is something you should keep in mind if you decide to mix the two styles.

Listing 9-7: Example demonstrating two types of layer controls: inflow and positioned

```
<HEAD>
<title>test</title>
</head>
<body>
<ilayer id=layer1>
<h1 style="color: blue">This is layer one</h1>
</ilayer>
<layer id=layer2 top=100px left=150px>
<h1 style="color: red">This is layer two</h1>
</layer>
<ilayer id=layer3>
<h1 style="color: green">This is layer three</h1>
</ilayer>
<layer id=layer4 top=200px left=50px>
<h1>This is layer four</h1>
</layer>
<NOLAYER>
<p>
This page uses the layer tag, implemented by Netscape Navigator 4.x
 and up
</NOLAYER>
</body>
</html>
```

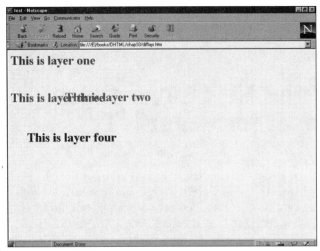

Figure 9-3: A page showing four layers, two positioned using absolute positioning, and two positioned using relative positioning

Notice in Listing 9-7 the use of the NOLAYER tags. These tags are read and interpreted only by browsers that do not support the LAYER tags, such as Internet Explorer 4.x. Figure 9-4 shows what the page would look like in IE 4.0. Also notice that the headers line up as they normally would without any positioning, and the message included between the NOLAYER and /NOLAYER tags displays beneath the headers.

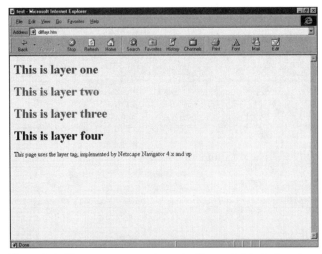

Figure 9-4: The same page as shown in Figure 9-3 but viewed with Internet Explorer 4.0

The Layer Object Properties

Layers have several different properties that can either be read from, written to, or both. You have seen a couple of these already with the last sample code that set both the left and top layer properties. The other properties are listed in Table 9-12.

TABLE 9-12 Layer Properties

Property	Description
name	Layer name, assigned using the ID or NAME attribute
left	Left edge of the layer in pixels, relative to the parent layer
top	Top edge of the layer in pixels, relative to the parent layer or document if placed directly in the document
pageX	Horizontal position of the layer relative to the Web page
pageY	Vertical position of the layer relative to the Web page
zIndex	The z-order of the layer, relative to siblings and the parent
visibility	Whether the layer is visible or not; allowable values are show and hide
clip.top	Top dimension of the layer clipping rectangle
clip.left	Left dimension of the layer clipping rectangle
clip.right	Right dimension of the layer clipping rectangle
clip.bottom	Bottom dimension of the layer clipping rectangle
clip.width	Width of the layer clipping rectangle
clip.height	Height of the layer clipping rectangle
background.src	Source file for the background image of the layer, if any
bgColor	Background color of the layer, if any, set to null for a transparent layer
siblingAbove	Sibling layer above the current layer in z-order, if any (otherwise null)
siblingBelow	Sibling layer below the current layer in z-order, if any (otherwise null)
above	Layer object above the current layer object among all layers in the document or the enclosing window object if this layer is top-most
below	Layer object below the current layer object among all layers in the document or null if this layer is bottom-most

continued

TABLE 9-12 **Additional Layer Properties** *(continued)*

Property	Description
parentLayer	Layer containing the current layer, or window if none
width	Width of the layer
height	Height of the layer
src	HTML source for the layer in URL format

The `clip` properties determine how much of the layer shows, while the `height` and `width` properties determine how big the layer is.

Listing 9-8, **layrprop.htm** on the CD-ROM, shows you how to use some of these properties. I created a page with four form elements and a layer. I use the `src` property to display another Web page within the layers, and the clipping properties to control the size. Notice how the `src` property displays another Web page within the layers, and the clipping properties control the size. The Web page reader can type a file into the first element, a text field, using either the standard *file URL* format (such as file:///E|/books/DHTML/chap9/layrprop.htm), or *http URL* format (such as http://www.somecom.com/somefile.htm).

Listing 9-8: Setting layer properties dynamically and loading an HTML source file into a layer

```
<HEAD>
<title>test</title>

<SCRIPT language="javascript1.2">

sample_width = 200;
sample_height = 200;

function open_source() {
  var filename=document.forms[0].elements[0].value;
  document.layers["file"].src=filename;
}

function make_bigger() {
  if (sample_width > 800)
      alert("Sorry, will not increase size of layer");
  else {
      sample_width+=50;
      sample_height+=50;
      document.layers["file"].clip.width=sample_width;
      document.layers[0].clip.height=sample_height;
      }
```

```
}

function make_smaller() {
 if (sample_width <= 50)
      alert("Sorry, will not decrease size of layer");
 else {
      sample_width-=50;
      sample_height-=50;
      document.layers["file"].clip.width=sample_width;
      document.layers[0].clip.height=sample_height;
      }
}
</SCRIPT>

</HEAD>
<BODY>
<FORM>
Enter URL of Layer Source: <INPUT type=text name="url_text"><p>
<INPUT type=button value="Make Smaller"
 onClick="make_smaller()">
<INPUT type=button value="Make Bigger"
 onClick="make_bigger()">
<INPUT type=button value="Open Source"
 onClick="open_source()">
</FORM>
<layer name="file" left=50 top=100 src="blank.htm">

</layer>
</BODY>
```

Pressing the Open Source button opens the file and stretches the layer to fit, as shown in Figure 9-5. Pressing either the Make Bigger or Make Smaller button increases or decreases, respectively, the clipping area for the layer, as shown in Figure 9-6. Try it yourself; run **layrprop.htm** and then open the file **nsloc.htm** into the layer. Also, take note of what happens to the Pathname property when it prints out. The Pathname is from the **layrprop.htm** file, not the original **nsloc.htm** file.

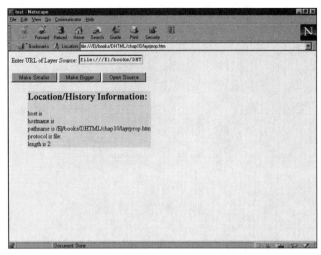

Figure 9-5: Loading a source file, nsloc.htm, into a layer

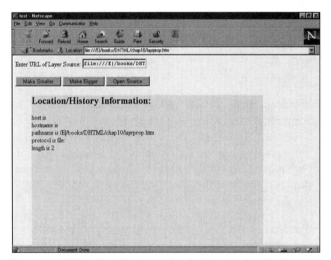

Figure 9-6: Using the clipping region buttons to size the layer

Take note in the listing that the original width and height of the clipping box are set to a value of 200 each, using the global variables sample_width and sample_height. My preference would be to set these variables to the block *after* I load the source code file, but until the clipping block is set specifically, no width and height clipping value exists.

The Layer Methods

In addition to having several properties, the `layer` object also has several methods. The methods mainly move or position a layer, or load a source file. Table 9-13 lists all of the available methods.

TABLE 9-13 Layer Object Methods

Method	Functionality	Parameters
moveBy	Changes the layer position using the difference	difference x, y
moveTo	Changes the layer position within the enclosing layer; for inflow layers, moves relative to the natural position	x, y
moveToAbsolute	Changes the layer position within the enclosing page	x, y
resizeBy	Resizes the layer by the specified height and width	difference width, height
resizeTo	Resizes the layer to the given width, height	width, height
moveAbove	Moves the layer to the layer above it in the stacking order	layer
moveBelow	Moves the layer to the layer below it in the stacking order	layer
load	Loads the external HTML file into the layer	source, width

The following example in Listing 9-9, **layrmthd.htm**, builds on Listing 9-8, using `layer` object methods. In this example you can move the loaded layer anywhere on the page by setting the x and y text fields and pressing the Move Layer button. You can also set its width and height fields and press the resize button to set the dimensions of the layer. This is accomplished by including the new functions, `move_layer` and `resize_layer`, and new form contents.

Listing 9-9: Applying layer methods to a layer

```
function move_layer() {
  var new_x = document.forms[0].elements[1].value;
  var new_y = document.forms[0].elements[2].value;
  document.layers["file"].moveTo(new_x, new_y);
}

function resize_layer() {
  var new_width = document.forms[0].elements[3].value;
  var new_height = document.forms[0].elements[4].value;
  document.layers["file"].resizeTo(new_width, new_height);
}
...
<FORM>
Enter URL of Layer Source: <INPUT type=text name="url_text"><p>
Enter new X: <INPUT type=text name="url_x"><br>
Enter new Y: <INPUT type=text name="url_y"><p>
Enter new width: <INPUT type=text><br>
Enter new height: <INPUT type=text><p>

<INPUT type=button value="Make Smaller"
 onClick="make_smaller()">
<INPUT type=button value="Make Bigger"
 onClick="make_bigger()">
<INPUT type=button value="Open Source"
 onClick="open_source()">
<INPUT type=button value="Move Layer"
 onClick="move_layer()">
<INPUT type=button value="Resize Layer"
 onClick="resize_layer()">
</FORM>
```

Now, you have some real choices as to what you want to do with this layer. Test the listing yourself by opening the file **layrmthd.htm** on the CD-ROM and trying out various files (access them both locally and via the Internet) set to different positions and dimensions.

The Layer Events

The events that can be trapped and processed for the `layer` object are:

- ◆ `mouseover`
- ◆ `mouseout`
- ◆ `load`
- ◆ `focus`
- ◆ `blur`

If multiple layers are stacked, the top layer receives the event unless the layer is hidden. Listing 9-10 provides an example of how to trap events for layers. It contains a Web page that implements an online tic-tac-toe game. This page, which you can find on the CD-ROM as file **nstictac.htm,** uses one layer to create a gray square to hold the other layers. When you click one of the playing boxes, the value of the image source is checked to see if the box has been played. If it hasn't, then the image source is changed to whichever player image is to be played next (either the o.gif or the x.gif file, depending on whose turn it is). Additionally, the background color of the layer changes to highlight a box that has been played.

Listing 9-10: A tic-tac-toe game using Navigator dynamic HTML and event handling for layers

```
<HEAD>
<title>X marks the spot</title>
<SCRIPT language="javascript1.2">
<!--

non_play = "";
figname="o.gif";

function make_play(layer_item) {
   // get clicked location and drop image
   var obj=
 document.layers[0].document.layers[layer_item].
       document.images[0].src;
   if (obj != non_play) return;
       figname = figname == "x.gif" ? "o.gif" : "x.gif"

 document.layers[0].document.layers[layer_item].
       document.images[0].src = figname;
   document.layers[0].document.layers[layer_item].
       bgColor="lime";
}

function display_status(layer_item) {
   var obj=
   document.layers[0].document.layers[layer_item].
   document.images[0].src;
   if (obj == non_play)
       document.layers[1].visibility="show";
   else
       document.layers[2].visibility="show";
}

function hide_status() {
 document.layers[1].visibility="hide";
 document.layers[2].visibility="hide";
}

//-->
</SCRIPT>
```

```
</HEAD>
<BODY>
<H1 id=header> Dynamic HTML tic-tac-toe</H1>
<p>
Now, I hope you know how to play this game...it's as old as time.
 Player 1 is 'X' and Player 2 is 'O'. The first player to get three
 boxes in a row, diagonally, horizontally, or vertically wins. If no
 player gets three boxes in a row, the game is a draw.
<p>
<layer left=100 top=250 bgColor=#eeeeee width=145
 height=145>
<layer left=10 top=10 width=35 height=35
 onLoad="non_play = this.document.images[0].src"
 onmouseover="display_status(0)"
 onmouseout="hide_status()">
<a href="" onclick="make_play(0);return false">
<img src="hold.gif" width=35 height=35 border=0></a>
</layer></a>
<layer left=55 top=10
 onmouseover="display_status(1)"
 onmouseout="hide_status()">
<a href="" onclick="make_play(1);return false">
<img src="hold.gif" width=35 height=35 border=0></a>
</layer>
<layer left=100 top=10
 onmouseover="display_status(2)"
 onmouseout="hide_status()">
<a href="" onclick="make_play(2);return false">
<img src="hold.gif" width=35 height=35 border=0></a>
</layer>

<layer left=10 top=55
 onmouseover="display_status(3)"
 onmouseout="hide_status()">
<a href="" onclick="make_play(3);return false">
<img src="hold.gif" width=35 height=35 border=0></a>
</layer>
<layer left=55 top=55
 onmouseover="display_status(4)"
 onmouseout="hide_status()">
<a href="" onclick="make_play(4);return false">
<img src="hold.gif" width=35 height=35 border=0></a>
</layer>
<layer left=100 top=55
 onmouseover="display_status(5)"
 onmouseout="hide_status()">
<a href="" onclick="make_play(5);return false">
<img src="hold.gif" width=35 height=35 border=0></a>
</layer>

<layer left=10 top=100
 onmouseover="display_status(6)"
 onmouseout="hide_status()">
```

```
<a href="" onclick="make_play(6);return false">
<img src="hold.gif" width=35 height=35 border=0></a>
</layer>
<layer left=55 top=100
 onmouseover="display_status(7)"
 onmouseout="hide_status()">
<a href="" onclick="make_play(7);return false">
<img src="hold.gif" width=35 height=35 border=0></a>
</layer>
<layer left=100 top=100
 onmouseover="display_status(8)"
 onmouseout="hide_status()">
<a href="" onclick="make_play(8);return false">
<img src="hold.gif" width=35 height=35 border=0></a>
</layer>
</layer>
<layer bgColor="lime" width=300 height=100 left=300 top=250
 visibility="hide">
<h2>Click on the square to make a play</h2>
</layer>
<layer bgColor="red" width=300 height=100 left=300 top=250
 visibility="hide">
<h2>sorry, square has been played already</h2>
</layer>
</BODY>
```

In this code, the load event is trapped for one layer in order to record a file reference. The mouseover and mouseout events for all boxes are trapped to display a message that indicates whether that box can be played (clicked) or not. The layer object does not have its own click event so an empty reference or stub HREF tag is placed around an image that is the same size as the layer.

Figure 9-7 shows the tic-tac-toe game after a couple of boxes have been played. Notice the status message to the right of the playing board, which tells the person playing the game whether the square has been played or not. Try the game for yourself by accessing the sample file nstictac.htm.

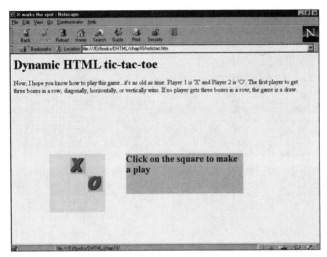

Figure 9-7: The tic-tac-toe game after a couple of boxes have
been played

This example can also be implemented using CSS1 positioning and DIV blocks. For more information on this topic, please see Chapter 11, which covers HTML element positioning.

The Document Is the Layer Is the Document

One interesting aspect of the layer object is that each layer contains its own document object. More than anything else, this characteristic has the potential to trip you up when you're working with code that includes layers.

For example, if you have an image enclosed within LAYER tags and you want to change the image source, you might try something like the following:

```
document.layers[0].images[0].src="somefile.gif";
```

If you do, you'll get an error. The following is actually the correct technique to use:

```
document.layers[0].document.images[0].src="some.gif";
```

In other words, you can access anything a document can access within a layer as long as you remember to use the second reference to the document. So, if you have a layer that contains layers that contain an image, the code would look like this:

```
document.layers[0].document.layers[0].document.images[0]
.src = "some.gif";
```

I would suggest, in cases such as this, that you consider assigning the first layer to a variable to keep track of what you are accessing:

```
var current_layer = document.layers[0];
current_layer.document.layers[0].document.images[0].
src = "some.gif";
```

The layer object is used extensively in the chapters to come, because it is Netscape's primary component for dynamic HTML.

 As you'll see in the next few chapters, the DIV block has many of the same capabilities as the layer object. The CSS1 positioning paper (you'll find the URL in Appendix A) described the positioning of *traditional* HTML block elements, such as DIV. So, when Netscape released Navigator 4.0, they also extended the CSS1 positioning capability to DIV blocks.

Console Mode and Signed Scripting

Beginning with Navigator 4.0, Netscape introduced *script signing* as a security measure. This is particularly important when you're using the new console mode to create Web pages. *Console mode* usually means that the Web page opens in a new browser window, full-screen, and is set to always stay on top. This feature is one of the JavaScript 1.2 enhancements that requires signing.

Script Signing

In this section, we'll cover enough of the basics of script signing to get you working with the new console mode. For a more detailed explanation of script signing, see Netscape's Web site (Appendix A lists the URL).

Script signing requires a couple of different steps. First, you need to obtain a certificate from one of several different companies. These certificates are used to sign the scripting, Java, or other file that is downloaded from a Web site. Verisign provides a certificate, free of charge, that can be used to test scripts locally. Netscape provides the URL and instructions for accessing this certificate. The process takes you through several steps and installs a certificate that can be used for testing scripts only. You may want to take a moment now to download this certificate if you haven't already downloaded or purchased a certificate.

Another approach you can take when developing and testing your scripts is to bypass the certificate signing by using the *activate codebase principals* line in your preferences file **(prefs.js)**. The line to add is:

```
user_pref("signed.applets.codebase_principal_support", true);
```

Once you've added the preceding line, you need to *be cautious* when exploring the Web, because it opens a door for unknown applets and script files to enter your machine from the Internet.

Once you have a certificate, you need to download the JAR Packager from the Netscape site (JAR stands for Java Archive Resources). This tool lets you package a script, applet, or plug-in together with a digital signature into one file. Appendix A includes Netscape's URL, and from there you can find the JAR Packager and script signing documentation.

After you've obtained your certificate and the packager, and have created your script file, sign the file by following the steps given next. Note that some packager versions run as applets from within Navigator, and others are stand-alone.

To sign the file using the applet version of the tool, follow these steps:

1. Run the applet by opening the packager HTML file in Navigator.

2. Select the Add Files option from the menu button bar.

3. Pick the file(s) you want to add to the archive.

4. After picking the files and returning to the main application, select the files you want to digitally sign. Sign the files by selecting them and pressing either the Sign All button or the Sign button.

5. Save the file, with the **.jar** extension. Exit the packager applet.

That's all you have to do. You will definitely want to read the Netscape's documentation on script signing and object signing. Note that if you change any of the files included in the JAR file, you will need to create the file again.

Console Mode

After you are all set to create signed scripts, you might want to create a Web page that takes advantage of the new Netscape console mode. This section walks you through the necessary steps of creating the files and digitally signing them.

Console mode requires the creation of a new Navigator browser window that may or may not be full-screen, and that usually remains either on top of all other windows all of the time, or below. This mode can be used with full-screen presentations, smaller dialog windows, and smaller tools windows. It can also be used with help-based windows that float unobtrusively above the main Web page window. Whatever your intended purpose, you'll most likely need to make some use of restricted JavaScript features to create the window, which means you need to sign the JavaScript.

I created a full-size example window that contains one of the Navigator dynamic HTML sample pages from my Web site. You can see this example by opening the file **openwin.htm** on the CD-ROM. (Note that I included the JAR file in the script tag, as well as the JavaScript source.) When the "press me" button is pressed, this page opens a new Navigator window. The window has only the toolbar, and scroll bars if any are needed. The window remains on top of all other windows in the Windows operating system, or if in the Macintosh environment, remains on top of other Navigator windows.

Listing 9-11 contains this simple code, which basically calls a function to open the window. It also includes a SCRIPT tag that includes an ARCHIVE attribute, which is essential for script signing and pointing to a JAR file created later in this section. The script used is loaded from the script file named **thescript.js** on the CD-ROM, shown in Listing 9-12, that creates the new console-mode-based browser window.

Listing 9-11: A simple HTML file that calls a JavaScript function when a button is pressed, and which contains a SCRIPT tag with both a JAR file and a JavaScript source file

```
<HEAD>
<SCRIPT ARCHIVE="myArchive.jar" src="thescript.js">
</script>
</HEAD>
<form>
<input type="button" value="press me" name="test"
 onclick="open_window()">
</form>
</BODY>
```

Listing 9-12: The contents of JavaScript file as it opens a new browser window in console mode

```
function open_window() {
   //Request privilege
   netscape.security.PrivilegeManager.enablePrivilege(
       "UniversalBrowserWrite");
   return open_win();
}

function open_win() {
  test = open("predesgn.htm", "ProgressiveDocument",
  "always_raised=yes, scrollbars=1,status=1");
}
```

In this code, the first function makes a call to a Netscape security object called the PrivilegeManager. Using any form of script signing requires making a request such as this to enable the security extension. In this example, the request is for UniversalBrowserWrite, which is the request to make when you're creating an odd-sized window, or a window that does not display a menu bar, toolbar, or one of the other features usually associated with console mode windows. Other privileges that can be requested are as follows:

♦ `UniversalBrowserRead` — reading privileged data

♦ `UniversalFileRead` — allowing an arbitrary local file to be uploaded to the server

♦ `UniversalSendMail` — allowing a page to send e-mail to a user's e-mail address

When the code makes a privilege request, the browser checks the signature associated with the file, and may display a dialog box that asks the Web page reader if he or she wants to grant the application the given privilege. The dialog box may also display the name of the person who wrote the application. If no problem exists, the privilege is then granted. In this example, a second function is called that does the actual window creation.

As mentioned earlier, you must create an archive file with a .jar extension that contains the digital signature that the browser uses to authenticate the application. This can be created with a couple of tools provided by Netscape, but I'll tell you step by step how to implement this technique. To create an archive using the Packager Applet, follow these steps:

1. Access the Packager HTML page, and then open the applet, as shown in Figure 9-8.

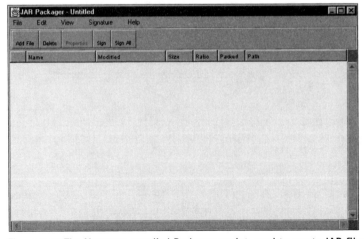

Figure 9-8: The Netscape-supplied Packager applet, used to create JAR files

2. Select the Add Files option from the menu that opens the directory.

3. Click your JavaScript file to select it, and then click the Add File button to add it to the list of files for the archive.

4. Click the Done button.

5. Once your file is listed, return to the main window, as shown in Figure 9-9.

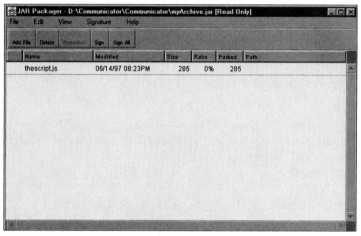

Figure 9-9: The Packager applet after adding the JavaScript file

6. Select the file and click the Sign button on the menu bar. Upon exiting the applet, it will prompt you to save the file. (In the previous project, I saved it as **myarchive.jar**, which is the name of the archive I use in Listing 9-11.)

7. The applet should then prompt you to enter the password you defined when installing your digital certificate.

Now, when a person accesses the example page and presses the button to open the new window, he or she should see a dialog box that provides information about the page, such as the name on the certificate, the e-mail address, and what security privileges are requested. You can try this yourself without having a digital certificate if you use the codebase principals option listed in the preceding section.

Before attempting any script signing, you should read all the documentation on this subject located at the Netscape site (see Appendix A for the URL).

Balance Hassles of Script Signing with Results

Script signing is not simple, and you will be charged to maintain a digital certificate (the cost of these certificates is not very high — usually less than 20.00 U.S. dollars per year). Before you run out and set all your pages to console mode, think of what you are truly hoping to accomplish. Most Web pages do not need more real estate than the content area of the normal browser window. And most Web pages do not need to "always remain on top," or send e-mail to the Web page reader, or upload a file. You will most likely never need to implement either a console mode window or script signing.

Summary

This chapter gave you a chance to work with many components of Netscape's dynamic HTML, including the `window` and `document` objects, Netscape cookies, forms and form elements, and the console mode.

In this chapter you learned:

◆ How to reference the basic HTML objects, such as `window` and `document`.

◆ About the new `window` object methods and events.

◆ How to work with Netscape cookies.

◆ The basics of the `navigator`, `location`, and `history` objects.

◆ How to work with forms and form elements.

◆ How to access the new `event` object.

◆ What the `layer` object is, and how it works.

◆ How to access and work with the new `layer` object methods.

◆ How event trapping works with layers.

◆ How to use JAR and script signing to protect scripts.

◆ How to implement a console-mode application using script signing.

In the next chapter we begin to use some of these objects as we explore ways to position, hide, display, move, and change the stacking order of HTML elements.

Chapter 10

Positioning HTML Elements

IN THIS CHAPTER

- ◆ HTML positioning basics

- ◆ Packaging elements into containers

- ◆ CSS positioning properties

- ◆ Layering elements

- ◆ Creating animations with layers

- ◆ Dynamically changing the positions of elements

- ◆ Using positioning to create animated effects

INTERNET EXPLORER 4.0 AND Netscape Navigator 4.0 have built-in capabilities that give you control over where an element is positioned, *absolutely*, according to specific *x* and *y* coordinates, or *relatively*, according to the element's position within the natural flow of the Web page contents. This chapter shows you how to position elements in Navigator, statically, using CSS positioning as well as using Netscape's <LAYER> tag. You'll also have a chance to try out dynamic positioning to create some interesting effects.

HTML Positioning — Introduction and Preview Example

To introduce you to HTML positioning with Netscape Navigator, I've created a "quick start" example that demonstrates a few of the techniques covered in more detail in the rest of this chapter. In this section, you'll get a hands-on preview of positioning as it's handled in Netscape Navigator. At the end of the chapter, after you've learned about positioning, the code for this example is shown along with more detail about the example.

To begin, open the sample file on the CD-ROM called **nsqckpos.htm.** Notice that the page has a button, and four images positioned in a semi-circle in the middle of the page, as shown in Figure 10-1. When you click the button, you'll notice that the images move in a clockwise circle around the page. Click the button several more times and the images continue to cycle around the middle of the page, as shown in Figure 10-2.

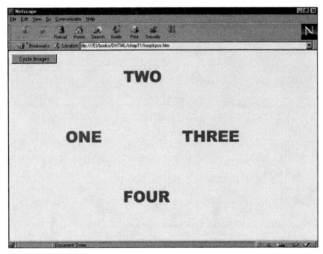

Figure 10-1: The preview example page after it first loads; notice the positioning of the images

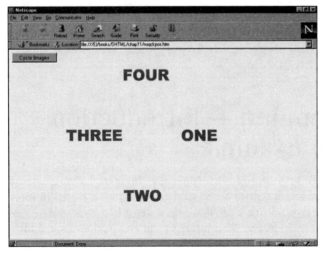

Figure 10-2: The preview example page after button has been clicked twice; notice the difference in the positions of the images compared to Figure 10-1

This example uses *absolute* positioning and layers to place four images and a button on a Web page. Eight arrays are created, two for each image, with one array containing the *x* coordinates of the path, the other array containing the *y* coordinates. Pressing the button cycles the images around the page. The images follow their designated path, which is changed every cycle. This cycle continues until each image has circled the page completely.

Packaging Elements into Containers

Before I go into detail on how to position elements, I'll show you how to group elements into containers, because at times you may want to position a group of elements rather than individual ones. Some elements have a natural grouping container, such as table rows and the contents of the rows contained within the table. Others, though, require the use of an external agent.

For example, the following code sets the position of a table to 50 pixels from the top of the Web page and 50 pixels from the left. All the items contained within the table definition are also positioned accordingly:

```
<HEAD>
<STYLE type="text/css">
#block1 {position: absolute; top: 50px;
     left: 50px; width: 300px}
</STYLE>
</HEAD>
<body>
<DIV id=block1>
<TABLE>
<tr><td>
<form>
Some text field: <INPUT type=text>
<p>
<INPUT type=button value="push me">
</form>
</td></tr>
</table>
</DIV>
</body>
```

Elements can be grouped using the HTML tags <DIV> and <SPAN>, and in the case of Navigator, the <LAYER> tag. The <DIV> and <LAYER> are block-level elements — a line break is implied before and after the block content. <SPAN> is an inline element — no breaks occur before or after the content enclosed within the <SPAN> tags. The <DIV> element can enclose and group any number of HTML elements including headers, paragraphs, and even other <DIV> blocks. The same also applies to the <LAYER> element. The <SPAN> element can enclose and group any number of inline elements, such as text, or inline text formatting elements such as the <strong> and <em> tags.

Because Netscape has promised to adhere to CSS positioning instead of its proprietary <LAYER> tag, you might want to use <DIV> for block-level grouping as much as possible. However, the examples in this chapter demonstrate the use of both types of block-level grouping.

The CSS Positioning Properties

Using CSS1, you can place an object anywhere on a Web page, either *absolutely* by specifying the element's top-left corner, or *relatively*, according to the natural position of an element among HTML contents. You can also set the element's container characteristics, such as how contents are clipped when the container is too small, how the browser treats overflow content, and whether the container is visible or hidden.

Absolute Positioning

To place an element absolutely in a Web page, set the position property to absolute and specify the top-left corner of an element using the left and top properties. The element is then placed at that coordinate, regardless of the location of other Web page objects. If more than one object is set to the same location, the objects are placed on top of each other, with the object defined last in the Web page document placed on top in the display.

For example, the following code positions the <DIV> block containing text at 250 pixels from the top and 200 pixels from the left.

```
<DIV
  style="background-color: red; position: absolute; top: 250px;
  left: 200px">
This is the beginning of a block of text that should start 250
  pixels from the top and 200 pixels from the left. The rectangle
  that is used to enclose this text will extend to the end of the
  text or object that is enclosed, and the height will be long enough
  to enclose the text or object, and no more.
</DIV>
```

This code creates a rectangle with its top-left corner at the coordinates of 250 (top) and 200 (left), with several attributes: a red background, a slightly jagged right edge, and with its height and width extending to accommodate the enclosed text.

Relative Positioning

Another type of positioning is *relative* positioning. Relative positioning places an object according to its natural position within the HTML flow. This includes any line breaks that may occur within the object. Relative positioning is the default for all HTML elements. To use CSS relative positioning, set the position property to relative and set the left and/or top properties to any number of pixels, including a negative number. The element will then be offset by that amount.

For example, the following code places the image included within the text block to the left of the starting point of the block, and overlaps the text at the end:

```
<DIV
style="position: absolute; top: 30px; left: 30px;
width=200px">
This is another block of text, but one that also includes an
<SPAN style="position: relative; left: 20px">
<img src="three.gif">
</SPAN>
image
</DIV>
```

Figure 10-3 shows the result of the relative positioning of the image. Note from the figure that the image overlaps the text that follows. If the image had been positioned within the natural flow of the HTML document, it would not have overlapped the text.

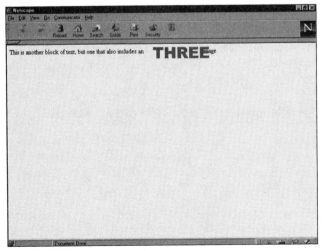

Figure 10-3: Using relative positioning to alter the location of an image relative to where it would occur naturally within the HTML document

Positioning and Style Sheets

Positioning styles do not need to be defined directly in the element – they can be defined using style sheets and then applied to one or more HTML elements, as the following code demonstrates:

```
<HEAD>
<STYLE type="text/css">
#block1 {position: absolute; top: 30px; left: 30px; width: 200px}
#image1 {position: relative; left: 20px }
</STYLE>
</HEAD>
<body>
<DIV id=block1>
This is another block of text, but one that also includes
an
<SPAN><img src="three.gif"></SPAN>
image.
</DIV>
</body>
```

Using the style sheet in this example results in the exact same presentation shown in Figure 10-3, which was created by code that embedded the style information directly into the HTML element using inline styles.

Combining Absolute and Relative Positioning

You can combine relative and absolute element positioning in a Web page. Listing 10-1 demonstrates this possibility by creating two separate <DIV> blocks, each containing an image and some text that describes the image. The first block is positioned relative to the HTML document, meaning that it is positioned relative to the margins set for the Web page body. The second block is positioned using absolute positioning, and ignores any other page elements.

Listing 10-1: Positioning multiple HTML elements using the <DIV> tags as containers

```
<HEAD>
<STYLE type="text/css">
BODY { margin-left: 0.25in; margin-top: 0.5in }
#block1 {position: relative; top: 50px;
        left: 20px; width: 300px;
        background-color: yellow }
#block2 {position: absolute; top: 50px;
        left: 400px; width: 300px;
        background-color: lime}
</STYLE>
</HEAD>
<body>
<DIV id=block1>
<img src="flourite3tn.JPG">
```

```
<strong>Fluorite</strong><p>
Fluorite is a member of the <em>halides</em>. Fluorite can come in
  various colors, and is a fairly common mineral. I collected this
  piece because of its unusual coloration, which the photograph
  demonstrates. This sample is one of my largest, being 4 inches
  across.
This makes it a 'hand' sample, and it comes from the Denton Mine,
  Hardin County, Illinois.
</DIV>
<DIV id=block2>
<img src="apophyllite2tn.JPG">
<strong>Apophyllite</strong><p>
Apophyllite is a member of the <em>Phyllosilicate</em> class. It is
  a colorless crystal, yet has a grayish cast. The sample is
  associated with Stilbite, which is not visible in the existing
  photograph. This sample is from Poone(Pune), India. This crystal
  can be differentiated from other clear crystals by its relative
  weight, it is a light stone, and a distinctly greasy feeling.
</DIV>
</body>
```

This example displays the two blocks side by side, as shown in Figure 10-4. Also note that the relative positioning of the first block sets the block slightly more to the right and much lower than would have occurred with absolute positioning, because the body margins are also applied to the block. In addition, the background colors of both blocks have been set to make the positioning rectangle more obvious. You can try this example yourself by opening the CD-ROM's sample file named **nstwoblk.htm**.

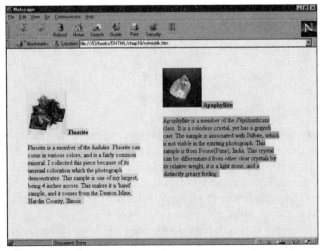

Figure 10-4: An example demonstrating how to pack one or more HTML elements into a block using the <DIV> tag, and then positioning the entire block at one time

Clip and Overflow

The `clip` property determines the shape and size of the clipping region. At this time, the clipping region can only be specified as a rectangle, and only works with absolute positioning. With Navigator, you can implement clipping on HTML block elements using CSS positioning, or with the `<LAYER>` tag. For example, the code in Listing 10-2 uses the `<LAYER>` tag to enclose an image. A timer is started and each firing of the timer shrinks the borders of the image, using the `<LAYER>` element's `clip` properties, until only the middle is showing.

Listing 10-2: The incredible shrinking image, courtesy of the <LAYER> tag and the clipping properties

```
<HEAD>
<STYLE type="text/css">
 LAYER.image1 { position: absolute; width: 295; height: 195}
</STYLE>
<SCRIPT language="javascript1.2">

current_count = 1
function shrink_image() {
  if (current_count < 15) {
        document.layers["image1"].clip.left+=5;
        document.layers["image1"].clip.right-=5;
        document.layers["image1"].clip.top+=5;
        document.layers["image1"].clip.bottom-=5;
        setTimeout("shrink_image()",200);
        }
  current_count++
}
</script>

</HEAD>
<BODY onLoad="setTimeout('shrink_image()',200)">
<LAYER name=image1 left=50 top=50>
<img src="barytocelstite.JPG" width=249 height=194>
</layer>
</BODY>
```

Notice from the code that the top- and left-hand clipping region moves inward and down by incrementing the existing clip values, while decrementing the right and bottom values moves the region inward and up. The negative or positive nature of the property determines the direction in which the clipping occurs. Adding more to the left and top clipping values moves the clipping region further to the right and bottom. Subtracting from these clipping properties moves the clipping region to the top and left side. The reverse is true for the bottom and right clipping properties. Subtracting from the bottom and right clipping values moves the clipping region further to the left and top, and adding to these properties moves the region to the right and down. You can try this yourself by opening the CD-ROM's sample file **nsclip.htm**.

Clipping also applies to other HTML elements. Taking the same Web page just demonstrated, I copied it and altered the block to be a `<DIV>` block, as shown next:

```
<DIV id=image1 style="position:absolute;left:50;top:50">
<img src="barytocelstite.JPG" width=249 height=194>
</DIV>
```

The differences between the first clipping example and the second is that the `<NAME>` attribute is used for the `<LAYER>` block in the first, and the `<id>` attribute is used to name the `<DIV>` block in the second. In addition, a style sheet is used to position the `<DIV>` block, while the positioning attributes of the `<LAYER>` tag are specified directly in the tag itself. Other than those two differences, the examples work exactly the same, as you can see for yourself by opening the sample file **nsclip2.htm**.

Clipping can be used with any HTML content, including text, and it works as well as it does with images. To demonstrate this potential, I positioned a header using a style sheet, and then shrank the header using the style `clip` properties, as follows:

```
<H1 id=header1
style="font-size:56pt;color:red;position:absolute;left:50;top:50">
This is some header
</H1>
```

The function to shrink the element is changed to `shrink_header` and the values used for the clipping are altered slightly to reflect the size of the content:

```
function shrink_header() {
  if (current_count < 15) {
      document.layers["header1"].clip.left+=10;
      document.layers["header1"].clip.right-=10;
      document.layers["header1"].clip.top+=5;
      document.layers["header1"].clip.bottom-=5;
      setTimeout("shrink_header()",200);
      }
  current_count++
}
```

This example also demonstrates that CSS positioning works on HTML elements other than just the `<DIV>` block (which has been used in most examples to this point). Read more about this in the sidebar "Navigator HTML Elements that Support CSSP Positioning." You can try out this example by accessing the sample file **nsclip3.htm**.

Navigator HTML Elements that Support CSSP Positioning

Netscape has implemented CSS positioning (referred to by Netscape as CSSP), with several HTML elements. I have tested it with headers (<H1> ... <H6> tags), paragraphs (<P>), unordered lists (<UL>), as well as the <DIV> and <SPAN> blocks, and found that all of these elements can be positioned using CSS positioning. I also tried it with forms, form elements, and images and found that these items would not position using CSS positioning, so I put these elements in either a <DIV> or <LAYER> block in order to control them using positioning attributes. Additionally, I have also found that the elements that can be positioned statically can also be positioned using the dynamic techniques demonstrated throughout this chapter.

To determine whether an element can or cannot be positioned or dynamically moved using CSS positioning, my personal recommendation is to try including the positioning attributes within the element, and if that doesn't work, enclose the element within a <SPAN> or <DIV> block and position these containers instead.

Throughout the book I mainly use the <DIV> or the <SPAN> blocks for CSS positioning, as these are the only two elements in IE that support this type of functionality.

The overflow property is used to determine what to do with content that extends beyond the rectangle defined using the positioning properties. Applicable values for this property are none, which is the default, clip, and scroll. The value of none means that no clipping is performed and the contents of the rectangle are allowed to extend beyond the boundaries. Note that this applies only to the width and height of the element set using the width and height properties. Setting values for the clipping region that are smaller than the element will clip the element, regardless of how the overflow property is set.

Visibility

The visibility property provides a way to specify whether the item is visible or hidden. The possible values for this property are:

- hidden — the item is not visible but takes up the same space it would normally take if the item were visible

- visible — the item is visible

- inherit — the default value, meaning that the item inherits its visibility property from the enclosing parent item

Note from the properties that setting an item to be hidden does not prevent the HTML document from reserving a space that would normally be required to hold the object. Also, note that by default if an enclosing element is invisible, any child element is also invisible. For example, the following code sets the image to be invisible within the <DIV> block:

```
<HEAD>
<STYLE type="text/css">
#block1 {position: absolute; top: 30px; left: 30px; width: 200px}
#image1 {position: relative; left: -20px; visibility: hidden }
</STYLE>
</HEAD>
<body>
<DIV id=block1>
This is another block of text, but one that also includes
an <SPAN id=image1><img src="three.gif"></SPAN>
image.
</DIV>
</body>
```

As shown in Figure 10-5, the text of the <DIV> block displays as it normally would with the image being present. Because no image is displayed, a gap occurs in the contents.

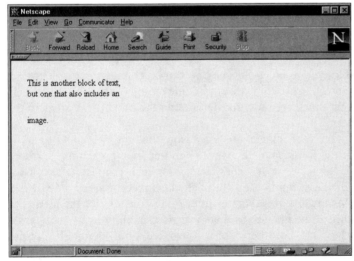

Figure 10-5: A demonstration of setting the visibility of an image to be hidden; notice that the image "space" is still provided

Setting the visibility of the <DIV> block to hidden, as the following code demonstrates, hides both the text and the image. This is because the enclosed child element, the image, inherits its visibility property from the parent element:

```
<HEAD>
<STYLE type="text/css">
#block1 {position: absolute; top: 30px;
      visibility: hidden; left: 30px; width: 200px}
#image1 {position: relative; left: -20px; }
</STYLE>
</HEAD>
<body>
<DIV id=block1>
This is another block of text, but one that also includes
an <img src="three.gif" id=image1>
image.
</DIV>
</body>
```

 When you change the visibility of an object dynamically with scripting, be careful when using the show versus the inherit values. The latter means that if the object is enclosed and the parent element is hidden, it is hidden also; the former means that the object shows regardless of the parent element's visibility.

Layering Elements

Positioning also enables you to layer objects. You can layer one or more objects by setting their absolute positions so they are placed one on top of the other in a stack. The objects lower in the stack are only visible through the transparent areas of the elements on top of them.

At my Web site I have four images on every page that act as a menu bar. The images are unchanging from page to page, enabling image caching for both Internet Explorer and Navigator. What *does* change for each page is the text associated with each of the images and the URL of the document that is loaded when an image is clicked. In versions of Navigator prior to 4.0, the text for the menu bar was located directly below the images, as there was no capability to layer objects. I never cared for this look but no other approach worked, and I definitely did not want to provide all new images for each Web page, which meant that the Web page reader had to download four new images for each newly accessed page.

But now, with absolute positioning, I can place the text of the link directly on the image, giving the images custom looks for each page without the addition of new images. With this approach, I can still take advantage of image caching and yet have a more customized look. It is also a simple process for me to change the images for the menu bar each month, as all the pages reference the same image files. All I have to do is change which image the image file contains.

The first step I took to convert my menu bar was to define style sheets for the page background and for each of the images:

```
BODY { background-image: url(snow.jpg) }
image { width: 100; height: 150 }
#logo { position: absolute; top: 20px; left: 50px;
        width: 102px }
#image1 { position: absolute; top: 20px; left: 180px}
#image2 { position: absolute; top: 20px; left: 290px}
#image3 { position: absolute; top: 20px; left: 400px}
#image4 { position: absolute; top: 20px; left: 510px}
```

Then I defined style sheets for each of my menu text bars. I also decided to use the <H2> header tag for the titles, so I added a style sheet for this, to change the font family, size, and color:

```
h2 { font-family: Cursive; font-size: 12pt;
     font-weight: 400; color: white }
#title1 { position: absolute; top: 20px; left: 185px;
     height: 20px }
#title2 { position: absolute; top: 20px; left: 295px;
     height: 20px }
#title3 { position: absolute; top: 20px; left: 405px;
     height: 20px }
#title4 { position: absolute; top: 20px; left: 515px;
     height: 20px }
```

Next, I placed the images and the titles on the page, using <DIV> blocks for the titles:

```
<body>

<!-- Set menu titles -->
<DIV id=title1>
<h2>Services</h2>
</DIV>
<DIV id=title2>
<h2>Sites</h2>
</DIV>
<DIV id=title3>
<h2>Scribbles</h2>
</DIV>
<DIV id=title4>
<h2>Samples</h2>
</DIV>

<!-- Set menu images-->
<img src="yasd.gif" id=logo>
<DIV id=image1>
```

```
<a href="http://www.yasd.com/services"><img src="menua.jpg" border=0
 id=image1></a>
</DIV>
<DIV id=image2>
<a href="http://www.yasd.com/sites"><img src="menub.jpg" border=0
 id=image2></a>
</DIV>
<DIV id=image3>
<a href="http://www.yasd.com/scribbles"><img src="menuc.jpg"
 border=0 id=image3></a>
</DIV>
<DIV id=image4>
<a href="http://www.yasd.com/samples"><img src="menud.jpg" border=0
 id=image4></a>
</DIV>
</body>
```

When all the pieces were in place, I loaded the page in the browser and all I saw were images and no titles. So what happened?

Objects are layered in the order in which they occur, with those occurring first in the document placed at the bottom of the stack, and those occurring later placed above. I embedded the images in the page last, so they were displayed on top. Because they are not transparent, the text of the menu option does not show through as demonstrated in Figure 10-6.

Figure 10-6: The image menu with menu titles not showing on images

To fix the problem of the images layered on top of the text, I could have moved the text of the titles in the HTML document so they occur last in the HTML code, but instead I decided to use the z-index positioning property. This removes any dependency on location of any element in the page, which can change each time content is added or removed from the page.

The z-index is a numeric property that determines the order in which objects are stacked. Objects with smaller z-index values are placed further down in the stack than those with larger z-index values. In other words, an object with a z-index of 2 is placed above that with a z-index of 1.

I modified the images and gave them a z-index value of 1, and gave the title styles a z-index value of 2. When I reloaded the page the titles were displayed on top of the images as planned. In order to test my example, I moved my mouse over the image. As I did, I noticed that the cursor changed from an active link cursor to the regular text cursor when it was over the titles. Because the titles now partially overlay the images, the hypertext link connection for the images didn't work when the mouse was over the text. To correct this problem, I also added the hypertext link to the titles as well as the images:

```
<!-- Set menu titles -->
<DIV id=title1>
<h2><a href="http://www.yasd.com/services">Services</a></h2>
</DIV>
<DIV id=title2>
<h2><a href="http://www.yasd.com/sites">Sites</a></h2>
</DIV>
<DIV id=title3>
<h2><a href="http://www.yasd.com/scribbles">Scribbles</a></h2>
</DIV>
<DIV id=title4>
<h2><a href="http://www.yasd.com/samples">Samples</a></h2>
</DIV>
```

Unfortunately, this triggered the visited and unvisited link colors set within my browser. I wanted to control the colors that appeared on the images so I added style sheet rules for the links to change the color to white for visited and unvisited links, and to remove the default underline text decoration from the link. As I only wanted this to have an impact on my image titles, I only applied this change to all hypertext links embedded within <H2> headers:

```
h2 A { text-decoration: none; color: white }
h2 A:link { color-white }
h2 A:visited { color: white }
```

When I reloaded the page after implementing these changes, the image titles displayed in the appropriate location and were white with no underlines, as shown in Figure 10-7.

Figure 10-7: The image menus with the menu titles showing
appropriately on the images

To make effective use of the image bar, I packaged the title and image style sheets
in a separate CSS1 style sheet file and linked it to every one of my pages. Then I
added the image and text HTML with the links and text appropriate to the page.
Listing 10-3 shows the use of the menu bar layering with my main Web page. Listing
10-4 shows how the menu bar would be modified for my JavaScript sample page.

Listing 10-3: The main Web page with the menu bar set to the main page menu hierarchy

```
<HEAD>
<LINK REL=STYLESHEET TYPE="text/css"
 HREF="nsmenu.css">
</HEAD>
<body>
<!-- Set menu images-->
<img src="yasd.gif" id=logo>
<DIV id=image1>
<a href="http://www.yasd.com/services"><img src="menua.jpg" border=0
 id=image1></a>
</DIV>
<DIV id=image2>
<a href="http://www.yasd.com/sites"><img src="menub.jpg" border=0
 id=image2></a>
</DIV>
<DIV id=image3>
<a href="http://www.yasd.com/scribbles"><img src="menuc.jpg"
 border=0 id=image3></a>
</DIV>
<DIV id=image4>
<a href="http://www.yasd.com/samples"><img src="menud.jpg" border=0
 id=image4></a>
```

```
</DIV>

<!-- Set menu titles -->
<DIV id=title1>
<h2><a href="http://www.yasd.com/services">Services</a></h2>
</DIV>
<DIV id=title2>
<h2><a href="http://www.yasd.com/sites">Sites</a></h2>
</DIV>
<DIV id=title3>
<h2><a href="http://www.yasd.com/scribbles">Scribbles</a></h2>
</DIV>
<DIV id=title4>
<h2><a href="http://www.yasd.com/samples">Samples</a></h2>
</DIV>

</body>
```

Listing 10-4: The same menu bar style sheet and layering with different URL targets and titles

```
<HEAD>
<LINK REL=STYLESHEET TYPE="text/css"
 HREF="nsmenu.css">
</HEAD>
<body>
<!-- Set menu images-->
<img src="yasd.gif" id=logo>
<DIV id=image1>
<a href="http://www.yasd.com/services"><img src="menua.jpg" border=0
 id=image1></a>
</DIV>
<DIV id=image2>
<a href="http://www.yasd.com/sites"><img src="menub.jpg" border=0
 id=image2></a>
</DIV>
<DIV id=image3>
<a href="http://www.yasd.com/scribbles"><img src="menuc.jpg"
 border=0 id=image3></a>
</DIV>
<DIV id=image4>
<a href="http://www.yasd.com/samples"><img src="menud.jpg" border=0
 id=image4></a>
</DIV>

<!-- Set menu titles -->
<DIV id=title1>
<h2><a href="http://www.yasd.com">Main</a></h2>
</DIV>
<DIV id=title2>
<h2><a href="http://www.yasd.com/samples">Samples</a></h2>
</DIV>
<DIV id=title3>
```

```
<h2><a
 href="http://www.yasd.com/samples/scripting">Scripting</a></h2>
</DIV>
<DIV id=title4>
<h2>JavaScript</h2>
</DIV>
</body>
```

You can try out these examples yourself. The main Web page is in the sample file **nsmain.htm** and the JavaScript sample page is in the file **nsjs.htm**. The CSS1 style sheet file is **nsmenu.css**. More complex uses of layering are provided in Chapter 15.

Dynamically Changing Positions of Elements

So far, the examples in this chapter have demonstrated how to position elements statically, using the `<LAYER>` tag, or using other HTML elements and CSS positioning, as defined by the CSS positioning draft specification currently under review by the W3C. For more information on CSS positioning, refer to Appendix A for the URL of the specification.

Navigator 4.0 also supports dynamic CSS positioning, again through the use of the `<LAYER>` element, and through the access of CSS positioning attributes. HTML elements can be accessed in script by their identifiers, directly, or from the built-in layers array. Once named, the element can be accessed using any of the following techniques:

```
document.layers["idname"]...
document.idname...
document.layers[index of element]
```

You can access layers created with the `<LAYER>` tag using these same approaches, but you must use the layer `<NAME>` attribute:

```
document.layers["name"]...
document.name...
document.layers[index of element]
```

To demonstrate dynamically altering the positioning properties of a `<LAYER>`, after the page containing it is loaded, I modified the code in Listing 10-1. The two blocks are still positioned, statically, within the Web page, but now I use the moveTo `<LAYER>` method. Clicking the button in the second block switches the position of both blocks, dynamically. The following code contains the code for the altered Web page. Notice that the two `<LAYER>` elements each enclose an image and the associated text, and that the second block also contains a form with one control — a button.

```
<HEAD>
<SCRIPT language="javascript">
function switch_blocks() {
    if (document.layers["block1"].x == 20) {
  document.layers["block1"].moveTo(350,50);
  document.layers["block2"].moveTo(20,50);
      }
    else {
  document.layers["block2"].moveTo(350,50);
  document.layers["block1"].moveTo(20,50);
      }
}
</SCRIPT>

</HEAD>
<body>
<layer id=block1 left=20 top=50 width=300>
<img src="flourite3tn.JPG">
<strong>Fluorite</strong><p>
Fluorite is a member of the <em>halides</em>. Fluorite can come in
  various colors, and is a fairly common mineral. I collected this
  piece because of its unusual coloration which the photograph
  demonstrates. This sample is one of my largest, being 4 inches
  across. This makes it a 'hand' sample, and it comes from the Denton
  Mine, Hardin County, Illinois.
</layer>

<layer id=block2 left=350 top=50 width=300>
<img src="apophyllite2tn.JPG">
<strong>Apophyllite</strong><p>
Apophyllite is a member of the <em>Phyllosilicate</em> class. It is
  a colorless crystal, yet has a grayish cast. The sample is
  associated with Stilbite, which is not visible in the existing
  photograph. This sample is from Poone(Pune), India. This crystal
  can be differentiated from other clear crystals by its relative
  weight, it is a light stone, and a distinctly greasy feeling.
<p>
<form>
<INPUT type=button name="transfer" value="Switch blocks"
  onclick="switch_blocks()">
</form>
</layer>
</body>
```

If I had used the moveBy method instead of moveTo, the blocks would be moved by the specified amount, which would mean that both blocks would literally fall off the sides of the Web page. You will want to exercise some caution and ensure that you use the correct method. You can see for yourself by opening the CD-ROM's sample file **nsmvblk.htm**.

Note that the values specified with the moveBy method can be negative as well as positive. A negative value moves the element in the opposite direction as a positive value. For movement along the y-axis, a negative value moves the element up the page as values of *y* increase from top to bottom. For movement along the x-axis, a negative value moves the element from the right to the left side of the page as values of *x* increase from left to right.

To produce the same Web page using CSS style sheets instead of layers, you first create the CSS style sheet, as follows:

```
<STYLE type="text/css">
  .block1 { position: absolute; left:20; top:50;
            width: 300}
  .block2 { position: absolute; left:350; top:50;
            width: 300 }
</STYLE>
```

The positions of the classes are exactly equivalent to the two layers in the previous version of the example. Next, instead of enclosing the content within layers, enclose it within <DIV> tags, as the following snippet demonstrates (I have only included the part of the page that is pertinent to the example here):

```
<DIV id=blk1 class=block1>
...
</DIV>
```

Finally, I modified the JavaScript code to reference the identifiers given to the two <DIV> blocks, and used the left property of these blocks to move their position:

```
<SCRIPT language="javascript">
function switch_blocks() {
   if (document.blk1.left == 20) {
 document.blk1.left=350;
 document.blk2.left=20;
   }
   else {
 document.blk1.left=20;
 document.blk2.left=350;
   }
}
</SCRIPT>
```

You can test this new version of the "switching blocks" example by accessing the sample file **nsmvdivs.htm** on the CD-ROM.

Again, to restate an earlier note, I have tested the CSS dynamic positioning technique with images, block-quotes, paragraphs, lists, tables, the <SPAN> tag, and the <DIV> tag. I found that dynamic positioning works with all of the elements except images (enclosed within <IMG> tags) and form elements. It even worked when I applied the technique to rows and cells within a table. However, a major limitation of the CSS technique is that most HTML elements do not trigger events based on user actions. Chapter 12, which covers interaction with the Web page reader, provides a workaround for this limitation.

Creating Animations with Layers

You can use the <LAYER> tag or any of the block-level HTML elements capable of being positioned to create animations. The real key is to load images into layers that are hidden, so that no breaks occur in the animation due to image loading once the animation starts.

I have a dynamic HTML example page at my Web site that shows an animated menu bar. I decided to use this example page here, but with an added little twist that is guaranteed to catch your Web page reader's attention. The surprise is an animated menu bar that moves away from Web page readers each time they approach it with their mouse.

To start, I added seven layers to the Web page, the first six set to enclose six different images and the seventh layer to contain the "images are loading . . ." message, so the Web page reader knows what's going on. Listing 10-5 contains the page contents.

Listing 10-5: The contents of the layer animation example page

```
<BODY bgcolor="white" onload="cycle()">
<layer name="menu1" left=0 top=0 visibility="hidden"
       onmouseover=
       "keep_away(event.pageX, event.pageY, 0)">
<img src="menu2.jpg"
 border=0 width=87 height=91>
</layer>

<layer name="menu2" left=142 top=0 visibility="hidden"
 onmouseover="keep_away(event.pageX, event.pageY, 1)">
<img src="menu3.jpg"
 width=87 height=91 border=0>
</layer>

<layer name="menu3" left=284 top=0 visibility="hidden"
 onmouseover="keep_away(event.pageX, event.pageY, 2)">
<img src="menu6.jpg"
 border=0 width=87 height=91>
</layer>

<layer name="menu4" left=0 top=192 visibility="hidden"
 onmouseover="keep_away(event.pageX, event.pageY, 3)">
<img src="menu1.jpg"
 border=0 width=87 height=91>
</layer>
```

```
<layer name="menu5" left=142 top=192 visibility="hidden"
 onmouseover="keep_away(event.pageX, event.pageY, 4)">
<img src="menu4.jpg"
 border=0 width=87 height=91>
</layer>

<layer name="menu6" left=284 top=192 visibility="hidden"
 onmouseover="keep_away(event.pageX, event.pageY, 5)">
<img src="menu5.jpg"
 border=0 width=87 height=91>
</layer>

<LAYER name="waitimage">
<DIV id=imagewait>
<h4>Images are loading...please wait</h4>
</DIV>
</LAYER>
```

Notice from the code that a function called cycle is called when the page finishes loading, and another function called keep_away is called as a result of a mouseover event for each of the layers that contain an image. The name of the latter function should give you an inkling of what the page is going to do when I am done.

In the head section of the Web page document, I created a style sheet for the layer that tells the reader the images are loaded, as shown next:

```
<STYLE type="text/css">
#imagewait { position: absolute; top: 125;
             left: 70 }
</STYLE>
```

I then created the JavaScript block that contains the functions that animate the images when the page first loads. The JavaScript block also contains functions that implement my little surprise. First, Listing 10-6 contains the function for the page-loading animation. The cycle function creates two new arrays, each containing the coordinates the individual images traverse when the animation begins. One array holds the x coordinates; the other holds the y coordinates. The images that were hidden until the page is finished loading are also exposed, and a timer is started to begin the animation.

Listing 10-6: A JavaScript function to animate the menu bar after the page loads

```
<SCRIPT language="javascript1.2">

// global variables
var TimingObjectsX
var TimingObjectsY
var currentTick = 0
var most_top
```

```
var most_right

// create arrays, set coordinates,
// expose images, hide image loading, and start timer
function cycle() {
 most_top = document.height;
 most_right = document.width;

 TimingObjectsX = new Array(6)
 TimingObjectsY = new Array(6)
 TimingObjectsX[0] = new
       Array(0,12,25,37,50,90,120,142)
 TimingObjectsY[0] = new Array(0,12,25,37,50,50,50,50)
 TimingObjectsX[1] = new
       Array(142,142,142,142,142,167,200,234)
 TimingObjectsY[1] = new Array(0,12,25,37,50,50,50,50)
 TimingObjectsX[2] = new
       Array(284,271,259,246,234,234,234,234)
 TimingObjectsY[2] = new
       Array(0,12,25,37,50,107,122,142)

 TimingObjectsX[3] = new Array(0,12,25,37,50,50,50,50)
 TimingObjectsY[3] = new
       Array(192,179,167,155,142,107,77,50)
 TimingObjectsX[4] = new
       Array(142,142,142,142,142,107,77,50)
 TimingObjectsY[4] = new
       Array(192,179,167,155,142,142,142,142)

 TimingObjectsX[5] = new
       Array(284,271,259,246,234,196,161,142)
 TimingObjectsY[5] = new
       Array(192,179,167,155,142,142,142,142)

 document.layers["menu1"].visibility="show"
 document.layers["menu2"].visibility="show"
 document.layers["menu3"].visibility="show"
 document.layers["menu4"].visibility="show"
 document.layers["menu5"].visibility="show"
 document.layers["menu6"].visibility="show"
 document.layers["waitimage"].visibility="hidden"

 setTimeout("MoveObjects()", 400)
}

// move each image along path
function MoveObjects() {
 document.layers["menu1"].moveTo
       (TimingObjectsX[0][currentTick],
TimingObjectsY[0][currentTick])
 document.layers["menu2"].moveTo
       (TimingObjectsX[1][currentTick],
TimingObjectsY[1][currentTick])
 document.layers["menu3"].moveTo
```

```
    (TimingObjectsX[2][currentTick],
TimingObjectsY[2][currentTick])
  document.layers["menu4"].moveTo
    (TimingObjectsX[3][currentTick],
TimingObjectsY[3][currentTick])
  document.layers["menu5"].moveTo
    (TimingObjectsX[4][currentTick],
TimingObjectsY[4][currentTick])
  document.layers["menu6"].moveTo
    (TimingObjectsX[5][currentTick],
TimingObjectsY[5][currentTick])

  currentTick++
  if (currentTick < 8)
    setTimeout("MoveObjects()", 400)
}
```

The JavaScript timer calls another function, MoveObjects, which uses the layer moveTo method to move each of the layers to the next coordinate, which is accessed from the *x* and *y* arrays. A new timer is created and the function is called again until all of the coordinates have been played and the images are in position.

That's all I needed to do to create an animated image menu bar. However, because I was having a little fun, I added that extra function I mentioned before. This function is shown in Listing 10-7 and is called keep_away. It checks to see which layer the mouse is over and then moves that layer. This results in the images literally moving all over the page as the reader chases them with the mouse.

Listing 10-7: The keep_away function, which moves the layer images away from the Web page reader's mouse

```
// prevent reader from clicking on image
function keep_away(x, y, layer_number) {
  if (layer_number < 2) {
    document.layers[layer_number].moveBy(0, 50);
    if (document.layers[layer_number].y >=
          most_top + 90)
      document.layers[layer_number].moveTo(0, 0);
    }
  else {
    document.layers[layer_number].moveBy(50, 0);
    if ((document.layers[layer_number].x) >=
          most_right + 90)
      document.layers[layer_number].moveTo(0,0);
    }
}
```

The function is relatively simple, but fairly effective. It is also a good demonstration of animation based on reader interaction, as well as more passive animation based on some other event. You can try this yourself, by accessing the CD-ROM's sample file **aniexmpl.htm**.

For a last demonstration, you will learn how to convert the animated menu map to using CSS positioning. You can dynamically move elements enclosed within <SPAN> or <DIV> or other block-level tags, based on CSS positioning. Because these elements will not capture events, you can use event trapping and make assignments to an event handler with the <DIV> blocks, an example of which is demonstrated next.

Taking the animated menu bar example just demonstrated, alter the blocks to be <DIV> blocks (remember, images cannot be positioned). First, add style sheets to the blocks and remove the embedded event handlers. An example of one of the <DIV> blocks is given next:

```
<DIV id=menu1
style="position:absolute;left:
  0;top:0;visibility:hidden">
<img src="menu2.jpg"
  border=0 width=87 height=91>
</DIV>
```

Next, alter the `cycle` function to add in the event trapping. Add this in after the page is loaded, otherwise you'll get a JavaScript error because nonfunction-based script is processed before all the elements in the page are created. The added cycle code follows:

```
// assign event to event handler
document.layers["menu1"].onmouseover=keep_away;
document.layers["menu2"].onmouseover=keep_away;
document.layers["menu3"].onmouseover=keep_away;
document.layers["menu4"].onmouseover=keep_away;
document.layers["menu5"].onmouseover=keep_away;
document.layers["menu6"].onmouseover=keep_away;
```

Finally, add a slight alteration to the `keep_away` function to pull in the ID of the <DIV> block to use in place of the layer index. Also, adjust the comparison operation of the conditional *if* statement to compare to the menu name rather than menu position. Because "menu1" is lexically less than "menu3," and so on, this is just as effective a method to use as the menu item index:

```
var layer_number = e.target.name;
if (layer_number < "menu3") {
```

That's all you have to do to convert the animated menu map to using CSS positioning. You can try this for yourself by opening the sample file **aniexmpl2.htm.**

Using Positioning to Create Animated Effects

Now that you have had a chance to work with absolute positioning to statically and dynamically manipulate elements on a page using various techniques, this section pulls all of these techniques together to show you how to add animated effects to the menu bar.

The animated effect I am about to illustrate dynamically pulls in the menu images from the sides of the Web page just after it is loaded. It then has them meet at the exact same time, and in the position in which they remain until the page is changed. I make use of the existing style sheets that were created with the menu bar previously, except that I add a timer and my array-based paths to animate the menu bar just after the page is loaded. Finally, the images are layered with the text, as defined in previous examples, to create the customized menu bar appearance I want. Open the **nstrns.htm** sample file on the CD-ROM to see this animated effect at work. Listing 10-8 provides the complete Web page code.

Listing 10-8: Using synchronized paths for an animated menu bar

```
<HEAD>
<STYLE TYPE="text/css">
  BODY { background-image: url(snow.jpg) }
  image { width: 100; height: 150 }
  h2 { font-family: Cursive; font-size: 12pt;
        font-weight: 700; color: yellow }
  h2 A { text-decoration: none; color: yellow }
  h2 A:link { color: yellow }
  h2 A:visited { color: yellow }
  #logo { position: absolute; top: 20px; left: 50px;
                width: 102px }
  #title1 { position: absolute; top: 20px; left: 185px;
                z-index: 2; height: 20px; width: 1px }
  #title2 { position: absolute; top: 20px; left: 295px;
                z-index: 2; height: 20px; width: 1px  }
  #title3 { position: absolute; top: 20px; left: 405px;
                z-index: 2; height: 20px; width: 1px  }
  #title4 { position: absolute; top: 20px; left: 515px;
                z-index: 2; height: 20px; width: 1px  }
</STYLE>

<SCRIPT language="javascript1.2">
<!--
currentTick = 0;

// global path arrays
TimingObjectsX = new Array(4);
TimingObjectsY = new Array(4);
TimingObjectsX[0] = new Array(-100,50,75,120,150,180);
TimingObjectsY[0] = new Array(400,350,220,150,100,20);
```

```
TimingObjectsX[1] = new Array(290,290,290,290,290,290);
TimingObjectsY[1] = new Array(600,500,400,300,200,20);

TimingObjectsX[2] = new Array(600,580,530,480,430,400);
TimingObjectsY[2] = new Array(600,500,400,300,200,20);

TimingObjectsX[3] = new Array(900,800,750,620,550,510);
TimingObjectsY[3] = new Array(400,350,220,150,100,20);

// timer variable
var hold = null;

// function to move objects to
// next coordinate
// checks to see if finished
// if yes, clear interval
function MoveObjects() {
 document.layers["image1"].moveTo
       (TimingObjectsX[0][currentTick],
       TimingObjectsY[0][currentTick]);
 document.layers["image2"].moveTo
       (TimingObjectsX[1][currentTick],
       TimingObjectsY[1][currentTick]);
 document.layers["image3"].moveTo
       (TimingObjectsX[2][currentTick],
       TimingObjectsY[2][currentTick]);
 document.layers["image4"].moveTo
       (TimingObjectsX[3][currentTick],
       TimingObjectsY[3][currentTick]);
 currentTick++;
 if (currentTick >=6 )
       clearInterval(hold);
}
</script>

<BODY onLoad="setInterval('MoveObjects()',200)">
<!-- Set menu images-->
<DIV id=logo>
<img src="yasd.gif">
</DIV>

<LAYER id=image1 left=-100 top=400>
 <a href="http://www.yasd.com/services">
 <img src="menua.jpg" border=0></a>
</LAYER>
<LAYER id=image2 left=290 top=600>
 <a href="http://www.yasd.com/sites">
 <img src="menub.jpg" border=0></a>
</LAYER>
<LAYER id=image3 left=600 top=600>
 <a href="http://www.yasd.com/scribbles">
 <img src="menuc.jpg" border=0></a>
</LAYER>
<LAYER id=image4 left=900 top=400>
```

```
<a href="http://www.yasd.com/samples">
<img src="menud.jpg" border=0></a>
</LAYER>

<!-- Set menu titles -->
<DIV id=title1>
<h2>
<a href="http://www.yasd.com/services">Services</a></h2>
</DIV>
<DIV id=title2>
<h2>
<a href="http://www.yasd.com/sites">Sites</a></h2>
</DIV>
<DIV id=title3>
<h2>
<a href="http://www.yasd.com/scribbles">Scribbles</a></h>
</DIV>
<DIV id=title4>
<h2>
<a href="http://www.yasd.com/samples">Samples</a></h2>
</DIV>
</body>
```

In this example, I modified the main page example to include this animated effect. First, to make things a bit simpler, I embedded the style sheet directly back into the Web page to make it easier to work with when testing changes. Then I added eight array-based paths and set the *x* and *y* coordinates for each. Finally, I trapped the onLoad event for the window, and created a function that sets the path targets and starts the synchronization timer.

Because I am mixing the <LAYER> and <DIV> tags in this example, the z-index ordering does not necessarily work in regard to each other. Due to this limitation, I placed the titles last in the document to ensure they load on top of the images. I also could have used the <LAYER> tags for the titles in addition to the images. Or I could have used the <DIV> tags for the entire application. However, I wanted to demonstrate how to mix the two techniques. Also, notice that I used timer *interval* functions, setInterval and clearInterval, instead of the setTimer function used in earlier examples. With these functions, the timer keeps firing until it is specifically cleared. The best thing about this effect is that it places no additional burden on either the server or the Internet, and results in no increased download times in order to implement this effect.

The Preview Example Revisited

At the beginning of this chapter you saw a preview example of positioning with Netscape Navigator (the **nsqckpos.htm** file on the CD-ROM, and its variation file **nsqckps2.htm)**. Now that you've learned about positioning, you'll see the details of that preview example as well as a variation.

To review, the preview example uses both absolute positioning and layers to place four images and a button on a Web page. Arrays are created for each image, and each array contains either the *x* or *y* coordinates of a path that the image follows each time the button is pressed. When the button is pressed, the images cycle, following their designated paths. The path changes for every cycle, and this process continues until each image has circled the page completely. Listing 10-9 shows the code for the "quick start" example.

Listing 10-9: Netscape Navigator's positioning capability, using absolute positioning, an array of coordinates, and a timer

```
<HEAD>
<SCRIPT LANGUAGE="JavaScript1.2">
<!--
// global variables
var TimingObjectsX
var TimingObjectsY
var object_order = new Array(4)
var currentTick = 0
var current_cycle = 3

// coordinate path arrays
TimingObjectsX = new Array(4)
TimingObjectsY = new Array(4)
TimingObjectsX[0] = new
      Array(150,165,180,195,210,225,240,255,270,285,30)
TimingObjectsY[0] = new
      Array(200,185,170,155,140,125,110,95,80,65,50)

TimingObjectsX[1] = new
      Array(300,315,330,345,360,375,390,405,420,435,45)
TimingObjectsY[1] = new
      Array(50,65,80,95,110,125,140,155,170,185,200)

TimingObjectsX[2] = new
      Array(450,435,420,405,390,375,360,345,330,315,30)
TimingObjectsY[2] = new
      Array(200,215,230,245,260,275,290,305,320,335,35)

TimingObjectsX[3] = new
      Array(300,285,270,255,240,225,210,195,180,165,15)
TimingObjectsY[3] = new
      Array(350,335,320,305,290,275,260,245,230,215,20)

// cycle function, determine image path
// and start timer
function cycle() {
 current_cycle++;
 if (current_cycle == 1) {
      object_order[0] = 1;
      object_order[1] = 2;
      object_order[2] = 3;
```

```
        object_order[3] = 0;
        }
else if (current_cycle == 2) {
        object_order[0] = 2;
        object_order[1] = 3;
        object_order[2] = 0;
        object_order[3] = 1;
        }
else if (current_cycle == 3) {
        object_order[0] = 3;
        object_order[1] = 0;
        object_order[2] = 1;
        object_order[3] = 2;
        }
else    {
        for (i = 0; i < 4; i++)
                object_order[i] = i;
        current_cycle = 0;
        }
setTimeout("MoveObjects()", 200)
}

// move object to next coordinate in path
function MoveObjects() {
var first = object_order[0];
var second = object_order[1];
var third = object_order[2];
var fourth = object_order[3];
document.layers["container1"].moveTo
        (TimingObjectsX[first][currentTick],
        TimingObjectsY[first][currentTick])
document.layers["container2"].moveTo
        (TimingObjectsX[second][currentTick],
        TimingObjectsY[second][currentTick])
document.layers["container3"].moveTo
        (TimingObjectsX[third][currentTick],
        TimingObjectsY[third][currentTick])
document.layers["container4"].moveTo
        (TimingObjectsX[fourth][currentTick],
        TimingObjectsY[fourth][currentTick])

  // if not at end of path, reset timer
currentTick++
if (currentTick < 11)
        setTimeout("MoveObjects()", 200)
else
        currentTick = 0;
}
//-->
</SCRIPT>


</HEAD>
<BODY>
```

```
<layer name=container1 top=200 left=150>
<img src="one.gif" width=90 height=29 >
</layer>
<layer name=container2 top=50 left=300>
<img src="two.gif" id=container2 width=97 height=30 >
</layer>
<layer id=container3 top=200 left=450>
<img src="three.gif" width=145 height=28 id=container3>
</layer>
<layer id=container4 top=350 left=300>
<img src="four.gif" width=119 height=29 >
</layer>
<layer id=container5 top=10 left=10>
<form>
<input type=button value="Cycle Images" onClick="cycle()">
</form>
</layer>
</BODY>
```

Notice in the code that the top-left corner of each image is set using the `layer` object properties `left` and `top`. Additionally, the button is also placed using absolute positioning, by setting its position with these same properties.

The location of the images when the page is loaded is determined from the initial layer settings (as shown previously in Figure 10-1). To move the image, the layer `moveTo` method is used, and the left and top coordinates from the arrays are passed to the `<LAYER>` method. Clicking the button a couple of times moves the images to their diametrically opposite positions (as previously seen in Figure 10-2). You can try this for yourself by accessing the sample file named **nsqckpos.htm**. For fun, try changing the timer value to a value of 50 instead of 200, and see what difference this makes in how the demonstration works.

This example of static and dynamic positioning would not be complete without demonstrating that the exact same Web page can be created using `<DIV>` blocks and CSS1 static and dynamic positioning.

You can find a variation of this example using dynamic style sheets in the **nsqckps2.htm** sample file. In this example, I enclosed the images and button within `<DIV>` blocks and instead of using the `moveTo` method, the images are moved by assigning new values to the `left` and `top` properties of the image block. In addition, each `<DIV>` block is referenced directly by its name.

The following portion of code from this second example shows the style sheet setting used to place the images and button when the page first loads, how the first image is moved, and how the first image is defined within the page:

```
<STYLE type="text/css">
 #container1 { position: absolute; top:200; left:150 }
 #container2 { position: absolute; top:50; left:300 }
 #container3 { position: absolute; top:200; left: 450 }
 #container4 { position: absolute; top: 350; left: 300 }
 #container5 { position: absolute; top:10; left: 10 }
</STYLE>
```

```
. . .
document.container1.left=
      TimingObjectsX[first][currentTick];
document.container1.top=
      TimingObjectsY[first][currentTick];
. . .
<DIV id=container1>
<img src="one.gif" width=90 height=29 >
</DIV>
```

The style sheet sets the original position of the images and button blocks using absolute positioning. I could also have set the style sheet values directly in the individual `<DIV>` tags, using a technique such as:

```
<DIV id=container1 style="position:absolute; top:100;left:300">
```

Notice that the individual elements are not accessed from the layers array (although this is possible), but instead access each element directly from the `docu-ment` object. Also, instead of a `moveTo` method, the `left` and `top` property values of the element are set. Finally, the images (and the form with the button) are enclosed within a `<DIV>` block, whose ID is set to the same style sheet that deter-mines its initial position. You can try this example by accessing the file **nsqckps2.htm** on the CD-ROM.

Summary

This chapter gave you a chance to work with some of the new HTML positioning capabilities Netscape has provided in Navigator 4.0. The chapter included many examples, and covered the key concepts. To find out more, Appendix A has several URLs that point to other sources of information on HTML positioning.

In this chapter you learned:

◆ How to package multiple HTML elements into packages using the `<DIV>`, `<LAYER>`, and `<SPAN>` tags

◆ How to use absolute and relative positioning for complete control over where an object is placed

◆ How to use the `<LAYER>` tag to position and move HTML content

◆ How script can be used to dynamically change the positions of HTML objects

◆ How layering techniques, including the `z-index` property, can provide you with the ability to control the foreground placement of objects in the same two-dimensional position

◆ How absolute positioning, layers, dynamic HTML, and array-based paths can be used to animate elements on a Web page

In the next chapter you will learn how to dynamically change the properties of HTML elements. You'll also learn about some workarounds that enable you to alter the styles of an element, or create some interesting animated effects.

Chapter 11

Dynamically Changing the Look of HTML Elements in Netscape Navigator

IN THIS CHAPTER

- ◆ JavaScript Accessible Style Sheets and a preview example
- ◆ JASS style setting properties
- ◆ Dynamic fonts
- ◆ Using layers to alter the appearance of traditional HTML elements
- ◆ Creating simple special effects

WITH ITS RELEASE OF Navigator 4.x, Netscape introduced *JavaScript Accessible Style Sheets* (JASS), which differed from the Cascading Style Sheet Standard, Level 1 (CSS1). JavaScript Accessible Style Sheets enable you to apply scripting techniques to alter the appearance of a Web page *before* the page is loaded. You'll get to see these style sheets in action in this chapter.

In Navigator 4.0, Netscape also introduced *dynamic fonts*, which are fonts that can be downloaded with the page. Unlike Microsoft, Netscape did not expose the CSS1 style sheet attributes of traditional HTML elements to their scripting model, which means you can't change the appearance of elements on the fly. What you can do, though, is use layers, and hide and reveal these layers, to give the illusion that you are altering Web page elements directly. I'll show you how to use these fonts later in this chapter, but first, I'll describe and demonstrate JASS.

JavaScript Accessible Style Sheets: A Preview Example

To quickly familiarize you with JavaScript Accessible Style Sheets, I developed an application that uses JASS to specify the look and layout of a Web page. The example uses a screen resolution object that formats the Web page according to screen resolution. To see JASS and this screen resolution object in action, open the sample file named **jssqst.htm** on the CD-ROM. If you open this file in different resolutions, you'll find that the Web page displays differently depending on screen resolution. Figure 11-1 shows the page displayed with 800 × 600 resolution. The last section of this chapter lists the code in this small application and describes its inner workings.

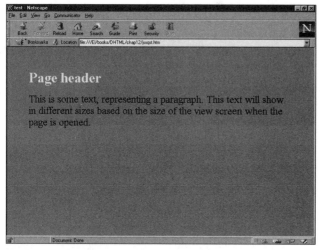

Figure 11-1: The example page at 800 × 600 resolution showing the impact of JASS script

Including JASS

As the example in the first section demonstrated, you can set HTML element styles by referencing the `tags` property of the `document` object. If the style setting had occurred within style blocks (delimited by `<STYLE>` and `</STYLE>`), the `document` specifier could have been dropped, as shown in the following code:

```
<STYLE type="text/jss">
tags.BODY.backgroundColor="red";
</STYLE>
```

In addition, the element's style can be specified directly within an element, as demonstrated here:

```
<H1 style="color='red'">
```

JASS can also be linked into a document using the CSS1 link technique, except the type needs to be `text/javascript` instead of `text/css` as the following code shows:

```
<LINK REL=STYLESHEET TYPE="text/JavaScript"
      HREF="somestyle.htm">
```

JASS styles can be combined with other JASS style settings, and they can be combined with CSS1. The rules that determine how the styles combine basically state that the last style listed has precedence, and more specific styles closer to the target element take precedence over the more generic ones. As the following code demonstrates, inline styles override those created from files or embedded styles (style blocks in the HEAD of the page):

```
<STYLE type="text/jss">
 tags.H1.color="green";
</STYLE>
...
<H1 STYLE="color='red'">This is the header</STYLE>
```

The header that has the inline style will display as red, while any other headers will display as green, because the inline style overrides the embedded style sheet.

JASS Tags, Classes, and IDs

You may have noticed that all the previous examples used the `tags` specifier for the style setting. The `tags` specifier sets a particular style setting to all HTML elements of that type within the Web page. Two other options are the `class` and the `ID` specifiers. The former is used for all specific HTML elements that share the same class name, and the latter is used with the HTML element(s) that have that specific ID.

The following example code applies the color, margin, and font changes only to the HTML elements that use the specified class name. All the other elements in the document display using the default format:

```
<SCRIPT language="javascript1.2">
 document.classes.NEWPARA.all.color="red";
 document.classes.NEWPARA.all.fontSize="18pt";
 document.classes.NEWPARA.all.backgroundColor="yellow";
 document.classes.NEWPARA.all.marginLeft="0.5in";
</SCRIPT>
```

Figure 11-2 shows the result when you apply this style sheet setting to a Web page that contains a couple of different paragraphs and a couple of different headers.

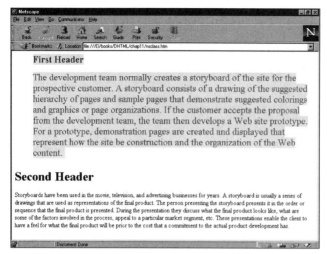

Figure 11-2: Applying the named class JavaScript style sheet
settings to the first header and paragraph

Notice in the figure that the first paragraph and header are displayed using the
style sheet settings, and the second header and paragraph are displayed using
default formatting. The code to apply these styles follows:

```
<H1 class=NEWPARA>
...
<P class=NEWPARA>
```

Using classes, you can apply a group of style settings to multiple HTML elements, and only the new settings will apply. You can try this yourself, and try out
different styles by accessing the sample file **nsclass.htm** on the CD-ROM.

The ID attribute, IDS, is used mainly to define an exception to the default formatting for a specific element. For example, the style settings in the previous code
can be extended to include an exception to the NEWPARA style setting. This exception would set the color to green instead of red:

```
<SCRIPT language="javascript1.2">
  document.classes.NEWPARA.all.color="red";
  document.classes.NEWPARA.all.fontSize="18pt";
  document.classes.NEWPARA.all.backgroundColor="yellow";
  document.classes.NEWPARA.all.marginLeft="0.5in";
  document.ids.except.color="green";
</SCRIPT>
```

You can apply this exception to a header, using the following code:

```
<H1 class=NEWPARA id=except>
```

Try this yourself by modifying the **nsclass.htm** sample file, and override any one of the existing style settings for any one of the HTML elements on the page.

JASS Style Properties

Not all aspects of a Web page can be set with JASS, but most can. This section details the properties that can be set, including font, text, and block-level properties, as well as background colors, images, lists, and white space.

FONT PROPERTIES

Several font properties can be set or altered using JASS, including the font family, font size, style, and weight. Table 11-1 lists each JASS font property.

TABLE 11-1 JASS Font Properties

Font Property	Description	Values
fontSize	Size of font	Absolute size (keyword), percentage, relative size, or number
fontFamily	Font family name	Name, such as "Arial"
fontWeight	Weight of the font	Keyword, and number from 100 to 900
fontStyle	Style of font	Keyword, such as italic

The following example uses the absolute size value keyword `large` with the `fontSize` property:

```
tags.P.fontSize = "large";
```

Other values that work with the `fontSize` property are:

- ◆ Percentage, such as 50%
- ◆ Relative size, such as `smaller` or `larger`
- ◆ A numeric value, such as 12
- ◆ Absolute values specified as a unit of measure, such as 12pt

The `fontWeight` property formats the weight of the font, making it slimmer or bolder. An example of using the `fontWeight` property to create a bold font with a numeric value is shown in the following code:

```
tags.P.fontWeight = 700;
```

Other values that work with the `fontWeight` property are:

- ◆ Keyword, such as `normal`, `bold`, `bolder`, or `lighter`
- ◆ Numeric value from 100 to 900

The `fontFamily` property specifies the font family. An example of this property, which sets all elements of the class to the font family "Arial," appears in the following snippet:

```
classes.newfont.all.fontFamily="Arial";
```

Not all fonts are available on all platforms, which can cause problems for Web page presentations that use specific or rare fonts. To be safe, be sure to include a generic font family in combination with a more desired, but possibly more rare, font family. These are the five generic font families:

- ◆ Serif
- ◆ Sans serif
- ◆ Cursive
- ◆ Monospace
- ◆ Fantasy

The `fontStyle` property can alter the appearance of the text, such as applying a slant to the letters. This property can be used to provide emphasis to a span of text using the `oblique` or `italic` value, as shown next:

```
ids.myem.fontStyle = "oblique";
...
<SPAN id=myem>This text is emphasized</SPAN>
```

 As with other font properties, the `fontStyle` property can appear differently on different operating systems.

Other values for the fontStyle property are:

- normal (default value)
- italic
- italic small-caps
- oblique
- oblique small-caps
- small-caps

Listing 11-1 pulls all of these font properties together into one font sampler. Each style is applied to a simple one-line paragraph so you can compare the effects.

Listing 11-1: The example page demonstrating how to apply different JASS style settings

```
<HTML>
<HEAD>
<SCRIPT language="javascript1.2">
 document.tags.BODY.margins("0.5in", "0.5in",
      "0.5in", "0.5in");
 document.ids.first.fontWeight="bold";
 document.ids.second.fontSize="large";
 document.ids.third.fontStyle="italic";
 document.ids.fourth.fontFamily="fantasy";
</SCRIPT>
</HEAD>
<BODY>
<p>This is the font as it appears by default</p>
<p id=first>This is an example of fontWeight</p>
<p id=second>This is an example of fontSize</p>
<p id=third>This is an example of fontStyle</p>
<p id=fourth>This is an example of fontFamily</p>
</BODY>
</HTML>
```

This is a simple Web page with only simple uses of JASS, but the results are very striking. The first line within the Web page uses the default font, and each succeeding line uses some variation of this font. One line alters the font family, one the font style, one the font size, and one the font weight. Figure 11-3 demonstrates these differences. Check out the example in the sample file **nsfont.htm** on the CD-ROM.

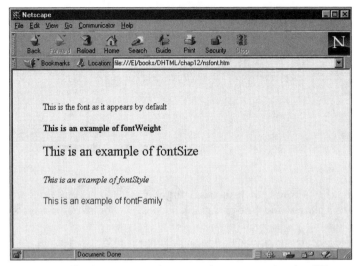

Figure 11-3: The font property demonstration page; notice the difference between the first line, which appears in the default font, and the other lines

TEXT PROPERTIES

In addition to changing font properties, you can also change the text properties within a Web page. Text properties include the underlining that occurs by default with hypertext links and text alignment. Table 11-2 lists the text properties you can alter.

TABLE 11-2 JASS Text Properties

Text Property	Description	Values
lineHeight	Within a block, sets the height of two lines adjacent to each other	Number, percentage, or length
textDecoration	Decoration added to the text	Keyword values such as underline
verticalAlign	Vertical positioning	Keyword or percentage
textTransform	Text case	Keyword such as lowercase
textAlign	Horizontal positioning	Keyword such as center
textIndent	Indentation at the beginning of the block	Length or percentage

The `lineHeight` property sets the distance between two adjacent lines. If a percentage is used, as demonstrated in the following code, the line height is based on the font size:

```
tags.P.lineHeight = 50%;
```

The `lineHeight` property compresses the vertical white space of the text and, depending on the size of the font, can cause the text to overlap. You want to be a little cautious when you use this property, and you may want to test the results on more than one machine. Allowable values for this property are:

◆ `number` — a number such as 2 increases the line height by 200 percent

◆ `length` — absolute length of the line height, such as 0.35 inch

◆ `percentage` — a percentage of the font size

The `textDecoration` property changes the appearance of text by adding or removing some specific type of decoration, such as an underline. This is helpful if you want to make a hypertext link appear as normal text, as demonstrated in the following code:

```
tags.A.textDecoration = "none";
tags.A.color="black";
```

This code removes the text decoration from links, and also sets the color to black. If you want the text of a link to appear exactly as the other text in a paragraph, you also need to change the color in addition to removing the underline. Otherwise the default color for hypertext links is used.

Using hypertext links and removing all references of a link's existence is a handy way of placing *hot spots* throughout a page. These are spots that only show as active when the Web page reader moves his or her mouse over the page.

Values you can use with the `textDecoration` property are:

◆ `none` — removes all text decoration

◆ `underline` — underlines the text

◆ `overline` — adds a line that appears over the text (note that the final release of Navigator 4.0 does not appear to implement this value)

◆ line-through – a line appears through the text, causing a strike-through effect

◆ blink – causes text to blink

 Many readers find blinking text irritating. I suggest that you use blinking text rarely, and only to highlight extremely critical and time-based information.

Positioning is important to the appearance of a Web page. Two properties, verticalAlign and textAlign, control the alignment of HTML elements. The verticalAlign property works with most HTML elements, but the textAlign property only works with block-level elements. An example of this is shown in the following code, which centers the text horizontally, but positions some of the text in a subscript position to the other words:

```
document.tags.P.textAlign="center";
...
The chemical makeup of water is H<sub>2</sub>O.
```

The allowable values for these two properties are listed in Table 11-3.

TABLE 11-3 Alignment Properties

Property	Value	Description
verticalAlign	baseline	Aligns the baseline of the element to the parent
verticalAlign	middle	Aligns the element to the baseline plus one half the vertical height of the parent
verticalAlign	sub	Subscript
verticalAlign	super	Superscript
verticalAlign	text-top	Aligns with the top of the parent element's font
verticalAlign	text-bottom	Aligns with the bottom of the parent element's font
verticalAlign	top	Aligns with the tallest element in a formatted line

continued

Property	Value	Description
verticalAlign	bottom	Aligns bottom with the lowest element in a formatted line
verticalAlign	percentage	Aligns to a percentage value of the line height
textAlign	left	Left justifies the text
textAlign	right	Right justifies the text
textAlign	center	Centers the text
textAlign	justify	Adds spaces to justify text on either end

The `textTransform` property changes the case of the text. For example, the following code capitalizes all of the first letters of the header, and sets all the letters of the paragraph to uppercase:

```
document.tags.H1.textTransform="capitalize";
document.tags.P.textTransform="uppercase";
```

The last text property is the `textIndent` property, which indents the first line of the text within the block by the specified amount. It is particularly effective with paragraphs. For example, the following code indents the first line of each paragraph within the page by half an inch:

```
document.tags.P.textIndent="0.5in";
```

The values specified for the `textIndent` property can be a specific numeric length, as just demonstrated, or it can be a percentage. Percentages are based on the parent (enclosing) element.

One approach to using the text properties is to provide consistent formatting for documents at a Web site. Once the font size is derived by calculation, other formatting can be applied to make plain text-based Web pages stand out a bit. Listing 11-2 contains the JASS settings for document formatting enclosed in a separate JavaScript file (with a .js extension).

Listing 11-2: Using text-based properties to define fairly standard document formatting styles

```
// apply document type formatting
document.tags.P.textIndent = "0.5in";
document.tags.BLOCKQUOTE.textTransform = "uppercase";
document.tags.BLOCKQUOTE.lineHeight="80%";
document.tags.A.textDecoration = "none";
document.tags.H1.textTransform = "capitalize";
```

```
document.tags.H1.textAlign="center";
document.tags.H2.textDecoration="underline";
```

Include this file in the target Web page with code like the following:

```
<SCRIPT src="nstext.js">
</SCRIPT>
```

A few simple lines of code can transform a document in some amazing ways. Figure 11-4 demonstrates this by displaying a sample Web page that includes the JASS file. Without the style settings, this page would be pretty plain, and the first paragraph would not stand out from the page as it does with the formatting. You can also try this for yourself by opening the sample file **nstext.htm** on the CD-ROM.

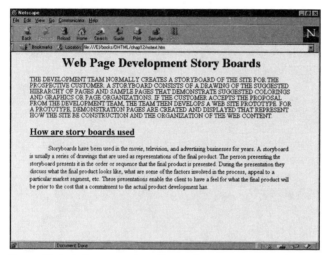

Figure 11-4: A demonstration of several text property settings within an otherwise plain text-based Web page

BLOCK-LEVEL PROPERTIES

Block-level formatting can be applied to change the margins of a document, the borders around elements, element padding, and the width and height of a block. Table 11-4 contains a listing of the block-level properties that can be altered using JASS.

TABLE 11-4 JASS Block-Level Properties

Block-Level Property	Description	Values
`marginLeft`	Left margin of block	length, percentage, or `auto`
`marginRight`	Right margin of block	length, percentage, or `auto`
`marginTop`	Top margin of block	length, percentage, or `auto`
`marginBottom`	Bottom margin of block	length, percentage, or `auto`
`margins()`	Sets all margins	length, percentage, or `auto`
`paddingTop`	Padding between border and top of content	length, percentage
`paddingRight`	Padding between border and right of content	length, percentage
`paddingLeft`	Padding between border and left of content	length, percentage
`paddingBottom`	Padding between border and bottom of content	length, percentage
`paddings()`	Sets all padding attributes of block element	length, percentage
`borderTopWidth`	Width of top border	number
`borderRigthWidth`	Width of right border	number
`borderLeftWidth`	Width of left border	number
`borderBottomWidth`	Width of bottom border	number
`borderWidths()`	Sets width of all borders	number
`borderStyle`	Style of border	keyword such as `none`, `solid`, and `3D`
`borderColor`	Color of border	none or color value
`width`	Width of block	length, percentage, or `auto`
`height`	Height of block	length, percentage, or `auto`
`align`	Alignment of block element	keyword such as `left`, `right`, or none

Specifying Color

Color can be specified in any of five ways:

- ◆ Use the RGB function with values for each entry in the range of 0–255, such as RGB(255,255,255) for the color white.

- ◆ Use named color such as "white" or "red."

- ◆ Use hexadecimal 6-digit format, such as "#FFFFFF" for white.

- ◆ Use the shortened hexadecimal color value, such as "#FFF" for white.

- ◆ Use the RGB function and percentages such as RGB (50%, 50%, 50%), which is a medium gray.

You'll probably use the margin properties extensively. But rather than just setting the margins for the document, try setting the margins for specific elements. The following code sets the document margins to a quarter inch, but sets the left and right margin of the headers in the page to a full inch:

```
<STYLE type="text/javascript">
  tags.BODY.margins("0.25in","0.25in",
      "0.25in","0.25in");
  tags.H1.marginLeft="1.0in";
  tags.H1.marginRight="1.0in";
</STYLE>
```

The header margins are actually displayed with a 1.25-inch margin because it includes the enclosing element (the document) margins, in addition to the header's margins. Note from the code that the `margins` function is used to set the document, while the specific right and left margin properties are used to set the headers.

Acceptable values for the margin properties are `auto`, which means that the value is automatically determined (inherited from the parent); a percentage such as 50%, which is a percentage based on the parent margins; and a specific length.

The padding properties also accept the same types of values as the margin properties except for the `auto` value. Padding specifies the amount of space between a block element's borders and the block element's contents. Again, as with margins, you can also specify the padding for all the sides using the `padding` function, demonstrated next:

```
<SCRIPT language="javascript1.2">
  document.tags.P.padding("0em", "3em", "0em", "3em");
</SCRIPT>
```

The JASS in the code sets the padding of paragraphs to 0 for the top and bottom of the paragraph, and to 3em for the right and left sides. The unit of measure, *em*, is the height of the element's font. Chapter 2 reviews the other sizing units.

The `borderWidth` properties set the borders' widths, and display them if they aren't already displayed. Before the release of Navigator 4.0, you could add a border only to images and tables. Now you can create a border around all block-level elements. For example, the following JASS creates a border for the Web page document, for each header, and for each paragraph. In addition, a border is also created around any unordered lists in the page:

```
<STYLE type="text/javascript">
 tags.BODY.borderWidths("0.25in","0.25in",
     "0.25in","0.25in");
 tags.P.borderLeftWidth="0.1in";
 tags.H1.borderTopWidth="0.3in";
 tags.H1.borderBottomWidth="0.3in";
 tags.UL.borderWidths("10px", "5px", "10px", "5px");
</STYLE>
```

You may have noticed in the code that you can set any one of the borders, or you can set all of them. Also, the borders do not have to be the same size. Figure 11-5 demonstrates the effect of using this JASS code. Notice the different size borders around the list, and that the paragraphs have a border only on the left.

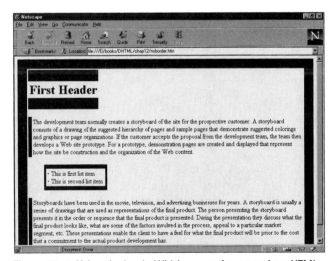

Figure 11-5: Using the borderWidth properties on various HTML block-level elements, including the Web page itself

The example shown in Figure 11-5 was created by the contents in the **nsborder.htm** sample file (on the CD-ROM). Try changing the border widths and which borders are displayed to get a feel for these properties.

So far, I have demonstrated the size-based block-level properties, such as borderWidths, margin, and padding. Now, take a look at other block-level properties you can set to dress up your block elements. For example, take the previous style setting but this time add a bit of color. In addition, change the border style of the document and header elements to 3D, as demonstrated in Listing 11-3.

Listing 11-3: Setting border color and border width

```
<STYLE type="text/javascript">
 tags.BODY.borderWidths("0.25in","0.25in","0.25in","0.25in");
 tags.BODY.borderColor="red";
 tags.BODY.borderStyle="3D";
 tags.P.borderLeftWidth="0.1in";
 tags.P.borderColor="yellow";
 tags.H1.borderTopWidth="0.3in";
 tags.H1.borderBottomWidth="0.3in";
 tags.H1.borderStyle="3D";
 tags.UL.borderWidths("10px", "5px", "10px", "5px");
 tags.UL.borderColor="green";
 tags.UL.borderStyle="3D";
</STYLE>
```

The sample file **nsbrder2.htm** contains the same Web page document contained in **nsborder.htm**, except with the JASS color settings. When you open the file, you'll notice that because the 3D style is used, the tops and left sides of the elements are a lighter color than the bottoms and right sides.

The final block-level properties I'll demonstrate are the width, height, and align properties. The width and height properties set the element's width and height, respectively, and align determines the position of the element within its space. The following code sets the width and height of a block containing an image, and the align property aligns it in the center:

```
tags.IMG.width="100";
tags.IMG.height="200";
tags.IMG.align="left";
```

Both the width and height properties can take auto as a value. Setting an image width or height that is larger or smaller than the actual image causes the browser to scale the image. Using the value auto for either the width or the height preserves the aspect ratio of the image. Also, the value left in an image's align property causes the text surrounding the image, if any, to flow to the right of the image (the image is placed to the right).

MISCELLANEOUS JASS PROPERTIES

The final properties I'll discuss are the backgroundColor and backgroundImage properties, the list properties, and the whiteSpace property. These properties are listed in Table 11-5.

TABLE 11-5 JASS Miscellaneous Properties

Miscellaneous Property	Description	Values
color	Text color of the element	Color values
backgroundColor	Background color of the element	Color values
backgroundImage	Background image of the element	Image source URL
display	Whether the element is displayed	Keyword value such as none
listStyleType	Type of graphic used with a list	Keyword such as disc or decimal
whiteSpace	Handling of white space	Keyword normal or pre

The following code alters the background color to "white," which is one of the named colors both Netscape and Microsoft support, and sets the paragraph font to red using the shortened hexadecimal format. The code also sets the body background to a gray color using the RGB function and percentage values:

```
<SCRIPT language="javascript">
 document.tags.BODY.backgroundColor=
      "RGB(75%, 75%, 75%)";
 document.tags.P.backgroundColor="white";
 document.tags.P.color="#F00";
</SCRIPT>
```

You can check this for out yourself by accessing the sample file **nscolor.htm** on the CD-ROM.

You can also use a background image for any HTML block element. This is most commonly used for backgrounds of Web pages, but you can create some interesting effects by using background images for other elements. For example, in addition to setting the background color of paragraphs, you can also set the background to an image, as the following code demonstrates:

```
document.tags.P.backgroundImage="snow.jpg";
```

Try this yourself by modifying the **nscolor.htm** file to include this line (the image is also on the CD-ROM, or you can use one of your own images). When you open the page, you'll probably get a surprise. If you assumed that, as with CSS1, the browser uses the background color only if the image can't load, you just learned that this isn't the case with JASS. What happens is that the background color is used for the areas containing text, and a background image is used to fill in the rest of the block! To dramatize this behavior with the figure, I used the color of "silver" instead of "white," which is the same color as the document background. When the Web page is silver all over, the block overlap that is filled in by the image stands out, as shown in Figure 11-6.

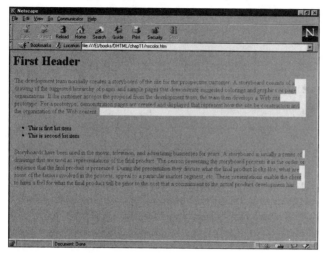

Figure 11-6: An example of using a JASS background image and color at same time

Another property that can add a little flair to your Web page is the listStyleType property, which alters the symbols that are used with ordered and unordered lists. By default, ordered lists display with plain decimal values. Unordered lists display with a disc (a filled circle). By specifying the listStyleType property, as the following code demonstrates, you can change both list types:

```
document.tags.UL.listStyleType = "square";
document.tags.OL.listStyleType = "upper-roman";
```

With this JASS style setting, unordered lists display with a square, and ordered lists display with uppercase roman letters. The allowable values for this property are:

- ◆ disc
- ◆ circle
- ◆ square
- ◆ decimal
- ◆ lower-roman

- ◆ upper-roman

- ◆ lower-alpha

- ◆ upper-alpha

- ◆ none

In addition to controlling the display of list items, you can also control the display of white space by using the whiteSpace property. If you want a block of text to display exactly as written, you can use the value of pre, as demonstrated in this example:

```
document.tags.P.whiteSpace="pre";
```

Now, no matter how the paragraph is typed in, the spacing of the text appears exactly as you type it, regardless of how the page is sized and resized. Try this line in some of the other example files and you'll see first-hand how this works.

Finally, you can choose not to display an HTML element at all. The display property has several different values that can be applied, but the one that is used most commonly is the value of none, as shown in the next code segment:

```
<SCRIPT language="javascript">
 with (document.tags) {
      UL.display="none";
 }
</SCRIPT>
```

This setting removes all unordered lists from the page, including the space they would normally take. Other values that could be specified for the display property are:

- ◆ block — as in a paragraph

- ◆ inline — as in an inline element

- ◆ list-item — a list item for an ordered or unordered list

- ◆ none

These are the last JASS properties this chapter covers. Again, the power of JASS lies in its capability to apply scripting to alter the styles as a page loads. The largest limitation of JavaScript Accessible Style Sheets is that once a Web page has been laid out (displayed), you can no longer change the styles. However, in the last section of this chapter, you'll find out how to emulate dynamic HTML element changes.

Dynamic Fonts

Navigator's technique called *dynamic fonts* enable users to view a page the way it is meant to be viewed, regardless of which fonts are currently installed on his or her machine, and regardless of what operating system is being used.

To use dynamic fonts, you need to include the font file in the Web page document. You can do this in a couple of different ways. The first is to use CSS1 syntax, and use the `@fontdef` keyword, as the following code demonstrates:

```
<STYLE TYPE="text/css">
@fontdef url(http://www.somecompany.com/somefile.pfr);
</STYLE>
```

Another approach is to link in the font file directly, using the following syntax:

```
<LINK REL=fontdef
  SRC="http://www.somecompany.com/somefile.pfr">
```

The fonts must be packaged on the server for the Web page to download them. Once they are downloaded, they are restricted for use with the Web page they are associated with.

You can access fonts using the JASS or CSS1 font specifications (as shown next), which reference a font currently being demonstrated at the Netscape Web site. Here's how to do access fonts using JASS:

```
tags.P.fontFamily="PosterBodoni BT";
```

Using CSS1:

```
P { font-family: PosterBodoni BT }
```

Appendix A contains a reference to the dynamic font Web site for Netscape, and a reference to Bitstream, which is the home of TrueDoc fonts.

Using Generic Fonts

If you don't have access to font files, your best bet for a standard look (regardless of where the client resides) is to use the generic fonts mentioned earlier in this chapter. These fonts are: serif, sans serif, cursive, monospace, and fantasy.

Using Layers to Alter the Appearance of Traditional HTML Elements

Microsoft has exposed all of the traditional HTML elements to their scripting object model in version 4.0 of Internet Explorer. This means that you can dynamically change the look of any HTML element even after the Web page displays. This definitely puts Netscape Navigator at a disadvantage when it comes to building dynamic HTML pages. It does not, however, mean that you can't *emulate* the dynamic modification of HTML elements.

To modify HTML elements after the Web page loads, define layers for every look you want to present the elements in, layer them so the "look" that displays when the Web page opens is the one on top, and set the other layers to be invisible. This doesn't add too much additional overhead unless you go a little crazy with what you want to change.

If you've worked with layers, you are probably aware of the fact that only the positioned layer element can capture mouse events; the inflow layer does not. However, the question is how to layer the objects within a Web page in such a way that the other objects in the page "flow" naturally with the layers. The real key is to position other objects as you normally would within the page, until you come to the part of the page that you want to alter dynamically. From that point on, all block-level elements need to be enclosed within layers.

This procedure probably raises the question of how to position the layers so their content flows within the page as it normally would. The answer is to use the inline technique of accessing the first layer's position and use this to calculate the second; then use the second layer's position to calculate the third, and so on.

For example, I took the first four paragraphs of this section, and the header, and created a Web page from the contents. Then, to modify the third paragraph to change the color, font, and background of the paragraph when Web page readers place their cursors over this paragraph, I created the CSS1 style sheet setting for the paragraph layer that shows only with the mouseover event, as shown next:

```
<STYLE type="text/css">
  LAYER.second { backgroundColor: black;
                 color: yellow;
                 font-family: Fantasy;
                 text-transform: uppercase;
                 font-size: 10pt }
</STYLE>
```

Then I created the script that handles the mouse event. Listing 11-4 contains a function, change, with one parameter that determines which of the paragraphs to hide and which to show. When the parameter has a value of 2, the original paragraph is hidden and the highlighted paragraph is displayed.

Listing 11-4: The change function, which hides one paragraph and displays another based on the value passed to it

```
<SCRIPT language="javascript1.2">

function change(version) {
  if (version == 2) {
      document.layers["para1"].visibility="hide";
      document.layers["para2"].visibility="show";
      }
  else  {
      document.layers["para2"].visibility="hide";
      document.layers["para1"].visibility="show";
      }
}

</SCRIPT>
```

When the value is 1, the highlighted paragraph is hidden, and the original paragraph is displayed.

The body of the document contains the four chapters, the first two of which I won't repeat here. However, the next *two* chapters (actually three) are important to understanding what I am doing, so I am including the whole document, starting with the third paragraph. Listing 11-5 contains two layers, both of which have the same content, but the second iteration of the paragraph has different style settings, using the style sheet created earlier, and is hidden when the document is first displayed.

Listing 11-5: Two layers, one hidden and one exposed, but both with the same content; the second displays when the mouse is over the paragraph

```
<layer id=para1
 onmouseover="change(2)">
If you have worked with layers, you are probably aware of the fact
 that only the positioned layer will capture mouse events. However,
 the question is how to layer the objects within a Web page in such
 a way that the other objects in the page "flow" naturally with the
 layers. The real key is to position other objects as you normally
 would within the page until you get to that part of the page that
 you want to alter dynamically. From that time on, all block-level
 elements will need to be enclosed within layers.
</layer>
<layer class=second id=para2 visibility="hide"
 TOP=&{document.layers[0].top;};
 onmouseout="change(1)">
```

```
If you have worked with layers, you are probably aware of the fact
that only the positioned layer will capture mouse events. However,
the question is how to layer the objects within a Web page in such
a way that the other objects in the page "flow" naturally with the
layers. The real key is to position other objects as you normally
would within the page until you get to that part of the page that
you want to alter dynamically. From that time on, all block-level
elements will need to be enclosed within layers.
</layer>
```

Pay particular attention to the second layer in Listing 11-5. This layer uses the inline positioning technique, developed by Netscape, to determine where to position the paragraph. This technique enables access to the value of the element that has not yet been created. In this case, because I want the new layer positioned in the exact same location as the first layer, I use the value of top from the first layer for the second.

Also notice from the listing that the code captures the mouseover event for the first paragraph in order to change to the highlighted paragraph, and captures the mouseout event for the highlighted paragraph in order to trigger the move to return the document to its original condition.

Finally, I added the last paragraph, as shown in Listing 11-6, which contains the final content for the page. Again, because I used positioned layers previously, I included this content within another layer and used the inline positioning technique to position it correctly.

Listing 11-6: The final layer on the page, using the inline positioning technique to ensure that it is positioned correctly

```
<layer
TOP=&{document.layers[1].top+document.layers[1].document.height+15;}
 ;>
This probably raises the question of how to position the layers so
that their content flows within the page as it normally would. The
answer to this is to use the inline technique of accessing the
first layer's position and use this to calculate the second; then
use the second layer's position to calculate the third, and so on.
</layer>
```

Notice, in the code, that I set the top of the layer to the previous layer's top position, plus the height of the document area contained within the layer, plus 15 to emulate the spacing of the paragraphs.

Figure 11-7 shows this page after it is first loaded, and Figure 11-8 shows it after the mouse is over the third paragraph. Note that it is difficult to tell that the third and fourth paragraphs aren't really paragraphs, just carefully positioned layers. Try this yourself by accessing the CD-ROM's **nschange.htm** sample file. Try resizing the window and you'll see that the page still works.

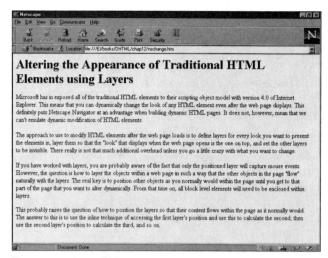

Figure 11-7: An ordinary Web page containing what seems to be a header and four paragraphs, but in actuality contains a couple of paragraphs and several layers

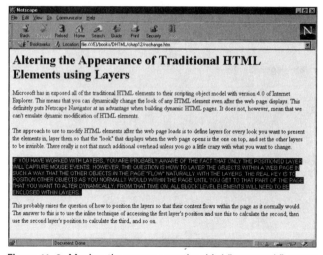

Figure 11-8: Moving the mouse over the third "paragraph" causes the paragraph to be highlighted

You can also use this approach with other block-level HTML elements such as <DIV> blocks and paragraphs.

In Chapter 7, you learned that Microsoft IE 4.0 contains several transition and visual filter properties that can alter the appearance of Web page elements by adding drop shadows to headers, changing the opacity of images, and applying other visual effects. You can emulate many of these special effects in Netscape Navigator — I'll show you how in the next section.

Creating Simple Special Effects

Chapter 10 showed you how to combine clip properties and a timer to create a transitional effect. This section demonstrates how you can emulate two of the IE 4.0 filter properties in Netscape Navigator: alpha, which changes the opacity of the filter, and shadow, which adds a shadow to an element.

My sample file contains a header and an image when the page first loads. When you move the cursor over the header, a drop shadow is applied to the text. You can see this effect in Figure 11-9, and you can try it out yourself by opening **effect.htm** on the CD-ROM.

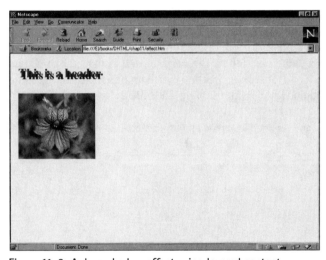

Figure 11–9: A drop-shadow effect using layered content

The drop shadow is created by placing a duplicate of the header slightly below and to the right of the original image. The code captures the `mouseover` and `mouseout` events for the header and displays or hides the shadow layer accordingly.

The second effect, opacity, also uses layered content. In this case, however, moving the cursor over the image causes a semitransparent version of the image to display, as shown in Figure 11-10.

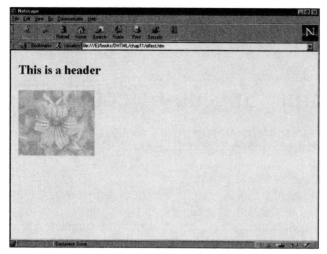

Figure 11-10: An opacity effect applied to an image

A semitransparent version of the original image creates the opacity effect, using whatever graphics program you used for the original image. This new version of the image is placed in the exact same position of the original, but is placed behind the original image, using the z-index attribute. Listing 11-7 contains the complete code for this special effects example (which is the sample file called **effect.htm**).

Listing 11-7: Using multiple images to emulate changing button states

```
<HTML>
<HEAD>
<STYLE type="text/css">
  #header1 { position: absolute; left: 20; top: 30;
            color: blue; z-index: 2 }
  #header2 { position: absolute; left: 25; top: 35;
            color: indigo; visibility:hidden;
            z-index: 1}
  #image1 { position: absolute; left: 20; top: 100;
            z-index: 2 }
  #image2 { position: absolute; left: 20; top: 100;
            z-index: 1}
</STYLE>

<SCRIPT language="javascript1.2">
<!--
// set the event trapping

header = 1;
image = 1;

function setup() {
  document.header1.onmouseover=change_header;
```

```
 document.header1.onmouseout=change_header;
 document.image1.onmouseover=change_image;
 document.image2.onmouseout=change_image;
}

// create or remove header effect
function change_header () {
 if (header == 1) {
      document.header2.visibility="inherit";
      header = 2;
      }
 else   {
      document.header2.visibility="hidden";
      header = 1;
      }
}

// create or remove image effect
function change_image() {
 if (image == 1) {
      document.image1.visibility="hidden";
      image = 2;
      }
 else {
      document.image1.visibility="inherit";
      image = 1;
      }
}
//-->
</SCRIPT>
</HEAD>
<BODY onload="setup()">
<DIV id="image1">
<img src="button.jpg">
</DIV>
<DIV id="image2">
<img src="button2.jpg">
</DIV>

<H1 id=header1>This is a header</H1>
<H1 id=header2>This is a header</H1>

</BODY>
</HTML>
```

The code in Listing 11-7 shows that it can actually be very simple to emulate IE 4.0 filters in Netscape by effectively using layers and absolute positioning.

The Preview Example Revisited

Now that you've had a chance to study how JavaScript Accessible Style Sheets are created, you can take a closer look at the preview example introduced at the beginning of this chapter. To create this JavaScript style sheet and screen resolution object application, I developed an application that creates a `window_format` object, and then creates a new instance of the object based on the screen resolution. The object creation occurs in a separate JavaScript file in a file named **format.jss**. Listing 11-8 shows the contents of this file.

Listing 11-8: The window_format object used to define page characteristics based on screen resolution

```
function window_format(font_size, background_color, header_size,
  header_color, page_margins) {
  this.font_size = font_size;
  this.background_color = background_color;
  this.header_size = header_size;
  this.header_color = header_color;
  this.page_margins = page_margins;
}

if (screen.width >= 1000)
  thisscreen =
      new window_format("24pt", "red", "36pt", "yellow",
      "1.0in");
else if (screen.width >= 800)
  thisscreen =
      new window_format("20pt", "lightcoral", "28pt",
      "ivory", "0.5in");
else
  thisscreen =
      new window_format("16pt", "beige", "20pt", "black",
"10px");
```

Note in the code that an object will be created whose properties reflect the screen resolution. For instance, a screen resolution width greater than or equal to 800 pixels will set the font size to "20pt," the background color to "lightcoral," the size and color of the header font to "28pt" and "ivory," and, finally, the page margin to "0.5in."

Afterward, I created a very simple HTML page that uses JASS to set the element styles. The JavaScript section includes the JavaScript file, and sets the styles based on the instantiated object, as shown in Listing 11-9.

Listing 11-9: An HTML page using an included object definition file to define properties based on resolution, and using JASS to format the window

```
<HEAD>
<title>test</title>
```

```
<SCRIPT language="javascript" src="format.js">
</SCRIPT>
<SCRIPT language="javascript1.2">
<!--
 with (document.tags.BODY) {
        backgroundColor=thisscreen.background_color;
        fontSize=thisscreen.font_size;
        marginTop=thisscreen.page_margins;
        marginLeft=thisscreen.page_margins;
        marginRight=thisscreen.page_margins;
        marginLeft=thisscreen.page_margins;
        }
 document.tags.H1.fontSize=thisscreen.header_size;
 document.tags.H1.color=thisscreen.header_color;
//-->
</SCRIPT>
</HEAD>
<BODY>
<h1>Page header</h1>
<P>
This is some text, representing a paragraph. This text will show in
 different sizes based on the size of the view screen when the page
 is opened.
</P>
</BODY>
```

The same JavaScript file can be used with many pages, and can also include the JASS code shown with the example page. Using this approach, you simply need to include the JavaScript file in a page.

Summary

This chapter covered some of the techniques that can be used to dynamically change HTML elements in Netscape Navigator 4.x.

In this chapter you learned how to:

- Use JavaScript Accessible Style Sheets to dynamically change style settings when the page loads

- Use JASS tags, `IDS`, and classes to determine how an element is displayed

- Modify font properties, such as `fontSize` and `fontFamily`

- Modify text properties, such as `textDecoration` and `textAlign`

- Modify block-level properties, such as `borderWidth` and `color`

- Change the background color, image, and text color

- Control white space with JASS

♦ Use dynamic fonts

♦ Use layers and the inline positioning technique to emulate the dynamic changing of HTML elements after the page loads

The next chapter combines the use of dynamic positioning, covered in the previous chapter, and dynamically altering HTML elements, covered in this chapter, to create interactive documents. You will also have a chance to work with keyboard and mouse event trapping.

Chapter 12

Adding Interactive Content to Web Pages

IN THIS CHAPTER

- ◆ Capturing mouse events
- ◆ Capturing keyboard events
- ◆ Capturing the `load` event
- ◆ Responding to user interaction
- ◆ Using visual effects to communicate with the user

INTERACTIVE PAGES ARE AN important part of successful Web sites. Dynamic HTML enables you to create Web pages that respond to the user's keyboard and mouse events.

This chapter covers Netscape-specific keyboard and mouse events, as well as other forms of reader interaction. To see the differences between how each browser handles the same events, compare this chapter with Chapter 8, which covers event handling in Internet Explorer.

Capturing Mouse Events

Several events are triggered by mouse use. These events can be categorized into movement-based events, such as mouseover, mousemove, mousedrag, and mouseout, or they can be click-based events, such as click, mousedown, mouseup, and dblclick. Each of these events has an associated event handler, such as onmousemove for mousemove, or onclick for click. The dragdrop event is a combination of the two and occurs when a Web page reader clicks content outside the Web page, drags it over the page, and then releases the mouse button.

Some events, such as mousemove, are only trapped if the event is explicitly captured using event capturing. Chapter 3 discusses event capturing in detail, but for your review, event capturing occurs whenever the `captureEvents` method is used, as demonstrated in the following code:

```
//explicitly capture event
Window.captureEvents(Event.MOUSEDOWN);
...
//define function for event
function handle_move(e) {
...
}
...
//register function with event for object
window.onMouseMove = handle_move;
```

This very abbreviated example demonstrates the three components of event capturing:

♦ Capture the event.

♦ Create a function to handle the event.

♦ Match the object, event, and function.

It is important to note a couple of features from the preceding code. First, the event used in the `captureEvents` function should be capitalized. Second, any use of case for the function registration function is acceptable. Thus, the following variation would be just as acceptable:

```
Window.onmousemove = handle_move;
```

In addition to capturing events, you can access information about the event. The events have parameters that can be accessed in the script processing the event. For example, the `mousemove` event has the following parameters:

♦ `layerY`, `pageY`, `screenY` — the vertical position of the event for the layer, page, and screen, respectively

♦ `layerX`, `pageX`, `screenX` — the horizontal position of the event for the layer, page, and screen, respectively

♦ `target` — the object to which the event was originally sent

♦ `type` — the type of event, such as `mousemove`

The properties just mentioned are accessed via the `event` object, which is a parameter that is passed with the event handling function. Do you notice the parameter labeled "e" in the previous code sample? This is the `event` object. The following code sample demonstrates the use of the `event` object:

```
//function to handle event
function handle_move(e) {
  var position_y = e.pageY;
  var position_x = e.pageX;
  ...
}
```

Only certain properties are available for each event. This topic is covered in detail in the following sections of this chapter.

Working with Mouse-Click Events

This section shows you an example of the `click` event, as it applies to events that occur when the mouse is clicked. The following mouse-click actions can trigger the `click` event (many of which are used in this chapter and in the last section of this book):

- Clicking with the left mouse button
- Clicking a hypertext link
- Clicking an item from a combo or list box to select it

Note that while the `click` event is described under this section about mouse events, it can also be triggered by the following *keyboard* events: selecting an item in a combo or list box by using the arrow keys and then pressing the Enter key, pressing the Enter key or the spacebar if the button, radio button, or checkbox has the focus, or pressing any command button.

With Navigator 4.0 you can access the `click` event for a document or the window, as well as form elements. If you want to capture a `click` event for other objects, you can use an anchor that has an empty link, or you can use event trapping. To use an empty link to trap the `click` event for a header and the text on a page, you can use the code in Listing 12-1.

Listing 12-1: Using an empty link to capture the click event for most HTML elements

```
<HTML>
<HEAD>
<STYLE type="text/css">
 A { text-decoration: none; color: black }
 H1 { color: red }
</STYLE>
</HEAD>
```

```
<BODY>
<a href="" onclick="alert('clicked on header');return
 false"><h1>test</h1></a>
<p>
<a href="" onclick="alert('clicked on paragraph');return false">
This is some content
</a>
</BODY>
</HTML>
```

This code displays a message about which object is clicked. Notice the use of the CSS1 style sheet. Without it, the header and paragraph code would be underlined, which is the normal behavior for links. Additionally, I need to specify a default color, otherwise the hypertext link color specified by the browser is applied. Finally, I override the color for the header by supplying my own.

To apply an empty link to trap `click` events, your code must return a `false` value as the last part of the event handler (as shown by the listing). This prevents the link from attempting to load the URL. Because the link is empty, this only results in displaying the directory of the Web page. Returning `false` ends the event handling.

Try this out for yourself by accessing the example file on the CD-ROM, **nsclick.htm.** Explore the options by adding other HTML element types, by extending the code to make the object invisible, or by changing its background color.

Another approach could be to use event trapping. To do this, the elements must be positioned using absolute positioning. The following code shows the alteration to the elements:

```
<H1 style="position:absolute; left:20;top:20" id=header1>test</h1>
<P style="position:absolute; left:20;top:80" id=para1>
This is some content
</p>
```

In addition, an event handler function must be created and the events for the elements directed to the event handler, as shown in the following code:

```
<script language="javascript1.2">
function click_element(e) {
 alert(e.target.name);
}

function setup() {
 document.para1.onmousedown=click_element;
 document.header1.onmousedown=click_element;
}
</SCRIPT>
```

Notice that the assignment of the event handler to the events occurs within another function. This is because the page must be loaded before this assignment takes place, because the elements have not yet been created. The setup function is called using the `onload` event handler for the document.

As you can see, this second approach is actually more complicated than need be for this simple application. However, if several objects exist within a page and each requires event trapping, and especially if the page undergoes constant change, using explicit assignment to event handlers is a better approach.

Finally, other events can be triggered indirectly by clicking with the mouse. For example, the `blurchange` event is triggered for one item when the Web page reader selects an entirely different item.

Working with Mouse-Movement Events

Tracking the movement of the user's mouse on a Web page requires you to trap mouse movement events, which are `mouseover`, `mouseout`, `mousedrag`, and `mousemove`.

When considering how these events can be used, two application possibilities come to mind. The first is to track the movement of the mouse so that colors or images change to highlight important text on the page when the mouse is over a particular HTML element. Altering the appearance of an element when the cursor is over it is sometimes referred to as the *rollover* effect.

For example, the sample file **nsbttns.htm** contains three button images when the page is first displayed. Moving the mouse over each image adds a highlighting effect, as shown in Figure 12-1. Moving the mouse away from the image sets the appearance back to its original state.

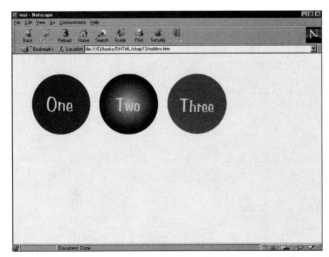

Figure 12-1: Changing the appearance of an element based on mouse movements

This page uses a style sheet to set the width and height of all images on the page to 150 pixels each, because the images are all the same size. Also, the background color for the page is set to white. The style sheet is placed in the head section of the document, as shown in the following code:

```
<HEAD>
<title>test</title>
<STYLE text="text/css">
    body      { background-color: white }
    img       { width: 150; height:150 }
</STYLE>
```

When you first view the page, it looks like it contains only three images (the other three images are hidden). These visible images, which are the nonhighlighted buttons, are placed on the page using absolute positioning. These three buttons are enclosed with layer tags, which in turn trap the mouseover event, as shown in the following code:

```
<layer left=50 top=50 onmouseover="show_highlight('one')">
<img src="button1.gif">
</layer>
<layer left=225 top=50 onmouseover="show_highlight('two')">
<img src="button2.gif">
</layer>
<layer left=400 top=50 onmouseover="show_highlight('three')">
<img src="button3.gif">
</layer>
```

The three highlighted images are placed on the page, each image in the exact same position as its associated nonhighlighted image, and each one is initially set to be invisible. This second set of images traps the mouseout event, and each image sets itself as invisible when this event is triggered:

```
<layer id=one left=50 top=50 visibility=hide
  onmouseout="this.visibility='hide'">
<img src="button1o.gif">
</layer>
<layer id=two left=225 top=50 visibility=hide
  onmouseout="this.visibility='hide'">
<img src="button2o.gif">
</layer>
<layer id=three left=400 top=50 visibility=hide
  onmouseout="this.visibility='hide'">
<img src="button3o.gif">
</layer>
```

For the nonhighlighted images, a function, show_highlight, is called. This function takes one parameter, which is the name of the layer that contains the associated highlight button for the image that receives the mouseover event, shown next:

```
<SCRIPT language="javascript1.2">
function show_highlight(button_item) {
 document.layers[button_item].visibility="show";
}

</SCRIPT>
</HEAD>
```

The mouseover event is trapped for the original images because the associated highlighted images are not visible, and cannot accept events. However, the mouseout event is trapped for the highlighted images because when they are visible, they appear on top of the other nonhighlighted images and receive all events at that point. In other words, when the highlighted red button, the first button, is invisible, its nonhighlighted associated button receives the trapped mouseover event, causing the highlighted button to be displayed. The mouse is still over the location of the two stacked images at this time. When the mouse moves out of this location, the mouseout event for the highlighted red button is triggered, causing the red button to be hidden, and the nonhighlighted button begins to receive events again.

The next section describes how to capture mouse events for pages that incorporate drag and drop.

Working with Drag-and-Drop Techniques

When Netscape released Navigator 4.0, the company also provided an example, called the "Vacation Planner," that demonstrated a drag-and-drop technique using their version of dynamic HTML. This demonstration was the most complex use of JavaScript I had ever seen.

I used some of the principles from the Netscape example to create a fun little drag-and-drop Web page that enables Web page readers to express their artistic natures by creating their own forest scene. The example can be found on the CD-ROM in the file called **nsdrgdrp.htm**, and you might want to try this out first before reading about how to create the page.

When the page opens, the elements are displayed with no apparent order, as shown in Figure 12-2. Click any of the elements with the left mouse button and move the mouse with the button still pressed. Notice that the element moves with the mouse. When the element is in the position desired, just let go of the mouse button.

Figure 12-2: The drag-and-drop forest scene demonstration after
the page is loaded

A fun little extension to this page enables you to move the object along the
z-axis, which means you can place one image in front of another. The application
contains code to trap the double-click event and to move the image that is the target of the event to the top, by adjusting its z-index value. Figure 12-3 shows the
same Web page after I have positioned the elements one way, and Figure 12-4 displays a second arrangement.

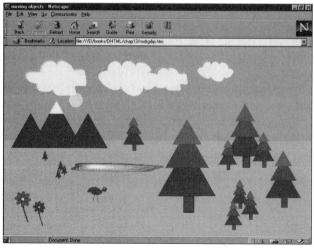

Figure 12-3: The drag-and-drop forest scene after elements are
moved into one arrangement

Figure 12-4: The drag-and-drop forest scene after elements are moved into a second arrangement

To create this page, I first set the background color to blue and added a layer that represents the ground:

```
<BODY bgcolor="skyblue">
<!-- add ground, no other contents -->
<layer id=ground left=0 top=50%
 bgcolor="lightgreen" height=50% width=100%></layer>
```

It is important to place the background as the first object because the other layers overlay it, and its entry in the layers array needs to be differentiated, as you'll see a bit later in the coding section.

Next, the images used to create the scenes are added. Each image is enclosed within a layer and each layer is set using absolute positioning, as shown in Listing 12-2.

Listing 12-2: Layers containing each of the individual images

```
<!-- add images to use for drawing -->
<layer id=one top=0 left=0>
<img src="bird.gif"
 height=36 width=54>
</layer>
<layer id=two top=0 left=60>
<img src="medtree.gif" height=143 width=91>
</layer>
<layer id=three top=0 left=150>
<img src="smltree.gif" height=86 width=54>
</layer>
<layer id=four top=0 left=200>
```

```
<img src="tnytree.gif" height=26 width=17>
</layer>
<layer id=five top=0 left=230>
<img src="smlgroup.gif" height=46 width=32>
</layer>
<layer top=0 left=260>
<img src="medgroup.gif" height=127 width=90>
</layer>
<layer top=0 left=350>
<img src="othgroup.gif" height=165 width=144>
</layer>
<layer top=0 left=400>
<img src="bigtree.gif" height=233 width=148>
</layer>
<layer top=145 left=0>
<img src="lake.gif" height=22 width=242>
</layer>
<layer top=145 left=250>
<img src="hills.gif" height=119 width=251>
</layer>
<layer top=270 left=0>
<img src="sun.gif" height=35 width=35>
</layer>
<layer top=270 left=50>
<img src="flower1.gif" height=62 width=34>
</layer>
<layer top=270 left=120>
<img src="flower2.gif" height=77 width=42>
</layer>
<layer top=270 left=260>
<img src="smlclda.gif" height=53 width=95>
</layer>
<layer top=270 left=370>
<img src="smlcldb.gif" height=59 width=106>
</layer>
<layer top=270 left=420>
<img src="bigclda.gif" height=92 width=162>
</layer>
<layer top=300 left=0>
<img src="bigcldb.gif" height=92 width=165>
</layer>
```

Note that the layers are named. Using named layers isn't essential for the drag-and-drop example, but it's good practice to name them. Named layers make it easy for you to access a specific element later using script and the element name.

Here is the JavaScript necessary to trap the mouse events, in which the mousedown, mouseup, and mousedrag events are captured for the window using event capturing:

```
window.captureEvents(Event.MOUSEDOWN | Event.MOUSEUP |
  Event.MOUSEDRAG);
```

```
window.onmousedown=begin_event;
window.onmouseup=end_event;
window.onmousemove=drag_event;
```

For each of the captured events, a function must be provided. First, a function is created that begins the drag process, and it is associated with the `mousedown` event. This function compares the *x* and *y* coordinates of the event with the location and width of the underlying layer elements using two helper functions, `check_width` and `check_height`. It does this by iterating through the layers array and compares each layer's dimensions with the coordinates of the event. If the event coordinates fall within the dimensions of a layer, the `current_layer` global variable is set to it, and the application quits iterating through the layers array. At the end of the `function` event, capturing is used to trap all `mousemove` events within the window, as shown in the Listing 12-3.

Listing 12-3: JavaScript functions to control image movement

```
function begin_event(e) {
  for (i = 1; i < document.layers.length; i++) {
      var test_layer = document.layers[i];
      var the_x = test_layer.pageX;
      var the_width = test_layer.clip.width;
      var the_y = test_layer.pageY;
      var the_height = test_layer.clip.height;
      var correct_width =
            check_width(e.pageX, the_x, the_width);
      var correct_height =
            check_height(e.pageY, the_y, the_height);
      if (correct_width && correct_height) {
            current_layer = test_layer;
            oldX = e.pageX;
            oldY = e.pageY;
            window.captureEvents(Event.MOUSEMOVE);
            break;
            }
      }
      return true;
}
function check_width(page_x, the_x, the_width) {
  if (page_x >= the_x && page_x <= the_x + the_width)
      return true
  else
      return false
}

function check_height(page_y, the_y, the_height) {
  if (page_y >= the_y && page_y <= the_y + the_height)
      return true
  else
      return false
}
```

As soon as a layer matching the coordinates is found, the enclosing `for` loop is exited with the `break` statement. The window `mousemove` event handler is set to the `drag-event` event handler function. This function processes each mouse movement and moves the captured layer accordingly, as shown next:

```
function drag_event(e) {
  if (current_layer != null) {
      current_layer.moveBy(e.pageX - oldX,
              e.pageY - oldY);
      oldX = e.pageX;
      oldY = e.pageY;
      }
  return false;
}
```

Each time a mouse movement occurs, the position of the location is set to global variables, which, in turn, are subtracted from the current mouse event coordinates in the `moveBy` function. When the drag-and-drop operation is complete, and the reader releases the mouse button, the event handler function created for the `mouseup` event is called to reset the `window` variables and release the `mousemove` event capturing for the window:

```
function end_event(e) {
  last_layer = current_layer;
  current_layer = null;
  window.releaseEvents(Event.MOUSEMOVE);
  return true;
}
```

That's all that's needed to create a drag-and-drop page. In addition to resetting the window events, the `end_event` function also assigns the value of `current_layer` to another global variable, `last_layer`. This variable holds the `layer` object that was previously moved. The reason for this is demonstrated next.

To create the double-click operation that changes the `z-index` ordering of an element, capture the double-click event for the document, as shown here:

```
document.captureEvents(Event.DBLCLICK);
document.ondblclick = key_press;
```

The `key_press` function, shown next, does nothing more than set the previous layer's `zIndex` property to a value of 5:

```
function key_press(e) {
  last_layer.zIndex=5;
}
```

The `key_press` function is not all that sophisticated. It just sets the previously trapped layer to a `zIndex` value that should set it above all other layers in the page.

Because the double-click event consists of the `mousedown` and `mouseup` events, the element that receives the double-click is the one that's moved.

Of course, with layering, you can click one image and instead of moving it, the image just below it moves instead. This is because the code is iterating through an array based on the original position of the elements, and more than one element can occupy the same position within the document. However, in spite of this option, the page works remarkably well — as you have had a chance to find out.

I could have placed all the images on top of each other and dispensed with the positioning definitions, but I wanted readers to see what they have to work with before they start dragging elements all over the place. Plus, because the page has many images, the reader sees changes occurring to the page, which provide some feedback as to why it is taking so much time to download.

Finally, I also could have used other HTML elements, such as the `DIV` element, to implement the drag-and-drop example. Most block-level HTML elements can also be found in the layers array as long as the element is named via its `ID` attribute.

Hypertext links created with the anchor tag (`<A>` `</A>`) will trap most mouse-based events, including `mousedown` and `mouseup`. Surrounding the images in the drag-and-drop example with hypertext links will trap the mouse events necessary for this type of application. Then, the hypertext link can be enclosed, in turn, by `<DIV>` tags. Because the image is enclosed in an element that can be moved, the image within this element can also be moved. To access event information, the `event` object is also passed to the function as is the `DIV` block. The following code shows what this looks like, based on the previous drag-and-drop example code:

```
<DIV id="bird"
 style="position: absolute;top: 0px; left: 0px;">
<a href=""
 onmousedown="begin_event(bird, event);return false"
 onmouseup="end_event();return false">
<img src="bird.gif" width=54 height=36
border=0></a></DIV>
```

The code also shows a function for the `mousedown` event. This function receives the `DIV` block `ID` and the `event` object as parameters. Remember that the `event` object maintains information about the event such as the location where it occurred. This function is listed next:

```
function begin_event(object,e) {
 current_object = object;
 objectX = e.pageX;
 objectY = e.pageY;
 window.captureEvents(Event.MOUSEMOVE);
}
```

I would say that this function is much more simplified than the one used in the drag-and-drop sample based on layers. The `end_event` function is about the same as shown next:

```
function end_event() {
 window.releaseEvents(Event.MOUSEMOVE);
 current_object = null;
}
```

I still used window event capturing for the mouse movement, as the two functions demonstrated. The event handler is still the `drag_event` function, as shown next in Listing 12-4.

Listing 12-4: The drag-and-drop page; the drag event is based on CSS1 positioning

```
function drag_event(e) {
 if (current_object != null) {
     current_object.left = current_object.left + (e.pageX -
objectX);
     current_object.top = current_object.top + (e.pageY -
objectY);
     objectX = e.pageX;
     objectY = e.pageY;
 }
 return false;
}
...
window.onmousemove=drag_event;
```

You'll find very little difference in the handling of the `zIndex` ordering. The document double-click event is still trapped and an event handler called `press_key` is still called for this event, as shown next:

```
document.captureEvents(Event.DBLCLICK);
document.ondblclick = key_press;
```

Then I assign a global variable, called `last_object`, the current value of the variable `current_object` just before setting `current_object` to `null` in the end_event function:

```
function end_event() {
 window.releaseEvents(Event.MOUSEMOVE);
 last_object = current_object;
 current_object = null;
}
```

Just as with the previous example, the `press_key` event sets only the `zIndex` property of `last_object`.

The code for the version of drag and drop based on CSS1 positioning is much simpler than that for layers, but the elements themselves are a bit more complicated. However, you can check out this second version of the technique by accessing the sample file **nsdrgdrp2.htm** on the CD-ROM.

One other approach I could have used with either example is to assign event handlers to each element when the page loads. I could also have captured the `mousedown` event for the entire document and then checked the `target` attribute of the `event` object to see which element received the event. However, this becomes a bit awkward with images enclosed within `DIV` blocks because the image itself receives the event, yet the block is the element that has to move (images cannot be moved). The approach I like to use the most is the one used in this example. However, I recommend that you open the file and practice modifying the page using a variety of techniques.

Capturing Keyboard Events

Keyboard activity can also explicitly trigger events. Events that are triggered by some form of keyboard activity are the `keydown`, `keypress`, and `keyup` events. The `keypress` event is a combination of `keydown` and `keyup`. These events have the following parameters:

- `type` – type of event
- `target` – object that receives the event
- `layerX`, `layerY`, `pageX`, `pageY`, `screenX`, and `screenY` – coordinates of the event for the layer, page, and screen respectively
- `which` – ASCII value of key
- `modifiers` – modifier keys held during the key press

The `which` property contains the ASCII value of the key being pressed, which can be translated using the `fromCharCode` function. The `modifier` value contains information that specifies whether one of the modifier keys is being held down. A modifier key is a key such as the Shift or Ctrl key.

I created a very simple application that could be handy if, like me, you can never remember the ASCII values of specific keys. The application traps the `keypress` event and displays the ASCII value. You can access the utility yourself by opening the file **nsascii.htm** on the CD-ROM. Listing 12-5 shows the contents of the file.

Listing 12-5: The Find ASCII key utility, used to find the ASCII value of the key pressed

```
<HTML>
<HEAD><TITLE>Finding the ASCII value</TITLE>
<SCRIPT language="javascript1.2">

function display_key(e) {
 document.forms[0].elements[0].value = e.which;
 document.forms[0].elements[1].value = e.modifiers;
}
```

```
document.captureEvents(Event.KEYPRESS);
document.onkeypress=display_key;
</SCRIPT>
</HEAD>

<BODY style="background-color: aqua; color: darkcoral; margin:
 0.5in">
<H1>ASCII Code Finder</H1>
Press any key and if there is an equivalent ASCII value for the key,
 it will be displayed here:
<p>
<form>
<INPUT type=text name="conversion">
<p>
Any modifiers will show here:
<p>
<INPUT type=text name="modifier">
</form>
</BODY>
</HTML>
```

You may notice that a value of false is returned at the end of the subroutine. This overrides the keystroke value and ensures that even if the text field has the focus, only the ASCII value shows and not the output of the keystroke.

Capturing the Load Event

Usually most of the events that are captured relate to either keyboard or mouse activity. However, you can also capture other events to provide feedback to the Web page reader.

For example, you might capture and process the load event in one of your Web pages. An excellent use for this event is to display an image-based menu bar, or other content, that requires the page to be entirely loaded before the reader interacts with it. Listing 12-6 demonstrates a Web page with three images contained within a layer block that isn't displayed until the entire page is loaded. While the page is loading, a message of "Please wait while images are downloading..." is displayed.

Listing 12-6: Trapping the load event for the Web page

```
<HTML>
<HEAD><TITLE>onLoad example</TITLE>
<SCRIPT language="javascript1.2">

function display_images() {
  document.layers["download"].visibility="hide";
  document.layers["thumbnails"].visibility="show";
}
```

```
</SCRIPT>
</HEAD>
<BODY onload="display_images()">
<layer id=download top=20 left=20>
<h1>Please wait while images are downloading...</h1>
</layer>
<layer id=thumbnails top=20 left=20 visibility=hide>
<img src="twinstn.JPG" width=99 height=86 hspace=5 id=image1>
<img src="apophylliteltn.JPG" width=101 height=99 hspace=5>
<img src="fluorite3tn.JPG" width=100 height=108 hspace=5>
</layer>

</BODY>
```

Use this approach whenever you want to hide page contents until some event is reached (such as when all the images are loaded, or when the entire contents of a page are loaded). You can try this out with the CD-ROM's sample file, **nsonload.htm**.

Responding to User Interaction

One very important reason to trap events for the keyboard and the mouse is to provide feedback to the Web page reader. Before Navigator 4.0, most Web pages provided readers with limited feedback — usually a message in the status bar at the bottom of the browser, or a message in an alert box. With Navigator 3.x, code could be used to change images when the reader had their cursor over a menu bar, or a page could load automatically if the reader's cursor was over a hypertext link.

These techniques were a start in providing useful feedback, but they were still pretty primitive when compared to the feedback techniques of applications such as Microsoft Word or Visual C++. However, with version 4.0 of Navigator, you can do so much more.

Most Web page authors and developers would like to provide some form of their own *tips window* — which is a little information window that pops up when the cursor moves over a particular item.

Using dynamic HTML in Navigator, you can create tips based on mouse activity on any HTML element, such as moving the mouse over an image or a block of text, or clicking a link. Using layer positioning and the `visibility` property, you can create hidden blocks of text, highlighted in some manner, that, based on keyboard or mouse movement, will display the text. Based on other events, you can then rehide the text.

The next two sections document ways of implementing user-responsive Web pages; one section shows how to reveal hidden information when users move their mouse over corresponding elements, and the other shows how to highlight elements in response to mouse and keyboard events.

Revealing Hidden Elements

As an example of hiding and revealing elements based on user interaction, Figure 12-5 shows a page, **nshelp.htm** (on the CD-ROM), containing two images and nothing else. Moving the mouse over either image displays a description to the right of the image. When the mouse leaves the image area, the description disappears. The effect is intensified because the description is exposed in a gradual "sliding" manner, and is hidden using the same process. Figure 12-6 demonstrates this technique by showing one description as it is in the process of being hidden and the second description as it is in the process of being exposed.

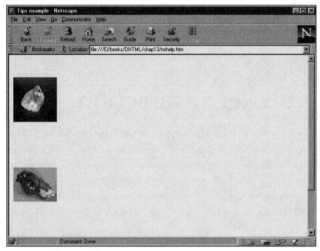

Figure 12-5: The page containing two images after the example page is first opened

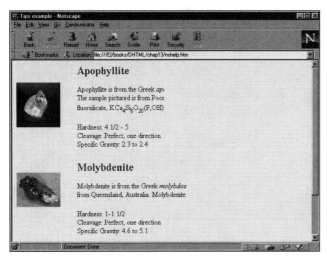

Figure 12-6: The example page after the mouse has just moved from the first image to slightly over the second image; the two descriptions are in the process of being hidden and exposed, respectively

Listing 12-7 contains the complete code for this example. Note from the listing that the same function is used to show each description, and the same function is used to hide each description, with the name of the appropriate layer being passed to the function.

Listing 12-7: Example code demonstrating how to hide and show text based on mouse movement over layers

```
<HTML>
<HEAD><TITLE>Tips example</TITLE>
<STYLE type="text/css">
    BODY { background-color: ivory; color: indigo }
    H2 { color: firebrick }
</STYLE>
<SCRIPT language="javascript1.2">

function show_message(message_name) {
 var current_layer = document.layers[message_name];
 current_layer.clip.right=-500;
 current_layer.visibility="show";
 thestep = 10;
 setTimeout(slide_contents, 75,
      current_layer, thestep-1)
}

function slide_contents(thelayer, thestep) {
 thelayer.clip.right += 50;
```

```
    if (thestep > 0)
        setTimeout(slide_contents, 75,
            thelayer, thestep-1);
}

function hide_message(message_name) {
 var current_layer = document.layers[message_name];
 thestep = 10;
 setTimeout(hide_contents, 75,
     current_layer, thestep-1)
}

function hide_contents(thelayer, thestep) {
 thelayer.clip.right -= 50;
 if (thestep > 0)
        setTimeout(hide_contents, 75,
            thelayer, thestep-1);
 else
        thelayer.visibility="hide";
}

</SCRIPT>
</HEAD>
<BODY>
<layer left=10 top=50 width=110 height=100
 onmouseover="show_message('help1')"
 onmouseout="hide_message('help1')">
<img src="apophyllite2tn.JPG" width=101 height=99>
</layer>
<layer id=help1 left=150 top=10 width=500
 height=200 visibility=hide>
<h2>Apophyllite</h2>
Apophyllite is from the Greek <em>apo</em> meaning "off" and
 <em>phyllon</em> meaning "leaves". The sample pictured is from
 Poone(Pune), India. It is Hydrous calcium potassium fluorsilicate,
KCa<sub>4</sub>Si<sub>8</sub>O<sub>20</sub>(F,OH)<sup>.</sup>8H<sub>
 2</sub>O.<p>
Hardness: 4 1/2 - 5<br>
Cleavage: Perfect, one direction<br>
Specific Gravity: 2.3 to 2.4
</layer>
<layer left=10 top=250 width=110 height=100
 onmouseover="show_message('help2')"
 onmouseout="hide_message('help2')">
<img src="vanadinite1tn.JPG" width=101 height=76>
</layer>
<layer id=help2 left=150 top=225 width=500
 height=300 visibility=hide>
<h2>Molybdenite</h2>
Molybdenite is from the Greek <em>molybdos</em> meaning "lead". The
 sample pictured is from Queensland, Australia. Molybdenite is
 Molybdenum Sulfide, MoS<sub>2</sub>.<p>
Hardness: 1-1 1/2<br>
```

```
Cleavage: Perfect, one direction<br>
Specific Gravity: 4.6 to 5.1
</layer>
</BODY>
```

Note that the functions displaying the description use the `clip.right` property. When the function `show_message` is first triggered, the `clip.right` property is set to a value of –500, which should clip the entire layer. Then it is set to be visible. Without this setting, the message would display all at once and you wouldn't get the slide effect. A timer is then called to increment the clip area, with each iteration, until the entire layer is exposed. Try this for yourself by opening the file **nshelp.htm** on the CD-ROM.

You can also display the text from both directions by using a combination of the `clip.right` and `clip.left` properties, and halving the increment size:

```
thelayer.clip.right+=increment;
thelayer.clip.left-=increment;
```

With this approach, the increment value would be 25 instead of 50. To achieve the effect of the text opening up from the center, the `clip.right` property is increased, but the `clip.left` property is decreased. These properties always move in opposite directions.

Another approach is to hide the text behind the object it is describing and use the `moveBy` method to slide the text layer either to the side, above, or below the target item.

Web page readers also prefer feedback when they click a page element such as a button. The draft specification for HTML 4.0 (see Appendix A for the URL) includes a solution – the new `<BUTTON>` element provides developers with an easy way to provide this type of feedback. The `<BUTTON>` element is a `container` object that can enclose any number of HTML elements and provides a button-like effect when the block is clicked.

I created my own example of a button-like block that encloses an image and some text. The block is surrounded by a frame, which has a light colored border on two sides and a dark colored border on the other two sides, as shown in Figure 12-7. When the Web page reader clicks the block, the border colors are reversed – the light colored sides become darker, and the dark colored sides become lighter, as shown in Figure 12-8. These borders create "button-up" and "button-down" effects.

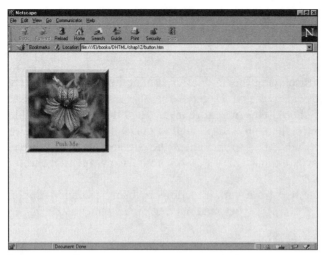

Figure 12-7: The image and text contained within a button-like background

Figure 12-8: The results of clicking the button

The example, shown in Listing 12-8, is actually very simple. Note that only an image and text were used to form the button contents of one layer: the "up" button border, which is another image enclosed in another layer, and a "down" button border, which is a third image enclosed in a third layer.

Listing 12-8: Using images and layers to create a button-up, button-down effect

```html
<HEAD>
<STYLE type="text/css">
 BODY { background-color: ivory }
 A { text-decoration: none; color: orchid; font-weight: 800; }
</STYLE>
<SCRIPT language="javascript1.2">
 function mouse_down() {
       document.layers["buttonup"].visibility="hide";
       document.layers["buttondown"].visibility="show";
       }

 function mouse_up() {
       document.layers["buttondown"].visibility="hide";
       document.layers["buttonup"].visibility="show";
       }

</SCRIPT>
</HEAD>
<body>
<layer name=buttonup width=220
      height=210 left=40 top=40>
<img src="buttonup.jpg" width=220
      height=210>
</LAYER>
<LAYER name=buttondown width=220
 height=210 left=40 top=40
 visibility="hide">
<img src="buttondn.jpg" width=220 height=210>
</LAYER>
<LAYER name=buttonblock bgcolor="lime"
 width=200 height=190 left=51 top=51 >
<a href="" onclick="return false" onmousedown="mouse_down()"
 onmouseup="mouse_up()">
<image src="button.jpg" width=200 height=164 border=0>
<center>Push Me</center>
</a>
</LAYER>
</body>
```

Again, in this example, I used the empty-link approach to capture the mousedown and mouseup events. Why not use event capturing and assignment to event handlers? Events such as mouseover and mouseout can be captured with a layer, but not click events such as click, mousedown, and mouseup. Because I wanted to capture the click event, I used the empty link.

Using Transitional Effects to Communicate with the Reader

Now it's time to apply some of the techniques discussed in this chapter. Using several of the techniques we just covered, I created an example page that provides users with feedback based on two types of events: mouse movement and key pressing.

The example page I have prepared to illustrate this technique has a header, two images with associated image titles, and two paragraphs displayed under the images. Moving a cursor over one of the images, let's say the second one, causes the descriptive paragraph associated with the image to highlight, with the font family and color changing as shown in Figure 12-9. Moving the cursor away from the image returns the paragraph to normal.

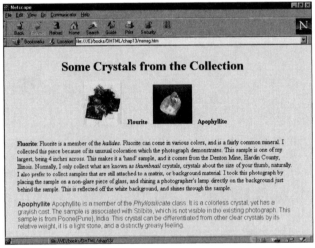

Figure 12-9: A paragraph (below) is highlighted when the cursor moves over the associated image (on the right)

The second effect occurs when the reader presses a lowercase *w* or a lowercase *h*. Pressing either key hides the normal contents of the page and displays a message associated with the specific key. For instance, Figure 12-10 shows the page when the reader presses the *h* key. The file containing the example is called **nsmsg.htm** (on the CD-ROM). The rest of this section discusses this file's contents.

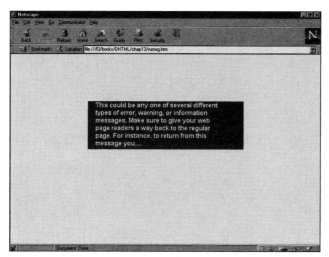

Figure 12-10: The page's content is hidden and a previously
hidden help message block is exposed

To create these effects, I first created the layers containing the two messages.
The first message uses a style sheet to define the contents of the paragraph, in addi-
tion to using inline styles for the layer. The second message uses just inline styles.
Both message layers are hidden, as shown in Listing 12-9.

Listing 12-9: The message layers, contents, and style settings

```
<layer id=messagebox1
 left=25% top=25% bgcolor="firebrick"
 width=400 height=120
 zIndex=2 visibility=hide>
<p class=msg1>
This could be any one of several different types of error, warning,
 or information messages. Make sure to give your Web page readers a
 way back to the regular page. For instance, to return from this
 message you...
</P>
</layer>
<layer id=messagebox2
 left=25% top=25% width=400 height=120
 zIndex=2 visibility=hide bgcolor="indigo">
<p style="width: 80%; margin: 20px; color: aqua">
This message was displayed because you, fair reader, pressed the
 lowercase 'w' key. Hit the ENTER key to return to normal.
</P>
</layer>
```

You always have a little room for humor, as the first message demonstrates. However, you want to make sure your Web page reader knows how to display and hide messages such as these.

Next, I created the document layer that includes all of the content that displays on the page when the messages are not displayed. This layer includes the two images and their associated titles, as well as image event capturing with an empty link, as shown in Listing 12-10.

Listing 12-10: The beginning of the document layer, including images and image event capturing

```
<layer id=wholedoc>
<H1 style="text-align: center; font-family: Cursive">
Some Crystals from the Collection
</H1>
<CENTER>
<a href="" onmouseover=
  "display_highlight('para1',true);return false"
onmouseout=
  "display_highlight('para1',false);return false">
<img src="fluorite3tn.JPG" hspace=10 id=pict1 border=0></a>
<strong>Flourite</strong>
<a href=""onmouseover=
  "display_highlight('para2',true);return false"  onmouseout=
  "display_highlight('para2',false);return false">
<img src="apophyllite2tn.JPG"
  hspace=10 id=pict2 border=0></a>
<strong>Apophyllite</strong>
</CENTER>
```

As the code shows, a value of `false` is returned when the empty-link technique is used. The next section of code includes the descriptive text for the first image. Note, though, the two identical blocks of text, each with different style settings One of these blocks is hidden, as shown in Listing 12-11. This is because Netscape did not, at least at the time this was written, expose all of the HTML elements to scripting. Because of this limitation, a second layer contains the altered formatting. It is positioned in the exact same spot as the original layer contents, and is hidden. When I want the formatting to be displayed, I set it to be visible.

Listing 12-11: Descriptive text for the first image and its associated highlighted layer

```
<layer top=200 left=0 style="color:black" id=para1>
<strong>Fluorite</strong>: Fluorite is a member of the
  <em>halides</em>.
Fluorite can come in various colors, and is a fairly common mineral.
  I collected this piece because of its unusual coloration which the
  photograph demonstrates. This sample is one of my largest, being 4
  inches across. This makes it a 'hand' sample, and it comes from the
  Denton Mine, Hardin County, Illinois. Normally, I only collect what
  are known as <em>thumbnail</em> crystals, crystals about the size
  of your thumb, naturally. I also prefer to collect samples that are
```

```
still attached to a matrix, or background material. I took this
photograph by placing the sample on a nonglare piece of glass, and
shining a photographer's lamp directly on the background just
behind the sample. This is reflected off the white background, and
shines through the sample.
</layer>
<layer top=200 left=0 style="color:red; font-family: fantasy"
visibility=hide id=para1r>
<strong>Fluorite</strong>: Fluorite is a member of the
<em>halides</em>.
Fluorite can come in various colors, and is a fairly common mineral.
I collected this piece because of its unusual coloration which the
photograph demonstrates. This sample is one of my largest, being 4
inches across. This makes it a 'hand' sample, and it comes from the
Denton Mine, Hardin County, Illinois. Normally, I only collect what
are known as <em>thumbnail</em> crystals, crystals about the size
of your thumb, naturally. I also prefer to collect samples that are
still attached to a matrix, or background material. I took this
photograph by placing the sample on a nonglare piece of glass, and
shining a photographer's lamp directly on the background just
behind the sample. This is reflected off the white background, and
shines through the sample.
</layer>
```

The next section of code contains the two layers for the next description, and this isn't listed here, but it is contained within the source file. Note that the description layers are all contained within the enclosing layer that represents the whole document.

The script to handle the page functionality is created next. First, I created the function that hides and shows the highlighted layer based on mouse movements over the images. The function, called display_highlight, takes two parameters, the root name of the layer and a Boolean value specifying whether to show the highlighted or normal text, as shown in Listing 12-12.

Listing 12-12: A function to show or hide the highlighted descriptive text layer

```
function display_highlight(root_layer, display) {
  if (display) {
    document.layers["wholedoc"].
      document.layers[root_layer].visibility="hide";
    root_layer = root_layer + "r";
      document.layers["wholedoc"].
    document.layers[root_layer].visibility="inherit";
    }
  else {
    document.layers["wholedoc"].
    document.layers[root_layer].visibility="inherit";
      root_layer = root_layer + "r";
    document.layers["wholedoc"].
      document.layers[root_layer].visibility="hide";
    }
}
```

To access the highlighted text, all I do is append an *r* to the end of the layer name. Notice the use of the value inherit instead of show for the visibility property. Because the example hides and displays the Web page contents, if the parent layer is hidden and the enclosed child layers are visible because they inherit their parent's visibility property, these layers are then hidden as well. Using a value of show leaves the text layer exposed when the Web page contents are hidden.

Next, the KEYPRESS event is captured for the window, and is associated with the function check_key, as shown next:

```
window.captureEvents(Event.KEYPRESS);
window.onkeypress=check_key;
```

The check_key function tests to see if either of the messages is displayed. If they aren't, the ASCII value of the key is tested to see if it maps to either a lowercase *w* (a value of 119) or a lowercase *h* (a value of 104). If it does, the appropriate message is displayed, and the original Web page contents are hidden. If the message is already displayed and the user has pressed the Enter key, the message is hidden and the Web page contents are then redisplayed, as shown in Listing 12-13.

Listing 12-13: Functions to process key presses

```
function check_key(e) {
  if (!displayed) {
    if (e.which == 104) {
      document.layers["wholedoc"].visibility="hide";
      document.layers["messagebox1"].visibility="show";
      }
    else if (e.which == 119) {
      document.layers["wholedoc"].visibility="hide";
      document.layers["messagebox2"].visibility="show";
      }
    displayed=true;
    }
  else {
    if (e.which == 13) {
      document.layers["messagebox1"].visibility="hide";
      document.layers["messagebox2"].visibility="hide";
      document.layers["wholedoc"].visibility="show";
      }
    displayed=false;
    }
  return false;
}
```

When the Enter key is pressed, both message visibility properties are set to hide, regardless of which is exposed.

This approach is a very effective one to take when you want to display highly critical or very important messages that require the Web page reader's immediate attention. Nothing is subtle about this approach and it should guarantee immediate response. Just make sure your reader knows how to return to "normal" after you display a message using this technique.

Summary

This chapter covered some of the techniques for capturing events and responding to the Web page reader.

In this chapter you learned how to:

◆ Capture mouse click events.

◆ Capture mouse movements.

◆ Capture keyboard events.

◆ Create drag-and-drop effects with layers.

◆ Create drag-and-drop effects with CSS1 positioning.

◆ Capture the load event.

◆ Use any element to emulate a button.

◆ Use dynamic HTML to respond to the user with dynamically changing content.

This is the last chapter of Netscape Navigator 4.0-specific examples. The next three chapters show you how to combine the Internet Explorer 4.0 and Netscape Navigator techniques you've learned so far to create cross-browser pages. In Chapter 13, you'll learn how to create a cross-browser interactive presentation page.

Part IV

Creating Cross-Browser
 Applications

Chapter 13

Creating an Interactive Presentation for Both Browsers

IN THIS CHAPTER

- Creating a cross-browser Web page object

- Positioning the basic Web page components

- Hiding, displaying, and clipping Web page contents

- Moving contents using CSS positioning

- Using hidden content to emulate dynamic changes to the `style` object

- Responding to the Web page reader

THIS CHAPTER SHOWS YOU how to use dynamic HTML to create a cross-browser interactive presentation. The topic of the presentation is something I am certain you're interested in – dynamic HTML itself. To get a sneak preview of this presentation, open the **present.htm** sample file on the CD-ROM in Netscape Navigator and then in Internet Explorer 4.0. Note that this example uses pure HTML text, no embedded controls, and no images, which means that the page downloads very quickly. As you can see, this presentation performs similarly in both browsers. When the cursor is over the word "Move," the elements move around the page and when it's over the word "Change," the elements change colors. In addition, when it's over the word, "Hide," the elements become invisible, albeit reluctantly, and when it's over the word "Respond" you, the Web page reader, are taken to another page that responds to mouse and keyboard events. The presentation page, when it is first loaded, is shown in Figure 13-1.

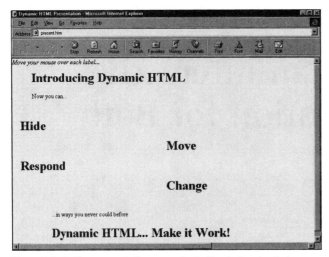

Figure 13-1: The presentation page just after being loaded

This cross-browser compatible presentation was created using the new scripting objects I call the *DHTML equalizers*, which overcome the differences in how Netscape and Explorer implement dynamic HTML. These objects, one for Internet Explorer and one for Navigator, provide a set of properties and functions that use browser-specific techniques internally, but can be controlled externally using common methods. Also, this presentation is an example of how you can use these equalizer objects to hide, display, and clip Web page contents in a manner that transcends browser differences. This is especially important when it comes to clipping, which is handled very differently by the two browsers. You can also use the objects to move HTML elements around the page.

This chapter discusses the creation and implementation of these equalizer objects and the cross-browser presentation, and also covers positioning, hiding, displaying, moving, and clipping elements, and responding to user interaction. Take note that the equalizer objects are also used in the next two chapters.

Creating a Cross-Browser Web Page Object

When I started creating this example, the first thing I noticed was how awkward it was to have to create different script blocks for Internet Explorer and Netscape Navigator. Although Microsoft and Netscape have complied with the CSS positioning (CSSP) standard, they have implemented dynamic positioning using very different techniques.

Microsoft's Internet Explorer exposes most of its dynamic HTML capability through a `style` object; Netscape's Navigator exposes the methods and properties directly off each HTML element. In addition, IE enables access to an HTML element using any one of the following techniques, given that the element is named "test" and its type is a `DIV` block, as shown next:

```
document.all(test-index)
document.all.test
document.all.tags("DIV").items("test")
document.all.item("test")
test
```

Using Navigator, accessing the element depends to some extent on what type of element it is. If it's a `layer` object, you can access it by its name or by its entry in the layer array:

```
document.layers[0]
document.layers["test"]
document.test
```

I have also found that the layer array contains the HTML block elements within the Web page, if these HTML elements have been positioned using CSS absolute positioning.

Regardless of what approach you take with either browser, it should be apparent that none of the approaches that work with one browser works with the other. So, to create content for both browsers, you have to differentiate between the two for every use of dynamic HTML.

One approach you can use is to test for the browser and use the appropriate technique based on the result. You can define a property, and attach it to the window object that contains the browser and version set, as the following code demonstrates:

```
var MS=navigator.appVersion.indexOf("MSIE")
window.isIE4 = ((parseInt(navigator.appVersion.substring(MS+5,MS+6))
 >= 4) && (navigator.appVersion.indexOf("MSIE"))>0)
var NSVER=parseInt(navigator.appVersion.substring(0,1))
if ((navigator.appName == "Netscape") &&
(NSVER == 4)){
 window.ISNS4 = true;
else
 window.ISNS4 = false;
```

This is just one technique you can use to test browser type and version number, but other ways also exist. Now, if you want to use one of the dynamic HTML techniques, such as moving an element by adjusting the value of its `left` property, you can use something like the following code:

```
if (window.ISIE4)
  document.all.theitem.style.left = 20;
else
  document.theitem.left = 20;
```

For more complex dynamic HTML routines, you can create separate scripting files and include them in the main document. Each file can contain either the Navigator implementation or the IE implementation. The same function names are used within each block, and the IE-specific script file is embedded after the Navigator script file. By default, both Navigator and IE access the last occurrence of a function if multiple functions are defined using the same name. For the IE-specific scripting file the jscript language value is used, which Navigator then ignores, as the following code demonstrates:

```
<SCRIPT src="nsobj.js" language="javascript1.2">
</SCRIPT>

<SCRIPT language="jscript" src="ieobj.js">
</SCRIPT>
```

This is definitely workable, but not an approach I recommend. The reasons why are, first, every time you want to create a new page and a new effect, you have to write code in separate blocks to handle the cross-browser compatibility problems. This seems to violate the concept of "code once, use many times." Also, if one or the other browser changes any of its properties, objects, or methods, you have to hunt through each implementation that uses that particular browser's code to make the change.

These reasons lead to my second approach, which is to create IE and Navigator objects that hide the implementation details, and then use them in all Web pages that include dynamic HTML. Because both Netscape and Microsoft support the concept of creating new objects, and the adding of methods and properties to these objects, you can create separate Navigator and IE objects.

Creating the Base Object

Each browser's "base" object is created in a separate scripting file so it can be referred to multiple times from different places. The first object is the IE object, which I call *ie_object*:

```
function ie_object(obj) {
  this.style = obj.style;
}
```

As you can see in this code, the object takes only one argument. Using JavaScript, a function is created with the name of the object, and then an instance of the object is created from the values passed through as arguments.

That's all it takes to create a new object. The parameter is assigned to an `object` property because IE does not support assignment directly to the keyword `this`. To use the new object, you must instantiate it. Because `ie_object` is, in essence, a *wrapper* object, you must pass in the basic IE element when the new object instance is created, as shown next:

```
theitem2 = new ie_object(document.all.theitem);
```

A wrapper object inherits from an existing object, and adds to or enhances the existing functionality of the object that is being wrapped. Now that the new object is created and instantiated, it can be used in the same manner as the original object. For example, the following code changes the visibility:

```
theitem2.style.visibility="hidden";
```

Now let's look at how to do the same with Navigator. As you can see, you can use the same approach. The new property is added to the object, and named `style`, as shown next:

```
function ns_object(obj) {
  this.style = obj;
}
```

Although creating an instance of this new object is very similar to creating the new instance for IE, the way the object is wrapped is different:

```
theitem2 = new ns_object(document.theitem);
```

The use of the new object is exactly the same in both browsers. Why is this? When the Navigator object was created, the object passed to the function was assigned to the `style` property, rather than to the object. When the IE object was created, the parameter object's `style` property was assigned to the new object's `style` property. Both now have a property called `style` that they can use to access and alter CSS attributes. This approach *equalizes* the IE and Navigator objects, which is why I call this technique *DHTML equalizing*, and the resulting objects *DHTML equalizers*.

An approach such as this breaks down when you try to set CSS attributes that are different between the two browsers. Good examples of this are the CSS clipping attributes. Both Navigator and IE support clipping, but in different ways. Navigator has exposed four rectangular clipping properties called `right`, `left`, `top`, and `bottom`. If you wanted to change the width of an element by using clipping using the new object, the code would be similar to the following:

```
theitem2.style.clip.left = 20;
theitem2.style.clip.right = 100;
```

IE, on the other hand, exposes CSS clipping through a function called rect, as shown next:

```
theitem2.style.clip = "rect(auto, 20, auto, 100)";
```

All the values for the clipping rectangle need to be provided, but the value of auto can be used to direct the rectangle clipping function to use existing values in place of literal values.

It's pretty obvious that the objects need to be extended in order to handle CSS attribute differences. In addition, IE and Navigator change their scripting model with each new release, so the example also needs to hide the object implementation as much as possible in order to minimize changes introduced in future browser versions. To meet these requirements, I extended the objects so they include methods to call that will access and set CSS attributes, rather than accessing or setting them directly. This approach is recommended with most object-oriented technologies, which suggest hiding the object data and exposing it only through functions.

Creating the Extended Objects

The following sections describe how to enable the extended DHTML equalizer objects to hide and show an object using the visibility property, described by the W3C positioning specification. The visibility attribute sets an element to either hidden, which makes the element invisible while reserving a space for it in the layout, and visible, which, of course, makes the object visible. Both IE and Navigator support this attribute, and the example shows how to alter this value dynamically.

Creating the DHTML Equalizer Objects for IE and Navigator

To create the DHTML equalizer objects, modify the IE object first, with the creation of two properties called hide and show, which are assigned to functions named hide_me and show_me, respectively. Also, test the current state of the visibility property by creating a method that returns the visibility property. The following code shows the extended object:

```
function ie_object(obj) {
  this.css1 = obj;
  this.hide = hide_me;
  this.show = show_me;
  this.get_visibility = get_visibility;
}
```

Note that I assigned the object to the css1 property in order to access all the properties of the object, not just the style properties, which is all I could access with my previous IE object definition.

Now create the three functions, as follows:

```
function hide_me() {
  this.css1.style.visibility = "hidden";
}

function show_me() {
  this.css1.style.visibility = "inherit";
}

function get_visibility() {
  return this.css1.style.visibility;
}
```

When you want to hide an object, the `hide` function is used rather than directly assigning a value to the CSS attribute, as the following code demonstrates:

```
theitem.hide();
```

To use the objects, they need to be instantiated, which is done within a function called `setup`. Also, because these objects need to be compatible between IE and Navigator, you should restrict which HTML elements you use to create the new extended objects. For example, both Navigator and IE expose `DIV` elements to positioning, so you should use the `DIV` element rather than some other element for cross-compatibility. Also, because you'll be picking up the `DIV` blocks from the layers array for Netscape, this also pulls in any layers within the Web page, an important concept to remember when implementing these techniques.

The next step is to create an array of equalizer objects that is equivalent to all the `DIV` blocks within the Web page. For IE, the `tags` functions are used to specifically access `DIV` blocks only, and are then assigned to the new array as equalizer objects:

```
function setup() {
   thegrp = document.all.tags("DIV");
   thegroup = new Array(thegrp.length);
   for (i = 0; i < thegrp.length; i++){
      thegroup[i] = new ie_object(thegrp[i]);
  }
}
```

Now you can access each `DIV` block within the page and alter its visibility with these two new methods. Unfortunately, with this approach, you can only access each element by its index value, which is the position it occupies when the page is first loaded. For more complex Web pages, this may be a bit difficult. Another approach you can take is to create the array but use the element's ID instead of its position as the array index, as shown next:

```
function setup() {
   thegrp = document.all.tags("DIV");
   thenamedgrp = new Array(thegrp.length);
   for (i = 0; i < thegrp.length; i++){
     thenamedgrp[thegrp[i].id] =
             new ie_object(thegrp[i]);
  }
}
```

With this approach, you can access the element by its identifier. However, a DIV block sometimes may not have a name, or you may want to do something for all the elements, in which case using the numeric index would be handier. The solution? Create both arrays, and use the objects that fit the situation best:

```
function setup() {
   thegrp = document.all.tags("DIV");
   thegroup = new Array(thegrp.length);
   thenamedgrp = new Array(thegrp.length);
   for (i = 0; i < thegrp.length; i++){
     thegroup[i] = new ie_object(thegrp[i]);
     thenamedgrp[thegrp[i].id] =
             new ie_object(thegrp[i]);
  }
}
```

Why use an ID instead of a name? At times you may want to access the element using the named group, and directly using the document.all.items(id) syntax. The latter only works with identifiers and won't work with names. The IE object code can be found in a sample file on the CD-ROM called **ieobj.js**.

You can use very similar code to create the Navigator equalizer object, as shown next:

```
function ns_object(obj) {
 this.style = obj;
 this.hide = hide_me;
 this.show = show_me;
 this.get_visibility = get_visibility;
  }
```

You can create the three methods for Navigator, just as you saw in the earlier code for IE:

```
function hide_me() {
 this.style.visibility = "hidden";
}

function show_me() {
 this.style.visibility = "inherit";
}
```

```
function get_visibility() {
  return this.style.visibility;
}
```

And finally, you can create the Navigator-specific setup function. Note that it has the same name as the function used to instantiate the IE equalizer objects. With this approach, and including the code for the objects in their own script blocks, each browser picks the setup code applicable for it:

```
function setup() {
    thegroup = new Array(document.layers.length);
    thenamedgrp = new Array(document.layers.length);
    for (i = 0; i < document.layers.length; i++){
        thegroup[i] = new ns_object(document.layers[i]);
        thenamedgrp[document.layers[i].id] =
               new ns_object(document.layers[i]);
  }
}
```

The Navigator equalizer object code is included in a file named **nsobj.js** on the CD-ROM .

At this point you have created the browser-specific objects, and the methods to hide and show the elements, and access the visibility property. You have also created a setup routine that creates arrays of these objects for each of the DIV blocks within the page. You're now ready to try out the code, and Listing 13-1 contains an example of using the objects. This code can also be accessed directly in the file **visobj.htm** on the CD-ROM.

Listing 13-1: A Web page to test the equalizer elements

```
<!DOCTYPE HTML PUBLIC "-//W3C//DTD W3 HTML 3.2//EN">
<HTML>
<HEAD><TITLE>test</TITLE>
<STYLE type="text/css">
 DIV {margin-top: 10 }
 H1 A { text-decoration: none; color: red }
</STYLE>
<SCRIPT language="javascript">
<!--
function clicked_header() {
   if (thenamedgrp["second"].get_visibility()
       == "inherit")
       thenamedgrp["second"].hide();
   else
       thenamedgrp["second"].show();
}
//-->
</SCRIPT>

<SCRIPT src="nsobj.js" language="javascript1.2">
</SCRIPT>
```

```
<SCRIPT language="jscript" src="ieobj.js">
</SCRIPT>
</HEAD>
<BODY onload="setup()">
<DIV name="first" style="position:relative">
<H1 id=head1><a href="" onclick="clicked_header();return
 false">Working with Images and Text</a></H1>
No matter what new HTML elements are supported by a browser, most of
 the content of a page will usually be some form of text, or some
 type of image.
</DIV>
<DIV name="second"
style="position:relative; visibility:inherit">
With dynamic HTML, you can now do much more with Web page text and
 images than just passively display them.
With text you can change the font family, size, or color, as well as
 move it to a different location, or alter it in some manner. You
 can hide images, move them also, flip them, or stack them one on
 each other for a slide show or online animation.
</DIV>
<DIV style="position:relative">
This section covers some fun changes you can make to text and images
 using dynamic HTML.
</DIV>
</BODY>
</HTML>
```

As you can see, the file **visobj.htm** on the CD-ROM contains three paragraphs and a header. In my example, I enclosed the header within a stubbed anchor to capture the click event for the header. Normally I wouldn't need to do this for IE, but Navigator also accesses this Web page and it doesn't have the capability to capture the click event for a header element. For Navigator, I could have taken another approach and captured the click event for the document and then used this to trigger the function, because both Navigator and IE support this type of event capturing. (See Chapter 14 for drag-and-drop examples that use both event techniques.)

The paragraphs within the page are enclosed with DIV blocks, and the first two are named first and second, respectively. I left the third unnamed. The click event handler accesses the named equalizer array, and calls the hide method for the element if it is visible, or the show method if it is hidden.

Also note from Listing 13-1 that source files for both the IE and Navigator objects are included in the Web page, each with its own scripting language attribute value, and the IE-specific file included last. The language used for the block they share is set to "JavaScript."

Figure 13-2 shows the Web page with the middle paragraph hidden as it would display in IE, and Figure 13-3 shows the same Web page loaded into Navigator, again with the second paragraph hidden.

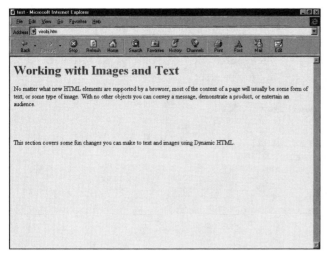

Figure 13-2: A Web page to test the equalizer object, displayed in IE

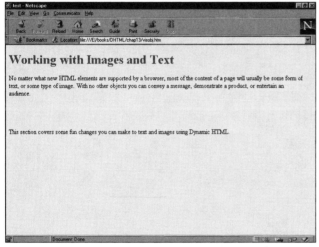

Figure 13-3: A Web page to test the equalizer object, displayed
in Navigator

Now that you have had a chance to test out the new objects, you can add new methods to the object. The following code includes many methods, some of which are used in the presentation example. You can always add or modify the methods in this code to suit specific projects, if need be. However, be aware that modifying or removing methods for one application will most likely break other applications that use the object. As a rule of thumb, your objects are less likely to break if you only make constructive changes to the methods, such as adding a parameter at the end of the parameter list, or adding a new function. Listing 13-2 shows my completed IE DHTML equalizer object source file that you can use to create cross-browser compatible dynamic HTML Web pages.

Listing 13-2: The IE equalizer object source code file

```
// function to instantiate equalizer objects
function setup() {
    thegrp = document.all.tags("DIV");
    thegroup = new Array(thegrp.length);
    thenamedgrp = new Array(thegrp.length);
    for (i = 0; i < thegrp.length; i++){
        thegroup[i] = new ie_object(thegrp[i]);
  thenamedgrp[thegrp[i].name] = new ie_object(thegrp[i]);
  }
}

// create IE DHTML equalizer object
function ie_object(obj) {
  this.css1 = obj;
  this.hide = hide_me;
  this.show = show_me;
  this.get_visibility = get_visibility;
  this.get_left = get_left;
  this.get_top = get_top;
  this.set_left = set_left;
  this.set_top = set_top;
  this.move = move_object;
  this.moveby = moveby;
  this.get_width = get_width;
  this.get_height = get_height;
  this.set_width = set_width;
  this.set_height = set_height;
  this.set_zindex = set_zindex;
  this.get_zindex = get_zindex;
  this.clip_obj = clip_obj;
  this.get_clip_right = get_clip_right;
  this.get_clip_top = get_clip_top;
  this.get_clip_left = get_clip_left;
  this.get_clip_bottom = get_clip_bottom;
}

// hide element
function hide_me() {
  this.css1.style.visibility = "hidden";
}

// show element
function show_me() {
  this.css1.style.visibility = "inherit";
}
```

```
// return element's visibility
function get_visibility() {
 return this.css1.style.visibility;
}

// element's left position
function get_left() {
 var left = this.css1.style.pixelLeft;
 return left;
}

// element's top position
function get_top () {
 var top = this.css1.style.pixelTop;
 return top;
}

// set element's top position
function set_top (top) {
 this.css1.style.top = top;
}

// set element's left position
function set_left(left) {
 this.css1.style.left = left;
}

// make absolute move
function move_object(newleft, newtop) {
 this.css1.style.left = newleft;
 this.css1.style.top = newtop;
}

// move relative to current location
function moveby(left, top) {
 this.css1.style.left= this.style.pixelLeft + left;
 this.css1.style.top = this.style.pixelTop + top;
}

// get element's width
function get_width() {
 return this.css1.style.pixelWidth;
}

// get element's height
function get_height() {
 return this.css1.style.height;
}

// get element's height
function set_height(height) {
 this.css1.style.pixelHeight = height;
}
```

```
// set element's width
function set_width(width) {
  this.css1.style.pixelWidth = width;
}

// set element's zindex order
function set_zindex(zindex) {
  this.css1.style.zIndex = zindex;
}

// get element's current zindex order
function get_zindex(zindex) {
  return this.css1.style.zIndex;
}

// clip object
function clip_obj(top,left, bottom, right) {
  var rectstring = "rect(" + top + "," + right + "," + bottom + "," +
  left + ")";
  this.css1.style.clip = rectstring;
}

// get current clip right
function get_clip_right() {
  var tmp = this.get_width();
  return tmp;
}

// get current clip left
function get_clip_left() {
  return this.get_left();
}

// get current clip top
function get_clip_top() {
  return this.get_top();
}

// get current clip bottom
function get_clip_bottom() {
  return this.get_height();
}
```

In this code, I created methods that move an element using absolute positioning or relative positioning, increase the element's size, change the clipping region, and change the element's z-order. Note the approach I used for setting the clipping region. I created a string that concatenates all four of the clipping region values and then applied the resulting value to the CSS attribute. The presentation shows how this technique can be used when only some of the values are changing.

Listing 13-3 contains the complete source code for the Navigator equalizer object.

Listing 13-3: The Navigator equalizer object

```
// function to instantiate equalizer objects
function setup() {
   thegroup = new Array(document.layers.length);
   thenamedgrp = new Array(document.layers.length);
   for (i = 0; i < document.layers.length; i++){
 thegroup[i] = new ns_object(document.layers[i]);
      thenamedgrp[document.layers[i].name] = new
 ns_object(document.layers[i]);
 }
}

// create NS DHTML equalizer object
function ns_object(obj) {
 this.style = obj;
 this.hide = hide_me;
 this.show = show_me;
 this.get_visibility = get_visibility;
 this.get_left = get_left;
 this.get_top = get_top;
 this.set_left = set_left;
 this.set_top = set_top;
 this.move = move_object;
 this.moveby = moveby;
 this.get_width = get_width;
 this.get_height = get_height;
 this.set_width = set_width;
 this.set_height = set_height;
 this.set_zindex = set_zindex;
 this.get_zindex = get_zindex;
 this.clip_obj = clip_obj;
 this.get_clip_right = get_clip_right;
 this.get_clip_top = get_clip_top;
 this.get_clip_left = get_clip_left;
 this.get_clip_bottom = get_clip_bottom;
}

// hide element
function hide_me() {
 this.style.visibility = "hidden";
}

// show element
function show_me() {
 this.style.visibility = "inherit";
}

// return element's visibility
function get_visibility() {
 return this.style.visibility;
}
```

```
// element's left position
function get_left() {
 var left = this.style.left;
 return left;
}

// element's top position
function get_top () {
 var top = this.style.top;
 return top;
}

// set element's top position
function set_top() {
 this.style.top = top;
}

// set element's left position
function set_left() {
 this.style.left = left;
}

// make absolute move
function move_object(newleft, newtop) {
 this.style.left = newleft;
 this.style.top = newtop;
}

// move relative to current location
function moveby(left, top) {
 this.style.left = this.style.left + left;
 this.style.top = this.style.top + top;
}

// get element's width
function get_width() {
 return this.style.width;
}

// get element's height
function get_height() {
 return this.style.height;
}

// set element's width
function set_width(width) {
 this.style.width = width;
}

// set element's height
function set_height(height) {
 this.style.height = height;
}
```

```
// set element's zindex order
function set_zindex(zindex) {
 this.style.zIndex = zindex;
}

// get element's current zindex order
function get_zindex() {
 return style.zIndex;
}

// clip object
function clip_obj (top,left,bottom,right) {
 this.style.clip.left = left;
 this.style.clip.right = right;
 this.style.clip.Top = top;
 this.style.clip.Bottom = bottom;
}

// get current clip right
function get_clip_right() {
 return this.style.clip.right;
}

// get current clip left
function get_clip_left() {
 return this.style.clip.left;
}

// get current clip top
function get_clip_top() {
 return this.style.clip.top;
}

// get current clip bottom
function get_clip_bottom() {
 return this.style.clip.bottom;
}
```

Notice from Listing 13-3 the different approach I had to take to handle clipping for Navigator. Unlike IE, Navigator has four exposed attributes that can be set individually.

That's it for the equalizer objects. The next section covers how these equalizer objects are used in the cross-browser dynamic HTML presentation.

Positioning the Basic Web Page Components

The presentation page is actually fairly plain, and primarily in black and white. This appearance makes it simple to download, and viewable on most machines.

You can view this page at any time by accessing the sample file **present.htm** on the CD-ROM.

In this example, the page contents are composed of several blocks of text evenly distributed throughout the page. Style sheet rules define the location and appearance of the blocks, using absolute positioning, as shown in Listing 13-4.

Listing 13-4: The style sheet for the demonstration page

```
<STYLE type="text/css">
 BODY { background-color: white; color: black }
 A { color: black; text-decoration: none }
 .demo {position: absolute; top:0; left: 0}
 .top { position: absolute; top:30px; left: 50px}
 .hide { position: absolute; top: 150; left: 20 }
 .move {position: absolute; top: 200; left: 400 }
 .change { position: absolute; top: 300; left: 400 }
 .respond { position: absolute; top: 250; left: 20 }
 .bottom { position: absolute; top: 380; left: 100;
              width:500}
</STYLE>
```

DIV blocks contain the visible page elements. To support the named element array for the equalizer object, each of the DIV blocks contains an ID attribute, as shown in Listing 13-5.

Listing 13-5: The presentation page's visible objects

```
<DIV id="thedemo" class="demo">
<em>Move your mouse over each label...</em>
</DIV>

<DIV id="thetop" class="top">
<a href="" onclick="if (effect == 0)alert('I am a lazy label...I do
 absolutely nothing');return false">
<h1>Introducing Dynamic HTML</h1>
Now you can...</a>
</DIV>

<DIV id="hideme" class="hide">
<H1><a href="" onclick="return false"
 onmouseover="hideall()">Hide</a></H1></DIV>
<DIV id="moveme" class="move">
<H1><a href="" onclick="return false"
 onmouseover="start_rotate()">Move</a></h1></DIV>
<DIV id="changeme" class="change">
<H1><a href="" onclick="return false"
 onmouseover="change_doc()">Change</a></H1></DIV>
<DIV id="respondme" class="respond">
<H1><a href="" onclick="return false"
 onmouseover="begin_respond()">Respond</a></h1>
</DIV>
```

```
<DIV id="thebottom" class="bottom">
...in ways you never could before
<H1><a href="" onclick="if (effect == 0)alert('I am a lazy label...I
  do absolutely nothing');return false">
Dynamic HTML...</a>
<a href="" onclick="theend();return false">Make it Work!</a></H1>
</DIV>
```

The page contains four actions: hide, move, change, and respond. The element that contains the text for each action calls an associated function to perform the specific action.

Speaking of these actions, it's time to look at how the first action functions, which runs when the Web page reader moves his or her mouse over the word "Hide."

Hiding, Displaying, and Clipping Web Page Contents

When the mouse is moved over the word "Hide," the elements within the page begin to disappear, starting with the top and ending with the "Dynamic HTML . . . Make it Work!" statement. For a little extra fun, the last text block does not seem to want to go willingly, an effect that is created by clipping and displaying a hidden block so that it seems as if the original block is crying out for help. This is an example of how you can hide and display elements with dynamic HTML using the new equalizer objects. Figure 13-4 shows the effect when the hidden message is displayed in Navigator.

Figure 13-4: The hide effect with the hidden message displayed, in Navigator

For this effect, divisions were extended to include text that are displayed when the last block on the page is hidden:

```
<DIV id="theno" class="message" style="visibility:hidden">
No!
<br>  No!
</DIV>
```

Also, a `message` style sheet class was added to handle the location and appearance of the element:

```
.message { position: absolute; top: 380; left: 20;
        font-weight: bold; color:red; width: 500}
```

Then a new global variable was added, called `effect`.

 When one effect is in operation, another effect shouldn't start, so remember, when you begin one effect, to set the `effect` variable to a value indicating that an effect is in operation. Then be sure to check this variable when starting an action.

Separate scripting files for each presentation action effect were created. In this example, for the "hide" effect, the sample file name containing the code to create the effect is named **hide.js** (on the CD-ROM). The first function called is `hideall`, which checks to make sure another effect is not in operation, and then starts a timer, which, in turn, invokes another function called `hide_object`. This latter function hides whichever object will be hidden next by using the equalizer object `hide` method, and then resets the timer. At the end of this routine, another function to hide the last text block is invoked, as shown in Listing 13-6.

Listing 13-6: The hide effect's hideall and hide_object functions

```
function hideall() {
      if (effect != 0) return;
      effect=1;
 window.setTimeout("hide_object()", 200);
}

function hide_object() {
 thegroup[count].hide();
 count++;
 if (count < lastitem)
      setTimeout("hide_object()",200);
 else {
      effect = 0;
```

```
        setTimeout("jiggled_hide()",200);
        hide_effect = 0;
        hide_right =
            thegroup[lastitem].get_clip_right() - 100;
    }
}
```

To create the block of text that is "reluctant" to hide, a function called
`jiggled_hide` is called last, and uses clipping for the effect. An array for
the `jiggled_hide` function is created to contain size difference information. This
information is used to reset the clipping region for the last text block each time the
object is resized and whenever the function is called. The clipping region grows
and shrinks in order to create the "unwillingness to disappear" look. Finally,
another function is called to re-expose the objects after they are all hidden. Listing
13-7 contains the clipping array and function.

**Listing 13-7: The clipping array, the hiding function, and the function to re-expose all the
objects at the end of the effect**

```
var hide_size = new Array(6);
hide_size[0] = 100;
hide_size[1] = -50;
hide_size[2] = -75;
hide_size[3] = 100;
hide_size[4] = -25;
hide_size[5] = -25;
hide_size[6] = 25;
hide_size[7] = 25;
hide_size[8] = -25;
hide_size[9] = 25;
hide_size[10] = 50;
hide_size[11] = 25;
hide_size[12] = -25;
hide_size[13] = 25;
hide_size[14] = -25;
hide_size[15] = 50;
hide_right = 0;
// jiggled_hide
function jiggled_hide() {
  var theright = thegroup[lastitem].get_clip_right();
  thegroup[lastitem].
        clip_obj("auto",hide_size[hide_effect],"auto",
        theright - hide_size[hide_effect]);
  hide_effect++;
  if (hide_effect < hide_size.length) {
        if(hide_effect ==
            Math.round(hide_size.length / 2))
            thegroup[7].show();
        setTimeout("jiggled_hide()",200);
        }
  else {
```

```
        thegroup[lastitem].hide();
        thegroup[lastitem+1].hide();
        thegroup[lastitem].
                clip_obj("auto",0,"auto",hide_right+100);
        setTimeout("expose_objects()", 3000);
        }
}

function expose_objects() {
  count = 0;
  for (i = 0; i <= lastitem; i++)
        thegroup[i].show();
  effect=0;
}
```

Notice the use of two of the equalizer object methods, get_clip_right and clip_obj, in addition to the hide method. The clip_obj method uses auto for the top and bottom parameters, because only the object width is being clipped. Using a value of auto should result in the specific style property being set to the value equal to its opposite, such as top and bottom. When both are set, neither clipping value changes. Also, in this code, the resizing value has been added to the left parameter, and is subtracted from the right parameter. Based on the positive or negative sign of the resizing array value, this either causes the object to grow or to shrink. Halfway through the effect the message block containing the words "No! No!" is shown.

That's it for the "hide" effect. The next effect implemented is the "move" effect.

Moving Contents Using CSS Positioning

The "move" effect dances the elements around the middle of the page, and exposes some supporting messages to compliment the effect.

To create this dancing effect, a couple more DIV blocks were added to hold the messages that are displayed during this effect. Because they are located in the same place on the page and have a similar appearance to the other messages on the page, these messages can use the same style sheet class as the message displayed during the "hide" action. The message blocks are shown here:

```
<DIV id="thegetdown" class="message" style="visibility:hidden">
Get Down<br>
Boogie On
</DIV>
<DIV id="eatdust" class="message" style="visibility:hidden">
DHTML<br>
Rocks!
</DIV>
```

New Elements Added to Object Arrays Automatically

One benefit of the Navigator layers array and the IE `tags` function is that as elements are added to the Web page for each new effect, they are automatically added to the equalizer object arrays. The only restriction is that the elements must match the type of element that is being searched for with the `tags` array for IE, and the block must use absolute positioning for Navigator.

The scripting source file for this animation is **move.js**, and the first function for it is `start_rotate`, which sets the action elements to their starting position and then creates a timer. The timer invokes another function that creates the motion of elements traveling to the center of the page, as shown in Listing 13-8. This motion is accomplished by using the dynamic relative positioning object methods of `get_left`, `get_top`, `move`, **and** `moveby`.

Listing 13-8: The start_rotate function that starts the "move" effect

```
function start_rotate() {
    if (effect != 0) return;
    effect=2;
    for (i =0; i < 4; i++) {
        hold_positions[i] = new position(
        thegroup[i+2].get_left(),
        thegroup[i+2].get_top())
        }
    thenamedgrp["hideme"].move(0,0);
    thenamedgrp["moveme"].move(window_width - 250, 0);
    thenamedgrp["changeme"].move(0,window_height - 200);
    thenamedgrp["respondme"].
        move(window_width - 250, window_height - 200);

    setTimeout("move_in()", 200);
}

function move_in() {
    thenamedgrp["hideme"].moveby(25,25);
    thenamedgrp["moveme"].moveby(-25,25);
    thenamedgrp["changeme"].moveby(25,-25);
    thenamedgrp["respondme"].moveby(-25,-25);
    count++;
    if (count < 8)
        setTimeout("move_in()",200);
    else {
        count=0;
        thenamedgrp["thegetdown"].show();
        setTimeout("cycle()", 200);
        }
    }
```

The `move` method uses absolute positioning, and the element is moved to whatever location is passed in as arguments. The `moveby` function uses relational positioning and moves the element the distance specified by the method arguments.

As you can see from Listing 13-8, the inward movement of the elements occurs because the top elements are moved down the page and the bottom elements are moved up the page. To do this, the top position of the upper elements is increased, and the top position of the bottom elements is decreased.

Furthermore, the left position is incremented for elements located on the left side of the page, and decremented for those elements on the right side of the page. At the end of the movement, another timer is created and another function is called that creates the second aspect of the element movement, `cycle`.

The `cycle` function moves the elements up and down, creating the dancing effect. The function also displays the complimentary messages during the movement, as you can see from Figure 13-5.

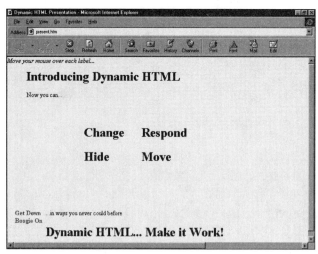

Figure 13-5: A snapshot of the "move" effect, with one of the supporting messages displayed

Listing 13-9 shows the `cycle` function, and the `reverse_cycle` function, which reverses the movement of the element in the middle of the page.

Listing 13-9: The cycle and reverse_cycle functions, which control the element "dancing"

```
function cycle() {
    thenamedgrp["hideme"].moveby(0,10);
    thenamedgrp["moveme"].moveby(0,10);
    thenamedgrp["changeme"].moveby(0,-10);
    thenamedgrp["respondme"].moveby(0,-10);
    count++;
    if (count < 4)
```

```
            setTimeout("cycle()",100);
    else {
        count=0;
        sequence++;
        if (sequence < 4) {
                if (sequence == 2) {
                        thenamedgrp["thegetdown"].hide();
                        thenamedgrp["rocks"].show();
                        }
                setTimeout("reverse_cycle()",100);
                }
        else
                setTimeout("move_out()",200);
 }
}

function reverse_cycle() {
    thenamedgrp["hideme"].moveby(0,-10);
    thenamedgrp["moveme"].moveby(0,-10);
    thenamedgrp["changeme"].moveby(0,10);
    thenamedgrp["respondme"].moveby(0,10);
    count++;
    if (count < 4)
        setTimeout("reverse_cycle()",100);
    else {
        count = 0;
        if (sequence < 4)
                setTimeout("cycle()",100);
        }
}
```

The cycle function invokes itself when its timer event occurs, until the counter reaches the specified value. Finally, at the end of the dance movement, the move_out function is called, which reverses the movement of the elements that occurred with the inward movement. Listing 13-10 contains this function and the original function, which returns all the elements to their original positions.

Listing 13-10: Returning the elements to their original positions by reversing the inward movement and resetting to the original position

```
function move_out() {
    thenamedgrp["hideme"].moveby( 25, 25);
    thenamedgrp["moveme"].moveby(25,-25);
    thenamedgrp["changeme"].moveby(-25,25);
    thenamedgrp["respondme"].moveby(25,25);
    count++;
    if (count < 8)
        setTimeout("move_out()",200);
    else {
        count=0;
        setTimeout("original()", 300);
        }
 }
```

```
function original() {
    thegroup[9].hide();
    for(i = 0; i < hold_positions.length; i++)
        thegroup[i+2].move(hold_positions[i].left,
        hold_positions[i].top);
    effect=0;
    count=0;
    sequence=0;
}
```

Notice from all these functions that the named equalizer object array is used for this presentation. The main reason for this is that specific elements are accessed for the effect, as opposed to what occurs with the "hide" action, which uses a generalized element array.

The next section covers how to dynamically alter the look of HTML elements, as demonstrated in the "change" action.

Using Hidden Content to Emulate HTML Change

One major difference between IE and Navigator 4.0 is that Microsoft enables you to alter the style settings of any HTML element, something that Navigator 4.0 doesn't let you do. This becomes a bit of a problem with the "change" effect because I cannot alter the HTML elements after a page has displayed.

With IE, to alter the color of an element, I can apply a change to the element's style property, as shown in the next code block:

```
document.all.hideme.style.color="red";
```

Unfortunately, this only works with IE 4.x at this time.

One thing Navigator lets me do is to access the document property of a layer or DIV object, and write new content to it, as demonstrated in the following code:

```
document.hideme.document.write("<H1 style='color:red'>Hide</H1>");
document.close();
```

This technique is very effective (and is also used in Chapter 14). However, it won't work with IE, and this example needs a cross-browser approach. For cross-browser compatibility, you can create new versions of existing elements with the properties you want to display, and keep them hidden until you need to display the "altered element" as shown in this Web page application. The downside to this approach is that you have to create new elements for each effect you want to implement, and this approach does increase the file size of the page because of the new elements. However, if the elements are text only, the impact is negligible as long as you don't get too carried away. So, as you can see, workarounds exist for browser differences.

The code for the new `DIV` blocks created for this presentation have the same content and same position as the first `DIV`s, except they are a different color and their `visibility` properties are set to `hidden`, as shown in Listing 13-11.

Listing 13-11: The new DIV blocks containing the elements with the altered style settings

```
<DIV id="rhideme" class="hide"
 style="visibility: hidden;color:red">
<H1>Hide</H1></DIV>
<DIV id="rmoveme" class="move"
 style="visibility: hidden;color:red">
<H1>Move</h1></DIV>
<DIV id="rchangeme" class="change"
 style="visibility: hidden;color:red">
<H1>Change</H1></DIV>
<DIV id="rrespondme" class="respond"
 style="visibility: hidden;color:red">
<H1>Respond</h1></DIV>

<DIV id="bhideme" class="hide"
style="visibility: hidden;color:blue">
<H1>Hide</H1></DIV>
<DIV id="bmoveme" class="move"
style="visibility: hidden;color:blue">
<H1>Move</h1></DIV>
<DIV id="bchangeme" class="change"
style="visibility: hidden;color:blue">
<H1>Change</H1></DIV>
<DIV id="brespondme" class="respond"
style="visibility: hidden;color:blue">
<H1>Respond</h1></DIV>

<DIV id="ghideme" class="hide"
style="visibility: hidden;color:lime">
<H1>Hide</H1></DIV>
<DIV id="gmoveme" class="move"
style="visibility: hidden;color:lime">
<H1>Move</h1></DIV>
<DIV id="gchangeme" class="change"
style="visibility: hidden;color:lime">
<H1>Change</H1></DIV>
<DIV id="grespondme" class="respond"
style="visibility: hidden;color:lime">
<H1>Respond</h1>
</DIV>
<DIV id="getout2"
 style="position:absolute; left:50; top:50; visibility:hidden; font-
 weight:bold">
Click on "Make it Work" to stop effect
</DIV>
```

Notice from the listing that each `DIV` block uses the same class as its corresponding original element, and then extends the style sheet with inline style settings, which changes the visibility and color. Also notice that the last `DIV` block contains the information about how the reader can stop the "change" effect.

The sample file on the CD-ROM that contains the source code for the "change" effect is **change.js**, and Listing 13-12 shows the code.

Listing 13-12: An example of the change color object and array, and a color-changing function

```
count = 0;

function change_clr(old, newobj) {
 this.old = old;
 this.newclr = newobj;
}

chgarray = new Array(4);
chgarray[0] = new change_clr(2,12);
chgarray[1] = new change_clr(12,16);
chgarray[2] = new change_clr(16,20);
chgarray[3] = new change_clr(20,2);

var color_timeout;
var shownew = 0;
var hideold = 0;

function theend() {
    if (effect != 4) return;
    clearTimeout(color_timeout);
    effect = 0;
    count = 0;
    hideold = shownew;
    shownew = 2;
    for(i = hideold; i < hideold + 4; i++)
  thegroup[i].hide();
    for(i = shownew; i < shownew + 4; i++) {
  thegroup[i].show();
  }
    thenamedgrp["getout2"].hide();
    thenamedgrp["thetop"].show();
}

function change_doc() {
    if (effect != 0)
    return;
    thenamedgrp["thetop"].hide();
    thenamedgrp["getout2"].show();
    effect = 4;
    change_divs();
}
```

```
function change_divs() {
   hideold = chgarray[count].old;
   shownew = chgarray[count].newclr;
   for(i = hideold; i < hideold + 4; i++)
 thegroup[i].hide();
   for(i = shownew; i < shownew + 4; i++) {
 thegroup[i].show();
 }
  count++;
  if (count == 4)
  count = 0
  color_timeout = setTimeout("change_divs()", 400);
}
```

In this example, the first function called is change_doc, which hides the top text block and displays a hidden text block that tells the reader how to stop the "change" effect

The change_divs function uses a timer to create the changing color effect, but this time assigns the timer to a global variable. It also uses an array of objects created for the effect. This array maintains the order of elements that will be displayed and hidden with each iteration of the timer. When you use this approach, the elements with the different colors are kept together and the same element content as the original elements are maintained (for example, red "Hide," "Change," "Move," and "Respond" action elements are displayed, then blue, and so on). The rest of the code creates the color object, the array, and the change_divs function.

As the listing shows, the color array provides the starting element for the action element DIV blocks. The first object element contains a reference to the block to hide, the second provides the reference to the block to display. A timer is used to set the event to trigger the next call of the function. No end point for this timer exists because the timer continues until the page is unloaded or until the reader ends it by clicking the target text.

When you take a second look at the DIV block that contains "Make it Work" and stops the "change" effect, you can see that it also contains a stub anchor to trap the click event and call a function called theend, as follows:

```
<DIV name="thebottom" class="bottom">
...in ways you never could before
<H1><a href=""
onclick="if (effect == 0)alert('I am a lazy label...I do absolutely
  nothing');return false">
Dynamic HTML...</a>
<a href="" onclick="theend();return false">Make it Work!</a></H1>
</DIV>
```

The theend function stops the timer by clearing it, hides whichever elements are currently displayed and then displays the original action elements. It also hides the information about how the effect is stopped, and redisplays the original document header:

```
function theend() {
    if (effect != 4) return;
    clearTimeout(color_timeout);
    effect = 0;
    count = 0;
    hideold = shownew;
    shownew = 2;
    for(i = hideold; i < hideold + 4; i++)
    thegroup[i].hide();
    for(i = shownew; i < shownew + 4; i++) {
    thegroup[i].show();
    }
    thenamedgrp["getout2"].hide();
    thenamedgrp["thetop"].show();
}
```

That's it for the "change" effect. You can see these tricks in action by accessing **present.htm** on the CD-ROM, or you can check out Figure 13-6, which shows the page in the process of changing. The color may not be apparent from the image in this book, but the altered header should be noticeable.

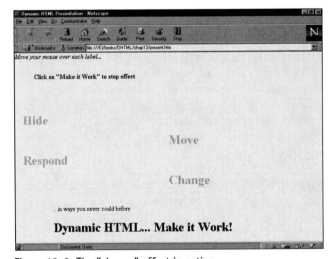

Figure 13-6: The "change" effect in action

Responding to the Web Page Reader

Another difference between the two browsers is how they support event handling. Both Navigator and IE have an `event` object, yet the properties for the object differ. Not only is event capturing different, but which elements trigger which events differs also.

However, just because the event handling differs doesn't mean you can't implement some of the same functionality for both browsers, though you may have to handle the events themselves differently.

The "respond" effect hides all of the elements on the page, changes the background color to yellow, and displays two messages. One message reads, "Ouch!" and marks where on the page the Web page reader clicks. The other message provides instructions to the Web page reader about how to end the effect. The effect is ended when the Web page reader presses the *s* or *S* key.

The functions to implement this effect are found in either the presentation file itself, **present.htm**, or in the script source file **respond.js** (on the CD-ROM). The effect begins with the begin_respond function, which hides all the elements on the page. Then the function tests the browser and sets the background color using the browser-specific code. For Navigator, the code also starts event capturing for the keyboard. You can see this function in Listing 13-13.

Listing 13-13: Beginning the "respond" effect by hiding all the elements

```
function begin_respond() {
 if (effect != 0) return;
 effect = 3;
 for (i = 0; i < thegroup.length; i++)
      thegroup[i].hide();
 if (window.ISIE4) {
      document.body.style.backgroundColor="yellow";
 }
 else {
    document.bgColor="yellow";
    window.captureEvents(Event.CLICK);
    window.onclick=mouseclick;
    document.captureEvents(Event.KEYPRESS);
    document.onkeypress = keypress;
 }
 thenamedgrp["ouch"].show();
 thenamedgrp["getout"].show();
}
```

As I said earlier, although there has to be code to handle the differences with the event handling, you can use the same code to hide all the elements on the page and display the two text blocks that will later be replaced by hidden ones. But aside from this function, all the functions are browser-specific except for the very last function that ends the effect.

For Navigator, I created a function to handle the mouse click, and a function to handle a key press, as shown next:

```
function mouseclick(e) {
 thenamedgrp["ouch"].move(e.x, e.y);
}
```

```
function keypress(e) {
   if (effect != 3) return;
   if (e.which == 83 || e.which == 115) {
      window.releaseEvents(Event.CLICK |
            Event.KEYPRESS);
      document.bgColor="white";
      end_respond();
      }
}
```

Again, the event handler for the mouse click uses the move method created for the equalizer object. The keypress function tests for the target keys and calls the end_respond function if the reader presses the effect-ending key (*s* or *S*). It also sets the background color back to white when the effect is ended.

The IE code is placed directly into the **present.htm** sample file, because the event-capturing technique is coded directly into the <SCRIPT> tag. This code is very similar to Navigator's in that it moves the element based on the mouse click, and checks each key press for the target key to end the effect. It also sets the background color back to white and calls end_respond when the reader presses *s* or *S*, as shown next:

```
<SCRIPT FOR=document EVENT=onclick language="jscript">
if (effect == 3)
  thenamedgrp["ouch"].move(event.x, event.y)
</SCRIPT>

<SCRIPT FOR=document EVENT=onkeypress language="jscript">
if (effect != 3) return;
if (event.keyCode == 83 || event.keyCode == 115) {
      document.body.style.backgroundColor="white";
      end_respond();
      }
</SCRIPT>
```

The final bit of code for this effect, and for the entire presentation, is end_respond, which redisplays the original element and hides the two text blocks used for the effect:

```
function end_respond() {
      for (i=0; i <= lastitem; i++)
      thegroup[i].show();
      thenamedgrp["ouch"].hide();
      thenamedgrp["getout"].hide();
   effect = 0;
}
```

This is a simple but effective demonstration of how a Web page can respond to the reader, based on both mouse and keyboard activity. As you can see from Figure 13-7, it also has a little humor, which my young nephew, who is just learning Web page development, particularly liked.

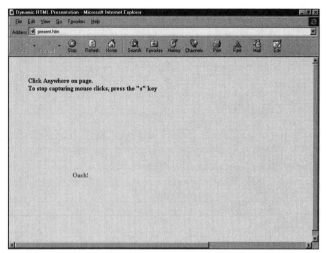

Figure 13-7: The word "Ouch!" moves to where the mouse click occurred

That's it for the effects and for the presentation.

Including Event Handlers in the Equalizer Objects

In this chapter, as well as Chapters 14 and 15, I did not include event handlers in the equalizer objects, though technically this could be done. I didn't include event handlers because I wanted the example to access different events for each Web application, and perform different actions based on the different events. So, I didn't necessarily want to "hide" the event handlers by embedding them into the objects.

However, if your Web applications capture the same events and perform the same processes over and over again, you also might want to use this technique to capture events for your equalizer objects.

For example, the following code extends the Navigator object to capture the mouseover event for each of the objects and assigns the event a function pointer:

```
// function to instantiate equalizer objects
function setup() {
    thegroup = new Array(document.layers.length);
    thenamedgrp = new Array(document.layers.length);
    for (i = 0; i < document.layers.length; i++){
thegroup[i] = new ns_object(document.layers[i]);
```

continued

Including Event Handlers in the Equalizer Objects
(continued)

```
        thenamedgrp[document.layers[i].name] =
        new ns_object(document.layers[i]);
  document.layers[i].onmouseover=mouse_over;
  }
}
```

The same approach can be used for IE as follows, using JScript:

```
// function to instantiate equalizer objects
function setup() {
    thegrp = document.all.tags("DIV");
    thegroup = new Array(thegrp.length);
    thenamedgrp = new Array(thegrp.length);
    for (i = 0; i < thegrp.length; i++){
        thegroup[i] = new ie_object(thegrp[i]);
  thenamedgrp[thegrp[i].id] = new ie_object(thegrp[i]);
  thegrp[i].onmouseover=mouse_over;
  }
}
```

If you are coding equalizer objects in VBScript, you can't assign a function pointer to the object, but you can assign the event handler to the function enclosed within quotes:

```
Thegrp(i).onmouseover="mouse_over(param1, param2)"
```

Now, moving the cursor over any of the elements that are included in either DHTML equalizer object results in a call to the function `mouse_over`.

Summary

This chapter showed how to use dynamic HTML, without controls or images, to create an online presentation that is cross-browser compatible. In addition, you've seen how to create what I call DHTML equalizer objects to handle browser differences, at least for CSS positioning. Once the equalizer objects are created, you can use them for any dynamic HTML purpose.

In this chapter, you learned how to:

◆ Create DHTML equalizer objects to handle browser differences.

◆ Add methods to the equalizer objects to control movement, visibility, and clipping.

♦ Use CSS positioning to hide and clip elements.

♦ Move elements using relative and absolute positioning.

♦ Emulate style changes by creating and layering elements and exposing them via code.

♦ Respond to the Web page reader by using each browser's event capturing, but sharing functionality whenever possible.

The next chapter discusses how to use the equalizer objects to create a kid's Web page, which, with a few code changes, is then converted into an interactive customer catalog page.

Chapter 14

Creating Interactive Pages for Both Browsers

IN THIS CHAPTER

- ◆ Different techniques for scripting interactivity

- ◆ Cross-browser drag and drop

- ◆ Creating a kids' page – introduction and the entry page

- ◆ The numbers page, including setting up the page, moving elements into a shopping cart, and dynamically modifying Web page elements

- ◆ Converting the kids' page into an online catalog

THIS CHAPTER COVERS HOW TO create a cross-browser, interactive kids' page, and an online shopping catalog using some of the same components in both pages. You'll find that interactive page components, such as event capturing and providing visual feedback, work equally well for both types of Web sites. In creating this cross-compatible application, this chapter makes extensive use of the DHTML equalizer objects created in Chapter 13, so if you haven't had a chance to read that chapter, I suggest that you do so before reading this one.

This chapter also explores the versatility of Microsoft's and Netscape's implementations of dynamic HTML and shows you how you usually have more than one way to script interactivity into your Web page.

Different Techniques for Scripting Interactivity

The thing I really like about both Microsoft's and Netscape's implementations of dynamic HTML is their versatility. At first, it may seem that Microsoft's approach, which exposes virtually every HTML element to scripting, is more flexible than Netscape's. But, as you'll see, the Netscape model is actually a little more adaptable than it first appears.

For example, in previous chapters, I used an empty (or *stub*) hypertext link, a link that does not open a page or move the page focus but instead is used for event capturing only. You can use this technique with Internet Explorer (IE) or you can capture the event directly within the element. Both techniques are shown in the following code:

```
<a href=""
onclick="some_function();return false"><img src="someimage.gif"></a>

-or-

<img src="someimage.gif" onclick="some_function()">
```

The second approach may be more efficient, but it only works in Internet Explorer. The first approach works with both browsers.

In Navigator, you can use the event model to capture events for any element that can be positioned dynamically, such as the DIV and LAYER elements. For example, the following code captures events for an image positioned absolutely within a DIV block:

```
<SCRIPT language="javascript1.2">

function response(e) {
  alert("You clicked " + e.target.id);
}

function setup() {
  document.divone.document.imgone.onclick = response;
}
</SCRIPT>
...
<BODY onload="setup()">
...
<DIV id="divone" style="position:absolute;left:10;top:10">
<img src="someimage.gif" name="imgone">
</DIV>
```

Because the element is located within the DIV block, it is really a part of the DIV document object rather than the overall document element. If the image were located directly in the Web page document you could access it with the following code:

```
document.imgone.onclick=response;
```

This approach can also be used with IE using *its* event model.

IE has the capability to create a scripting block for a specific event for a specific, named HTML element. Based on this capability, you can use the following code to perform the same event capturing as was just demonstrated for Navigator:

```
<SCRIPT language="jscript" FOR="imgone" EVENT="onclick">
alert("You clicked " + window.event.srcElement.name);
</SCRIPT>
```

As you can see, you have a lot of options when scripting interactivity into your Web pages. It's all a matter of which browser(s) you wish to support and the techniques you prefer to use.

The kids' Web page created in this chapter has a numbers game that invites its readers to "buy" numbers in order to add them up toward a target number. This page is a good example of the options you have when using dynamic HTML.

You have a couple of interactive and animated ways to implement this "buy" functionality. First, you can implement drag and drop and let your visitor drag the number to a bin, in which case the number is considered "bought." Another approach is to have the reader click the number with the mouse, or use the keyboard to dictate the action — a feasible and workable option that helps familiarize kids with keyboards and mouse handling.

To keep this page simple, I decided to use the `click` event combined with an animation to move the element, rather than use the drag-and-drop technique. I didn't feel the drag-and-drop effect rightly justified the added complexity it required. Its use would require having to test the location of the drop, to ensure the location is over the bin, and provide feedback to the reader. Then, if the drop was incorrect, the dragged element would need to be moved back to the original location. All of this takes a lot of code, and probably produces some frustration for the reader. In addition, the click approach makes the page more manageable for younger kids who have a little trouble holding a mouse button down while moving the mouse, for older people with limited hand movement, and for people using laptops.

Although I'll use the click technique in the kids' Web page, the following section discusses a couple of ways to implement the drag-and-drop technique.

Drag and Drop

Drag and drop is an engaging feature to implement in your Web pages. Although this technique is not used in the featured Web page examples of this chapter, I feel it is important to give drag and drop some attention so you can use it in your own Web pages. As you saw in Chapter 13, you can take advantage of the flexibility inherent in Explorer and Navigator to script this kind of interactivity into your Web pages in different ways. The next two sections show you two ways to capture events when creating the drag-and-drop effect: event capturing using hypertext links and event capturing using the object model.

EVENT CAPTURING USING HYPERTEXT LINKS

I have a simple example of drag and drop at my Web site that was originally implemented for Netscape Navigator. For this book, in order to illustrate how to write cross-browser script, I decided to take this Web page example and extend the code to support Internet Explorer. The following paragraphs outline the steps I took to make event capturing cross-browser compatible, and you can find this example in its entirety in the **drgdrp2.htm** sample file on the CD-ROM.

First, because I used CSS positioning to position the elements in the page, I included my new equalizer objects to handle all the elements' movements. To enable these objects, I captured the load event for the Web page body and called the equalizer objects' setup function.

As you saw in Chapter 12, you can use DIV blocks and stub hypertext links to create a drag-and-drop effect by capturing the mousedown event and calling a function to begin the drag operation. The actual DIV block id *and* the event object are passed to the event handler function as parameters. As you will see demonstrated in the next technique of drag and drop, using the event model and event capturing automatically passes the event object as a function parameter.

Using the actual DIV block as a parameter generates an error for IE. Because the equalizer objects access the Web page DIV blocks using their *identifiers*, I altered the approach to pass the block identifier as well as the event object, as shown next:

```
<DIV id="theblock" style="position: absolute;top: 50px; left: 20px;
  width:300px ">
<a href="" onmousedown="begin_event('theblock',event)"
  onmouseup="end_event()" onclick="return false">
```

The code also captures the mouseup event for the link, which calls the onmouseup event handler function, end_event, to end the drag operation.

The mousemove events are handled through event capturing. Because each browser has its own event object model, I used two separate script blocks to capture events. For Navigator, the code captures all mouse movements within the page, including mousemove and mousedrag. However, the mousemove event isn't captured until the drag begins, thus preventing unnecessary burden for the Web page. Also, I coded different browser versions of the end_event and begin_event functions because, again, each function uses the browser-specific event operations. Listing 14-1 contains the event handling source code for Navigator.

Listing 14-1: Navigator-specific drag-and-drop functions

```
<SCRIPT language="javascript1.2">

current_object = null;
objectX = 0;
objectY = 0;

function begin_event(object,e) {
        current_object = thenamedgrp[object];
        objectX = e.pageX;
        objectY = e.pageY;
        window.captureEvents(Event.MOUSEMOVE);
```

```
}
function drag_event(e) {
  if (current_object != null) {
        var distX = e.pageX - objectX;
        var distY = e.pageY - objectY;
        current_object.moveby(distX, distY);
        objectX = e.pageX;
        objectY = e.pageY;
  }
  return false;
}

function end_event() {
  window.releaseEvents(Event.MOUSEMOVE);
  last_object = current_object;
  current_object = null;
}

if (navigator.appName != "Microsoft Internet Explorer")
    window.onmousemove=drag_event;

</SCRIPT>
```

Notice from the listing that the event capturing is not turned on for the document until after the drag operation begins. Also notice the use of the equalizer object thenamedgrp, which is an array of DIV or LAYER block elements that are accessible by their identifiers. Also, to prevent IE from processing the event handler assignment statement, I check for the Navigator application name before the assignment.

For Internet Explorer, a separate script block is created for the specific event and specific element. In addition, because the event object for IE is not available until the event occurs, the object passed through to the begin_event routine is ignored. Listing 14-2 contains the IE-specific event-handling routines.

Listing 14-2: IE code to begin the drag event, move the element based on mousemove, and end the dragging event

```
<SCRIPT language="jscript">

var Event = null;
current_object = null;

// begin drag operation
function begin_event(object, e) {
  e = window.event;
  current_object = object;
  objectX = e.clientX;
  objectY = e.clientY;
}

// end drag operation
```

```
function end_event() {
 last_object = current_object;
 current_object = null;
}
</SCRIPT>

<SCRIPT language="jscript"
 FOR=document EVENT=onmousemove>

 // if mouse move and dragging object
 if (current_object != null) {
      var xdist = window.event.clientX - objectX;
      var ydist = window.event.clientY - objectY;
      thenamedgrp[current_object].moveby(xdist, ydist);
      objectX = window.event.clientX;
      objectY = window.event.clientY;
      }
 return false;
</SCRIPT>
```

Again, the IE approach also uses the `thenamedgrp` equalizer object, though the event has different properties for the event location than the `navigator` object.

I applied the drag-and-drop routine to two blocks, one containing text and one containing an image. Also, because I didn't want the text to be underlined, and because the code includes an empty hypertext link, I turned off text decoration for the HTML element using a style sheet. Listing 14-3 contains the style sheet settings and the body of the application document.

Listing 14-3: The drag-and-drop application style sheet setting and document body

```
<STYLE>
 BODY {background-image: background-color: white }
 A {text-decoration: none; color: firebrick}
</STYLE>
...
<DIV id="theblock" style="position: absolute;top: 50px; left: 20px;
 width:300px ">
<a href="" onmousedown="begin_event('theblock',event)"
 onmouseup="end_event()" onclick="return false">
This is an example of drag-n-drop with DIV blocks, and event
 capturing. You can click on and drag either the text or the image
 on this page. Also, place one in front of the other, such as the
 image over this text, and then double-click on the text. This moves
 the object up through the z order.
<p>
Click on the View...Page Source to see how this works!
</a>
</DIV>
<DIV id="yasd" style="position: absolute;top:50px; left: 350px;">
<a href="" onmousedown="begin_event('yasd', event)"
 onmouseup="end_event()" onclick="return false">
<img src="yasd.gif" width=104 height=152 border=0></a></DIV>
```

You can try the example yourself by opening the **drgdrp2.htm** sample file on the CD-ROM in either Navigator or IE.

Event Capturing Using the Object Model

The second approach to creating a drag-and-drop operation that's cross-browser compatible is to use the event-capturing technique using the event model. This means you need to capture all of the events, including mousedown and mouseup using the event model rather than capturing the events at the elements themselves.

Internet Explorer captures events for any element, but Navigator only captures events for any element that is contained within a predefined element array. As stated earlier, this includes elements such as DIV blocks, accessible via the layers array, and images, accessible via the images array. However, this poses a problem because multiple types of elements can be contained within DIV blocks, such as images and paragraphs. So how can you move the appropriate elements within blocks or the blocks themselves?

To solve this problem, first, for IE, you can capture events for images separately from the other document events, and then set the cancelBubble event to true to prevent the event from bubbling up to the document. When you capture the event for the image, you can send the ID for the parent element for the object, which is the DIV block that contains the image.

Trapping the mousedown event for the specific element overrides the document event trapping as the image receives the event before the document does. However, once you have captured which element is being dragged then you can use the mouseup and mousemove events for the rest of the event handling, as shown in Listing 14-4.

Listing 14-4: Event handling for IE using the event model

```
<SCRIPT language="jscript">
<!--
var Event = null;
current_object = null;

// begin capture
function begin_event(object, e) {
 e = window.event;
 current_object = object;
 objectX = e.clientX;
 objectY = e.clientY;
}

// release captured element
function end_event() {
 last_object = current_object;
 current_object = null;
}
```

```
// dummy function - to counter Navigator function
function setup2() {
}
//-->
</SCRIPT>

<SCRIPT language="jscript" FOR=document EVENT=onmousemove>
 // move object
 if (current_object != null) {
      var xdist = window.event.clientX - objectX;
      var ydist = window.event.clientY - objectY;
      thenamedgrp[current_object].moveby(xdist, ydist);
      objectX = window.event.clientX;
      objectY = window.event.clientY;
      }
 return false;
</SCRIPT>

<SCRIPT language="jscript" FOR="yasd" EVENT=onmousedown>
 begin_event(window.event.srcElement.parentElement.id,
 window.event);
 window.event.cancelBubble=true;
</SCRIPT>
<SCRIPT language="jscript" FOR=document EVENT=onmousedown>
 begin_event(window.event.srcElement.id, window.event);
</SCRIPT>
<SCRIPT language="jscript" FOR=document EVENT=onmouseup>
 end_event();
</SCRIPT>
```

Notice that, in this code, I am still using the same functions for the pertinent drag-and-drop operations. I could have chosen to handle the code directly in the event.

The Navigator event handling also has to use event capturing using the event model. Because the two DIV blocks used to position the page contents actually have different elements, such as paragraphs of text for the one and an image for the other, I didn't capture all of the events for these blocks at the DIV block level. I wouldn't get any of the events for the text-based DIV block, as paragraphs don't support event trapping. However, the image can trap events, so I can forgo explicitly capturing events at the DIV level for this element. However, if the block contained other elements along with the image, I would need to capture events for the block.

If I do capture the events within a block, I can't directly reference which block receives the event because the target property of the event references the element that received the event, which could be the image, or the paragraphs. So, in order to determine which block received the event, I use the check_width and check_height functions I created in Chapter 12, in the example file **nsdrgdrp.htm** on the CD-ROM. These functions compare the click point to the parameters of the element's occupied space, and return which element received the event. To bring the old and the new together (the application from Chapter 12 and the equalizer objects from Chapter 13), I use the new equalizer object methods `get_left`, `get_top`, `get_clip_width`, and `get_clip_height` in the functions. Of course, another approach would be to implement these drag-and-drop functions within the objects, but for now I'll leave the objects the way they are.

Listing 14-5 contains the script block for trapping and handling the events for Navigator.

Listing 14-5: Navigator-specific scripting using the event model

```
<SCRIPT language="javascript1.2">
<!--
current_object = null;
objectX = 0;
objectY = 0;

// begin drag operation
function begin_event(e) {
 var elem = -1;
 for (i = 0; i < thegroup.length; i++) {
      var isobjwidth =
              check_width(e.pageX, thegroup[i].get_left(),
 thegroup[i].get_clip_width());
      var isobjheight =
              check_height(e.pageY, thegroup[i].get_top(),
 thegroup[i].get_clip_height());
      if (isobjwidth && isobjheight) {
              elem = i;
              break;
              }
      }
 current_object = elem;
 objectX = e.pageX;
 objectY = e.pageY;
 window.captureEvents(Event.MOUSEMOVE);

}

// check to see if event is within object area by width
function check_width(page_x, the_x, the_width) {
 if (page_x >= the_x && page_x <= the_x + the_width)
      return true;
 else
      return false;
}

// check to see if event is within object are by height
function check_height(page_y, the_y, the_height) {
 if (page_y >= the_y && page_y <= the_y + the_height)
      return true;
 else
      return false;
}
```

```
// drag operation
function drag_event(e) {
 if (current_object != null) {
      var distX = e.pageX - objectX;
      var distY = e.pageY - objectY;
      thegroup[current_object].moveby(distX, distY);
      objectX = e.pageX;
      objectY = e.pageY;
 }
 return false;
}

// end operation
function end_event() {
 window.releaseEvents(Event.MOUSEMOVE);
 last_object = current_object;
 current_object = null;
}

// assign event to handler
if (navigator.appName != "Microsoft Internet Explorer")
   window.onmousemove=drag_event;

// capture events for blocks
function setup2() {
 document.theblock.captureEvents(Event.MOUSEDOWN);
 document.theblock.captureEvents(Event.MOUSEUP);
 document.theblock.onMouseDown=begin_event;
 document.theblock.onmouseup=end_event;
 document.yasdd.captureEvents(Event.MOUSEDOWN);
 document.yasdd.onMouseDown=begin_event;
 document.yasdd.document.yasd.onmouseup=end_event;
}
//-->
</SCRIPT>
```

You can try out the second drag-and-drop technique by accessing the sample file **drgdrp2a.htm** on the CD-ROM. To get in a little practice, try converting the IE-specific code to use equivalent `check_width` and `check_height` code to determine which block received the event.

Now that you have a better understanding of how to take advantage of DHTML's versatility, you'll see how I created a cross-browser application, and then used some of the same components to create a second.

Creating Interactive Kids' Pages

Just because you can layer Web page elements and hide and display content, all within one page, doesn't mean you'll want to include all of your content within the boundaries of a single page. The interactive kids' application you will see in this section uses a multiple-page approach, with the entry and instruction pages placed in separate smaller windows. This section also includes the numbers site, which you can link to from the introduction page.

The Introduction Page

To begin the construction of the kids' Web page, I created a backdrop image, to be used in all the pages, and wrote a simple introductory document with a link that the reader can click to enter the site. Figure 14-1 shows this page when it first loads. When the reader clicks the hypertext link, a separate smaller window is opened above this main window, and this new window accesses the entry code for the site.

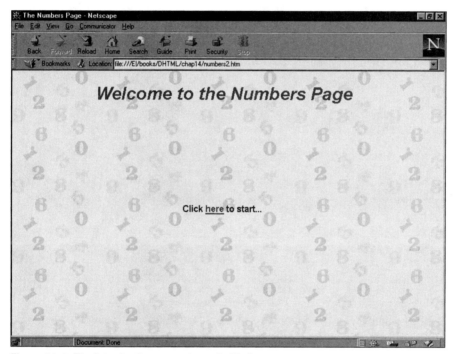

Figure 14-1: The introduction page, shown in Navigator

Because IE and Navigator have different attributes for an open window event, I wrote two separate code blocks for the event, one for each browser, as shown next:

```
<SCRIPT language="javascript">

function open_page() {
  window.open("numbers.htm", "Numbers",
      "Width=600,Height=400,left=0,top=0");
}
</SCRIPT>
```

```
<SCRIPT language="javascript1.2">
function open_page() {
 window.open("numbers.htm", "Numbers",
       "innerWidth=600,innerHeight=400, left=0,top=0");
}
</SCRIPT>
```

In addition, I wrote two blocks for style sheets, one a JSS style sheet block and the other a traditional CSS1 style sheet. I found that if I didn't include the JSS style sheet, Navigator didn't display the font that I wanted for the page, most likely a bug that could be fixed by the time you read this. The style sheets for the introduction are shown in Listing 14-6, and they are the beginnings of the style sheets that were created for the entire application.

Listing 14-6: The style sheet for the introduction page

```
<STYLE type="text/css">
 BODY { background-image: url(backgrnd.jpg); background-color:
 white;
             color: blue; font-family: Arial;
             font-size: 18pt; text-align:center }
 A {color: red }
 H1 { color: red; font-family: Cursive;
       text-align: center; margin: 15 }
 P { margin-top: 1.5in; font-size: 12pt;
 font-style: arial; font-weight: bold }
 STRONG { color: red }
</STYLE>
<STYLE type="text/javascript">
   with(tags.H1) {
 fontFamily="sans-serif";
 fontStyle="italic";
 fontSize="24pt";
 }
</STYLE>
```

Both browsers have the same background, STRONG tag, and paragraph settings. The only difference is in the header. You can see the page yourself by accessing the sample file **numbers2.htm** on the CD-ROM.

The Entry Page

When you click the hypertext link in the introduction page, a smaller entry page is displayed, as shown in Figure 14-2. Notice also from the figure that this time the page is displayed in Internet Explorer.

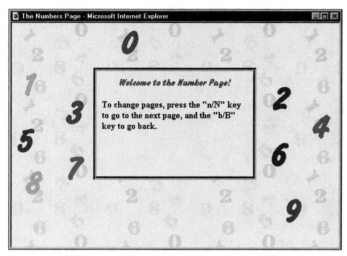

Figure 14-2: The entry page, opened in IE

For the numbers application, I presented four numbers-based questions for kids to answer. If they get all four answers correct, they will obtain entry to the numbers Web site, and the numbers game. Notice from the page contents that pressing either *N* for Next or *B* for Back moves the reader through the question pages. You can see this for yourself by clicking the link from the **numbers2.htm** sample file, or accessing the file directly from the file **numbers.htm** on the CD-ROM. Note, though, that the file will expect the parent window to exist when all four questions are answered, so you may want to access it through the introduction page.

SETTING UP THE ENTRY PAGE DISPLAY

The style sheet for the page handles the page elements, including the placement of the question block and the appearance of the numbers, as shown in Listing 14-7. From here on, I won't list any additional style sheets for this application, because for the most part little changes from page to page of the application. Where changes occur I list them individually.

Listing 14-7: The style sheet setting for the entry page

```
<STYLE type="text/javascript">
   with(document.tags.A) {
 fontWeight="bold";
 fontSize="56pt";
 textDecoration="none";
 fontFamily="sans-serif";
 }
</STYLE>
<STYLE type="text/css">
 BODY { background-image: url(backgrnd.jpg);
```

```
                    background-color: white }
        DIV { position:absolute }
        A { font-family:sans-serif; font-weight: bold;
              font-size: 62; text-decoration: none }
        H1 { font-size: 48pt; font-family: sans-serif;
                  font-weight: bold; width: 60; }
        .question { position: absolute;
                    width: 300; height:200;
                    background-color:white; left: 150; top: 80;
                    border-width: 6; border-color: lime;
                    border-style: groove;
                    margin-top: 10 }
        H3 { color: red; font-family: sans-serif;
                    text-align: center; margin-top: 5;
                    margin-bottom: 5 }
        P { margin-left: 10; margin-right: 10;
                    font-size: 12pt;
                    font-style: arial; font-weight: bold }
        STRONG { color: red }
        #zero { color: red}
        #one {color:lime}
        #two { color:blue}
        #three { color:red}
        #four { color:magenta }
        #five { color:blue }
        #six { color:blue }
        #seven { color:magenta }
        #eight { color:lime }
        #nine { color: red}
        </STYLE>
```

You might notice that I am using the ID "selector" approach for the numbers. I have found, at least with the version of Navigator in use when I wrote this, that using a new inline style with hypertext links overrides all the styles that follow the element that used the inline style. Again, I consider that this is most likely a bug. For now though I want to have each number be a different color, so I use ID selectors. Also, I have placed a border around the question DIV block to make it stand out in the page.

I am using the empty hypertext link approach to trap events for the numbers. You could also use event trapping using the event model if you prefer. Listing 14-8 shows the DIV blocks for the numbers used in the page.

Listing 14-8: The entry page "number" DIV blocks

```
<DIV style="left:200;top:0">
<a href="" id="zero" onclick="pick_number(0);return false">0</a>
</DIV>
<DIV style="left:20; top:75">
<a href="" id="one" onclick="pick_number(1);return false">1</a>
</DIV>
<DIV style="left: 480; top: 100">
```

```
<a href="" id="two" onclick="pick_number(2);return false">2</a>
</DIV>
<DIV style="left: 100; top: 125">
<a href="" id="three" onclick="pick_number(3);return false">3</a>
</DIV>
<DIV style="left: 550; top: 150">
<a href="" id="four" onclick="pick_number(4);return false">4</a>
</DIV>
<DIV style="left: 10; top: 175">
<a href="" id="five" onclick="pick_number(5);return false">5</a>
</DIV>

<DIV style="left: 475; top: 200">
<a href="" id="six" onclick="pick_number(6);return false">6</a>
</DIV>
<DIV style="left: 100; top: 225">
<a href="" id="seven" onclick="pick_number(7);return false">7</a>
</DIV>
<DIV style="left: 25; top: 250">
<a href="" id="eight" onclick="pick_number(8);return false">8</a>
</DIV>
<DIV style="left: 500; top: 300">
<a href="" id="nine" onclick="pick_number(9);return false">9</a>
</DIV>
```

If you want a chance to try out some of the technology you've learned, you can adapt this page to use event trapping with the event model instead of the hypertext link. Remember that you have to include the two check_width and check_height functions for Navigator in order to test which block receives the event.

When clicked, each of the number DIV blocks calls a function, pick_number, and passes the number represented in the block as a parameter. I cover this function a little later in this section.

In addition to the number DIV blocks, I also use DIV blocks for each "page" of the question block, and hide all but the top-most page. You can see these blocks in Listing 14-9.

Listing 14-9: The numbers entry page components

```
<DIV id="page1" class="question">
<H3>Welcome to the Number Page!</H3>
<p>
To change pages, press the "n/N" key to go to the next page, and the
  "b/B" key to go back.
</DIV>
<DIV id="page2" class="question" style="visibility:hidden">
<p>
To enter the Numbers Page, you have to find the combination for the
  entry.
</p>
<P>
```

```
Four questions will be given. To find the entry combination, click
  on the number that answers each question. When you have all four
  numbers, you will have found the entry <strong> key</strong>.
</P>
</DIV>
<DIV id="question1" class="question" style="visibility:hidden">
<P>
I am 18, take away 3, but add 6, and then divide by 3. What am I?
</P>
</DIV>
<DIV id="question2" class="question" style="visibility:hidden">
<P>
If you slice an apple once, and then cut each slice in half, and
  then cut each of these slices in half, how many apple slices would
  you have?
</P>
</DIV>
<DIV id="question3" class="question" style="visibility:hidden">
<P>
As 16 is to hexadecimal, and 8 is to octal, this number is to
  binary. What is the number?
</P>
</DIV>
<DIV id="question4" class="question" style="visibility:hidden">
<P>
Multiply me, or divide me, I'll always be me. What am I?
</P>
</DIV>
```

Notice that I use the same `question` class for each block. They all share the same style sheet setting, because only one of the blocks will be visible at any one time. To me, this is the most powerful feature that dynamic HTML provides: the capability to position and layer elements and control their visibility.

Speaking of control, the next section shows you how the entry page is controlled.

ACTIVATING THE ENTRY PAGE

I have included some source code for the entry page as content in the Web page itself, and some in a source code file called **respond.js**. I also use the equalizer objects, and include their source code files (**ieobjs.js** and **nsobjs.js**).

To create the entry page for the application, I wrote two functions to handle the next and previous page navigation. Because I am using the equalizer objects, and all that the functions are doing is hiding and displaying blocks, I can use the same functions for both browsers, as shown in Listing 14-10.

Listing 14-10: Next page and previous page functions

```
<SCRIPT language="javascript">
current_page = 0;
```

```
function next_page() {
   if (current_page < thegroup.length - 1) {
       thegroup[current_page].hide();
       current_page++;
       thegroup[current_page].show();
   }
}

function prev_page() {
  if (current_page > 0) {
       thegroup[current_page].hide();
       current_page = current_page - 1;
       thegroup[current_page].show();
       }
   }
</SCRIPT>
```

I used event trapping in the code to capture all keyboard activity for the page, and to determine which key has been pressed. The value determining which page to hide and which to display is based on the global variable current_page. A next-page action increments this variable, and a previous-page action decrements it in response to whether the Web page reader presses the *N* key or the *B* key. Again, because event trapping differs between Navigator and IE, this is coded separately.

For IE the script block event trapping is used, and keyboard actions are captured for the Web page, as shown next:

```
<SCRIPT FOR=document EVENT=onkeypress language="jscript">
if (event.keyCode == 110 || event.keyCode == 78)
 next_page();
else if (event.keyCode == 98 || event.keyCode == 66)
 prev_page();
else if (event.keyCode >= 48 && event.keyCode <= 57)
 pick_number(event.keyCode - 48);
</SCRIPT>
```

Notice that I also trap the keyboard events for numbers and use them to call the pick_number function, after converting them to a type of number that the function is expecting. The function is expecting a value of from zero (0) to nine (9). For example, the ASCII code for 1 is 49, and the value of 1 can be derived by subtracting 48 from the ASCII code. The pick_number function is discussed later in this section.

To find out what the different ASCII values are for the keys, use the **fndascii.htm** program for IE from Chapter 8, or the **nsascii.htm** application for Navigator from Chapter 12.

For Navigator, I capture all key-press events for the document, and send them to a function for processing, as shown next:

```
<SCRIPT language="javascript1.2">

function keypress(e) {
    if (e.which == 110 || e.which == 78)
  next_page();
    else if (e.which == 98 || e.which == 66)
  prev_page();
    else if (e.which >= 48 && e.which <= 57)
  pick_number(e.which - 48);

}

if (navigator.appName != "Microsoft Internet Explorer") {
    document.captureEvents(Event.KEYPRESS);
    document.onkeypress = keypress;
}
</SCRIPT>
```

Again, because both Navigator and IE use different `event` objects, I decided to keep the two operations separate, and check the Navigator application name when assigning my event handlers to events in the Navigator code section.

The last function to take note of in the entry page is `pick_number`, included in **respond.js** on the CD-ROM. This function accesses an answer value array and determines whether the answer given equals the one in the array for the specific question. If it is the correct value, another array is used to mark that the question has been answered successfully, by setting the value of the array element to 1. After successfully answering a question, this array is checked to see if all array entries have been set to 1. If so, then the page is closed and the numbers page is opened. If the question was answered successfully, but all of the questions have not been answered yet, the question page focus is changed based on the current page, as seen in Listing 14-11.

Listing 14-11: The pick_number function

```
var answer_array = new Array(4);
for (i = 0; i < answer_array.length; i++)
  answer_array[i] = 0;

// the answers - no peeking
var value_array = new Array(4);
value_array[0] = 7;
value_array[1] = 8;
value_array[2] = 2;
value_array[3] = 0;

// check answer
function pick_number(num) {
```

```
var answer_index = current_page - 2;
var answer = value_array[answer_index];
if (answer == num) {
   alert("The answer of " + answer + " is correct!");
   answer_array[current_page - 2] = 1;
   var test_result = 0;
   for (i = 0; i < answer_array.length; i++)
      test_result+= answer_array[i];

   // if all questions answered successfully, open
      numbers page
   if (test_result == 4) {
      window.opener.location="nummain.htm";
      window.close();
      }
   else
      if (current_page < thegroup.length - 1)
            next_page();
      else
            prev_page();
}
else
      alert("Sorry, that is not correct. Please try
      again.");
}
```

I use an array because a natural extension to this application is to display the unanswered question closest to the current question. You can try this out yourself by modifying the function included with the files on the CD-ROM, and running the modified function.

Notice from the listing that messages are displayed to let readers know whether they answered the question correctly or not. Also, when the numbers page is opened, it's opened in the parent window, using the opener property. This property is discussed in more detail in Chapters 3 and 4, the scripting review chapters.

That's it for the entry window. Once the reader successfully answers each of the questions, the numbers game page is opened in the parent window. Note that the appearance of all of these pages is very similar between browsers, except for the border surrounding the DIV block within the entry page. With IE, this is stretched to fit the DIV block width and height; with Navigator it is resized to fit the contents.

The Numbers Page

Open **numbers2.htm** from the CD-ROM in IE 4.0 or Navigator to get a feel for how this example looks and functions. The object of the numbers page game is to have kids (and adults) "buy" numbers that are added to match the current target number. For example, if the target number is 12, the kids can buy the number 6, the number 4, and the number 2. They cannot buy two 6s because the number can only be bought once per target entry.

The strategy of the game is to use only enough of the ten target numbers to match the winning number count. For the game, this value is hard-coded in to be 33. This means that, to win the game, the Web page reader has to use exactly 33 numbers to get all target number values. In a real-world application, this winning number count could change on a regular basis to keep the game more interesting.

When the reader selects a number to buy, by clicking it or typing the number into the keyboard, the number is moved from the number section at the top of the page to the shopping cart and the value is subtracted from the current number. When the user finally reaches zero, the program displays a new target number and the available numbers (1 through 9) reappear at the top of the page so the user can play the next round. The sections that follow show you how the page was set up and activated for use in both browsers.

SETTING UP THE NUMBERS PAGE

When the numbers page is first opened, an instruction page appears. This page uses a small window placed over the main window, as shown in Figure 14-3. To close the window, click the link that does nothing more than call the close window function on itself.

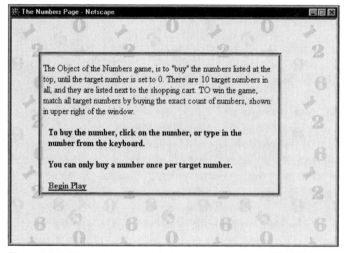

Figure 14-3: The numbers page instruction page, opened in Navigator

The numbers page uses the same style sheet setting as the previous windows, except that the background image is repeated along the x-axis only, and shows only along the top. Also, it does not make use of the `question` style sheet class, which is removed.

Note that I could have also used a CSS1 style sheet file for all of the application windows, and then overridden the locally changed elements by including local style sheet settings. The file could have been linked in using the following syntax:

```
<LINK REL=STYLESHEET TYPE="text/css"
 HREF="samples.css" TITLE="style1">
<STYLE>
```

The page also uses the equalizer objects, and the functions included in the **respond.js** scripting source code file.

Several elements are added to the page, including the numbers, a couple of text blocks for keeping track of totals, a shopping cart image, and a listing of target numbers. These are positioned using absolute positioning on the DIV blocks enclosing them. I won't include the HTML for all of them here, but you can view the setup in the **nummain.htm** file on the CD-ROM.

The numbers in this page are given another function to call, buy_number, that handles all of the processing for the page. This is also called whenever the reader uses the keyboard to select a number. You've seen this technology in the previous section, so I won't go over it again here.

The next section covers the animation of moving the numbers to the shopping cart based on the reader's actions.

MOVING ELEMENTS INTO A SHOPPING CART

As stated previously, when the reader selects a number to buy (either by a mouse click or by typing the number into the keyboard) the number moves from the number section at the top of the page to the shopping cart. In the code, the target numbers are loaded into an array based on the target number turn, providing access to which number is the next target. Also, a couple of global numbers are created, one to track the turn, and one to track how many numbers have been "bought" to that point. Also, my apologies for the name of the global variable for the total number count, but I couldn't resist, as shown next:

```
var turn = 0;
var numnums = 0;

var current_number = new Array(10);
current_number[0] = 25;
current_number[1] = 11;
current_number[2] = 23;
current_number[3] = 30;
current_number[4] = 17;
current_number[5] = 28;
current_number[6] = 9;
current_number[7] = 15;
current_number[8] = 20;
current_number[9] = 5;
```

Next, an array with nine entries is created and each member of the array is set to a value of 0. This array is used to keep track of whether a specific number has been played or not:

```
var array_hold = new Array(9);
for (i = 0; i < 10; i++)
  array_hold[i+1] = 0;
```

Now for the buy_number function. The first thing this function does is check to see whether the number has been bought previously within the turn. If it has, the function is exited. If not, the array_hold array member for the number is marked with a value of 1, indicating that this number has been used. Then the number is subtracted from the value of the current target number. Finally, another function is called, move_number, to move the number to the shopping cart:

```
function buy_number(num) {
  if (array_hold[num-1] == 1) return
  array_hold[num-1] = 1;
  numnums++;
  current_number[turn]-=num;
  move_number(num);
}
```

The function is pretty simple. The next function, move_number, determines the distance between the number being moved and the basket, with a little positioning to prevent all of the numbers from ending up in the same position in the basket. It creates a timer that calls a function to make each individual move of the number element, as shown next:

```
xincr =0;
yincr = 0;
objnum = 0;
move = 0;
function move_number(num) {
  move = 1;
  objnum = num -1;
  var objleft = (thenamedgrp["cartd"].get_left() +
        20 + (num * 10)) - thegroup[objnum].get_left();
  var objtop = (thenamedgrp["cartd"].get_top() + 20) -
              thegroup[objnum].get_top();
  xincr = objleft / 10;
  yincr = objtop / 10;
  setTimeout("make_move()",100);
}
```

Notice the use of the equalizer object thenamedgrp to access the location of the shopping cart. The next function, make_move, uses the other equalizer object thegroup, which can be accessed by position index, and moves the object incrementally:

```
function make_move() {
 thegroup[objnum].moveby(xincr,yincr);
 move++;
 if (move < 11)
       setTimeout("make_move()",100);
 else {
       move = 0;
       objnum = 0;
       xincr = 0;
       yincr = 0;
       end_move();
       }
}
```

The make_move function moves the element and then checks to see if the current move is still less than 11. Only ten moves are allowed per element. If the number is less than 11, it creates a timer that recalls itself. If the number is equal to 11, it resets the global variables used in the move and calls another function, end_move, to finish the target number turn.

Note that I could also have used the setInterval timer event instead of repeated calls to setTimeout. The setInterval timer would have continued to fire until a specific function call occurred to clear the interval using clearInterval. You might try both functions with this code to see which you prefer.

The end_move function checks to see if the target number has reached zero yet. If it has, it moves all of the numbers back to the number section, using the array_hold array to determine which numbers have been moved and need to be repositioned, as shown in Listing 14-12.

Listing 14-12: The end_move and end_game functions

```
function end_move() {
 if (current_number[turn] == 0) {
       turn++;
       for (i = 0; i < 9; i++)
             if (array_hold[i] == 1)
                 thegroup[i].move((20 + i * 50), 20);
       if (turn == 10)
             end_of_game();
       else {
          for (i = 0; i < 10; i++)
             array_hold[i] = 0;
             start_number();
             }
       }
}
function end_of_game() {
 alert("end of game" + numnums);
}
```

The listing also contains the end_game function, which could do some kind of processing when the game is over. At this time, all it does is display a message and a count of the numbers bought.

Figure 14-4 shows the numbers page in action, with the number 1 in the process of being moved after it has been purchased.

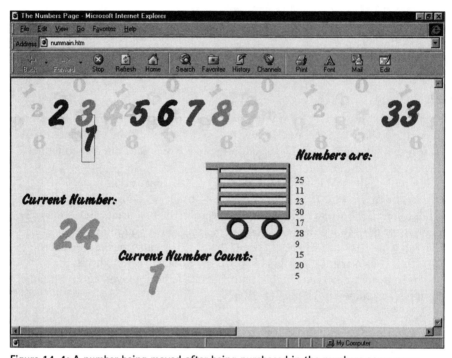

Figure 14-4: A number being moved after being purchased in the numbers game page

Figure 14-5 shows the number after it is in the shopping cart. Notice that the numbers appear behind the shopping cart, primarily because the z-order value for the cart is set to 2, and the z-order for the numbers is 1, the default value. Higher z-order objects are placed on top of those with lower-value z-orders.

You also might notice from the figures that some text within the window is updated based on the current total for the target value, and how many numbers have been bought. The code to accomplish this is discussed in the next section.

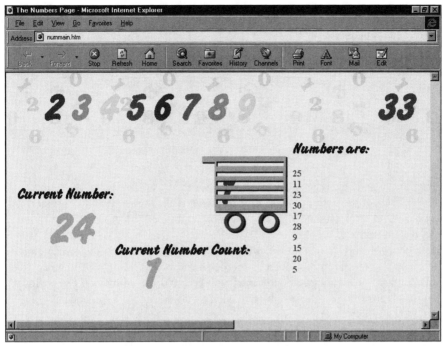

Figure 14-5: A number in the shopping cart after being purchased in the numbers game page

DYNAMICALLY MODIFYING WEB PAGE ELEMENTS

As discussed in the previous section, some text blocks in the window display different values when the reader makes a choice.

IE provides the capability to replace the HTML or the text associated with any HTML element within the page. Something that may not be as well known is that Navigator provides the capability to access the document property of a DIV or LAYER block and, using the write and close functions, replaces the contents of these blocks.

First, as each target number is displayed, the block that shows the current value of the target number must be set. This also needs to occur when the page is first loaded. So I created a function, called start_number, that accesses the next target number to be displayed, as well as the block where the number will be displayed, and then uses each browser's unique techniques to alter the block. The code for this is shown next:

```
function start_number() {
 var strng = "<H1>" + current_number[turn] + "</H1>";
 if (navigator.appName ==
       "Microsoft Internet Explorer")
       thenamedgrp["total"].css1.innerHTML =
             strng;
 else {
       document.layers["total"].document.
             write(strng);
       document.layers["total"].document.close();
       }
}
```

First, the type of browser is accessed through the navigator object property, appName. Then, if the browser accessing the page is IE, the innerHTML property of the DIV block is set to the new HTML. I use the equalizer object for this and for the Navigator section.

The equalizer objects extend the underlying object, which means for IE you still have access to the underlying object's methods and properties. Unfortunately, this doesn't hold true for Navigator. However, you can add the additional properties and methods for the navigator object easily, or do as shown here, and access the DIV or LAYER object directly.

If you have not read Chapter 5, which discusses the innerHTML property for IE, you might want to take a look at it now before continuing on.

For Navigator, I access the document property of the block and, using the write method, replace the contents of the block. Once done, I close the document so the element will repaint.

For IE 4.0 and Navigator, I am replacing the HTML of the element and I can use the same replacement string with both browsers. The string must include any HTML tags I want to use in addition to any other content, including new style sheet information.

To handle each number as it is bought, I extend the buy_number function to also include the dynamic alteration of the total DIV blocks. The adjusted function is shown in Listing 14-13.

Listing 14-13: The buy_number function with HTML modification added

```
function buy_number(num) {
 if (array_hold[num-1] == 1) return
 array_hold[num-1] = 1;
 numnums++;
 current_number[turn]-=num;
 var strng1 = "<H1>" + numnums + "</H1>";
 var strng2 ="<H1>" + current_number[turn] + "</H1>";
 if (navigator.appName ==
       "Microsoft Internet Explorer"){
       thenamedgrp["totalnum"].css1.innerHTML =
             strng1;
```

```
    thenamedgrp["total"].css1.innerHTML =
            strng2;
    }
else {
    document.layers["total"].document.
            write(strng2);
    document.layers["total"].document.close();
    document.layers["totalnum"].document.
            write(strng1);
    document.layers["totalnum"].document.close();
    }
move_number(num);
}
```

For this function, two text blocks are actually modified: one to hold the current value of the target number, the other to hold the count of numbers that have been bought so far in the game. I use two strings to create the content, and then use them both with the appropriate browser technique. Note that, with Navigator, I have to remember to close both DIV and LAYER block documents.

The buy_number function calls another function, move_number, to begin the process of moving the purchased number to the cart. It, in turn, determines the distance between the number and cart, divides it by the number of move increments, and starts a timer to begin the movement. This timer calls a function, end_move, to move the number each increment. Listing 14-14 contains the code for these functions.

Listing 14-14: Number movement after it has been purchased is handled by these functions

```
xincr =0;
yincr = 0;
objnum = 0;
move = 0;
// find distance between number
// and cart and begin move
function move_number(num) {
  move = 1;
  objnum = num -1;
  var objleft = (thenamedgrp["cartd"].get_left() + 20 + (num * 10)) -
            thegroup[objnum].get_left();
  var objtop = (thenamedgrp["cartd"].get_top() + 20) -
            thegroup[objnum].get_top();
  xincr = objleft / 10;
  yincr = objtop / 10;
  setTimeout("make_move()",100);
}

// move number by increment
function make_move() {
  thegroup[objnum].moveby(xincr,yincr);
  move++;
```

```
    if (move < 11)
         setTimeout("make_move()",100);
    else {
         move = 0;
         objnum = 0;
         xincr = 0;
         yincr = 0;
         end_move();
         }
}

// return numbers if done
function end_move() {
  if (current_number[turn] == 0) {
         turn++;
         for (i = 0; i < 9; i++)
              if (array_hold[i] == 1)
                  thegroup[i].move((20 + i * 50), 20);
         if (turn == 10)
              end_of_game();
         else {
             for (i = 0; i < 10; i++)
                 array_hold[i] = 0;
                 start_number();
                 }
         }
}

// end of game, output count
function end_of_game() {
  alert("end of game, count of numbers " + numnums);
}
```

Notice the use of the equalizer object arrays to move the elements. Without these objects the Navigator and IE sections would need to be coded separately. The code also contains one more function, end_of_game, that is called when the application determines the last number has been bought.

That's all it takes to dynamically alter any HTML element within the Web page, for either browser. Figure 14-6 shows the application in IE, just after several numbers have been purchased and moved into the shopping cart. Figure 14-7 shows this same page in Navigator. That's it, too, for the application. Again, you can try out the example yourself by accessing the CD-ROM's **numbers2.htm** file from Navigator or IE.

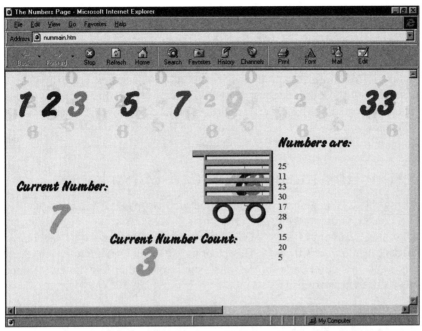

Figure 14-6: The display of numbers game in IE after several numbers have been purchased

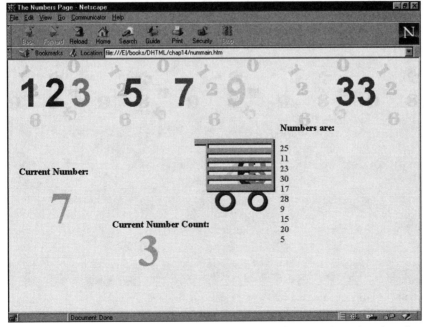

Figure 14-7: The display of numbers game in Navigator after several numbers have been purchased

Converting the Kids' Page into an Online Catalog

Most dynamic HTML routines can be used for multiple applications. For example, layering works with the kids' page just presented, and also with the progressive document that is presented in Chapter 15. To further explore this concept of reusable code, I will show you how to convert the kids' page for use in a simple one-page online shopping catalog for buying rare minerals that I call the rock shop.

Converting the Introduction and Entry Pages

In converting the kids' page into an online shopping cart page, I first changed the background image to one more suited to the new content, as you can see in the introduction page shown in Figure 14-8. You can look at this page by accessing the file **rocks2.htm** on the CD-ROM. This page uses the same technology implemented in the introduction page for the kids' page, except that it uses new content and opens a different entry page.

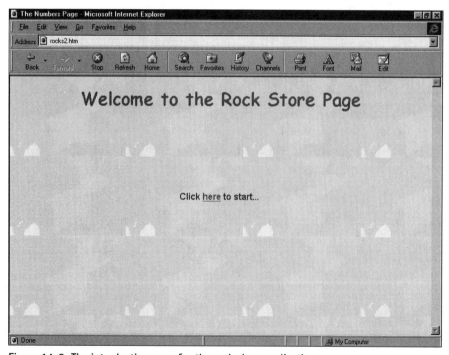

Figure 14-8: The introduction page for the rock shop application

The entry page for the store looks and acts a little differently than the entry page the kids' page. First, the central block for the entry page has just one message asking the reader to enter his or her account number. In addition, readers receive no feedback when they enter their account numbers, and if they make a mistake, they need to re-enter the whole account number. The entry page uses a function, still called `pick_number`, from a source code file called **coresp.js** (available on the CD-ROM) that processes the account number as it is entered. The modified `pick_number` function is shown in Listing 14-15.

Listing 14-15: The pick_number function, which checks the accuracy of the Web page reader's account number

```
var answer_array = new Array(4);
for (i = 0; i < answer_array.length; i++)
 answer_array[i] = 0;

var value_array = new Array(4);
value_array[0] = 1;
value_array[1] = 2;
value_array[2] = 3;
value_array[3] = 4;

answer_index = 0;
// check account number
function pick_number(num) {
 var answer = value_array[answer_index];

 // check to see if last number - if so open main window
 if (answer == num) {
    answer_index++;
    if (answer_index == 4) {
       window.opener.location="rckmain.htm";
       window.close();
       }
 }
 else {
       answer_index=0; // start over if incorrect number
       alert(
"Sorry, that is not correct. Please try again.");
       }
}
```

Of course, the code shows that only one account number is checked, and it is hard-coded in. To have true account number checking requires access to data on the server or stored in a cookie on the client machine.

Figure 14-9 shows the new entry window, with the slightly altered look and different message.

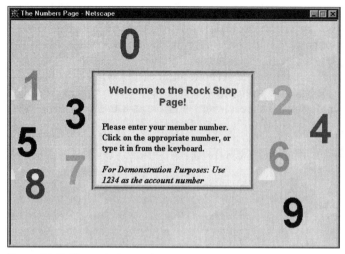

Figure 14-9: The rock shop entry page

Once the account number is entered, the main rock shop catalog page is opened. You can view the source code for the entry page by looking at the CD-ROM's **rocks.htm** sample file.

Converting the Main Page

As with the kids' page, when the main Web page is opened, a smaller window is opened to display any instructions needed to work with the page. Figure 14-10 shows the instruction page for the rock shop Web page.

The script to control the rock shop page, from animating the rocks toward the basket, to calculating and displaying the total for the order, is very similar to the script created for the kids' page. The main differences are that it has no target value array, and that a cost array displays the value of the purchased crystal. Listing 14-16 shows the adjusted `buy_number` function, and the new function to empty the cart, `empty_cart`. The `empty_cart` function is called when the reader clicks a new text-based `DIV` block, with the words "Empty Cart."

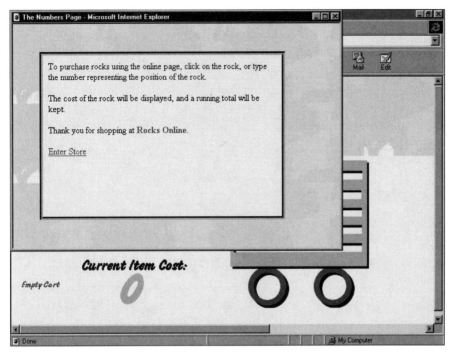

Figure 14-10: The rock shop instruction page

Listing 14-16: Code to control rock purchase and movement, and redisplay of totals

```
var turn = 0;
var total_cost = 0;

// used to mark which rocks already purchased
var array_hold = new Array(5);
for (i = 0; i < 5; i++)
 array_hold[i+1] = 0;

// cost array
var cost_array = new Array(5);
cost_array[0] = 150.00;
cost_array[1] = 375.00;
cost_array[2] = 320.00;
cost_array[3] = 90.00;
cost_array[4] = 495.00;

// purchase the rock
function buy_number(num) {

  // if rock already purchased, return
  if (array_hold[num-1] == 1) return
```

```
        array_hold[num-1] = 1;

        // add cost
        total_cost+= cost_array[num-1];
        strng1 = "<H1>$" + cost_array[num-1] + "</H1>";
        strng2 = "<H1>$" + total_cost + "</H1>";
        // redraw the display
        if (navigator.appName == "Microsoft Internet Explorer"){
            thenamedgrp["totalnum"].css1.innerHTML =
                    strng1;
            thenamedgrp["total"].css1.innerHTML =
            strng2;
            }
        else {
            document.layers["total"].document.
                    write(strng2);
            document.layers["total"].document.close();
            document.layers["totalnum"].document.
                    write(strng1);
            document.layers["totalnum"].document.close();
            }
      move_rock(num);
}

xincr =0;
yincr = 0;
objnum = 0;
move = 0;

// move rock to basket
function move_rock(num) {
  move = 1;
  objnum = num -1;
  var objleft = (thenamedgrp["cartd"].get_left() + 70 + (num * 20)) -
            thegroup[objnum].get_left();
  var objtop = (thenamedgrp["cartd"].get_top() + 50) -
            thegroup[objnum].get_top();
  xincr = objleft / 10;
  yincr = objtop / 10;
  setTimeout("make_move()",100);
}

// make next object move
function make_move() {
  thegroup[objnum].moveby(xincr,yincr);
  move++;
  if (move < 11)
        setTimeout("make_move()",100);
  else {
        move = 0;
        objnum = 0;
        xincr = 0;
        yincr = 0;
```

```
            end_move();
            }
   }

// setup for next turn, test if end of rocks and redisplay
function end_move() {
 turn++;
 if (turn < 5) return;
 for (i = 0; i < 5; i++) {
    if (array_hold[i] == 1)
        thegroup[i].move((20 + i * 120), 20);
    }
 if (turn == 5)
        end_of_sale();
      for (i = 0; i < 5; i++)
      array_hold[i] = 0;
      // redraw the display
 if (navigator.appName == "Microsoft Internet Explorer"){
        thenamedgrp["totalnum"].css1.innerHTML =
            "<H1>$0</H1>";
        thenamedgrp["total"].css1.innerHTML =
        "<H1>$0</H1>";
        }
 else {
        document.layers["total"].document.
            write("<H1>$0</H1>");
        document.layers["total"].document.close();
        document.layers["totalnum"].document.
            write("<H1>$0</H1>");
        document.layers["totalnum"].document.close();
        }
 turn = 0;
 total_cost = 0;
}

function empty_cart() {
 turn = 4;
 end_move();
 }

function end_of_sale() {
 window.status="returning items to shelves";
}
```

As the listing shows, the empty_cart function does nothing more than set the turn variable to the end of the number of rocks, and call the end_move function.

Notice from the code that I repeat the number of crystals in several places. This would be a good opportunity to use a global variable to specify this number. With this, all you would have to do is replace the variable if you added more crystals.

You can check out the source for this application by opening the **rckmain.htm** sample file on the CD-ROM. Figure 14-11 shows the main rock shop Web page with three crystals already in the basket. As the figure shows, the cart used is larger, the winning number count is gone, and a dollar sign is used with the text values, in addition to the small "Empty Cart" block.

Figure 14-11: The rock shop main Web page

The code in this example can be converted for use with drag and drop or by using event capturing rather than embedded hypertext links. For practice, you might want to consider altering the pages to use these approaches.

If you extend the page to use drag and drop, remember to test where the reader drops the element, and that the reader is only dragging the rocks, not any of the other elements. If you use event capturing with the event model, you might want to try converting the `check_width` and `check_height` functions to IE and use these to check which object is the focus of the event.

Summary

This chapter explored some of the available options when scripting for dynamic HTML. Although the technologies in both browsers differ, and although you may find certain aspects of cross-browser scripting to be restrictive, with a little creativity and ingenuity, you can usually find a way to resolve the differences and accomplish what you set out to do.

The real key to successful Web page development, particularly when developing pages for both Internet Explorer and Navigator is to keep your mind open to different ways of doing things. When you run into problems, with an open-minded attitude you are more likely to look for a different way of doing something rather than spending days fighting the technology to get one specific method to work.

In this chapter you learned how to:

♦ Create drag-and-drop techniques that work with both Navigator and IE.

♦ Use CSS1 to organize Web page contents.

♦ Use IE 4.0 and Navigator open attributes to open small entry windows.

♦ Use layers to hide and expose Web page content.

♦ Capture and view keyboard content.

♦ Animate an item based on reader input.

♦ Create reusable code for use in multiple applications.

One problem with the Web application just demonstrated is that the version of Navigator used to create this application does not handle window resizing very well. If you resize the application page, it will not redisplay correctly with Navigator. The next chapter addresses the resize issue and makes use of some of the techniques discussed in this chapter and in Chapter 13 to create a fairly extensive online *progressive document*. In a progressive document, the reader's actions are noted and tracked. When the reader closes the document, and then reopens it, the document is presented in the same state as the reader left it.

Chapter 15

Creating a Progressive Document for Both Browsers

IN THIS CHAPTER

- ◆ Introduction to the progressive document

- ◆ Picking the tools

- ◆ Common tools

- ◆ Creating the Navigator-specific application

- ◆ Creating the IE-specific application

- ◆ Combining the two approaches to create a cross-browser application

FOR SEVERAL REASONS, ONLINE documents and electronic magazines, called *e-zines*, are ideally suited to take advantage of the features in Cascading Style Sheets (CSS1) and dynamic HTML. First, because e-zines need to change frequently, Cascading Style Sheets help to make the updating process much simpler by enabling you to establish an external master style sheet for all pages in a Web site, separating content from style. This way, updates to the Web site may only require changes to the content, without having to reestablish the style for every page. With dynamic HTML and CSS1, you can also create content that is nicely laid out, tailored to the user's screen resolution, and visually organized in such a manner as to *invite* the reader, rather than confuse them.

This chapter shows you how to create an interactive, progressive document that's an online e-zine called *Oregon Naturalist*. It features photographs and small articles, composed of three pages, with each page broken into three separate articles or presentations. To maximize the ease with which the articles are viewed, only one article is presented at a time at the largest font the screen resolution and page size can support. The reader can get to other articles by requesting another page or another article, and by accessing a table of contents (TOC) window.

In addition, if the Web page reader chooses, persistent information is maintained that tracks where he or she was when they last accessed the site, and returns them to that position when they revisit the site.

Another purpose for this chapter is to show how to combine applications that are created specifically for each browser into one application that is cross-browser compatible.

The first section of the chapter covers creating the entire application using Netscape's Navigator and the second section presents the same application, in its entirety, using Microsoft's Internet Explorer (IE). The third section details how to combine both of these applications into one that works with both browsers. You can choose to read either or both of the browser-specific sections and then progress to the final section. Note that the last section assumes that both browser versions have been created, and creates the cross-browser version of the application by combining the techniques.

What Is a Progressive Document?

I coined the phrase *progressive document* to represent any online document in which the content displayed is based on reader interaction, and that usually, but not always, tracks the reader's progress in some manner. Unlike multiple Web page documents that are hypertext-linked together, an interactive document is usually one page, with contents hidden until displayed in response to the reader's actions.

The first exposure I had to DHTML was at a workshop for authors held at the Microsoft campus, when the speaker brought up a document containing headers only. As he spoke, he clicked the top header and the subtopics for that header displayed just below the heading, instantly. I have seen more sophisticated uses of DHTML since then, but this is still the one that, to me, symbolizes what dynamic HTML is all about — information logically organized and revealed to the user at his or her request.

Picking the Tools

As you know, if you want to create sophisticated layouts, your best bet is to use Cascading Style Sheets. They are also imperative when using any of the features in dynamic HTML. In Navigator, you can use JavaScript Style Sheets to set the page dimensions and fonts before each page is loaded. In IE 4.0, you can set these styles dynamically throughout the presentation.

Because the site also hides and displays content, scripting for Navigator and IE is necessary to take advantage of layers in Navigator and the exposed HTML object model in IE 4.0.

To keep the browser-specific code handling for IE 4.0 separate from Navigator, the scripting for IE is done with VBScript or using the JScript tag, and the scripting for Navigator is done with JavaScript 1.2 where possible conflicts may occur. Though IE 4.0 also processes JavaScript 1.2 source, the browser accesses the functions contained in the last scripting block listed in the document. This means that if a function listed in a JavaScript 1.2 block is also listed in a JScript block, IE 4.0 will pick up the JScript block because it is located after the JavaScript 1.2 block. This is demonstrated in more detail later in this chapter.

JavaScript (without a version number) is used where both browsers can share code. Netscape cookies are used to maintain the information that tracks the reader's progress.

Common Elements

This section covers the elements that I used to create this application and that are common to both Internet Explorer and Navigator, including style sheets, the screen-resolution object and cookies.

Style Sheets

The first things that need to be created are the style sheets. Because the look of the pages is the same for both applications, I used CSS1 style sheets to design the look of the pages and used script to adjust the font for both browsers based on screen resolution. I also implemented Netscape cookies for persistence. Each one of these components of the application uses common code, so I include this code here to prevent having to duplicate it in the next two sections.

The first component of the application is the general formatting for all of the HTML pages. For each displayed document page, I decided on a forest green border, and then a smaller inset that displays an ivory color if images are turned off, or displays a background image that I created from a photograph of a forest scene.

I had some choices here as to where I could include the style settings for these two page components, such as an embedded or linked style sheet. Because I was dealing with five separate pages, and each of the pages share some of the same styles, I chose to put the styles into an externally linked style sheet. The following syntax links the style sheet to a document:

```
<LINK REL=STYLESHEET TYPE="text/css"
 HREF="nature.css">
```

At this time, the only feature I wanted to control from a global CSS1 style sheet is the background color of the page, the text color, and the font family. The CSS1 file contains the following definitions:

```
BODY { background-color : #339933;
       font-family: Arial; color: #336633}
```

This style sheet sets the background color of the document to a dark green, the font color to a darker green, and the default font to Arial.

The Screen-Resolution Object

Because I wanted my online magazine to display nicely regardless of the screen resolution, I change the default font size for general text and headers based on screen size. You can do this by using the **format.js** file created in Chapter 10, and modifying it to contain what you need for the current application. Format.js contains a technique to create an object that has properties that are specific to the screen resolution (or to color depth if this is also tracked). For this example, I modified the file to include changes to the font size for both headers and general body text, and to differentiate the size of the content navigation menu. Listing 15-1 shows the modified **format.js** file.

Listing 15-1: The format.js screen-resolution object for the naturalist online magazine

```
function window_format(font_size, header_size, menusize) {
  this.font_size = font_size;
  this.header_size = header_size;
  this.menusize = menusize;
}

if (screen.width >= 1000)
  thisscreen = new window_format("14pt", "24pt",
"lrgmenubar");
else if (screen.width >= 800)
  thisscreen = new window_format("10pt","18pt",
"lrgmenubar");
else
  thisscreen = new window_format("8pt", "16pt",
"smmenubar");
```

Checking for Color Depth

Modify the **format.js** file to add whatever resolution, or color depth, attributes you wish. Just add the new attributes, and alter the code that instantiates the object. For example, you can test for a color depth of 8, which is 256-color mode, and set the background color to white instead of ivory, and the text color to black instead of dark green.

If you find later that you need other properties added, it isn't that difficult to redefine the object and create new instantiations. Then, you need only alter the code in other documents to handle the new properties.

Cookies

I use Netscape-style cookies extensively with both the Navigator- and IE-specific applications. To create these cookies, I copied the `set_cookie` and `get_cookie` functions that Netscape provides in its JavaScript Guide (you'll find the URL in Appendix A), and added a few minor modifications of my own, mainly setting a long or short term for the cookie. Long-term cookies are stored for ten days, and short-term cookies are only stored for sixty seconds. Listing 15-2 contains these two functions.

Listing 15-2: The set_cookie and get_cookie functions to set and retrieve Netscape cookies

```
function set_cookie(name, value, expire) {
   var cookieDate = new Date();
   if (expire=="short")
      cookieDate.setTime (cookieDate.getTime() +
      (1000 * 60 * 60));
   else
      cookieDate.setTime (cookieDate.getTime() +
      (1000 * 60 * 60 * 24 * 10));
   document.cookie = name + "=" + escape(value) +
      "; expires=" + cookieDate.toGMTString();
}

function get_cookie(Name) {
  var search = Name + "="
  var returnvalue = "";
  if (document.cookie.length > 0) {
    offset = document.cookie.indexOf(search)
    if (offset != -1) { // if cookie exists
      offset += search.length
      // set index of beginning of value
      end = document.cookie.indexOf(";", offset)
      // set index of end of cookie value
      if (end == -1) {
        end = document.cookie.length
        returnvalue=
            unescape(document.cookie.substring(offset, end))
      }
    }
  }
  return returnvalue;
}
```

You can use this code, as is, for your own purposes, or you can use the third parameter as a string containing the expiration date for the cookie, which is Netscape's approach. These functions will go into the reusable code source file for the application when it is created.

At this point, the rest of the applications differ by browser, and the details are covered in the following sections.

Always Add, Never Delete

I read somewhere, I can't remember where now, that the true key to a successful implementation of object-oriented technologies is when you make constructive rather than destructive changes with the objects. (A *constructive* change is one in which a property, object, or method is added. A *destructive* change is one in which a property, object, or method is removed.)

Keeping this in mind ensures the success of your object-oriented project, and is also excellent advice for scripting, and splitting content into separate files. As long as you are adding methods and properties, and making constructive changes, the only modifications that occur due to these changes are in those files and in that code that needs to take advantage of the change.

Creating the Navigator-Specific Application

You can see the Navigator-only version of the online magazine at any time by accessing the application introduction file, **nnature.htm**, located on the CD-ROM that comes with this book. The example consists of three separate physical HTML documents (each containing three separate "articles"), a table of contents, an introduction page, a CSS1 style sheet file, a JSS file, and a JavaScript code file. This application can be modified for your own interactive documents.

Creating the Layout

After creating the global style sheet and formatting script file, detailed in the previous section, I created the first of the article pages, **nnature1.htm**, and added in the links to these two files, as shown next:

```
<LINK REL=STYLESHEET TYPE="text/css"
 HREF="nature.css">
<SCRIPT language="javascript" src="format.js">
</SCRIPT>
```

Because I have created a screen-resolution object in the **format.js** file, the logical next step is to use this object and alter the general page styles. Again, because this needs to be included in all the e-zine HTML pages, I encapsulated the code into a separate file so that whatever changes I make later are reflected in all my pages. I created a new file called **reusable.js** that contains all of my reusable code and functions. Listing 15-3 contains the first section of code, which sets the general style definitions, creates the global variables, and sets some of the global values that need to be accessible later in the code.

Listing 15-3: The first entry in reusable.js, to check for a browser and its version and to set the page fonts accordingly, using the object created in format.js

```
// global variables

// browser/version
var NSVER = 0
var MSVER = 0

// constant values
MAXPAGE = 3
MAXARTICLE = 3
MAXMENU = 6
MAXDISABLEDMENU=4

// background inset size
background_offset = 0;
background_width = 0;

document.tags.H1.fontSize = thisscreen.header_size;
document.tags.BODY.fontSize = thisscreen.font_size;

// set current window width and height
window_height = window.innerHeight;
window_width = window.innerWidth;

// set base inset values
background_offset = Math.round(window_height * .95);
background_width = Math.round(window_width * .95);
```

Listing 15-3 contains several global variables, used throughout the application, that define the size of the background inset. The inset, created next, visually encloses the document menu, images, and article text for each article. Normally the inset is set to 95 percent of the width and height of the Web page. However, the article may sometimes extend beyond the inset height. To prevent the article text from overflowing the inset, it's adjusted to fit the article if the article does extend beyond the inset's boundary. The `background_inset` and `background_width` variables trap and maintain what the inset boundary should be each time the page is opened.

In the article document pages, I needed to add in a reference to **reusable.js**:

```
<SCRIPT language="javascript" src="reusable.js">
</SCRIPT>
```

I added a layer to each of the article pages to create the inset. This forms the backdrop for each article and the associated image(s). The main reason I used a layer is that I wanted to fill the entire inset with a different background regardless of the size of content. Using the DIV tags only fills in the background of the content, such as the text, rather than the entire rectangle. The code for the layer is:

```
<LAYER
 bgColor="#ffffcc" width=95% height=95%
 top=2.5% left=2.5%
 background="back3.jpg">
</layer>
```

The layer definition sets the background color to a light ivory, for those browsers that turn off image downloading, and uses a forest graphic as the background image. The width and height are set to 95 percent of the parent element, which is the Web page document. To center the layer, I set the top-left corner to 2.5 percent.

My first inclination was to create the inset layer and use it to enclose the images and text for each article. This way, I could just hide or expose the whole layer at a time. But there were two problems with something like this. First, I also have buttons that will be available for all the articles, and most of them won't change when the articles change. Secondly, I found that, at least with release 4.01 of Navigator for Windows 95, that the JavaScript Style Sheet doesn't work with content that is embedded in two or more levels of layers. So, when I tried to set the font size of the header, and it was contained in one layer that was, in turn, contained in another layer, the JSS wouldn't work. Finally, I found that nesting layers too deeply makes the Web page document more difficult to read and work with.

Next, I created the content for the menu section of the article page, consisting of two layers, one to hold the larger menu and made up of larger button graphics, and one to hold the smaller menu. I would have liked to create one menu layer and then set the images and the image sizes after testing the screen resolution. However, I found that setting the image sizes using JSS just didn't work, as the following code shows:

```
document.classes.img1.all.width=100;
document.classes.img1.all.height=27;
...
<img class="img1" src="plcehldr.jpg"
    hspace=5 border=0>
```

I tried using the generic tags approach in addition to the more defined IDs approach (for more information on JSS, check out Chapter 10), but none of these techniques worked. Using CSS1 styles settings did not work either. I checked with Netscape and was told this was a bug. So, I decided it was time to improvise. However, if you are using a version of Navigator 4.x later than 4.01, try using the preceding code to see if it works in your version.

After weighing my options, the approach I finally took was to create two separate layers, one for large menu buttons and one for smaller blocks. I set the width and height of the images in both to the graphics files I created for both menus, and hid both layers on loading. As you can see in Listing 15-4, I also used only one very small file size image for all the image statements.

Listing 15-4: Two layers making up the large and small menu blocks

```
<!-- large menu bar, screen resolutions larger than
     or equal to 800 -->
<LAYER id=lrgmenubar top=30 left=30 width=300 height=130
 visibility="hide">
<a href="" onclick="change_article(0,0); return false">
<img src="plcehldr.jpg"  width=100 height=27
 border=0 hspace=5 ></a>
<a href="" onclick="remember(); return false">
<img src="plcehldr.jpg"  width=100 height=27
 border=0></a><p>
<a href="" onclick="change_article(0,1); return false">
<img src="plcehldr.jpg" width=100 height=27 hspace=5 border=0></a>
<a href="" onclick="change_article(0,-1); return false">
<img src="plcehldr.jpg" width=100 height=27 border=0></a><p>
<a href="" onclick="change_article(1,0); return false">
<img src="plcehldr.jpg" width=100 height=27 hspace=5 border=0></a>
<a href="" onclick="change_article(-1,0); return false">
<img src="plcehldr.jpg" width=100 height=27 border=0></a>
</LAYER>

<!-- small menu bar, screen resolutions less than 800 -->
<LAYER id=smmenubar top=15 left=30 width=250 height=100
 visibility="hide">
<a href="" onclick="change_article(0,0); return false">
<img src="plcehldr.jpg"  width=60 height=16
 border=0 hspace=5 ></a>
<a href="" onclick="remember(); return false">
<img src="plcehldr.jpg"  width=60 height=16
 border=0></a><p>
<a href="" onclick="change_article(0,1); return false">
<img src="plcehldr.jpg" width=60 height=16 hspace=5 border=0></a>
<a href="" onclick="change_article(0,-1); return false">
<img src="plcehldr.jpg" width=60 height=16 border=0></a><p>
<a href="" onclick="change_article(1,0); return false">
<img src="plcehldr.jpg" width=60 height=16 hspace=5 border=0></a>
<a href="" onclick="change_article(-1,0); return false">
<img src="plcehldr.jpg" width=60 height=16 border=0></a>
</LAYER>
```

Notice from the code that I also include event trapping for the click event, using an empty link and calling a function called change_article. The code returns "false," to keep the event from any further processing. This function will be explained in more detail later in this chapter.

Why am I using a small image as a placeholder for the menu? The reason is because I use code, covered in the next section, that checks to see what the screen resolution is and then creates an array of images based on the results. Because of this process and using the placeholder image, I am only loading the images used in the displayed menu. Anytime I can find a method that doesn't include download-ing additional images, I use it. The only additional cost in this approach is the few bytes necessary for the code included in the document and the placeholder image and the small amount of processing time necessary to check the screen resolution and load the correct menu images.

Because both layers are not visible, I won't show you the page as it looks after this placement; there isn't anything to see, yet.

Each article has at least one image, displayed just below the menu bar and a text section. I used dummy content when setting up the initial display and then fine-tuned the layout when the real content was ready. The first layer is the image and the second is the associated text, as shown in Listing 15-5. The image used in the example is the cityscape image associated with the e-zine's first article.

Listing 15-5: The first article image layer, which will be the prototype for additional article image layers

```
<!-- first article image and text -->
<layer left=30 width=300 height=200 top=200
 id="image1" visibility="hide">
<DIV class="imgbrd">
<img src="city.jpg" width=299 height=169 border=0>
<em>The Portland CityScape from Forest Park</em>
</DIV>
</layer>
<LAYER id="text1" left=425 top=30 zIndex=5
 width=200  visibility="hide"
 style="margin-left: 10; margin-top: 10">
<H1> The Oregon Naturalist</H1>
<p>
Dummy text.
</p>
</LAYER>
```

Notice from the code that I use a DIV block surrounding the article image and subtitle. This block also uses a CSS1 style sheet called imgbrd that looks like the following:

```
DIV.imgbrd {border-width:4; border-color: #339933;
 border-style:groove}
```

This creates a grooved and colored border surrounding whatever content is included within the layer. The reason I don't use this style sheet setting with the layer is that when the page resizes, the border is drawn incorrectly when associated with the layer. Regardless of how many times the page resizes, when using the DIV block, the border always draws correctly. Because this style setting needs to be available to all three of the article pages, it's added to the **nature.css** file.

To check the layer positioning at this point, I changed the visibility property to show for the large menu bar. Figure 15-1 demonstrates the layout as it exists at this stage of production. Note from the figure that the menu bar buttons use the one-pixel placeholder JPEG file.

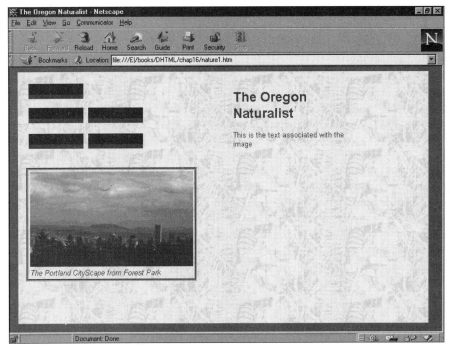

Figure 15-1: Layout of the first article with dummy content, displayed as visible to test placement

With these changes made, I was satisfied with my preliminary layout. Because each page has three articles, I copied the image layer, added an id of image1 to it and created two more image layers named image2 and image3 respectively. I set both of these new layers to hidden. I did the same for the article text layer, except I used the id names text1, text2, and text3. I also added the real content to the first article Web page. Now I was ready to start adding some script.

Activating the Buttons

Three separate areas of activation exist for the online magazine application: the interactive navigation menu buttons, the TOC window, and the application persistence, which uses Netscape cookies to store information about where the reader was the last time he or she accessed the e-zine, and returns them to that place.

THE ARTICLE AND PAGE BUTTONS: BUILDING THE MENU AND IMPLEMENTING NAVIGATION

Because each HTML document for the e-zine must use the same menu, and each has multiple articles, the code for building and activating the article buttons should be accessible globally by the application. This code is placed in the **reusable.js** file, created in the previous section.

First, the menu bar contains six buttons, one for the TOC window, one that enables the application to "remember" a specific page and article, one to open the previous article for the reader, one for the next article, one for the previous page, and one for opening the next page. Not all actions are available with every article or every page. For instance, if the reader is at the last article within the page, the "next article" action is not valid. The same holds true for the first article and the "previous article" action. To communicate this behavior, I wanted to provide a visual clue to the reader that these actions are not available.

I could have implemented this visual clue in several ways. I could have added more layers to the menu bar, enclosing each image within a layer and then hiding the images when the action is not available. Or I could have left the images and layer as they were and replaced the button with a totally transparent image that wouldn't show. However, the approach I used was to create a second version of the button that is semi-transparent and which takes the place of the original button to demonstrate that the action is "disabled" at that time.

To implement the buttons, active and disabled, I created two arrays: one to hold the original menu buttons, and one to hold the disabled button images. The first array contains six images, the second only four, as the TOC and Remember buttons are never disabled. Listing 15-6 contains the definition and creation of these two arrays.

Listing 15-6: The definition and creation of two arrays to hold menu bar buttons

```
// create arrays to hold images, large, small, and disable
var images_array = new Array(MAXMENU);
for (i = 0; i < MAXMENU; i++)
  images_array[i] = new Image();
var images_disabled_array = new Array(MAXDISABLEDMENU);
for (i = 0; i < MAXDISABLEDMENU; i++)
  images_disabled_array[i] = new Image();
```

Each entry in the array must be set to a new image object. Note that no reference to the image size occurs at this point, though size parameters can be used when creating a new image. Size is specified with the image embedding, and which images are loaded into the array, the larger or the smaller, occurs next. Also, a global variable is used in place of the maximum size of the enabled and disabled button arrays. This makes it easier to do global changes later if I decide to add more buttons to the arrays.

Listing 15-7 uses the screen object to test the screen resolution to determine whether to load the larger or smaller images into the arrays.

Listing 15-7: Code to check screen resolution and to load appropriate images

```
// setup based on size
if (screen.width >= 800) { // larger screen resolution
  // all displayed menu
```

```
for (i=0; i < MAXMENU; i++) {
     var menuname = "menu" + i + "l.jpg";
     images_array[i].src = menuname;
     }
// disabled button menu
for (i=0; i < MAXDISABLEDMENU; i++) {
     var menuname = "menu" + i + "dl.jpg";
     images_disabled_array[i].src = menuname;
     }
}
else    {       // smaller menu, less than 800 resolution
// all displayed menu
for (i=0; i < MAXMENU; i++) {
     var menuname = "menu" + i + ".jpg";
     images_array[i].src = menuname;
     }
// disabled button menu
for (i=0; i < MAXDISABLEDMENU; i++) {
     var menuname = "menu" + i + "d.jpg";
     images_disabled_array[i].src = menuname;
     }
}
```

The image files are named to represent their locations in the menu arrays. Also, if the resolution is larger, the image name also includes the letter "l" to represent a larger image. The disabled images contain the letter "d" and their array is smaller.

Referencing an image file in code will not load the image. The file must be used to create either an image variable or used in an inline-image HTML statement in order to be loaded. Based on this, only the images appropriate to the resolution are loaded with the application.

In addition to creating and loading the menu arrays, I also needed to create arrays to hold the inset width and height for each article. Remember that, in the last section, I captured the insert height and width based on the size of the page. Here I needed a place to store the information about whether these sizes will be used for the inset, or for the article width and height:

```
// array to contain inset vertical and horizontal offsets
article_voffset = new Array(0,0,0);
article_hoffset = new Array(0,0,0);
```

After this, I created a function, set_articles, that loads the images from the arrays into the layer containing the menu bar. Which menu is used is determined by the screen-resolution object. Also, because the inset is size-dependent, I placed the code to calculate the offsets into the same function, which is contained in Listing 15-8.

Listing 15-8: A function to set the menu images and display the appropriate menu, and to calculate the inset offsets

```
function set_articles() {
  // setup inset offsets
  for (i = 0; i < MAXARTICLE; i++) {
      var textvar = "text" + (i + 1);
      article_voffset[i] =
            document.layers[textvar].clip.height + 20;
      article_hoffset[i] =
            document.layers[textvar].clip.width + 400;
      if (article_voffset[i] < background_offset)
            article_voffset[i] = background_offset;
      if (article_hoffset[i] < background_width)
            article_hoffset[i] = background_width;
      }
  // setup and display menu
  the_menu = document.layers[thisscreen.menusize];
  for (i = 0; i < MAXMENU; i++) {
      the_menu.document.images[i].src = images_array[i].src;
      }
  the_menu.visibility="show";
}
```

I made use of consistent layer naming in order to use a for...loop statement to generically calculate each set of offsets. This way, I can add more articles and the code will literally not change. The function needs to be called just after the document is loaded, so the load event is trapped and a new function, post_load, is created to handle any post-document-loading activity.

If I did not add in the insert resizing information, longer articles would overflow the inset and the result is not very attractive, as shown in Figure 15-2.

With the resizing capability, the inset is resized to fit the article, a much more attractive result, as shown in Figure 15-3.

Now, regardless of what size the article is, the inset either expands to fit the article size, or remains the same as when the page was first opened or after a resize event.

Along with the load event, I also needed to trap the resize event (first available in Navigator 4.0), because, if the document is resized, the set_articles function needs to be called again to recalculate the inset offsets and to redisplay the menu. I found that loading a document always triggers a resize event, and resizing the window always triggers the load event. Because both of these events are so closely associated, I used the same function to process both events, but sent a parameter through to differentiate the activity, as Listing 15-9 demonstrates.

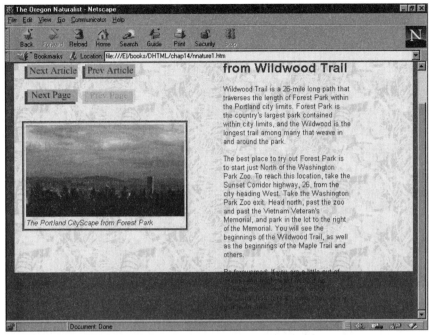

Figure 15-2: The results of a longer article and application inset not resizing

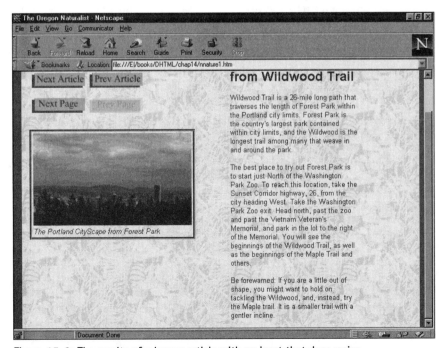

Figure 15-3: The results of a longer article with an inset that does resize

Listing 15-9: The post_load function that responds to both the load and resize events

```
function post_load(resizing) {
 var article = current_article;
 resizing = parseInt(resizing);
 // if resizing
 set_articles();
 if (resizing == 0) {
        article=get_cookie("naturalist_article");
        if (article == "") article = 1;
        load_article(article);
        update_menu(article, true);
        }
 else {
        show_article(article);
        update_menu(article, false);
        }
}
```

I also could have created two separate functions and there would have been no difference. If a resizing event occurs, I could include a call to a function, show_article, that resizes the inset and redraws the article. If a load event occurs, I could include a call to load_article, which also hides the previous article in addition to redisplaying the new article. Using both, I can update the menu by calling the function update_menu, passing a value of true for the second parameter for loading, and a value of false for a resize event. As you will see a little later in this section, this parameter tells the function whether it should reset any disabled buttons before setting the menu to the buttons that should be displayed for the current article. For a resize event, the buttons only need to be redisplayed.

Also, I call get_cookie when a load event occurs. This is for the persistence handling and to process the TOC window request, both of which are discussed in a later section.

The load_article function is next in the code, and all it does is hide the current article image and text, update the global variables of current_txt and current_img, and call show_article, as shown next:

```
function load_article(article) {
 document.layers[current_txt].visibility="hide";
 document.layers[current_img].visibility="hide";
 current_img = "image" + article;
 current_txt = "text" + article;

 show_article(article);
}
```

Next, I created the function show_article. It uses the offset arrays to resize the inset layer, checks the screen resolution to see if the text and image layers need to be moved to compensate for the smaller resolution, and shows the article. Listing 15-10 contains this function.

Resizing and Loading Events

In tracking the calls to the `post_load` function, I discovered that reloading a document actually calls this function several times. Resizing a page, by using the menu bar, for example, causes several `resize` events, and occasionally a `load` event (if the page is maximized). You can check this out for yourself with your version of Navigator by placing an alert in the `post_load` function and printing out the resizing variable. The downside to this is that the page can flicker quite a bit during a resize, and the page may even paint incorrectly during a resize operation.

Listing 15-10: The show_article function that resets the inset size, moves the image and text layers based on screen resolution, and then shows the article

```
function show_article(article) {
 // resize inset
 document.layers["article_background"].
     ResizeTo(article_hoffset[article-
             1],article_voffset[article-1]);

 // if smaller screens, move layers
 if (screen.width < 800) {
     document.layers[current_img].moveTo(30,105);
     document.layers[current_txt].moveTo(350,30);
     }
 document.layers[current_img].visibility="show";
 document.layers[current_txt].visibility="show";
}
```

Next I created the `update_menu` function, which checks the parameters to see if previously disabled buttons need to be enabled, and to disable any buttons that need to be disabled based on the article and page. Why do these need to be updated if the article has not changed and the current buttons aren't changed? When the page is resized or reloaded, the in-page menu bar is redrawn. Based on this behavior, the menu needs to be updated to fit the current article and page, as shown in Listing 15-11.

Listing 15-11: The update_menu function, which sets the enabled and disabled buttons depending on page and article number

```
function update_menu(new_article, change_current) {
    new_article = parseInt(new_article);
    if (change_current) {
        if (current_article == 1)
            the_menu.document.images[3].src =
            images_array[3].src;
        else if (current_article == 3)
            the_menu.document.images[2].src =
```

```
                images_array[2].src;
        }

  if (new_article == 1) {
        the_menu.document.images[3].src =
        images_disabled_array[1].src;
  }
    else if (new_article == 3){
        the_menu.document.images[2].src =
        images_disabled_array[0].src;
  }

current_article = new_article;
if (current_page == 1)
        the_menu.document.images[5].src =
        images_disabled_array[3].src;
  else if (current_page == MAXPAGE)
        the_menu.document.images[4].src =
        images_disabled_array[2].src;
}
```

Figure 15-4 shows the Web page article with the disabled buttons. Notice from the display that the article displayed is the first article on the first page so neither the previous article nor the previous page buttons are enabled.

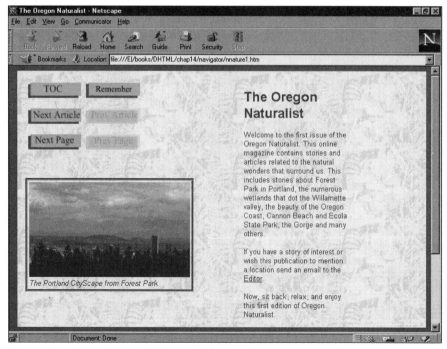

Figure 15-4: The application Web page with menu images, including disabled menu images representing disabled choices

Finally, I created a function to process mouse clicks on the Next and Previous Article buttons. The function, change_article, is shown in Listing 15-12, and it checks to see if the TOC window is being opened, or whether the article or page buttons were pressed. The open_toc function is discussed in the next section.

Listing 15-12: Functions to handle clicks on the Previous Article, Next Article, Previous Page, and Next Page buttons and to update the menu accordingly

```
function change_article(page, article) {
 // if open TOC window
 if (page == 0 && article == 0)
     open_toc();

 // if change article
 else if (page == 0) {
    article = parseInt(current_article) +
            parseInt(article);
    if (article > 0 && article < MAXARTICLE + 1) {
       load_article(article);
       update_menu(article,true);
       set_cookie("naturalist_article",article,"short");
       }
 }

 // change page
 else {
    page = current_page + page;
    if (page > 0 && page < MAXPAGE + 1) {
       set_cookie("naturalist_article",1,"short");
       var move_page = "nnature" + page + ".htm";
       current_page=page;
       location = move_page;
       }
 }
}
```

The function has two parameters, representing the difference between the current page and the requested page and between the current article and the requested article. Each one of these parameters can receive a value of –1, 0, or 1. If both the page and article are 0, the TOC window is opened. If the page is 0 and the article is not, the direction of the change is tested. The variables current_article and current_page are set outside a function, making them available to all functions. The current_article is set to whatever value is found in the Netscape cookie when the page is loaded, or a value of 1. The current_page variable is set to whatever page is currently loaded.

The article parameter's value is added to current_article and this value is tested. If current_article has a value of 1, meaning that the first article is being displayed, and the reader clicks the Previous Article button, the value would be set to 0 (1 + – 1 = 0). If the reader clicks the Next Article button, the value would be set to 2 (1 + 1 = 2). This value is then used in an expression to see if it falls between the values of 0 and `MAXARTICLE` + 1. `MAXARTICLE` is a global variable set to the maximum number of articles per Web page, in this case set to a value of 3. Because this value is used with all three pages, it is set in **reusable.js.**

Based on the expression, the Web page reader's action of pressing the Previous Article button on the first article is ignored. If the current article were the last, which is article three in this example, pressing the Next Article button is ignored. If the value meets the expression, the `load_article` and `update_menu` functions are called. In addition, the function `set_cookie` is called to set the stored Netscape cookie to the new article. Again, this is discussed in more detail in the next section, but be aware that setting this value means this is the article that is redisplayed if the reader hits the reload key. Without this setting, the reader would always get the first article on the page every time a `reload` or `resize` event occurs.

If the reader clicks either the Next Page or Previous Page buttons, the function uses the same logic to test to see if the action is allowable. If it is, the current location of the window is set to the new page.

Figure 15-5 shows the prototype page after the Next Article button has been pressed twice, and the third article layer is displayed. This time, the Next Article button is disabled, and the Previous Article button is enabled.

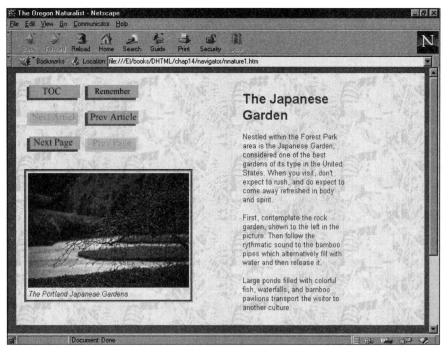

Figure 15-5: The prototype page demonstrating the state of the Next and Previous Article buttons based on the user reading the last article

At this time, I also decided to add the rest of the pages. I copied the prototype page into two new files, **nnature2.htm**, and **nnature3.htm** (available on the CD-ROM). Then I replaced the prototype image and text with ones appropriate to the article and page. Because this content gets fairly large at times, I won't repeat the contents here, but you can check this out for yourself by opening any one of these pages.

THE TOC BUTTON: ADDING A TABLE OF CONTENTS WINDOW

After activating the article and page buttons, I activated the TOC button. Because communication needs to be tracked between Web pages, I also added in the functions to the **reusable.js** file, discussed in the previous section, to control Netscape cookies.

To add the TOC window, I first needed to create the TOC window. I used the same style sheet files of **nature.css** and **format.js** to maintain a consistent look among all the pages associated with the application. In addition, I created an embedded style sheet to set some styles that are unique to the TOC document:

```
<STYLE type="text/css">
 BODY { font-size: 10pt }
 H2 { color: #993333; font-size: 14pt }
 A { color: #993333 }
</STYLE>
```

Then I added in menu items for each of the articles, and a brief description of each article. Listing 15-13 contains the first section of this menu. You can check out the full Web page by accessing the sample file **ntoc.htm** on the CD-ROM. Figure 15-6 also shows the TOC page. Note the lack of menus, which are unnecessary for this type of Web page, and only take up valuable screen space.

Listing 15-13: The body of the TOC Web page

```
<LAYER
 bgColor="ivory" width=95% height=95%
 top=2.5% left=2.5%
 background="back3.jpg">
</layer>
<layer left=10% top=10%>
<H2>Welcome to the Oregon Naturalist</H2>
<a href="" onclick="go_topage(1,1);return false">
<img src="flower.jpg" width=25 height=24
 border=0 hspace=5 align=top>
Page One First Article</a> Welcome to the first issue of the Oregon
 Naturalist
<p>
<a href="" onclick="go_topage(1,2);return false">
<img src="flower.jpg" width=25 height=24
 border=0 hspace=5 align=top>
Page One Second Article</a> The Top of the Trail for the Wildcat
 Trail
<p>
```

```
<a href="" onclick="go_topage(1,3);return false">
<img src="flower.jpg" width=25 height=24
 border=0 hspace=5 align=top>
Page One Third Article</a> The Rose Garden, an island of serenity
```

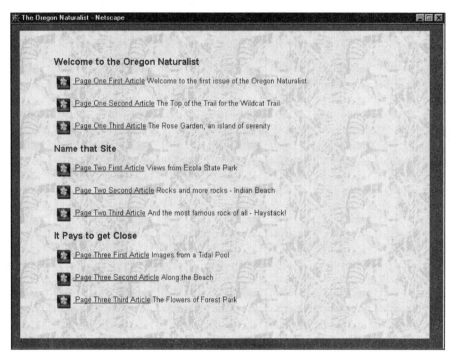

Figure 15-6: The TOC page, opened full screen

Each entry in the page traps the onclick event for the hypertext link associated with the item, and calls a function called go_topage. This function is actually quite simple. For the window that opened it, found by accessing the opener property, it calls a function called toc_page and passes the page and article to this function. Lastly, the TOC window closes itself, as shown next:

```
function go_topage(page, article) {
 window.opener.toc_page(page, article);
 window.close();
}
</SCRIPT>
```

Because the go_topage function called another function that must be available for all three article pages, I needed to create the new function, toc_page, in **reusable.js**. My first instinct was to set the location property to the new page, and then call change_article to change to the appropriate article. However, some timing issues crop up here. What happens is that the new page is still loading while the function call to `change_article` is being processed. Needless to say, some erratic results occur. The solution? I used Netscape cookies to store the article number and then, during the `post_load` function call, I set the page to the article number found in this cookie.

The function `toc_page`, using the new cookie function, follows:

```
function toc_page(page,article) {
  page = "nnature" + page + ".htm";
  set_cookie("naturalist_article",article,"short");
  location = page;
}
```

Remember from Listing 15-9 that the `post_load` function calls the `get_cookie` function to get the article that should be loaded.

Finally, I needed to add the code to open the TOC window, which is the function `open_toc`. The code for this little function is provided next:

```
function open_toc() {
  toc_window = open("ntoc.htm", "TableOfContents",
             "scrollbars=yes")
}
```

This code opens the TOC window into a full size console-mode window, with scroll bars if the content is too large to display in one screen length.

By this point, you've seen how to implement the functions for the Next and Previous Article buttons, as well as the TOC button. You have also seen how to handle problems such as resizing the inset to fit the article size. The next section discusses how to implement the Web application's persistence functionality, through the Remember button, and the introduction page.

THE REMEMBER BUTTON: IMPLEMENTING PERSISTENCE

If the Web page reader presses the Remember button, the application needs to trap both the page and the current article and store this information in Netscape cookies. The function call to start this process is `remember`, called when the button is pressed. This is the last function I added to **reusable.js**. Here is the code for this simple function:

```
function remember() {
   set_cookie("naturalist_rem_article",current_article,
       "long");
   set_cookie("naturalist_page",current_page,"long");
}
```

The `remember` function calls `set_cookie` twice, once to set the value for the current article, and once to set the value for the current page. Because a cookie is already being used for tracking the article accessed by the TOC window, a different name is used for the remember article.

I created a new document, the introduction page, and named it **nnature.htm**.
This Web page checks for the page and article that is persistently stored, and loads
the target page, if any — otherwise it loads page one. Also, it sets the current article
cookie used by the post_load function to the article that should be loaded. The
page also incorporates the formatting files of **nature.css** and **format.js**. The
reusable code file, **reusable.js**, is not used because it contains much more functionality than this page needs and I wanted the page to load as quickly as possible. The
page also uses an embedded style sheet to define styles local only to it. The complete page can be found in Listing 15-14.

Listing 15-14: The introduction page for the Netscape-specific progressive document
application

```
<HTML><HEAD>
<TITLE>The Oregon Naturalist</TITLE>
<!--
Add in the standard CSS1
and JSS style sheet files
-->
<LINK REL=STYLESHEET TYPE="text/css"
 HREF="nature.css">
<STYLE type="text/css">
 H1 { color: #993333; font-size: 36pt }
</STYLE>
<SCRIPT language="javascript" src="format.js">
</SCRIPT>

<SCRIPT language="javascript1.2">

// set_current_article
// sets cookie to target article
function set_current_article(article) {
   var cookieDate = new Date();
   cookieDate.setTime (cookieDate.getTime() +
      (1000 * 60));
   document.cookie = "naturalist_article=" + article +
      "; expires=" + cookieDate.toGMTString();


}
// get_current_page_article
// gets cookies containing page and article if any
// If no cookies are found, 1 is used for both values
function get_current_page_article() {
 var content = document.cookie;
 var article=1;
 var page=1;
 var loc = content.indexOf("naturalist_rem_article");
 if (loc >= 0)
      article = content.substring(loc+23,
            loc+24);
 loc = content.indexOf("naturalist_page");
```

```
if (loc >= 0)
      page = content.substring(loc+16,loc+17);

set_current_article(article);
window.location="nnature" + page + ".htm";
}

</SCRIPT>

</HEAD>
<BODY onload="get_current_page_article()">
<LAYER
 bgColor="#ffffcc" width=95% height=95%
 top=2.5% left=2.5%
 background="back3.jpg">
</layer>
<layer left=10% top=10%>
<H1>Welcome to the <strong>Oregon Naturalist</H1>
</layer>
</BODY></HTML>
```

The post_load function used with the article pages already checks for the current article when the page loads so no change to the code is necessary. The page also uses cookie functions, which means that these functions are probably best placed into their own separate script file. This topic is addressed in this chapter's last section.

If you haven't had a chance to try out the application, access the file **nnature.htm** on the CD-ROM and navigate through the pages, open the TOC window, and test for persistence.

That's all for the Navigator-specific version of the progressive document application. If you want, you can read the next section to see how to create the same application for IE, or you can skip directly to the concluding section to see how to create this same application for both browsers.

Creating the IE 4.0-Specific Application

You can see the IE-specific version of the online magazine at any time by accessing the introduction file for the application, **ienature.htm**, located on the CD-ROM that comes with this book. The example consists of three separate physical HTML documents, each containing three separate "articles," a table of contents, an introduction page, a CSS1 style sheet file, and a JavaScript code file. The example can easily be modified for your own interactive documents.

Creating the Layout

After creating the global style sheet, detailed in the section covering common code, I created the first of the article pages, **ienature1.htm**, and added in the links to the file, as shown next:

```
<LINK REL=STYLESHEET TYPE="text/css"
  HREF="nature.css">
```

Next, I created the `inset` object that forms the background for all of the articles. I used a `DIV` block for this and used inline styling to set the appearance of the block, as shown next:

```
<DIV id="article_background"
style="position: absolute; z-index: -1; background-color:#ffffcc ;
  width:95%; height:95%; top:2.5%; left:2.5%; background-
  image:url('back3.jpg')">
</DIV>
```

The `z-index` value of the block is set to a negative value to force it to remain in the background. Note that I set the background color as well as the image, in case the reader has turned off image loading.

Next, I created the menu block. IE provides techniques to resize the images dynamically after a Web page is loaded, so only one set of menu block images is needed. Also, the image tags form placeholders for the document so no actual images are loaded at this time. Image loading occurs later in the script section. Listing 15-15 contains the definition for the menu block.

Listing 15-15: The menu bar image block

```
<!-- menu bar -->
<DIV style="position:absolute; left:30; top:30; width: 300; height:
  130">
<img id="menu1" onclick="change_article(0,0)">
<img id="menu2" onclick="remember()"><p>
<img class="menu" id="menu3" onclick="change_article(0,1)">
<img class="menu" id="menu4" onclick="change_article(0,-1)"><p>
<img class="menu" id="menu5" onclick="change_article(1,0)">
<img class="menu" id="menu6" onclick="change_article(-1,0)"><p>
</DIV>
```

IE provides event trapping for all elements, including images, and the `onclick` event is trapped for the menu bar images. The `click` event handler, `change_article`, is discussed in a later section.

Next, I added in the prototype image and text sections. In this stage of preliminary layout design, I didn't include any actual content, although I did use an actual image so I could have a better view of the layout, as shown next:

```
<!-- first article image and text -->
<DIV class="imgbrd" id="image1">
<img src="city.jpg" width=299 height=169 border=0>
<em>The Portland CityScape from Forest Park</em>
</DIV>

<DIV id="text1"
style="position:absolute; left:425; top:30; z-index:5; width:200">
<H1> The Oregon Naturalist</H1>
<p>
Dummy text
</p>
</DIV>
```

Figure 15-7 shows the page at this point, with empty image tags and dummy content.

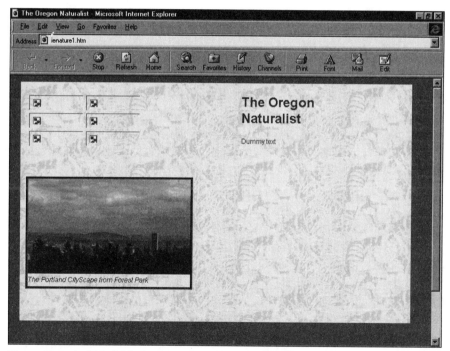

Figure 15-7: An IE article's first page with dummy content and empty images

The DIV block surrounding the image and its title has a border, which is called imgbrd, and is defined as:

```
DIV.imgbrd {border-width:4; border-color:#33cc33;
  border-style:groove;
```

```
position:absolute; top: 180; left:30;
width:300; height:200;
visibility:hidden;
FILTER:revealTrans(Duration=3.0,Transition=23)}
```

This code creates a grooved and colored border surrounding whatever content is included within the layer. In addition to creating the colored border, the image contained within the block is hidden when initially displayed, and is assigned the revealTrans transition filter in order to add transitioning effects to the article images. Because this style setting needs to be available to all three of the article pages, it's added to the **nature.css** file. Each time the article changes, and the image changes, the random transitioning effect will be applied, meaning that the transitioning effect will differ each time an article image is displayed.

I copied the image and text blocks and created two new versions of each, naming the image blocks image2 and image3 respectively, and the text blocks text2 and text3. I also added the real articles and images, and hid all of the articles and images by setting the visibility of each to hidden as shown next for the first article:

```
<!-- first article image and text -->
<DIV class="imgbrd" id="image1" style="visibility:hidden">
<img src="city.jpg" width=299 height=169 border=0>
<em>The Portland CityScape from Forest Park</em>
</DIV>

<DIV id="text1"
style="position:absolute; left:425; top:30; z-index:5;
 width:200;visibility:hidden">
<H1> The Oregon Naturalist</H1>
<p>
...
</p>
</DIV>
```

The appropriate article and matching image will be displayed using scripting, which is discussed in the next section.

Activating the Buttons

Three separate areas of activation exist for the online magazine application: the interactive navigation menu buttons, the TOC button, and the Remember button, which uses Netscape cookies to store information about where the reader was the last time they accessed the e-zine, and returns them to that place.

THE ARTICLE AND PAGE BUTTONS:
BUILDING THE MENU AND IMPLEMENTING NAVIGATION

Because I had created a screen-resolution object in the **format.js** file, the logical next step was to use this object and alter the general page styles. Again, because this is pertinent in all the e-zine HTML pages, I encapsulated the code into a separate file so that whatever changes I might make later would be reflected in all my pages. Thus I created a new file called **iereusable.js** that contains all of my reusable code and functions. Listing 15-16 contains the first section of code, which sets the general style definitions, creates the global variables, and sets some of the global values that need to be accessible later in the code.

Listing 15-16: The global variable section of the source code file

```
// global variables

// browser/version
var NSVER = 0
var MSVER = 0

// constant values
MAXPAGE = 3
MAXARTICLE = 3
MAXMENU = 6
MAXDISABLEDMENU=4

// background inset size
background_offset = 0;
background_width = 0;
```

I can't use the screen-specific object that I created in **format.js** just yet because the document must be fully loaded before I can alter any of the element styles.

Next, I created the array to hold the menu images and the vertical and horizontal inset offset arrays. The menu array contains the larger or smaller images based on the screen width. The inset offset arrays are used to help resize the inset based on which article is currently displayed. This is discussed in more detail a little later. Listing 15-17 shows the code to create these arrays.

Listing 15-17: Creating the menu bar image array and the inset offset arrays

```
// set base inset values

// create arrays to hold images, large and small
var images_array = new Array(MAXMENU);
for (i = 0; i < MAXMENU; i++)
 images_array[i] = new Image();

// setup menu display based on size
if (screen.width >= 800) { // larger screen resolution
 // all displayed menu
 for (i=0; i < MAXMENU; i++) {
     var menuname = "menu" + i + "1.jpg";
     images_array[i].src = menuname;
     }
 }
else  {       // smaller menu, less than 800 resolution
 // all displayed menu
```

```
for (i=0; i < MAXMENU; i++) {
    var menuname = "menu" + i + ".jpg";
    images_array[i].src = menuname;
    }
}

// array to contain inset vertical and horizontal offsets
article_voffset = new Array(0,0,0);
article_hoffset = new Array(0,0,0);
```

As you can see from Listing 15-17, the offset arrays are created with three members, each set to a value of zero (0).

The next section of code is a function called `set_articles` that checks the dimensions of each of the articles and adds in the appropriate value to the offset arrays. What this means is that if the article is longer than the offset, the offset is increased to fit the size of the article. Otherwise, the offset is kept at the same size as when the Web page is first loaded, which is 95 percent of the Web page and centered. This function will be called any time a new article is loaded, and is shown in Listing 15-18.

Listing 15-18: The set_articles function measures and sets offsets for inset based on the article size

```
// set_articles
// get width and height of articles
// compare to inset and set inset to whichever is
// larger
function set_articles() {
  for (i = 0; i < MAXARTICLE; i++) {
    var textvar = "text" + (i + 1);
    article_voffset[i] =
        document.all.item(textvar).clientHeight + 20;
    article_hoffset[i] =
        document.all.item(textvar).clientWidth + 400;
    if (article_voffset[i] < background_offset)
        article_voffset[i] = background_offset;
    if (article_hoffset[i] < background_width)
        article_hoffset[i] = background_width;
    }
}
```

The `set_articles` function is called whenever the Web page is loaded, and whenever the current article is changed. Several other functions are also called whenever the Web page is loaded, and they are all processed in a function called `post_load`.

The `post_load` function does several things. First, it captures the default inset width and height as the page is first loaded. The function also accesses all of the H1 headers within the page and sets the font size for these elements using the `thisscreen` object. It then calls `get_cookie` to get the article it should display, and `set_menu`, which sets the menu images and image sizes. Finally, it loads the current article and updates the menu buttons to reflect the article number by calling the function `update_menu`. Listing 15-19 contains the code for the `post_load` function. The other functions are given in detail later in this section.

Listing 15-19: The post_load function, which redefines the page based on screen resolution and calls the functions to load the appropriate article and set up the menu

```
// post_load
// called whenever page is reloaded
function post_load() {
  background_offset = document.body.clientHeight * 0.95;
  background_width = document.body.clientWidth * 0.95;

  set_articles();
  article=get_cookie("naturalist_article");
  if (article == "") article = 1;
  set_menu();
  load_article(article);
  update_menu(article, true);
}
```

The images for the menu bar are loaded next. The function `set_menu` checks the screen resolution and loads the appropriate images into the menu bar image locations. In addition, it also changes the width and height of the images, using the `style` property. If the smaller menu bar is used, the space from the top and side of the menu bar, and between the menu images, is compressed. Listing 15-20 shows this function.

Listing 15-20: The set_menu function sets the menu images and sizes

```
// set_menu
// function checks screen size
// and loads appropriate menu images
// it also sizes image tags to fit image files,
// and compresses space for the smaller image
function set_menu() {
  if (screen.width < 800) {
      for (i = 1; i < 7; i++) {
            var menuname = "menu" + i;
            var menufile = "menu" + (i-1) + ".jpg";
            document.images[menuname].style.width=60;
            document.images[menuname].style.height=16;
            document.images[menuname].src = menufile;
            document.images[menuname].style.top =
                document.images[menuname].style.pixelTop - 20;
            if (i % 2 == 0)
                document.images[menuname].style.left =
                document.images[menuname].style.pixelLeft - 40;
            else
                document.images[menuname].style.left =
```

```
                    document.images[menuname].style.pixelLeft - 5;
        }
    }
else
    for (i = 1; i < 7; i++) {
        var menuname = "menu" + i;
        var menufile = "menu" + (i-1) + "l.jpg";
        document.images[menuname].style.width=100;
        document.images[menuname].style.height=27;
        document.images[menuname].src = menufile;
        }
}
```

Without compressing the space when using the smaller images, the menu bar will look a bit funny and will take up too much space, conflicting with the other elements on the Web page. Figure 15-8 shows the Web page, in 640 × 480 resolution, without using this compression code. As you can see, the menu images are spaced too far apart, ruining the cohesive nature of the menu, as well as cutting into the space needed for the article image.

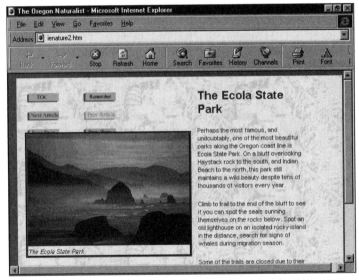

Figure 15-8: The menu bar images without compression, in 640 × 480 resolution

Figure 15-9 shows the same page in the same resolution while using the compression code. The appearance is better, and the menu images no longer overlap the article image.

The next two functions I created in the source code file are the load_article and show_article functions. The load_article function hides the current image and article for the page, and determines the nature of the new article and image. It also calls the `show_article` function.

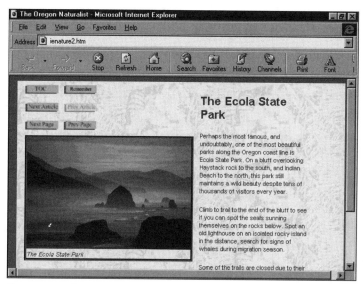

Figure 15-9: The menu bar images with compression, in 640 × 480 resolution

The `show_article` function resizes the inset for the Web page based on the article offsets. It also moves the article if the screen width is less than 800, in order to fit the article horizontally into the Web page for lower-resolution monitors. The function also sets the image and article text blocks to be visible. I also found that I needed to set the `overflow` property to be visible for the article text. This property can be set to visible or hidden to display or clip text that overflows the block size. This property inherits its original value from the object when it is first displayed in the page, and needs to be reset when the object is reset.

Feature or bug? Having to reset the overflow `visibility` property could either be a feature or it could be a bug. My recommendation is to test this code with your version of IE 4.x. Try the code without setting the `overflow` property. If it works, then it was a bug that has since been fixed. If it doesn't, then you can assume it is either a bug that has not been fixed or a feature.

Listing 15-21 contains the code for the `load_article` and `show_article` functions.

Listing 15-21: Functions to load a specific article and resize the inset to fit the article size

```
// load_article
// hide current article
function load_article(article) {
 var textobj = document.all.item(current_txt);
 var imgobj = document.all.item(current_img);
 textobj.style.visibility="hidden";
 imgobj.style.visibility="hidden";
 current_img = "image" + article;
 current_txt = "text" + article;
 show_article(article);
}

// show_article
// resize inset to fit article width/height
// set image top just below menu if screen resolution
//    is less than 800
// show new article image and text
function show_article(article) {
 // resize inset
 var new_width = article_hoffset[article-1];
 var new_height = article_voffset[article-1];
 var background =
      document.all.item("article_background");
 background.style.width = new_width;
 background.style.height = new_height;

 // if smaller screens, move layers
 if (screen.width < 800) {
      document.all.item(current_img).style.left=30;
      document.all.item(current_img).style.top = 105;
      document.all.item(current_txt).style.left=350;
      document.all.item(current_txt).style.top=30;
      }
 document.all.item(current_img).style.
      visibility="inherit";
 document.all.item(current_txt).style.
      visibility="inherit";
 imgobj.filters.item(0).Apply();
 imgobj.filters.item(0).Play(2.0);
 document.all.item(current_txt).style.
      overflow="visible";
}
```

Notice that I use the current_img and current_txt strings to determine which items are made visible. The item method for the all property takes either item indexes, or the item name. I also use the transition filter methods Apply and Play to stop any painting on the image and reapply the transitioning effect.

The next function, update_menu, is called by post_load and the change_article function, discussed later. The update_menu function checks to see which article and which page is currently loaded, and disables the menu buttons that are no longer applicable based on the article and page.

IE has built-in properties to alter the appearance of HTML elements. Among these is the visual filter, discussed in detail in Chapter 7, which alters the appearance of a visual block. I decided to use this filter to alter the opacity of the image using the Alpha visual filter property, giving the button a disabled appearance. The actual behavior of an enabled and disabled button is included in change_article. Listing 15-22 contains the code for the update_menu function.

Listing 15-22: A function to update the menu when the article changes

```
// update_menu
// if update_menu called from change_article
//     if current_article is first or last
//     adjust menu
// if first article, disable previous article button
// if last article, disable next article button
// if first page, disable previous page button
// if last page, disable next page button
function update_menu(new_article, change_current) {
    if (change_current) {
      if (current_article == 1)
         document.images[3].style.filter="";
      else if (current_article == 3)
         document.images[2].style.filter="";
    }
    if (new_article == 1) {
         document.images[3].style.filter="";
         document.images[3].style.
         filter= "Alpha(opacity: 50)";
         }
    else if (new_article == 3){
         document.images[2].style.filter="";
         document.images[2].style.
         filter="Alpha(opacity: 50)";
         }
    current_article = new_article;
    if (current_page == 1) {
         document.images[5].style.filter="";
         document.images[5].style.
         filter="Alpha(opacity: 50)";
         }
    else if (current_page == MAXPAGE) {
         document.images[4].style.filter="";
         document.images[4].style.
         filter="Alpha(opacity: 50)";
         }
}
```

To remove the opaque filter, the `style` filter property is set to an empty string.

Finally, I wrote a function that covers the page and article movement called the `change_article` function, shown in Listing 15-23. This function checks to see if the TOC window is being opened, in which case the `open_toc` function, discussed later, is called. If the article buttons are pressed or the page buttons are pressed, the function processes the actions accordingly.

Listing 15-23: The change_article function, which determines whether to open the TOC window, to change the article, or to change the page

```
// change_article
// called when previous or next article button is
// pressed
//     call load article and update menu
// or next page or previous page button is pressed
//       change page
function change_article(page, article) {
  // if open TOC window
  if (page == 0 && article == 0)
      open_toc();

  // if change article
  else if (page == 0) {
     article = parseInt(current_article) +
             parseInt(article);
     if (article > 0 && article < MAXARTICLE + 1) {
        load_article(article);
        update_menu(article,true);
        set_cookie("naturalist_article",article,"short");
        }
     }
  // change page
  else {
     page = current_page + page;
     if (page > 0 && page < MAXPAGE + 1) {
        set_cookie("naturalist_article",1,"short");
        var move_page = "ienature" + page + ".htm";
        current_page=page;
        location = move_page;
        }
   }
 }
```

The function has two parameters, representing the difference between the current page and the requested page and between the current article and requested article. Each one of these parameters could get a value of –1, 0, or 1. If both the page and article are zero (0), the TOC window is opened. If the page is 0 and the article is not, the direction of the change is tested. The variables `current_article` and `current_page` are set outside a function, making them available to all functions. The `current_article` is set to whatever value is found in the Netscape cookie when the page is loaded, or a value of 1. The `current_page` variable is set to whatever page is currently loaded.

The article parameter's value is added to `current_article` and this value is tested. If `current_article` has a value of 1, meaning that the first article is being displayed, and the reader clicks the Previous Article button, the value will be set to 0 (1 + −1 = 0). If the reader clicks the Next Article button, the value will be set to two 2 (1 + 1 = 2). This value is then used in an expression to see if it falls between the values of 0 and `MAXARTICLE` + 1. `MAXARTICLE` is a global variable set to the maximum number of articles per Web page, in this case set to a value of 3. Because this value is used with all three pages, it is set in **iereusable.js**.

Based on the expression, the Web page reader's action of pressing the Previous Article button on the first article is ignored. If the current article were the last, which is article three in this example, pressing the Next Article button is ignored. If the value meets the expression, the `load_article` and `update_menu` functions are called. In addition, the function `set_cookie` is called to set the stored Netscape cookie to the new article. Again, this is discussed in more detail in the next section, but be aware that setting this value means this is the article that is redisplayed if the reader hits the reload key. Without this setting, the reader would always get the first article on the page every time a reload or `resize` event occurs.

If the reader clicks either the Next Page or Previous Page buttons, the function uses the same logic to test to see if the action is allowable. If it is, the current location of the window is set to the new page.

Once the button movement functions were created, I copied the template page, **ienature1.htm**, to **ienature2.htm** and **ienature3.htm** (available on the CD-ROM), and added in the content for these pages. The additional content is the only change at this stage, and because I don't want to take the space to include it in this chapter, you should open each of these files to view the contents.

Figure 15-10 shows the application with the second page loaded, and the third article displayed. Notice that both of the application page buttons are enabled because navigation can occur in both directions from this page.

Figure 15-11 shows the third page and second article. In this case, both of the article buttons are enabled, because you can move in both directions with these buttons. However, the Next Page button is disabled because the last page in the application is currently open.

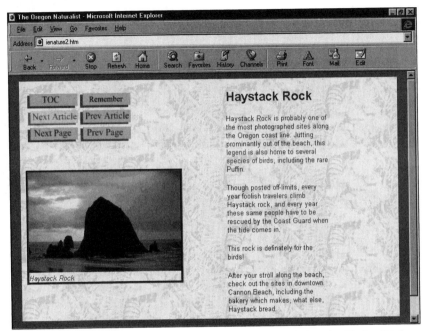

Figure 15-10: The progressive document with page two loaded, and with the third article displayed

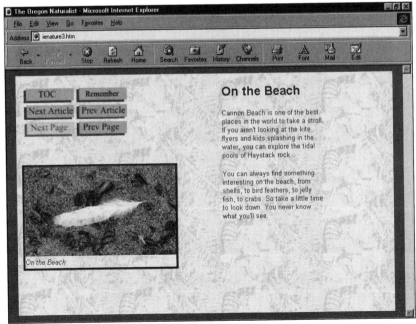

Figure 15-11: The progressive document with page three loaded, and with the second article displayed

THE TOC BUTTON: ADDING A TABLE OF CONTENTS WINDOW

Next, I wrote the code to activate the TOC button. Because communication needs to be tracked between Web pages, I also added in the functions to the **iereusable.js** file, discussed in the previous section, to control cookies.

The function to open the TOC window is fairly simple, and opens the window in console mode by opening it full screen:

```
// open_toc
// open TOC window in console mode
function open_toc() {
  toc_window = open("ietoc.htm", "TableOfContents",
            "scrollbars=yes,fullscreen=yes")
}
```

To call the TOC window, I first needed to create the TOC window. I used the same style sheet file, **nature.css**, to maintain a consistent look among all the pages associated with the application. In addition, I created an embedded style sheet to set some styles that are unique to the TOC document:

```
<STYLE type="text/css">
 BODY { font-size: 10pt }
 H2 { color: firebrick; font-size: 14pt }
 A { color: firebrick }
 .backgrnd { margin-left: 10px; margin-top: 10px;
          background-color: ivory;
          background-image: url(back3.jpg);
          position:absolute; width: 95%;
          height: 95%; top: 2.5%; left: 2.5% }
</STYLE>
```

Next, I added in menu items for each of the articles, and a brief description of each article. Listing 15-24 contains menu items that form the document body of the file. You can also see the source code by opening the sample file **ietoc.htm** on the CD-ROM.

Listing 15-24: Body elements of the TOC page

```
<DIV class="backgrnd">
<H2>Welcome to the Oregon Naturalist</H2>
<a href="" onclick="go_topage(1,1);return false">
<img src="flower.jpg" width=25 height=24
 border=0 hspace=5 align=top>
Page One First Article</a> Welcome to the first issue of the Oregon
 Naturalist
<p>
<a href="" onclick="go_topage(1,2);return false">
<img src="flower.jpg" width=25 height=24
 border=0 hspace=5 align=top>
```

```
Page One Second Article</a> The Top of the Trail for the Wildcat
  Trail
<p>
<a href="" onclick="go_topage(1,3);return false">
<img src="flower.jpg" width=25 height=24
  border=0 hspace=5 align=top>
Page One Third Article</a> The Rose Garden, an island of serenity
<p>
<H2>Name that Site</H2>
<a href="" onclick="go_topage(2,1);return false">
<img src="flower.jpg" width=25 height=24
  border=0 hspace=5 align=top>
Page Two First Article</a> Views from Ecola State Park
<p>
<a href="" onclick="go_topage(2,2);return false">
<img src="flower.jpg" width=25 height=24
  border=0 hspace=5 align=top>
Page Two Second Article</a> Rocks and more rocks - Indian Beach
<p>
<a href="" onclick="go_topage(2,3);return false">
<img src="flower.jpg" width=25 height=24
  border=0 hspace=5 align=top>
Page Two Third Article</a> And the most famous rock of all -
  Haystack!
<p>
<h2> It Pays to get Close</h2>
<a href="" onclick="go_topage(3,1);return false">
<img src="flower.jpg" width=25 height=24
  border=0 hspace=5 align=top>
Page Three First Article</a> Images from a Tidal Pool
<p>
<a href="" onclick="go_topage(3,2);return false">
<img src="flower.jpg" width=25 height=24
  border=0 hspace=5 align=top>
Page Three Second Article</a> Along the Beach
<p>
<a href="" onclick="go_topage(3,3);return false">
<img src="flower.jpg" width=25 height=24
  border=0 hspace=5 align=top>
Page Three Third Article</a> The Flowers of Forest Park
<p>
</DIV>
```

Each of the menu items calls a function called go_topage when clicked. The function takes two arguments, the page and the article. This function, shown next, calls a function, toc_page, within the parent window that calls the TOC window. It then closes itself:

```
<SCRIPT language="javascript">

// function go_topage
// open page in window that opened TOC
```

```
// call change_article to change
// to requested article
function go_topage(page, article) {
 window.opener.toc_page(page, article);
 window.close();
}
</SCRIPT>
```

The `toc_page` function is created in the **iereusable.js** file, and it uses the cookie function `set_cookie` to set the article, and sets the `location` property of the window to the new page:

```
// TOC window choice
function toc_page(page,article) {
 page = "ienature" + page + ".htm";
 set_cookie("naturalist_article",article,"short");
 window.location=page;
}
```

Up to this point, you have seen how to create functionality for Web-page navigation buttons and how to handle problems such as resizing the inset to fit the article size. The final addition to this application is the introduction page, and the persistence behind the Remember button. This is covered in the next section.

THE REMEMBER BUTTON: IMPLEMENTING PERSISTENCE

If the Web page reader presses the Remember button, the application needs to trap both the page and the current article and store this information in Netscape cookies. The function call to start this process is `remember`, called when the button is pressed. This is the last function I added to **iereusable.js**. The code for this simple function is shown here:

```
// remember
// record page and article as netscape cookies
function remember() {
    set_cookie("naturalist_rem_article",
        current_article,"long");
    set_cookie("naturalist_page",current_page,"long");
}
```

The `remember` function calls `set_cookie` twice, once to set the value for the current article, and once to set the value for the current page. Because a cookie is already being used for tracking the article accessed by the TOC window, a different name is used for the remember article.

I then created the introduction page and named it **ienature.htm**. This Web page checks for the page and article that is persistently stored, and loads the target page, if any — otherwise it loads page one. Also, it sets the current article cookie used by the `post_load` function to the correct article. The page also incorporates the formatting file, **nature.css.** The reusable code file, **iereusable.js,** is not used because it contains much more functionality than this page needs and I wanted the page to load as quickly as possible. The page also uses an embedded style sheet to define local styles. The complete page can be found in Listing 15-25.

Listing 15-25: The introduction page, which loads the correct article, incorporates the formatting file, and uses an embedded style sheet to define local styles

```
<HTML><HEAD>
<TITLE>The Oregon Naturalist</TITLE>
<!--
 Add in the standard CSS1
 and JSS style sheet files
-->
<LINK REL=STYLESHEET TYPE="text/css"
 HREF="nature.css">
<STYLE type="text/css">
 H1 { color: firebrick; font-size: 36pt;
      text-align:center }
 .backgrnd { margin-left: 10px; margin-top: 10px;
             background-color: ivory;
             background-image: url(back3.jpg);
             position:absolute; width: 95%;
             height: 95%; top: 2.5%; left: 2.5% }
</STYLE>

<SCRIPT language="javascript">

// set_current_article
// sets cookie to target article
function set_current_article(article) {
    var cookieDate = new Date();
    cookieDate.setTime (cookieDate.getTime() +
        (1000 * 60));
    document.cookie = "naturalist_article=" + article +
        "; expires=" + cookieDate.toGMTString();

}
// get_current_page_article
// gets cookies containing page and article if any
// If no cookies are found, 1 is used for both values
function get_current_page_article() {
  var content = document.cookie;
  var article=1;
  var page=1;
  var loc = content.indexOf("naturalist_rem_article");
  if (loc >= 0)
        article = content.substring(loc+23,
                loc+24);
  loc = content.indexOf("naturalist_page");
  if (loc >= 0)
        page = content.substring(loc+16,loc+17);
```

```
  set_current_article(article);
  window.location="ienature" + page + ".htm";
}

</SCRIPT>

</HEAD>
<BODY onload="get_current_page_article()">
<DIV class="backgrnd">
<H1>Welcome to the Oregon Naturalist</H1>
</DIV>
</BODY></HTML>
```

This page uses Netscape cookie technology to check and see if an application page and article have been stored via the `remember` function. If so, the stored page is loaded and the stored article is re-stored into the article cookie that is always checked when any of the pages are loaded. As a result, when the page loads, the correct article loads. If no page and article are stored, the first page is accessed and the first article is shown.

That's it for the IE-specific application pages. If you want, you can review the Navigator-specific application pages, or you can continue to the next section, which implements the application for both browsers.

Combining the Two Approaches to Create a Cross-Browser Application

The advantages of building cross-browser applications are obvious – they reach wider audiences, while still taking advantage of technologies particular to certain browsers. To reach a broader audience, you may want to extend your Navigator- or IE-specific application to include the other browser. Or, you may be currently maintaining a separate Web page for each browser, and want to combine the two to minimize site maintenance.

This section examines how to combine the browser-specific applications created in this chapter's main two sections into a single cross-browser application.

Combining the Layouts

The first element I needed to combine from the browser-specific applications was the style sheet, which differed between browsers because of the transition style attribute for IE. Because Navigator does not ignore CSS1 attributes it doesn't understand, I removed the transition attribute from the global style sheet file, **nature.css**. I then added the filter transition attribute to each of the elements' inline style sheet settings, which for some reason, Navigator does ignore.

Only Navigator uses the JSS style sheet, in addition to the **format.js** file that checks the screen resolution in order to modify the fonts. However, because IE will ignore these files and Navigator needs them, I included them.

The Navigator application uses two menu bars, one for smaller resolutions and one for higher resolutions. IE only uses one and resizes the images. Because I had to find the common denominator here, I included both menu bars. I then handled the differences between the two browsers in the code.

IE uses a `DIV` block for the inset layer, which forms the backdrop for the page. Navigator uses a `LAYER` block. I used both for the cross-browser platform pages. The `LAYER` tag is the only method to create a block that fills the dimensions I give, and IE must have the `DIV` block. However, because IE ignores the `LAYER` block, and the `DIV` block is totally contained within the `LAYER` element, using both will be compatible for both browsers.

For the rest of the application Web page contents, the Navigator-specific Web pages use the `LAYER` tag to create all of the article blocks. The IE application uses the `DIV` block. I could have continued using both `LAYER` and `DIV` for the cross-browser pages, but I really didn't want to continue to use duplicate blocks for everything. Unlike the inset block, I didn't need to have the background of the article blocks filled, which is my main reason for using the `LAYER` tag with inset. Also, Navigator can hide, move, and display `DIV` blocks as well as layers. Because of this capability, I chose to contain the rest of the content using `DIV` blocks.

To summarize, here's the status of the document after I combined the layout techniques for both browsers: each of the progressive document application Web pages uses the same global CSS1 style sheet; also, the JSS styles and the **format.js** file necessary for Navigator to control the appearance of the Web pages are included. Both the small and large menu bars are included, the page inset is created with both a `LAYER` and a `DIV` block, and the rest of the content in enclosed with `DIV` blocks.

Combining the Code for the TOC and Remember Buttons

The Web page layout is the easiest part of this cross-platform application. The toughest is getting the code to work together.

The two versions have no incompatibility when it comes to activating the TOC button and implementing the TOC page, which is the example file called **toc.htm**. This page uses only the global CSS1 page and nondynamic HTML JavaScript.

Furthermore, in regard to the Remember button, the cookie functions `get_cookie` and `set_cookie`, as well as the function to "remember" the Web page and article, don't differ by browser and are pulled from the browser-specific reusable source code files into a browser-neutral source code file named **reusable.js**.

However, the entry or introduction page, called **ienature.htm** for IE and **nsnature.htm** for Navigator, needs to change and this is due, surprisingly enough, to the Navigator resize problem. In the Navigator section of this chapter, I trapped the `resize` event and called the `post_load` function to redraw certain page elements. Without doing this, the page will not redraw correctly. I tried the same approach with the cross-browser application but it would not work. The main reason why is that when a `resize` event occurs with Netscape, it parses the global variables and nonfunctional code sections of the scripting blocks. As you will see later in this section, I use the equalizer objects, created in Chapter 13 and refined in Chapter 14, to handle all the page movement and article visibility. However, during a `resize` event the equalizer object arrays are getting reset to empty arrays. When I created the array of inset sizes based on each article, the articles should be accessible by the equalizer arrays, but because these are now empty, I get JavaScript errors.

My attempts to work around these resizing limitations just weren't working, so I did the next best thing: I opened the application into a new browser window, full size, and turned off resizing. After testing this, I found that the only problem I had to worry about was the resize that occurs when the page is minimized and, as you will see, I created a not very elegant but workable solution to this problem. Through conversations with Netscape, I found out that the resize issue is a major one, and hopefully, by the time you read this, the problem might be fixed. However, the application as it is written should work regardless of the presence of resize bugs.

I renamed the existing **nsnature.htm** file to **nature.htm**, and replaced the `get_current_page_article` function with the one shown in Listing 15-26.

Listing 15-26: Nature.htm, which uses a workaround to open the new window to maximum size

```
// get_current_page_article
// gets cookies containing page and article if any
// If no cookies are found, 1 is used for both values
function get_current_page_article() {
 var content = document.cookie;
 var article=1;
 var page=1;
 var loc = content.indexOf("naturalist_rem_article");
 if (loc >= 0)
        article = content.substring(loc+23,
              loc+24);
 loc = content.indexOf("naturalist_page");
 if (loc >= 0)
        page = content.substring(loc+16,loc+17);

 set_current_article(article);
 if (navigator.appName ==
        "Microsoft Internet Explorer")
        window.open("nature" + page + ".htm", "",
        "fullscreen=yes,menubars=yes,resizeable=no");
 else {
        newwin=window.open("nature" + page + ".htm", "",
        "");
        if (newwin != null) {
                newwin=
                window.open("nature" + page + ".htm", "",
```

```
                "scrollbars=yes");
            }
    }
  this.location="natend.htm";
}

</SCRIPT>
```

This function opens the new window to its maximum size, as shown in Figure 15-12.

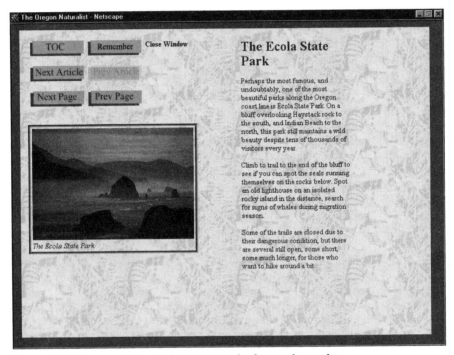

Figure 15-12: The application Web page opened using maximum size

---

What Happens with Resize?

I experimented a bit with resizing and found that if I have a Web page with a scroll bar, three resize events occur: the first resizes the page, the second removes the existing scroll bar, and the third replaces the scroll bar. I also found, when using hidden blocks and scroll bars, that many times CSS1 sheets are not being reloaded after the resizing occurs, and the page does not reflect the existence of these sheets. Also, variables that are dependent on measurements during a reload are not always being set correctly following a resize event.

Creating compatibility with the other code sections, such as the article and page buttons, is detailed in the following sections.

Combining the Code for the Menu and Article and the Page Buttons

I wanted to use CSS1 positioning with the articles, and because I used DIV blocks to enclose the article contents, I decided to use the DHTML equalizer objects I created in Chapter 13 to get CSS1 positioning to work in one cross-browser compatible application.

I used the **nsobjs.js** file, discussed in Chapter 13, to create objects for use with Navigator, and **ieobjs.js** to create the IE objects. Instead of using the get_width and get_height functions with the invisible text sections, which only return "undefined," I created two new functions to get the clip width and height, called get_clip_width and get_clip_height. The comparable functions for IE use the object's clientHeight and clientWidth properties.

The global variables are the same for both browsers, so these got put into **reusable.js**. Additionally, both the small and large image menu arrays are the same for both browsers and were put into the common source code file. However, in the specific applications, Navigator uses alternate button images to indicate when an option is not available, while IE uses the Alpha opacity filter on the same images. For the cross-browser application, I decided to keep the code separate so that those readers using Netscape would have to download the additional images, and those using IE 4.0 wouldn't have to download additional images because their browser supports the opacity filter. To me, the cost of downloading unnecessary additional images is higher than the cost of maintaining the separate blocks of code to handle the menu changes.

Based on my decision to not use the disabled menu images with IE, I created the arrays for these images only in the Navigator-specific source code file, **nsreusable.js**. To ensure that all the nonfunctional code in this JavaScript code file is not parsed by IE, I enclosed the code in a conditional statement that checks the application name of the navigator object to ensure that the browser is not IE:

```
// check to make sure not IE
if (navigator.appName != "Microsoft Internet Explorer") {
```

The vertical and horizontal offset arrays are the same for both browsers and these are pulled into the common file. What's more, the set_articles function was modified to pull in the code that populates these offset arrays into a commonly shared function, shown in Listing 15-27.

Listing 15-27: Creating the inset sizing array, based on sizes of articles

```
// set_articles
// get width and height of articles
//   compare to inset and set inset to whichever is
```

```
//    larger
function set_articles() {
 // setup inset offsets
 for (i = 0; i < MAXARTICLE; i++) {
        var textvar = "text" + (i + 1);
        article_voffset[i] =
               thenamedgrp[textvar].get_clip_height() + 20;
        article_hoffset[i] =
               thenamedgrp[textvar].get_clip_width() + 400;
        if (article_voffset[i] < background_offset)
               article_voffset[i] = background_offset;
        if (article_hoffset[i] < background_width)
               article_hoffset[i] = background_width;
        }
 }
```

Note the use of the new `get_clip_height` and `get_clip_width` equalizer object methods. With these, I was able to use the same code for both browsers.

The second part of this function handles setting up the image array for Navigator, and this array was pulled into a separate function called `set_menu` that exposes the applicable menu and loads the menu images for Navigator, as shown next:

```
function set_menu() {
 // setup and display menu
 document.lrgmenu.visibility="hidden";
        if (thisscreen.menusize == "lrgmenubar") {
        thenamedgrp["largemenu"].show();
        the_menu = document.largemenu.document;
        }
        else {
        thenamedgrp["smallmenu"].show();
        the_menu = document.smallmenu.document;
        }
 for (i = 0; i < MAXMENU; i++) {
        the_menu.images[i].src = images_array[i].src;
        }
 }
```

The menu setup routine was already pulled into a separate `set_menu` function for IE.

The `post_load` functions remain specific to each browser and were left in the respective browser source code files. However, the `load_article`, `show_article`, and `change_article` functions were tweaked and moved to the common source code file.

All of these functions hide or show specific article blocks, and possibly move the text blocks based on the screen resolution, or use common scripting techniques. Because all of this is manageable with the equalizer object methods, these functions easily made the transition to shareable code, as shown in Listing 15-28.

Listing 15-28: Processing a change article request, loading the new article, and resizing the inset to match the article size

```
// load_article
// hide current article
function load_article(article) {
 thenamedgrp[current_txt].hide();
 thenamedgrp[current_img].hide();
 current_img = "image" + article;
 current_txt = "text" + article;

 show_article(article);
}


// show_article
// resize inset to fit article width/height
// set image top just below menu if screen resolution
//    is less than 800
// show new article image and text
function show_article(article) {
 // resize inset
 if
 (navigator.appName == "Microsoft Internet Explorer") {
   var new_width = article_hoffset[article-1];
   var new_height = article_voffset[article-1];
   var background =
      document.all.item("article_background");
   background.style.width = new_width;
   background.style.height = new_height;
   }
 else
   document.layers["article_background"].
    ResizeTo(article_hoffset[article-
     1],article_voffset[article-1]);

 // if smaller screens, move layers
 if (screen.width < 800) {
     thenamedgrp[current_img].move(30,105);
     thenamedgrp[current_txt].move(350,30);
     }
 thenamedgrp[current_img].show();
 thenamedgrp[current_txt].show();

 // add effects
 if (navigator.appName ==
     "Microsoft Internet Explorer") {
     var imgobj = document.all.item(current_img);
     imgobj.filters.item(0).Apply();
     imgobj.filters.item(0).Play(2.0);
     }

}
```

```
// change_article
// called when previous or next article button is pressed
//     call load article and update menu
// or next page or previous page button is pressed
//       change page
function change_article(page, article) {
  // if open TOC window
  if (page == 0 && article == 0)
        open_toc();

  // if change article
  else if (page == 0) {
     article = parseInt(current_article) +
        parseInt(article);
     if (article > 0 && article < MAXARTICLE + 1) {
        load_article(article);
        update_menu(article,true);
        set_cookie("naturalist_article",article,"short");
        }
  }
  // change page
  else {
     page = current_page + page;
     if (page > 0 && page < MAXPAGE + 1) {
        set_cookie("naturalist_article",1,"short");
        var move_page = "nature" + page + ".htm";
        current_page=page;
        location = move_page;
        }
  }
}
```

I was able to move the change_article function without consequence because all it does is determine whether the article or page move will occur, or whether the TOC window should be opened. The load_article function hides the existing article and sets the global variables that hold the next article to be displayed. It then calls show_article.

The show_article function sets the width and height of the Web page document inset. Because Navigator uses a LAYER tag for the inset, and IE uses a DIV block, I created separate sub-blocks for each browser. Optionally, I could also have pulled this code into the browser-specific source code files, but the differences are so minute, I decide to keep it as is. The rest of the function moves the image block for a smaller resolution screen, and makes both it and the article text blocks visible, again using the equalizer object methods. Finally, for IE only, I added in the filter transition methods to create the transition. If you read the section on the IE-specific application earlier in this chapter, you saw how the transition filter adds a nice transition to the images when they switch. I had considered creating a "box-out" effect for Navigator, in which I set the clipping size of the image to a very small box and then increase the size of the clipping region using timers to have the image "grow" to fit its original size. But the amount of work to create this effect is fairly significant compared to the resulting effect, so I decided to not create this effect for Navigator.

After taking these steps, the only other code that I needed to combine was the `update_menu` functions and the `open_toc` function. The Navigator `update_menu` function disables or enables the menu buttons using the disabled images. The IE `update_menu` function performs the same action using the opacity filter.

Also, each browser has a different technique of opening a window to fill the window. I didn't use the full-console mode technique for Navigator because I didn't use signed script for the application, as discussed in Chapter 9. However, I do open the TOC window full screen and minimize the "chrome" that surrounds the window. For IE I use the new `fullscreen` attribute when I open the window.

Though I am prohibiting resizing in the application, the Web page reader can minimize and maximize the application. Doing so triggers `resize` events. Because I need to refresh the page due to the resize problems with Navigator, I created a rather kludgy workaround to the problem, shown in the following code:

```
function reload() {
  turn++;
  if (window.scrollbars)
        if (turn == 3)
                window.location=
                "nature" + current_page + ".htm";
  else
                window.location=
                "nature" + current_page + ".htm";

  return false;
}
```

This code keeps a count of the resizes that occur and, on the last one, reloads the Web page. If the code did not compensate for the resizing event, the results would be unpredictable, and undesirable, as shown in Figure 15-13. The global variable `turn` is reset to 0 when the Web page loads or reloads.

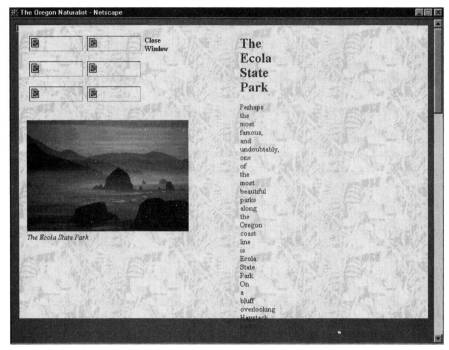

Figure 15-13: The resized Web page when compensation for the resizing event is not incorporated

That's all for the source code files. You can test this cross-browser example by opening the **nature.htm** file in either IE or Navigator.

The Unknown Resize Event

I found that two different types of `resize` events happen. You can trap the `resize` event for the document and window, as well as capture it inline within the BODY tag. When the Web page loads, you get a window `resize` event, followed by a document `resize` event, the page `load` event, and finally, one of the mysterious body `resize` events. When you resize the page, or minimize it and restore it to its original size, all three of the `resize` events are from the body `resize` event, not the `document` or `window` events. I found that trying to trap the `resize` event directly for the body does not alter this behavior.

Summary

This rather long chapter created a progressive document Web application, first as a stand-alone application for Netscape Navigator, and then as a stand-alone application for Internet Explorer. This chapter then discussed how to combine these applications while incorporating the DHTML equalizer objects, created in Chapter 13, to create a single cross-browser compatible application.

In this chapter you learned how to:

◆ Create a style sheet file, shareable by multiple Web pages.

◆ Create a window resolution object to alter style settings to handle screen resolution differences.

◆ Create multiple image menu bars for different screen resolutions.

◆ Resize images in IE based on screen resolution.

◆ Use alternate images to emulate a disabled button.

◆ Use the `Alpha` filter in IE to emulate a disabled button.

◆ Store and retrieve persistent information with Netscape cookies.

◆ Use cookies to synchronize efforts between multiple Web pages.

◆ Store long-term information about a Web page to restore the page when the Web page reader revisits your Web site.

◆ Create a resizable page with an inset that resizes to the content.

◆ Open a full-size window in both IE and Navigator.

◆ Use the equalizer objects, created in Chapter 13, to handle all movement, clipping, and hiding of Web page contents for a cross-browser compatible application.

◆ Achieve common functionality in both browsers using common and browser-specific techniques.

This chapter concludes the book. The Quick Reference, provided next, pulls together the objects, properties, methods, and events discussed in several of this book's chapters. After that, Appendix A contains many helpful URLs.

Dynamic HTML is the great new wave of Web page programming. With the information you've learned in this book, I hope that you're well on your way to catching the DHTML wave.

Quick Reference

THIS SECTION ASSEMBLES the book's most pertinent tables into a single reference guide. You'll find reference tables for the following subjects in this order:

- ◆ CSS1 attributes
- ◆ Microsoft's dynamic HTML
- ◆ Netscape's dynamic HTML

CSS1 Attributes

This section repeats the information in Chapter 2 on CSS1 attributes.

CSS1 Syntactic Conventions

Lexical Symbol	Description
<VALUE>	Designates a value appropriate for a property, such as a numeric value for size (for example, "1"), or a keyword value such as color (for example, "red")
<PERCENTAGE>	Indicates a numeric value with a percent sign (%); specifies that the value is a percentage of the associated value of the parent (containing) HTML object
|	Delimits optional choices
[ ]	Elements contained between brackets are grouped together
{#1,#2}	Denotes that the group or option just specified can be repeated from 1 to 2 times
*	Indicates that the group or option is optionally repeated 0 or more times

---

Block-Level Attributes

Block-level attributes control the width and height of an element or group of elements, in addition to the type and size of border, and whether padding is used.

This Quick Reference section uses syntactic notation to describe the attributes. This notation provides you with information about what is optional or required when using the attribute, and identifies some of the permissible values.

Margin Properties

Property	Values
margin:	[<length> | <percentage> | auto]{1,4}
margin-left:	<value> | <percentage> | auto
margin-right:	<value> | <percentage> | auto
margin-top:	<value> | <percentage> | auto
margin-bottom:	<value> | <percentage> | auto

Border Properties

Property	Values
border-left-width:	<value> | thin | medium | thick
border-right-width:	<value> | thin | medium | thick
border-bottom-width:	<value> | thin | medium | thick
border-top-width:	<value> | thin | medium | thick
border-width:	[<value> | thin | medium | thick]{1,4}
border-color:	[<color>]{1,4}
border-style:	[none | dotted | dashed | solid | double | groove | ridge | inset | outset]

Padding Properties

Property	Values
padding:	[<length> | <percentage>]{1,4}
padding-top:	<length> | <percentage>
padding-left:	<length> | <percentage>
padding-top:	<length> | <percentage>
padding-bottom:	<length> | <percentage>

Font Attributes

Font attributes control what type of font is used, including any special display characteristics such as the use of italics, and the font size, family, and whether any font variants are used.

Font Properties

Property	Values
font-family:	[<family-name> | <generic-family>],]* [<family-name> | <generic-family>]
font-style:	normal | italic | oblique
font-size:	<absolute-size> | <relative-size> | length | percentage
font-weight:	normal | bold | lighter | 100 | 200 |300 | 400 | 500 | 600 | 700 | 800 | 900
font-variant:	normal | small-caps

Colors and Background

Colors can be applied to the background of an element, or to the text of an element. In addition, other background attributes control whether a background image is used and, if one is used, whether the image repeats horizontally or vertically, is fixed in location, or doesn't repeat at all.

Background Properties

Property	Values
background	[<background-color> || <background-image> || <background-repeat> || <background-attachment> || <background-position]
background-color:	<color>
background-image:	<url> | none
background-repeat:	repeat | repeat-x | repeat-y | no-repeat
background-attachment:	scroll | fixed
background-position:	[<percentage> | <length>]{1,2} | [top | center | bottom] || [left | center | right]

Document and Text Layout

Layout controls such things as spacing between and within elements. It can also control how list items and list bullets are related to each other.

Text Properties

Property	Values
text-indent:	<length> | <percentage>
text-align:	left | right | center | justify
letter-spacing:	<length>
word-spacing:	<length>
text-decoration:	none | [underline || overline || line-through || blink]

continued

Property	Values
text-transform:	capitalize | uppercase | lowercase | none
vertical-align:	baseline | sub | super | top | text-top | middle | bottom | text-bottom | \<percentage\>

List Properties

Property	Values
list-style:	\<keyword\> || \<position\> || \<url\>
list-style-type:	disc | circle | square | decimal | lower-roman | upper-roman | lower-alpha | upper-alpha | none
list-style-image:	\<url\> | none
list-style-position:	inside | outside

Microsoft's Dynamic HTML

This section provides highlights from the chapters that cover Microsoft's dynamic HTML. It starts off with one of the most basic elements of Microsoft's object model, the window object.

The Window Object

Chapter 5 provides an overview of the window object, including this object's properties and methods. Normally you can access these properties without having to use the window reference, such as using document... rather than window.document....

Window Properties

Property	Description
client	Browser
closed	Boolean value indicating whether the reference window is closed
defaultStatus	Message that is displayed, by default, in the status bar
dialogArguments	Variable or array of variables passed to the dialog
dialogHeight	Height of dialog
dialogWidth	Width of dialog
dialogTop	Window top
dialogLeft	Window left
document	document object
event	event object
history	history object
length	When used with the frames collection, the number of frames (read-only)
location	location object
navigator	navigator object
name	Name of window if one has been assigned; set to a value when a new browser window is opened using open and the name is specified, or when a frame and a name is given in the FRAMESET (read-only)
offscreenBuffering	Specifies whether to use the offscreen buffer
opener	Reference to the window that opened the current window
parent	If a window is a frame, returns FRAMESET window (read-only)
returnValue	Used with modal dialog windows; set this value to return the value to the calling routine
self	Current window (read-only)
status	Message displayed in the status bar
top	Top-most ancestor window (read-only)

Window Object Methods

Method	Functionality	Parameters
alert	Displays alert message	message
blur	Loses focus and triggers onBlur	
clearTimeout	Cancels an existing timer	timer id
clearInterval	Cancels an existing interval timer	timer id
close	Closes a window	
confirm	Displays confirmation message	message
execScript	Executes script	script, language (such as JScript)
focus	gets focus and triggers onFocus	
navigate	Sets the URL (VBScript only)	URL
open	Opens a new browser window	URL, title, attributes, replace
prompt	Displays prompt message and input field	message, default
setTimeout	Creates a timer that evaluates an expression	expr, time, language
setInterval	Creates an interval timer that evaluates an expression	expr, time
scroll	Turns scroll bar on or off	'yes' | 'no'
showHelp	Shows a help file	URL, arguments
showModalDialog	Opens a modal dialog	URL, title, attributes

Opening an IE Browser Window

Chapter 4 provides demonstrations of how to open new browser windows for IE. The channelmode and fullscreen attributes listed in the following table are very important for creating full-screen browser windows, or channel-specific Web pages.

Window Object Properties

Property	Allowable Values
fullscreen	[yes|no] [0|1]
channelmode	[yes|no] [0|1]
location	[yes|no] [0|1]
directories	[yes|no] [0|1]
status	[yes|no] [0|1]
menubar	[yes|no] [0|1]
scrollbars	[yes|no] [0|1]
resizable	[yes|no] [0|1]
toolbar	[yes|no] [0|1]
width	number of pixels
height	number of pixels
top	number of pixels
left	number of pixels

Opening a Modal Dialog

Microsoft included a new feature in IE 4.0 that lets you open a modal dialog window. This window is opened with the showModalDialog function, and the following table includes the attributes that you can specify with this function. This is a particularly effective technique for querying the Web page reader just prior to an event.

Modal Dialog Properties

Property	Valid Values
dialogWidth	dialogWidth:number
dialogHeight	dialogHeight:number

continued

Property	Valid Values
dialogTop	dialogTop:number
dialogLeft	dialogLeft:number
center	center:[yes|no] [0|1]
font	font:CSS1 value
font-family	font-family:CSS1 value
font-style	font-style:CSS1 value
font-weight	font-weight:CSS1 value
font-style	font-style:CSS1 value
font-variant	font-variant:CSS1 value
border	border:[thick | thin]
help	help: [yes|no] [0|1]
minimize	minimize: [yes|no] [0|1]
maximize	maximize: [yes|no] [0|1]

The Document Object

Chapter 5 provides examples of using the document object, its properties, and its methods. In particular, the use of Netscape-style cookies is demonstrated.

Document Object Properties

Property	Description
alinkColor	Color of the active links within the document
activeElement	Element that currently has focus (read-only)
bgColor	Background color of the object
cookie	Information that can be persistently stored on the client machine

continued

Document Object Properties *(continued)*

Property	Description
domain	Domain suffix, to enable pages to share code, though server host name may differ (read-only)
fgColor	Color of foreground text
linkColor	Color of the links within the document
lastModified	Date and time the Web page was last modified (read-only)
location	location object
parentWindow	Window that owns document
referrer	URL of previous location (read-only)
readyState	Status of object being loaded with values of: complete(4), interactive(3), loading(2), uninitialized(1) (read-only)
title	Title of document
URL	URL of document (read-only)
vlinkColor	Color of the unvisited links within the document

Document Object Methods

Method	Functionality	Parameters
close	Closes the document and displays contents	
blur	Removes focus from document	
open	Opens document for write methods	mimeType
clear	Clears document	
createElement	Creates element of type IMG or OPTION	tag of element
write	Writes HTML to document	HTML expression
writeln	Writes HTML/carriage return to document	HTML expression
execCommand	Runs command over range	cmd, value, UI flag

continued

Method	Functionality	Parameters
elementFromPoint	Returns element at position	x,y
queryCommandEnabled	Is command enabled	command
queryCommandText	String associated with command	command
queryCommandSupported	Specifies whether command is on/off	command
queryCommandState	Returns true, false, null — current state	command
queryCommandIndeterm	Specifies whether command is indeterminate	command
queryCommandValue	Value of current command	

The Location, History, and Navigator Objects

The location, history, and especially the navigator objects can be useful with dynamic HTML Web applications. The navigator object is used to query the type of browser accessing the page and direct the browser to the browser-specific code, or hide noncompatible code. The location object is used to open a new Web page in the current browser.

Location, History, and Navigator Object Properties

Object	Property	Description
location	hash	The string minus the pound sign (#) with a named anchor tag
location	host	Host name concatenated with port, if any
location	hostname	Host name of the Web page
location	href	URL that is the target of the link
location	pathname	Relative path of the Web page
location	port	Port number, if any
location	protocol	Type of protocol used to access the page, such as HTTP:

continued

Location, History, and Navigator Object Properties *(continued)*

Object	Property	Description
location	search	Form data or query string
history	length	Number of URLs currently maintained in history
navigator	appName	Name of the browser
navigator	appVersion	Version of the browser
navigator	codeName	Code name of the browser
navigator	cookieEnabled	Specifies whether cookies are enabled
navigator	plugins	Collection; plug-ins loaded for the browser
navigator	mimeTypes	Collection; MIME types defined for the browser
navigator	userAgent	User agent header sent with HTTP protocol

Navigator, History, and Location Object Methods

Method	Functionality	Parameters
navigator.javaEnabled	Call to determine if Java is enabled	
navigator.taintEnabled	Call to determine if data tainting is enabled; returns false for IE 4.0 as data tainting is not enabled	
history.back	Loads previous URL	
history.forward	Loads next URL	
history.go	Loads specific URL	location delta | URL
location.reload	Refreshes current document	
location.replace	Replaces current document, including history list	URL
location.assign	Sets current location to given URL	URL

The Style Object

The style object was created expressly to apply CSS1 attribute modifications dynamically to any HTML element. To use CSS1 positioning, such as the left or top property, or to modify CSS1 attributes, such as backgroundColor, this object must be referenced.

Style Object Properties

Property	Description
background	Shortcut method for setting background properties
backgroundColor	Color of element background
backgroundImage	Image of element background
backgroundRepeat	Indicates how the background image repeats
backgroundAttachment	Indicates how the background image is attached
backgroundPosition	Position where the background image is attached
backgroundPositionX	Left position for the background image
backgroundPositionY	Top position for the background image
border	Shortcut method for setting border properties
borderBottom	Shortcut method for setting border bottom properties
borderTop	Shortcut method for setting border top properties
borderRight	Shortcut method for setting right border properties
borderLeft	Shortcut method for setting left border properties
borderStyle	Shortcut method for setting border style
borderTopColor	Top border color
borderRightColor	Right border color
borderBottomColor	Bottom border color
borderLeftColor	Left border color
borderTopWidth	Width of top border
borderRightWidth	Width of right border

continued

Style Object Properties *(continued)*

Property	Description
borderLeftWidth	Width of left border
borderBottomWidth	Width of bottom border
borderBottomStyle	Style of bottom border
borderTopStyle	Style of top border
borderLeftStyle	Style of left border
borderRightStyle	Style of right border
clear	Vertical space for text alignment around an image
clip	Clipping dimensions for element
color	Color of text
cssText	Persisted representation of style rule, which is the style sheet set for the individual element explicitly within the tag for the element
cursor	Sets type of mouse cursor when over element
display	Whether the item is displayed or not
filter	Any filters applied to element
font	Shortcut method for setting font properties
fontSize	Size of font
fontStyle	Style of font
fontVariant	Font variant
fontWeight	Weight of font
fontFamily	Font family
height	Height in absolute units or percentages
left	Left location of element including units
letterSpacing	Spacing between letters
lineHeight	Distance between the baselines of two adjacent lines
listStyleType	Type of style for list element

continued

Property	Description
listStyleImage	Image used with list elements
listStylePosition	Indicates how the list marker is drawn
margin	Shortcut method for setting margins
marginLeft	Left margin of element
marginRight	Right margin of element
marginTop	Top margin of element
marginBottom	Bottom margin of element
overflow	Indicates how content overflow is handled
paddingTop	White space between contents and top border
paddingRight	White space between contents and right border
paddingBottom	White space between contents and bottom border
paddingLeft	White space between contents and left border
pageBreakBefore	Page break before element
pageBreakAfter	Page break after element
pixelHeight	Height of element in pixels
pixelWidth	Width of element in pixels
pixelLeft	Location of the left side of the element in pixels
pixelTop	Location of the top side of the element in pixels
position	Type of positioning used with the element
posLeft	Location of the left side of the element in style-based units
posTop	Location of the top of the element in style-based units
posHeight	Height of the element in style-based units
posWidth	Width of the element in style-based units
styleFloat	Specifies whether the image floats left or right
textAlign	Horizontal alignment of text
textDecoration	Decoration applied to text, such as underlining

continued

Style Object Properties *(continued)*

Property	Description
textDecorationBlink	Specifies whether text blinks
textDecorationUnderline	Specifies whether text is underlined
textDecorationOverline	Specifies whether text is overlined
textDecorationLineThrough	Specifies whether a line is drawn through text
textIndent	Indentation of text for the first line
textTransform	Transformation of text, such as all caps
top	Top position of the element
verticalAlign	Vertical alignment of text
visibility	Specifies whether the element is visible, or visibility is inherited
width	Length in absolute units or percentages
zIndex	Z-index of the element; indicates how elements layer

The Screen Object

Microsoft also added the screen object with IE 4.0. This object contains information about the Web page reader's monitor, such as color depth and screen resolution. Use this object to modify the style sheet settings to match the resolution and color depth.

Screen Object Properties

Property	Description
bufferDepth	Enables buffering for bitmaps
colorDepth	Represents the BPI (bits per inch) of the current screen color settings; a value of 8 is equivalent to 256-color mode
updateInterval	Timing that determines how long between updates of window
width	Horizontal pixel settings
height	Vertical pixel settings

The TextRange Object

The TextRange object is a container element that can hold text and HTML for a specific HTML element, or an entire Web page. The TextRange object has only two properties:

◆ htmlText — HTML source as an HTML fragment

◆ text — Actual text from the selection

However, this object has several methods, given in the following table.

TextRange Object Methods

Method	Functionality	Parameters
collapse	Creates empty range at the beginning/end of range	true/false
compareEndPoints	Compares endpoints between two TextRange objects	numeric comparison
duplicate	Duplicates range	
execCommand	Runs command over range	cmd, value, UI flag
expand	Expands the range to include a component	component
findText	Searches for text within the range	text string
getBookmark	Creates a bookmark, which is an opaque string and is used to return to a previous text range	
inRange	Specifies whether the given range is within the current range	range to compare
isEqual	Specifies whether the given range is equal to the range	range to compare
move	Moves the range over the text	unit to move, number
moveEnd	Adjusts the size of the range at the end	unit to size, number
moveStart	Adjusts the size of the range at the beginning	unit to size, number

continued

TextRange Object Methods *(continued)*

Method	Functionality	Parameters
moveToBookmark	Moves to the bookmark	
moveToElementText	Moves to the text range encompassed within the element	element
moveToPoint	Moves to the point within TextRange	x,y
parentElement	Parent of the element	
pasteHTML	Pastes HTML into the current range	HTML string
queryCommandEnabled	Is command enabled	command
queryCommandText	String associated with the command	command
queryCommandSupported	Specifies whether the command is on/off	command
queryCommandState	Returns true, false, null; current state	command
queryCommandIndeterm	Specifies whether the command is indeterminate	command
queryCommandValue	Value of the current command	
scrollIntoView	Specifies whether to go to beginning of the range	true/false
select	Actively selects the range	
setEndPoint	Sets endpoint on the TextRange element based on another TextRange	element type, range

---

The Event Object

Microsoft introduced a new `event` object with IE 4.0. The following table contains a list of this object's properties.

Event Properties

Property	Description
altKey	Specifies whether the Alt key is pressed during an event
button	Button pressed to generate an event
cancelBubble	Prevents the current event from passing to other objects in the hierarchy
clientX	Left position of the event within client units
clientY	Top position of the event within client units
ctrlKey	Specifies whether the Ctrl key is pressed during an event
fromElement	Element being moved with the mouseOver and mouseOut events
keyCode	ASCII value of the key currently pressed
offsetX	Left position of the element relative to a container element
offsetY	Top position of the element relative to a container element
returnValue	Return value of an event
shiftKey	Specifies whether the Shift key is pressed during an event
srcElement	Element within which an event originated
srcFilter	Filter that caused the event
toElement	Target element for the mouseOver and mouseOut events
type	Type of event
x	Horizontal position where the event occurred
y	Vertical position where the event occurred

Event Handlers

Event handlers are functions or routines that perform some functionality when an event occurs. The following table from Chapter 4 lists several event handlers, what triggers them, and how the event is trapped using the VBScript object_event-handler syntax.

VBScript Events

Event Handler	Triggered By	Event Handler
onAbort	image loading is aborted, usually by reader pressing Stop button	object_onabort()
onbeforeunload	immediately before page unloads	window_onbeforeunload
onBlur	object losing focus	object_onblur()
onBounce	object reaches side (marquee)	object_onbounce()
onChange	object value has changed	object_onchange()
onClick	object is clicked	object_onclick()
onDblClick	object is double-clicked	object_ondblclick()
onDragStart	selected object is dragged	object_ondragstart()
onError	image loading error	object_onerror()
onFinish	object loop is complete (marquee)	object_onfinish()
onFocus	object gets focus	object_onfocus()
onHelp	user presses F1 or help key	object_onhelp()
onKeyDown	user presses any key	object_onkeydown()
onKeyPress	user presses a key	object_onkeypress()
onKeyUp	user releases a key	object_onkeyup()
onLoad	object is loaded	object_onload()
onMouseDown	user presses mouse button	object_onmousedown()
onMouseMove	user moves mouse	object_onmousemove()
onMouseOut	when cursor leaves element	object_onmouseout()
onMouseOver	when cursor is over element	object_onmouseover()
onMouseUp	user releases mouse button	object_onmouseup()
onReadyStateChange	ready state for object changes	object_onreadystatechange()
onReset	form is reset	object_onreset()
onRowEnter	current row has changed	object_onrowenter()

continued

Event Handler	Triggered By	Event Handler
onRowExit	current row is changing	object_onrowexit()
onScroll	scroll box has changed	object_onscroll()
onSelect	user selects text	object_onselect()
onStart	loop starts (marquee)	object_onstart()
onSubmit	user submits form	object_onsubmit()
onUnload	exit frame or window	object_onunload()

Netscape's Dynamic HTML

This section features the most important tables from the chapters on Netscape's dynamic HTML. It begins with one of the most basic objects in the Netscape object model, the window object.

The Window Object

Chapter 9 provides an overview of the window object, including this object's properties and methods.

Window Properties

Window Property	Description
closed	Boolean; indicates whether the window is open or not
innerHeight	Height of window contents; signed script only if the dimensions are less than 100 × 100
innerWidth	Width of window contents; signed script only if the dimensions are less than 100 × 100
locationbar.visible	Hide or show locationbar; signed script only
menubar.visible	Hide or show menubar; signed script only

continued

Window Properties *(continued)*

Window Property	Description
outerHeight	Height of the window's outer boundary; signed script only if the dimensions are less than 100 × 100
outerWidth	Width of the window's outer boundary; signed script only if the dimensions are less than 100 × 100
pageXOffset	Current *x*-position of viewed page; read-only
pageYOffset	Current *y*-position of viewed page; read-only
personalbar.visible	Hide or show the personal bar; signed script only
scrollbars.visible	Hide or show scroll bars; signed script only
statusbar.visible	Hide or show the status bar; signed script only
toolbar.visible	Hide or show the toolbar; signed script only
status	Message displayed in the status bar
defaultStatus	Message displayed, by default, in the status bar
name	Name of the window if a name has been assigned; set to a value when a new browser window is opened via the open method with a name specified, or through a frame with a name given in the FRAMESET; read-only
self	Current window; read-only
length	The number of frames when used with the frames collection; read-only
top	Top-most ancestor window; read-only
parent	If a frame, returns FRAMESET window; read-only
opener	Reference to the window that opened the current window
window	Refers to the current window, equivalent to self
frames	Array of frames contained within FRAMESET for the window

Window Object Methods

Method	Functionality	Parameters
alert	Displays an alert dialog with the message	Message
blur	Removes focus from the window/frame	
clearTimeout	Removes the time-out	
close	Closes the window	
confirm	Displays a confirmation message	Message
eval	Evaluates a JavaScript string in the context of the object	JavaScript string
focus	Sets focus to window	
open	Opens a new browser window	Strings containing an HTML content file, if any, name of the window, and attribute lists
prompt	Displays a prompt message	Message, default
scroll	Scrolls the window	X value, y value
setTimeout	Creates a time-out for the window that will call a specified function or evaluate a specified expression	Expressions, time
toString	Converts the object into a string	
valueOf	Primitive value of the object (if one exists), or object itself	
back	Returns to the previous URL in the history list	
enableExternalCapture	Enables the frames window to capture events in other pages; signed script only	
disableExternalCapture	Disables event capturing	
find	Finds the specified string in the page	String, case-sensitive, backward-search

continued

Window Object Methods *(continued)*

Method	Functionality	Parameters
forward	Moves to the next URL in the history list	
home	Moves to the page designated as the home page	
moveBy	Moves the window by amount specified	Horizontal, vertical
moveTo	Moves the window to the specified coordinates	*X*-position, *y*-position
resizeBy	Resizes the window by moving the lower-right corner	Horizontal, vertical
resizeTo	Resizes the window to the specified dimensions	Width, height
scrollBy	Scrolls the viewing area by the given amount	Horizontal, vertical
scrollTo	Scrolls the viewing area to specific coordinates	*X*-position, *y*-position
stop	Stops the current document from downloading	

Window and Document Shared Methods

Method	Functionality	Parameters
captureEvents	Capture events of specified type	Event type
clearInterval	Release interval timer	
handleEvent	Invokes the handler for the event	Event
print	Prints the window or frame contents	
releaseEvents	Releases all event capturing for type	Event type

continued

Method	Functionality	Parameters
routeEvent	Passes the event along the hierarchy	Event
toString	Converts object, arrays to literals, including a listing of all properties	

Opening an Navigator Browser Window

The following table from Chapter 3 contains the window.open method attributes supported for Navigator.

Window Object Properties

Property	Valid Values	Requires Signed Script
alwaysLowered	[yes|no] [0|1]	yes
alwaysRaised	[yes|no] [0|1]	yes
hotkeys	[yes|no] [0|1]	no
innerWidth	pixels	yes if window smaller than 100 × 100
innerHeight	pixels	yes if window smaller than 100 × 100
outerWidth	pixels	yes if window smaller than 100 × 100
outerHeight	pixels	yes if window smaller than 100 × 100
dependent	[yes|no] [0|1]	no
screenX	pixels	yes if window placed offscreen
screenY	pixels	yes if window placed offscreen
titlebar	[yes|no] [0|1]	yes if set to *false* ('no' or 0)
z-lock	[yes|no] [0|1]	yes
location	[yes|no] [0|1]	no
directories	[yes|no] [0|1]	no
status	[yes|no] [0|1]	no

continued

Window Object Properties *(continued)*

Property	Valid Values	Requires Signed Script
menubar	[yes|no] [0|1]	no
scrollbars	[yes|no] [0|1]	no
resizable	[yes|no] [0|1]	no
toolbar	[yes|no] [0|1]	no

The Document Object

Chapter 9 provides examples of using the document object, its properties, and its methods, including the use of Netscape-style cookies.

Document Object Properties

Document Object Property	Attribute
alinkColor	Color of the active links within the document
linkColor	Color of the links within the document
vlinkColor	Color of the unvisited links within the document
title	Title of the document
bgColor	Background color of the object
cookie	Information that can be persistently stored on the client machine
lastModified	Date and time the Web page was last modified (read-only)
referrer	URL of the previous location (read-only)
fgColor	Color of the foreground text
URL	URL of the document (read-only)
domain	Domain of the server

Document Object Methods

Method	Functionality	Parameters
GetSelection	Returns a string with the current selection	
close	Closes the document and displays the contents	
open	Opens the document for write methods	mimeType
write	Writes HTML to the document	HTML expression
writeln	Writes HTML/carriage return to the document	HTML expression
eval	Evaluate a JavaScript string in the document context	string
toString	Convert a document to string format	
valueOf	Primitive value of the object, if it exists, or the object itself	

The Location, History, and Navigator Objects

The navigator object maintains information about which browser and version is accessing the page. The location object contains information about the URL currently loaded, and the history object contains information about which URLs have been visited, and in what order.

Location, History, and Navigator Object Properties

Property	Description
location.hash	With a NAME attribute, it is the string minus the pound sign (#)
location.host	Host name concatenated with the port, if any
location.hostname	Host name of the Web page
location.href	URL that is the target of a link
location.pathname	Relative path of the Web page
location.port	Port number, if any

continued

Location, History, and Navigator Object Properties *(continued)*

Property	Description
location.protocol	Protocol used to access the Web page, such as "http:"
location.search	Form data or query string
history.length	Number of URLs currently maintained in the history
history.current	URL of the current Web page
history.next	Next URL in the history list
history.previous	Previous URL in the history list
navigator.language	Two-letter code representing the browser's language
navigator.platform	Platform of the browser
navigator.appName	Name of the browser
navigator.appVersion	Version of the browser
navigator.appCodeName	Code name of the browser
navigator.plugins	Array of plug-ins installed on the client
navigator.mimeTypes	Arrays of MIME types supported by the client
navigator.userAgent	User-agent header

Location, History, and Navigator Object Methods

Method	Functionality	Parameters
location|history.back	Previous URL in the history list	
location|history.go	Go to a specific object in the history list	Object index
location|history|navigator.eval	Evaluate JavaScript in the context of the object	JavaScript string

continued

Method	Functionality	Parameters
location|history|navigator.toString	Convert the object to a string	
location|history|navigator.valueOf	Primitive value of the object, if it exists, or the object itself	
location|history.forward	Next object in the history list	
navigator.javaEnabled	Whether Java is enabled	
navigator.taint	Enabled	Whether data tainting is enabled

Form Object

Chapter 9 covers the form object, which differs little between Navigator and IE.

Input Objects Owned by the Form Object

Input Object	Description
Button	Standard button
Checkbox	Checkbox that the reader can click to check or uncheck
FileUpload	Special input text component that accesses a file name for uploading
Hidden	Hidden component, commonly used for containing nondisplay values
Password	Password field that does not display the password as entered
Radio	Radio button, representing exclusive or choices (only one choice)
Reset	Resets the form (puts form components back to loading state)
Select	A select list is a control that lists several different options for the reader to pick from
Submit	A special type of button that submits the form to the server

continued

Input Objects Owned by the Form Object *(continued)*

Input Object	Description
Text	Text field
Textarea	Multiple column, row text field

The Event Object

The Navigator event model is discussed in Chapters 3 and 9.

Event Object Properties

Property	Description
type	Type of event
layerX	Object width during resize, or horizontal position relative to the layer and expressed in pixels
layerY	Object height during resize, or vertical position relative to the layer and expressed in pixels
pageX	Pixel value of horizontal position relative to the page
pageY	Pixel value of vertical position relative to the page
screenX	Pixel value of horizontal position relative to the screen
screenY	Pixel value of vertical position relative to the screen
which	Number of mouse button pressed or ASCII value of pressed key
modifiers	Used to check for presence of modifier keys (for use with ALT_MASK, CONTROL_MASK, SHIFT_MASK, or META_MASK)
data	Array of strings with the URLs of dropped objects

List of JavaScript Events

Event Handler	Triggered By	Object
onabort	Stop loading image	Image
onblur	Object losing focus	Radio Button, Button, Window, Submit
onchange	Object value changed	Select, Text, Textarea, Fileupload
onclick	Object is clicked	Button, Checkbox, Link, Radio Button
onerror	Scripting error	Image, Window
onfocus	Object gets focus	Radio Button, Button, Window, Submit
onload	When object is loaded	Window, Image
onmouseout	When mouse leaves	Area, Link
onmouseover	When mouse is over	Area, Link
onreset	Form is reset	Form
onselect	User selects text	Text, Textarea
onsubmit	User submits form	Form
onunload	Exit document	Window
ondragdrop	User drops object on window	Window
onkeydown	User presses key	Document, Image, Link, Textarea
onkeyup	User releases key	Document, Image, Link, Textarea
onmousedown	User presses mouse button	Button, Document, Link
onmousemove	User moves mouse	Occurs only with event capturing
onmouseout	Cursor moves out of object	Area, Layer, Link
onmouseover	Cursor moves over object	Area, Layer, Link
onmouseup	User releases mouse button	Button, Link, Document
onmove	User moves window or frame	Window, Frame
onresize	User resizes window or frame	Window, Frame

The Screen Object

The `screen` object contains information about the color depth and resolution of the client monitor.

Screen Object Properties

Screen Object Property	Description
colorDepth	Represents the BPI (bits per inch) of the current screen color settings; a value of 8 is equivalent to 256-color mode
availHeight	Height of the screen in pixels minus features such as task bars
availWidth	Width of the screen in pixels minus features such as task bars
width	Width of the screen in pixels
height	Height of the screen in pixels
pixelDepth	Bits per pixel of the display

Layer Object

With Navigator 4.0, Netscape introduced another container element, the LAYER element.

Layer Properties

Property	Description
name	Layer name, assigned using the ID or NAME attribute
left	Left edge of the layer in pixels, relative to the parent layer
top	Top edge of the layer in pixels, relative to the parent layer or document if placed directly in the document
pageX	Horizontal position of the layer relative to the Web page
pageY	Vertical position of the layer relative to the Web page
zIndex	The z-order of the layer, relative to siblings and the parent

continued

Property	Description
visibility	Whether the layer is visible or not; allowable values are show and hide
clip.top	Top dimension of the layer clipping rectangle
clip.left	Left dimension of the layer clipping rectangle
clip.right	Right dimension of the layer clipping rectangle
clip.bottom	Bottom dimension of the layer clipping rectangle
clip.width	Width of the layer clipping rectangle
clip.height	Height of the layer clipping rectangle
background.src	Source file for the background image of the layer, if any
bgColor	Background color of the layer, if any, set to null for a transparent layer
siblingAbove	Sibling layer above the current layer in z-order, if any (otherwise null)
siblingBelow	Sibling layer below the current layer in z-order, if any (otherwise null)
above	Layer object above the current layer among all layers in the document or the enclosing window object if this layer is top-most
below	Layer object below the current layer among all layers in the document or null if this layer is bottom-most
parentLayer	Layer containing the current layer, or window if none
width	Width of the layer
height	Height of the layer
src	HTML source for the layer in URL format

Layer Object Methods

Method	Functionality	Parameters
moveBy	Changes the layer position using the difference	difference x, y
moveTo	Changes the layer position within the enclosing layer; for inflow layers, moves relative to the natural position	x, y
moveToAbsolute	Changes the layer position within the enclosing page	x, y
resizeBy	Resizes the layer by the specified height and width	difference width, height
resizeTo	Resizes the layer to the given width, height	width, height
moveAbove	Moves the layer to the layer above it in the stacking order	layer
moveBelow	Moves the layer to the layer below it in the stacking order	layer
load	Loads the external HTML file into the layer	source, width

Part V

Appendixes

Appendix A

Web Site URLs

THIS APPENDIX INCLUDES Web site URLs mentioned in the book, as well as a few others that may be helpful to you when you work with dynamic HTML.

 Be forewarned that URLs tend to change fairly frequently and, although this reference was up to date at the time of publication, one or more of these links may be outdated by the time you read this.

URLs Related to This Book

IDG BOOKS WORLDWIDE RESOURCE CENTER FOR WEB PUBLISHING

```
http://www.idgbooks.com/rc/publish/index.html
```

This site contains additional information or updated material for this book.

SHELLEY POWERS' WEB PAGE

```
http://www.yasd.com
```

This is the author's main Web page. Additional examples of dynamic HTML, including the use of channels and DirectAnimation will be posted here.

Standards

This section provides links to standards organizations and specific standards that this book references. Main Web pages are listed first; the rest are alphabetized.

The World Wide Web Consortium (W3C)

W3C MAIN WEB PAGE

`http://www.w3.org`

Cascading Style Sheet Level 1 Standard (published December 17, 1996)
`http://www.w3.org/TR/REC-CSS1`

Document Object Model Activity Page
`http://www.w3.org/MarkUp/DOM`

Extensible Markup Language (XML)
`http://www.w3.org/TR/WD-xml`

Web Fonts
`http://www.w3.org/TR/WD-font`

HTML Activity Page
`http://www.w3.org/MarkUp`

HTML 3.2 Reference Specification
`http://www.w3.org/TR/REC-html32`

HTML 4.0 Working Draft Release
`http://www.w3.org/TR/WD-html40`

W3C Style Sheets
`http://www.w3.org/Style`

Technical Reports and Publications
`http://www.w3.org/TR`

European Computer Manufacturers Association (ECMA)

THE ECMA MAIN WEB PAGE

`http://www.ecma.ch`

The ECMAScript Scripting Standard
`http://www.ecma.ch/stand/ecma-262.htm`

Microsoft-Specific Pages

This section provides URLs for Microsoft and Internet Explorer Web pages.

THE MICROSOFT MAIN WEB PAGE

http://www.microsoft.com

Dynamic HTML Page
http://www.microsoft.com/workshop/author/dhtml

Internet Client SDK (download page)
http://www.microsoft.com/msdn/sdk/inetsdk/asetup/default.asp

Internet Explorer
http://www.microsoft.com/ie

Internet Explorer 4.0
http://www.microsoft.com/ie/ie40

Internet Explorer 4.0 Features
http://www.microsoft.com/ie/ie40/features

Internet Explorer Web Authors and Developers
http://www.microsoft.com/ie/authors

The JScript Page
http://www.microsoft.com/jscript

Resource Gallery for Web Authors
http://www.microsoft.com/ie/authors/resource-f.htm

Site Builder Page
http://www.microsoft.com/sitebuilder

The VBScript Page
http://www.microsoft.com/vbscript

Web Casting (Push Technology) White Paper
http://www.microsoft.com/ie/press/techinfo-
  f.htm?/ie/press/whitepaper/pushwp.htm

Netscape-Specific Pages

This section provides URLs for Netscape and Navigator Web pages.

NETSCAPE'S MAIN WEB PAGE

```
http://www.netscape.com
```

DevEdge Online (Developer's Home Page)
```
http://developer.netscape.com
```

Dynamic HTML Developer Central
```
http://developer.netscape.com/one/dynhtml/index.html
```

Dynamic HTML in Netscape Communicator Guide
```
http://developer.netscape.com/library/documentation/communicator/
  dynhtml/index.htm
```

HTML Reference Guide
```
http://developer.netscape.com/library/documentation/htmlguid/
  index.htm
```

JavaScript Guide
```
http://home.netscape.com/eng/mozilla/3.0/handbook/javascript/
  index.html
```

JavaScript: What's New in JavaScript for Navigator 4.0?
```
http://developer.netscape.com/library/documentation/communicator/
  jsguide/js1_2.htm
```

Navigator Home Page
```
http://www.netscape.com/comprod/products/communicator/navigator_
  frameset.html
```

The Netcaster Developer's Guide
```
http://developer.netscape.com/library/documentation/netcast/devguide
  /index.html
```

Object Signing: Resources
```
http://developer.netscape.com/library/documentation/signedobj/
  overview.html
```

Object Signing: Establishing Trust for Downloaded Software
```
http://developer.netscape.com/library/documentation/signedobj/trust/
  index.htm
```

Software Download Site
```
http://home.netscape.com/flash1/download/index.html
```

Appendix B

What's On the CD-ROM

THE COMPANION **CD-ROM** at the back of this book contains Microsoft's and Netscape's popular Internet browser software, as well as numerous files designed to help you master dynamic HTML, as follows:

- ◆ Files for the examples presented throughout this book
- ◆ Microsoft Internet Explorer 4.0
- ◆ Netscape Navigator 4.0

CD-ROM Organization

This book's CD-ROM is organized into 17 folders, one folder for each of the book's 15 chapters, plus one folder apiece for Internet Explorer 4.0 and Netscape Navigator 4.0. The chapter folders contain the example files for each chapter. For example, all of the files for Chapter 1 appear in the \CHAPTER01\ folder. You'll find Internet Explorer 4.0 in the \InternetExplorer4\ folder, and Netscape Navigator 4.0 in the \NetscapeNavigator4\ folder.

All example files as well as Internet Explorer 4.0 and Netscape Navigator 4.0 work with both Windows 95 and Windows NT 4.0. Note that the example files have been named in **boldface** type throughout the book for easy identification.

Installing the Example Files

You can copy the example files from the CD-ROM directly to your hard drive by selecting and then dragging them to the location you desire. The examples were created without using any specialized tools, and you will probably want to work with them directly because many HTML and script-generation tools have not yet been adapted for use with dynamic HTML.

The example files have been tested with IE 4.0 for Windows 95 and Windows NT, and Navigator 4.03 for Windows 95 and NT. If you are using a later version of either browser, the sample files may not always perform as intended. Be aware, as well, that the examples may look a little different from the images in the book because of differences between operating systems, fonts, and so forth. Also, if the technology changes after this book shipped to the printer, new versions of the samples will be posted at the IDG Books Worldwide Web Resource Center site for Web publishing – you can find the URL in Appendix A.

Installing the Browsers

You'll find the setup files for the two browsers on the CD-ROM in the following folders:

- Internet Explorer 4.0: \InternetExplorer4\
- Netscape Navigator 4.0: \NetscapeNavigator4\

To install the browsers, double-click the file called **ie.exe** for Internet Explorer and **setup.exe** for Netscape Navigator and follow the directions.

Index

Symbols

* (asterisk) in CSS1 syntax, 21
&& (Boolean "and") JavaScript operator, 58
|| (Boolean "or") JavaScript operator, 58
[ ] (brackets) in CSS1 syntax, 20
{ } (curly brackets) for style sheet rule
    declarations, 19
(pound sign) in CSS1 syntax, 21
; (semicolon) in style definitions, 20
| (vertical bar)
    Boolean "or" (||), 58
    in CSS1 syntax, 20

A

absolute positioning (IE)
    layering elements, 161–163
    overview, 155
    relative positioning combined with,
        157–158
absolute positioning (Navigator)
    layering elements, 298–304
    overview, 290
    relative positioning combined with,
        292–293
activate codebase principals, 281–282
ActiveX controls, 5
Add parameter
    blur filter, 203
    wave filter, 204
addAmbient method (light filter), 207
addCone method (light filter), 207
addPoint method (light filter), 207
"Alien Head" example, 224
all collection, 141–143
alpha filter
    described, 194
    emulating in Netscape, 345–347
    example, 195–196
    parameters, 195
    syntax, 194
ambient light filter effect, 206–211
ampersands (&& Boolean "and"), 58
"and", Boolean, 58
animation
    moving button gag, 184–186
    moving image show, 267–269

using layers (Navigator), 307–311
using positioning (IE), 171–173
using positioning (Navigator), 312–314
Apply method (transition filter), 211
array-based objects (Navigator), 266–269
    accessing example, 267–269
    table of, 267
arrays
    animating objects using, 171–173
    array-based objects (Navigator), 266–269
    for article inset height and width, 469,
        503–504
    dense arrays, 56
    description property for, 56
    dynamic arrays, 80–81
    in JavaScript variables, 55–56
    for menu bar, 485–486
    for menu bar buttons, 468
    in number kid's page, 439–440
    Path Control versus, 173
    pick_number function, 436–437
    in VBScript variables, 80–81
article and page buttons
    cross-browser, 503–508
    IE, 484–494
    Navigator, 467–477
ASCII key value
    finding (IE), 230–231
    finding (Navigator), 365–366
asterisk (*) in CSS1 syntax, 21
attaching filters to objects, 193
audio messages, 240
auto property (JASS), 333, 336

B

background images
    adding dynamically, 184–186
    CSS1 property for, 38, 39–40
    JASS property for, 337–338
background properties (CSS1), 37–40
    examples, 37–40
    for script references, 181–182
    syntax, 38–39, 514
background-attachment property (CSS1), 38, 39
backgroundColor property (CSS1)
    changing with click event, 186–187
    changing with mouse movement, 182–184

background-color property (CSS1)
   changing with mouse movement, 355–357
   example, 39–40
   overview, 23
   syntax, 38
backgroundColor property (JASS), 337
background-image property (CSS1), 38, 39–40
backgroundImage property (JASS), 337–338
background_inset variable, 463
background-position property (CSS1), 38, 39
background-repeat property (CSS1)
   examples, 37, 38
   syntax, 38, 39
background_width variable, 463
baseline keyword value (vertical-align
      property), 36
begin_event function, 361, 363
begin_respond function, 413
blink value of text-decoration property, 37
block-level attributes (CSS1), 511–513
block-level properties (JASS), 332–336
blur events
   help tips example, 235–236
   triggering indirectly, 223
blur filter
   described, 203
   example, 204–206
   parameters, 203–204
   syntax, 203
Boolean "and" or "or," 58
border properties (CSS1), 28–31, 512
   border-width, 28–29
   keyword values, 29, 30
   style values, 30
   syntax, 30
border properties (JASS), 333, 335–336
Bosworth, Adam, 3
box properties (CSS1), 23–31, 511–513
   border, 28–31, 512
   margin, 24–26, 512
   overview, 23–24
   padding, 26–28, 513
brackets ([ ]) in CSS1 syntax, 20
break statement (JavaScript), with switch
      statement, 59
browsers. See Internet Explorer; Netscape
      Navigator; Web browsers
Button object (Navigator), 261
buttons
   article and page buttons (cross-browser),
      503–508
   article and page buttons (IE), 484–494
   article and page buttons (Navigator), 467–477

highlighting, 371–373
input objects owned by form object
      (Navigator), 261, 539–540
moving button gag, 184–186
moving images gag, 310–311
Remember button (cross-browser), 500–503
Remember button (IE), 497–499
Remember button (Navigator), 479–481
slide show effect, 191–193
TOC button (cross-browser), 500–503
TOC button (IE), 495–497
TOC button (Navigator), 477–479
See also click events
buy_number function, 440, 444–445, 451–452

C

caching images (Navigator), 268
cancelBubble property of event object (IE),
      228, 425
captureEvents method, 66–68, 352
capturing user events (cross-browser)
   using hypertext links, 420, 421–425
   using the object model, 420–421, 425–428
capturing user events (IE)
   keyboard events, 230–231
   load event, 231–232
   mouse events, 219–230
   responding to user interaction, 232–237
   visual feedback for user, 237–240
capturing user events (JavaScript), 62–68
   document- and window-level capturing,
      66–68
   event handlers, 62–64, 541
   event object, 64–66, 540–541
capturing user events (Navigator)
   keyboard events, 365–366
   load event, 366–367
   mouse events, 351–365
   responding to user interaction, 367–373
   visual feedback for user, 374–379
capturing user events (VBScript), 88–93
   event handlers, 88–92, 529–531
   event object, 92–93, 529–531
Cascading Style Sheets (CSS1), 15–49, 511–515
   adding style sheet rules directly to elements,
      45
   background properties, 37–40, 514
   block-level attributes, 511–513
   box properties, 23–31, 511–513
   collections, 141, 148–149
   color units, 22–23
   combining style sheet rules, 45–48

cross-browser compatibility and, 16
embedded, 44
e-zines and, 457–458
font properties, 31–34, 513
imported, 43
inheritance of styles, 46, 47
for layers (Navigator), 341
linked, 43
list properties, 40–42, 515
measurement units, 21–22
overview, 7–8, 16
positioning elements with, 8, 156–157, 292,
  306–307, 404–408
positioning properties (IE), 154–161
positioning properties (Navigator), 290–298
progressive document example, 459–460
properties, 17
quick reference, 511–515
simple example, 18–19
<STYLE> tags, 19–20
switching, for dynamic positioning,
  167–169
syntactic conventions, 20–21, 511
text properties, 34–37, 514–515
in Web pages, 43–45
See also positioning HTML elements (IE);
  positioning HTML elements (Navigator)
catalog, online
introduction and entry pages, 448–450
main page, 450–454
cells collection, 143–146
with data binding, 145
example, 143–145, 146
overview, 413
certificates for script signing, 281–282
CGI, 4
change events, triggering indirectly, 223
change function, 341–342
change_article function
cross-browser, 504, 506
IE, 491, 492–493
Navigator, 475–476, 478–479
change_clr function, 410
changeColor method (light filter), 207
change_divs function, 411
change_doc function, 410
changeStrength method (light filter), 208
Checkbox object (Navigator), 261
check_height function, 361, 423, 426, 454
check_key function, 378
check_width function, 361, 423, 426, 454

chroma filter
color parameter, 195
described, 194
example, 195–196
syntax, 194
class specifier (JASS), 323–324
Clear method (light filter), 208
click events
capturing (IE), 221–223
capturing (Navigator), 353–355
capturing and changing background color,
  186–187
cross-browser example, 412–415
dblclick event, 219–220, 362
drag-and-drop versus, 421
ID assignments, 222–223
keyboard events triggering, 222, 353
making hidden listing visible, 124
tic-tac-toe example, 277–279
transition filter effect, 211
See also mouse events
Clicked event handler (transition filter), 211
clip property
IE, 158–159
Navigator, 294–295, 371
clipping
clip property (IE), 158–159
clip property (Navigator), 294–295, 371
clipping region, 158
cross-browser compatibility issues, 387–388
cross-browser implementation, 403–404
Microsoft implementation, 158–159
Netscape implementation, 294–295
closing window, button for, 110–111
cm, measurement unit, 21
collections, 140–149
all, 141–143
cells, 143–146
defined, 140
frames, 147–148
images, 146–147
imports, 141, 148–149
overview, 140–141
rows, 143–146
scripts, 148
styleSheets, 141, 148–149
color parameter
drop shadow filter, 197
glow filter, 194, 195
mask filter, 195
shadow filter, 197

color property (CSS1)
    changing with mouse movement, 182–184
    emulating dynamic change (cross-browser),
        408–412
    overview, 23
color property (JASS), 337
colors
    changing background on load event,
        116–118, 258–259
    changing background with click event,
        186–187
    changing to grayscale, 201–203
    changing with mouse movement, 182–184,
        355–357
    CSS1 color units, 22–23
    emulating dynamic change (cross-browser),
        408–412
    keyword names, 22–23
    light filter effect, 206–211
    "negative" effect, 201–203
    setting with JASS, 322–324, 337
    testing color depth and resolution (cross-
        browser), 460
    testing color depth and resolution (IE),
        126–128
    testing color depth and resolution
        (Navigator), 265–266
    x-ray effect, 201–203
combining
    absolute and relative positioning (IE),
        157–158
    absolute and relative positioning
        (Navigator), 292–293
    CSS1 style sheet rules, 45–48
    JASS styles with other style settings, 323
compatibility. See cross-browser compatibility
conditional statements
    JavaScript, 57–59
    VBScript, 82–84
cone light filter effect, 206–211
console mode (Navigator), 282–286
constructive changes, 462
containers for elements
    built-in arrays (Navigator), 266–269
    form object (Navigator), 260–264, 539–540
    grouping elements (IE), 153–154
    grouping elements (Navigator), 289–290
    See also collections
cookie property
    Open Profiling Standard (OPS) versus
        cookies, 256
    setting and getting (cross-browser), 461
    setting and getting (IE), 113–115

setting and getting (Navigator), 254–256
cross-browser compatibility
    "base" objects to hide implementation
        details, 386–388
    color keywords and, 23
    CSS1 style sheets and, 16
    data binding and, 145
    DHTML equalizer objects, 388–399
    extended objects for, 388
    JavaScript and, 6
    object models and, 6–7
    positioning and, 385
    scripting and, 9, 385–386
    ten-step plan for, 12–13
CSS1. See Cascading Style Sheets (CSS1)
Ctrl key, testing for, 228
curly brackets ({}) for style sheet rule
    declarations, 19
cycle function, 308, 406–407

D

dashed border style value, 30
data binding, 145
data types
    JavaScript scalar data types, 53–55
    VBScript scalar data types, 77–80
dblclick event (IE)
    event sequence for, 219–220
    example, 220
dblclick event (Navigator), z-index ordering
    for, 362
deleting. See removing
dense arrays, 56
description property for arrays, 56
destructive changes, 462
DHTML equalizer objects
    creating, 388–391
    event handlers in, 415–416
    overview, 387
    source code, 394–399
    testing, 391–394
DHTML equalizing, 387
Digital Cats, 6
Direction parameter
    blur filter, 204
    shadow filter, 197
display property
    hiding and showing paragraphs (IE), 191
    hiding and showing text (Navigator),
        374–378
    JASS, 337, 339
    visibility property versus, 188–191, 234

Do...Loop statement (VBScript), 85–86
do...while statement (JavaScript), 60–61
document load event. *See* load event
document object (IE), 111–115
    cookie property example, 113–115
    methods, 112–113, 520–521
    overview, 107, 111
    properties, 111–112, 519–520
    tags property, 322–323
document object (Navigator), 252–257
    cookie property example, 254–256
    in layer objects, 280–281
    methods, 252–253, 257, 537
    overview, 253–254
    properties, 253–254, 536
document-level event capturing (JavaScript),
    66–68
dotted border style value, 30
double border style value, 30
drag-and-drop techniques
    IE, 224–230
    Navigator, 357–365
    using hypertext links (cross-browser), 421–425
    using the object model (cross-browser),
        425–428
drag_event function, 362, 364
drop shadow filter
    described, 196
    emulating in Netscape, 345–347
    example, 197–198
    parameters, 197
    syntax, 196
dynamic arrays (VBScript), 80–81
dynamic fonts (Navigator), 11, 340
dynamic HTML
    need for, 11–12
    ten-step plan, 12–13
    Web page content prior to, 4–7
dynamic positioning (IE)
    animating elements, 171–173
    changing element positions, 167–170
dynamic positioning (Navigator)
    animating elements with layers, 307–311
    animating the menu bar, 312–314
    changing element positions, 304–307
dynamically changing HTML elements (IE),
    179–217
    background color with click event, 186–188
    background properties for scripts (CSS1),
        181–182
    display property, 188–191
    example Web page, 179–181, 214–216
    font properties for scripts (CSS1), 182
    hiding and showing elements, 188–193
    image properties, 184
    moving button gag, 184–186
    text properties for scripts (CSS1), 182
    transition filter, 211–214
    visibility property, 188–193
    visual filters, 193–211
dynamically changing HTML elements
    (Navigator), 321–350
    drop shadows, 345–347
    dynamic fonts, 340
    example, 321–322, 348–349
    JASS, 321–339
    layer properties, 272–274
    opacity changes, 345–347
    using layers, 341–347
    See also JavaScript Accessible Style Sheets
        (JASS)

E

ECMAScript, 10
effect variable, 402
elements. *See* collections; HTML elements
em, measurement unit, 21
embedding CSS1 style sheets, 44
empty hypertext links, event capturing with,
    353–354, 363, 420, 421–425
Empty value for VBScript variables, 79
empty_cart function, 450, 453
end_event function, 362, 363–364
end_move function, 441, 446, 453
end_of_game function, 441–442, 446
end_of_sale function, 453
entry kid's page
    activating, 434–437
    converting to online catalog, 448–450
    creating, 430–437
    display setup, 431–434
erasing. *See* removing
error event, 232
error messages. *See* messages to user
event capturing. *See* capturing user events
event handlers
    in DHTML equalizer objects, 415–416
    JavaScript, 62–64, 541
    layer object (Navigator), 276–280
    VBScript, 88–92, 529–531
event object (IE)
    cancelBubble property, 228
    event handlers, 88–92, 529–531

(continued)

event object (IE) *(continued)*
   intrinsic events, 10
   keyCode property, 230, 239
   mouse events, 219–220
   overview, 10–11, 92, 135
   properties, 92–93, 135, 220–221, 529
   returnValue property, 228, 231
   srcElement property, 134, 187
event object (Navigator)
   direct function calls, 264–265
   event handlers, 62–64, 264, 541
   intrinsic events, 10
   overview, 10–11, 64–65, 264–265
   properties, 65, 265, 540
event trapping for click events, 354–355
ex, measurement unit, 21
execCommand method, 113
expose_objects function, 404

F

feedback to user
   audio messages, 240
   button highlight, 371–373
   error, warning, or information messages,
      237–240, 367–371, 378–379
   help tips example, 232–237
   information hide-and-show example,
      367–371
   interactive forms, 232–237
   on load event, 231, 366–367
   visual effects, 237–240
FileUpload object (Navigator), 261
filter properties (IE), 193–214
   alpha filter, 194–196
   assigning to variables, 194
   attaching filters to objects, 193
   blur filter, 203–206
   chroma filter, 194–196
   drop shadow filter, 196–198
   filter effects, 193
   flip horizontal filter, 198–200
   flip vertical filter, 198–200
   glow filter, 194
   grayscale filter, 201–203
   invert filter, 201–203
   light filter, 206–211
   mask filter, 194–195
   multiple effects for one object, 194
   overview, 11, 193–194
   removing, 194
   shadow filter, 196–198
   transition filter, 211–214

wave filter, 203–206
   x-ray filter, 201–203
Find ASCII key utility
   IE, 230–231
   Navigator, 365–366
finishopacity parameter (alpha filter), 195
finishX parameter (alpha filter), 195
finishY parameter (alpha filter), 195
flip horizontal filter, 198–200
flip vertical filter, 198–200
focus events
   help tips example, 235–236
   triggering indirectly, 223
<FONT> tag, limitations of, 16
font properties (CSS1), 31–34
   examples, 32–34
   matching font algorithms, 33
   overview, 31
   for script references, 182
   syntax, 31, 513
font-family property (CSS1), 32
fontFamily property (CSS1), 182–184
fontFamily property (JASS), 326
fonts
   changing with mouse movement, 182–184
   dynamic fonts (Navigator), 11, 340
   font properties (CSS1), 31–34, 513
   generic families, 32
   JASS font properties, 325–328
   setting with JASS, 323–324
font-size property (CSS1), 32
fontSize property (JASS), 325
font-style property (CSS1), 32
fontStyle property (JASS), 326–327
font-variant property (CSS1), 33
font-weight property (CSS1), 32–33
fontWeight property (JASS), 326
For...Next statement (VBScript), 84–85
for statement (JavaScript), 60, 361–362
ForEach...Next statement (VBScript), 85
forest scene drag-and-drop example
   IE, 224–230
   Navigator, 357–365
form object (Navigator), 260–264
   input objects owned by, 261, 539–540
   multiple form example, 261–264
forms, interactive
   form object (Navigator), 260–264, 539–540
   help messages (IE), 232–237
   multiple form example (Navigator), 261–264
frames collection, 147, 148
Freq parameter (wave filter), 204

functions
    creating and calling in JavaScript, 61–62
    JavaScript timer functions, 68–70
    in JavaScript variables, 54–55
    VBScript procedures, 86–87
Furman, Scott, 8

G

get_clip_height function, 503
get_clip_width function, 503
get_cookie function
    IE, 114
    Navigator, 255
    progressive document example, 461, 472, 500
get_current_page_article function
    cross-browser, 501–502
    IE, 498–499
    Navigator, 480–481
get_visibility function, 388–391
GIFs, one-pixel, 5, 151
global variables
    for article and page buttons, 485
    JavaScript, 52–53
    VBScript script-level variables, 76, 77
glow filter, 194
go_topage function
    IE, 496–497
    Navigator, 478
graphics. See images
grayscale filter
    described, 201
    example, 201–203
    syntax, 201
groove border style value, 30

H

hash sign (#) in CSS1 syntax, 21
<HEAD> section, <STYLE> tags in, 19
header
    adding background image dynamically,
        184–186
    changing dynamically on loading, 184
height property (JASS), 333, 336
help event (IE), 230
help messages for interactive forms, 232–237
Hidden object (Navigator), 261
hideall function, 402
hide_me function, 388–391
hide_object function, 402–403
hiding and showing elements
    "base" objects to hide implementation

    details, 386–388
    DHTML equalizer objects for, 388–399
    display property, 191, 374–378
    display property (JASS), 337, 339
    to emulate HTML change, 408–416
    emulating HTML change (cross-browser),
        408–412
    help tips example, 232–237
    information hide-and-show example,
        367–371
    for keyboard events, 239–240, 374,
        378–379, 412–415
    messages to user, 237–240
    mouse-movement events and (IE), 223–224
    mouse-movement events and (Navigator),
        355–357
    multiple form example (Navigator), 261–264
    paragraphs, 190–191
    presentation page contents (cross-browser),
        401–404
    slide show effect, 191–193
    using layers (Navigator), 341–345
    visibility property (IE), 159–161
    visibility property (Navigator), 296–298
    visibility versus display property,
        188–191, 234
hierarchies in Microsoft object model, 106
highlighting buttons, 371–373
history object (IE), 115–118
    example, 116–118
    methods, 116, 522
    overview, 115–116
    properties, 116, 521–522
history object (Navigator), 257–260
    example, 258–259
    methods, 260, 538–539
    overview, 257
    properties, 258, 537–538
<Hn> tags, limitations of, 15
HTML elements, 136–140
    accessing, 138
    accessing with tagname property, 188
    adding CSS1 style sheet rules to, 45
    collections, 140–149
    CSSP positioning support for, 296
    dynamically changing (IE), 179–217
    dynamically changing (Navigator), 321–350
    layering (IE), 161–167
    layering (Navigator), 298–311
    marquee element example, 139–140
    Microsoft elements exposed to scripting,
        137–138
    positioning (IE), 151–177

(continued)

HTML elements *(continued)*
    positioning (Navigator), 287–319
    See also collections; dynamically changing
        HTML elements (IE); dynamically
        changing HTML elements (Navigator);
        positioning HTML elements (IE);
        positioning HTML elements (Navigator)
hypertext links, event capturing with, 353–354,
    363, 420, 421–425

I

ID specifier (JASS), 324–325
ie_object, creating, 386–388
if...then...else statements
    JavaScript, 57–58, 361–362
    VBScript, 82–83, 227–228
images
    adding background image dynamically,
        184–186
    background-image property (CSS1), 38,
        39–40
    backgroundImage property (JASS), 337–338
    caching (Navigator), 268
    dynamically changing, 184
    hiding and showing with mouse movement,
        223–224, 355–357
    moving button gag, 184–186
    moving image show, 267–269
    shrinking with clip property, 294–295
    slide show effect, 191–193
    testing color depth and resolution (cross-
        browser), 460
    testing color depth and resolution (IE),
        126–128
    testing color depth and resolution
        (Navigator), 265–266
images collection, 146–147
importing CSS1 style sheets, 43
imports collection, 141, 148–149
in, measurement unit, 21
information messages
    hiding and showing (IE), 237–240
    hiding and showing (Navigator), 367–371,
        374–379
inheritance
    of CSS1 style sheet rules, 46, 47
    of properties from containing parent, 187
inline CSS1 style sheets, 45
innerHTML property (IE), 132–134
innerText property (IE)
    marquee element example, 140

overview, 132
tic-tac-toe example, 132–134
input objects owned by form object (Navigator),
    261, 539–540
insertAdjacentHTML method (IE), 134
insertAdjacentText method (IE), 134
inset border style value, 30
inset object, 482
interactive content (IE), 219–241
    capturing keyboard events, 230–231
    capturing mouse events, 219–230
    capturing the load event, 231–232
    responding to user interaction, 232–237
    using hidden content to emulate HTML
        change, 408–416
    visual feedback for user, 237–240
interactive content (Navigator), 351–379
    capturing keyboard events, 365–366
    capturing mouse events, 351–365
    capturing the load event, 366–367
    responding to user interaction, 367–373
    visual feedback for user, 374–379
interactive pages (cross-browser), 419–455
    drag-and-drop techniques, 421–428
    kid's page, 428–455
    scripting techniques, 419–421
    See also kid's Web page
interactive presentation (cross-browser),
    383–417
    clipping, 503–504
    creating a cross-browser Web page object,
        384–389
    creating "base" objects to hide
        implementation details, 386–388
    creating DHTML equalizer objects, 388–399
    creating extended objects, 388
    emulating HTML change, 408–412
    hiding and showing contents, 401–404
    moving contents using CSS1 positioning,
        404–408
    overview, 383–384
    positioning components, 399–401
    responding to user, 412–415
Internet Explorer
    new features, 9–11
    object model, 6–7, 105–150
    opening browser window, 517–518
    testing for browser type and version,
        116–118, 258–259, 385, 444, 463
    See also cross-browser compatibility;
        Microsoft object model
intrinsic events, 10
introduction kid's page

converting to online catalog, 448–450
creating, 429–430
invert filter
　described, 201
　example, 201–203
　syntax, 201
invisibility. *See* display property; hiding and
　　showing elements; visibility property
Isaacs, Scott, 8

J

JAR Packager, 282–285
JASS. *See* JavaScript Accessible Style Sheets
　　(JASS)
Java applets
　activate codebase principals and, 282
　JAR Packager, 282–285
　limitations of, 5
Java Archive Resources (JAR) Packager,
　　282–285
JavaScript, 51–74
　arrays, 55–56
　capturing user events, 62–68
　collections, 140–149
　conditional statements, 57–59
　creating objects, 54
　creating variables, 52
　cross-browser compatibility and, 6
　functions, creating and calling, 61–62
　functions in variables, 54–55
　global variables, 52–53
　JScript versus, 73
　local variables, 52
　looping statements, 60–61
　multiple windows, working with, 70–72
　naming variables, 52
　operators for expressions, 58
　overview, 6
　scalar data types, 53–55
　signing, 246, 249
　timer functions, 68–70
　VBScript versus, 110
　VBScript with, 142
　See also scripting; VBScript
JavaScript Accessible Style Sheets (JASS),
　　321–339
　block-level properties, 332–336
　class specifier, 323–324
　combining JASS styles with other style
　　settings, 323
　example, 321–322, 348–349
　font properties, 325–328

ID specifier, 324–325
layers and, 464
linking into documents, 323
miscellaneous properties, 336–339
overview, 9
setting HTML element styles, 322
tags specifier, 322–323
text properties, 328–332
jiggled_hide function, 403–404
JScript
　JavaScript versus, 73
　See also JavaScript
JSS. *See* JavaScript Accessible Style Sheets
　　(JASS)

K

keep_away function, 308, 310–311
keyboard events
　capturing (IE), 230–231
　capturing (Navigator), 365–366
　click events triggered by, 222, 353
　cross-browser example, 412–415
　displaying messages for, 239–240, 374,
　　378–379
　kid's entry page example, 435–436
　testing for Shift or Ctrl key, 228
keyCode property of event object (IE), 230, 239
keydown events, capturing (IE), 230
keypress events
　cross-browser example, 412–415
　displaying messages, 239–240, 374,
　　378–379
　finding ASCII value (IE), 230–231
　finding ASCII value (Navigator), 365–366
　kid's entry page example, 435–436
key_press function, 362–363, 436
keyup events, capturing (IE), 230
keyword names
　for border properties (CSS1), 29, 30
　for colors, 22–23
　for vertical-align property (CSS1), 36
kid's Web page, 428–455
　converting to online catalog, 448–454
　entry page, 430–437, 448–450
　introduction page, 429–430, 448–450
　numbers page, 437–447, 450–454
　overview, 421, 428–429

L

LAYER element, 9

layer object (Navigator), 269–281
applying methods, 275–276
document objects in, 280–281
event handling, 276–280
example, 269–270
inflow layer, 269–270
methods, 275, 544
overview, 269
positioned or out-of-flow layer, 269–270
properties, 271–272, 542–543
setting properties dynamically, 272–274
tic-tac-toe example, 277–280
layering elements (IE)
using absolute positioning, 161–163
using z-index property, 163–167
layering elements (Navigator)
animation with layers, 307–311
button highlight example, 371–373
drop shadow effect, 345–347
dynamic positioning, 304–306
emulating dynamic modification of HTML
elements, 341–345
hiding and showing text, 367–371, 374–379
layer object, 269–281
opacity effect, 345–347
positioning with inline technique, 341–342
progressive document layout, 463–466
using absolute positioning, 298–304
using z-index property, 300–304
See also layer object (Navigator)
layout for progressive document
cross-browser, 499–500
IE, 482–484
Navigator, 462–467
letter-spacing property (CSS1)
defined, 35
stretching words, 35
syntax, 36
light filter
described, 206
example, 208–211
methods and parameters, 206–208
syntax, 206
Light parameter (wave filter), 204
lineHeight property (JASS), 329
linking
CSS1 style sheets, 43
event capturing using links, 353–354, 363,
420, 421–425
JASS into documents, 323
list properties (CSS1), 40–42
examples, 40–42
syntax, 41, 515

listStyleType property (JASS), 337, 338–339
load event
animated menu bar, 312–314
capturing (IE), 231–232
capturing (Navigator), 366–367
changing background color, 116–118,
258–259
changing page dynamically, 184
progressive document example, 470, 472
load_article function
cross-browser, 504–505
IE, 488–489, 490
Navigator, 472, 476
local variables
JavaScript, 52
VBScript procedural-level variables, 76
location object (IE), 115–118
example, 116–118
methods, 116, 522
Netscape Navigator object versus, 257
overview, 115–116
properties, 116, 521–522
location object (Navigator), 257–260
example, 258–259
Internet Explorer object versus, 257
methods, 260, 538–539
overview, 257
properties, 258, 537–538
looping statements
JavaScript, 60–61
VBScript, 84–86

M

make_move function, 440–441, 445–446,
452–453
margin properties (CSS1), 24–26, 512
shorthand, 24–25
syntax, 25
values totaling over 100 percent, 26
margins (JASS)
properties, 333, 334
setting, 323–324
marquee element example, 139–140
mask filter
color parameter, 195
described, 194
syntax, 194
measurement units
for CSS1 properties, 21–22
for window object (IE), 107
menu bar examples
animating dynamically (Navigator), 312–314

using absolute positioning (IE), 161–163
using absolute positioning (Navigator), 298–304
using z-index property (IE), 163–167
using z-index property (Navigator), 300–304
menus for progressive documents
    article and page buttons (cross-browser), 503–508
    article and page buttons (IE), 484–494
    article and page buttons (Navigator), 467–477
    Remember button (cross-browser), 500–503
    Remember button (IE), 497–499
    Remember button (Navigator), 479–481
    TOC button (cross-browser), 495–497
    TOC button (IE), 500–503
    TOC button (Navigator), 477–479
messages to user
    audio messages, 240
    error, warning, or information messages, 237–240, 367–371, 374–379
    help tips example, 232–237
    on keypress event, 239–240, 374, 378–379
    on load event, 231, 366–367
methods
    document object (IE), 112–113, 519–520
    document object (Navigator), 252–253, 257, 537
    history object (IE), 116, 522
    history object (Navigator), 260, 538–539
    layer object (Navigator), 275, 544
    light filter, 206–208
    location object (IE), 116, 522
    location object (Navigator), 260, 538–539
    navigator object (IE), 116, 522
    navigator object (Navigator), 260, 538–539
    selection object (IE), 136
    shareable (Navigator), 252–253, 534–535
    signing, 249
    TextRange object (IE), 130–132, 527–528
    transition filter, 211
    window object (IE), 109, 517
    window object (Navigator), 250–253, 533–535
Microsoft Internet Explorer. See Internet Explorer
Microsoft object model, 105–150, 515–531
    collections for HTML elements, 140–149
    document object, 107, 111–115, 519–521
    event object, 88–93, 135, 528–529
    hierarchy, 106
    history object, 115–118, 521–522
    HTML elements, 136–140
    innerHTML property, 132–134
    innerText property, 132–134
    location object, 115–118
    navigator object, 115–118, 521–522
    Netscape object model versus, 6–7
    outerHTML property, 132–134
    outerText property, 132–134
    quick reference, 515–531
    screen object, 126–128, 526
    selection object, 136
    style object, 118–126, 523–526
    TextRange object, 128–132, 527–528
    window object, 107–111, 515–517
    See also object models
mm, measurement unit, 21
mouse events
    accessing event information (IE), 220–221
    accessing event information (Navigator), 352–353
    capturing (IE), 219–230
    capturing (Navigator), 351–365
    click events (IE), 221–223
    click events (Navigator), 353–355
    drag-and-drop techniques (IE), 224–230
    drag-and-drop techniques (Navigator), 357–365
    movement events (IE), 223–224
    movement events (Navigator), 355–357
    overview, 219–220
    properties (IE), 220–221
    See also click events; specific events by name
mouseclick function, 413–414
mousedown event
    button highlight example, 371–373
    trapping for drag-and-drop, 227, 360–361, 363, 425–426
mousedrag event, 422
mousemove event
    drag-and-drop examples, 227–230, 360–365, 422–424, 427–428
    parameters (Navigator), 352–353
mouseout events
    background, font, and text changes, 183
    drop shadow effect, 345–347
    hiding and showing images, 223–224, 355–357
    hiding and showing layers, 343
    hiding and showing text, 235–236, 238–239, 370, 374–378
    tic-tac-toe example, 277–279

`mouseover` events
  animation with layers, 307–308
  background, font, and text changes,
    182–183
  changing header color, 124, 125
  changing paragraph style, 124
  drop shadow effect, 345–347
  hiding and showing images, 223–224,
    355–357
  hiding and showing layers, 343
  hiding and showing text, 235–236,
    238–239, 370, 374–378
  moving button gag, 184–186
  for pop-up text, 124, 125
  rollover effect, 182–183, 355–357
  tic-tac-toe example, 277–279
`mouseup` event
  overview, 67, 68
  trapping for drag-and-drop, 227, 360–361,
    363, 422, 425–426
`moveBy` method (Navigator), 305–306
`move_in` function, 405–406
`MoveLight` method (light filter), 208
`move_number` function, 440, 445
`MoveObjects` function, 310
`move_out` function, 407–408
`move_rock` function, 452
`moveTo` method (Navigator), 305
moving button gag, 184–186
moving image show, 267–269
multiple windows
  JavaScript with, 70–72
  VBScript with, 96–100

N

naming
  JavaScript variables, 52
  VBScript variables, 76–77
Navigator. *See* Netscape Navigator
`navigator` object (IE), 115–118
  example, 116–118
  methods, 116, 522
  overview, 115–116
  properties, 116, 521–522
`navigator` object (Navigator), 257–260
  example, 258–259
  methods, 260, 538–539
  overview, 257
  properties, 258, 537–538
"negative" color effect, 201–203
Netscape Navigator
  new features, 9–11

object model, 6–7, 245–286
opening browser window, 535–536
testing for browser type and version,
  116–118, 258–259, 385, 444, 463
See also cross-browser compatibility;
  Netscape object model
Netscape object model, 245–286, 531–544
  array-based objects, 266–269
  console mode, 282–286
  `document` object, 252–257, 280–281,
    536–537
  `event` object, 264–265, 540–541
  `form` object, 260–264, 539–540
  `history` object, 257–260, 537–539
  `layer` object, 269–281, 542–544
  `location` object, 257–260, 537–539
  Microsoft object model versus, 6–7
  `navigator` object, 257–260
  quick reference, 531–544
  `screen` object, 265–266, 542
  shareable methods, 252–253, 534–535
  signed scripting, 246, 249, 281–282, 286
  `window` object, 246–253, 531–535
  See also object models
`next_page` function, 435
`none` border style value, 30
`Null` value for VBScript variables, 79
number sign (#) in CSS1 syntax, 21
numbers kid's page
  converting to online catalog, 450–454
  creating, 437–447
  dynamically modifying page elements,
    443–447
  moving elements to shopping cart, 439–443
  setup, 438–439

O

object models
  cross-browser compatibility and, 6–7
  event capturing using (cross-browser),
    420–421, 425–428
  Netscape and Microsoft differences, 6–7
  scripting languages versus, 6, 75, 105
  W3C standardization, 9
  See also Microsoft object model; Netscape
    object model
objects
  attaching filters to, 193
  creating "base" objects to hide
    implementation details, 386–388
  creating DHTML equalizer objects, 388–399
  creating extended objects, 388

creating with JavaScript, 54
See also Microsoft object model; Netscape
    object model
OffX parameter (drop shadow filter), 197
OffY parameter (drop shadow filter), 197
one-pixel GIFs, 5, 151
online catalog
    introduction and entry pages, 448–450
    main page, 450–454
opacity effect in Netscape, 345–347
opacity parameter (alpha filter), 195
Open Profiling Standard (OPS), cookies versus,
    256
opener property (JavaScript), 70–71
Opener property (VBScript), 96
opening
    browser window (IE), 517–518
    browser window (Navigator), 525–526
    new window, button for, 110–111
open_toc function
    cross-browser, 507
    IE, 495
    Navigator, 479
operators
    JavaScript, 58
    VBScript, 83
OPS (Open Profiling Standard), cookies versus,
    256
Option Explicit flag (VBScript), 77
"or", Boolean, 58
Oregon Naturalist e-zine example. See
    progressive documents (cross-browser)
outerHTML property (IE)
    marquee element example, 140
    overview, 132
    tic-tac-toe example, 132–134
outerText property (IE)
    overview, 132
    tic-tac-toe example, 132–134
outset border style value, 30
overflow property
    IE, 159, 489
    Navigator, 296

P

padding properties (CSS1), 26–28, 513
    style rules and, 27
    syntax, 27
padding properties (JASS), 333, 334–335
page buttons. *See* article and page buttons
Password object (Navigator), 261
Path Control (IE), 173

pc, measurement unit, 21
Phase parameter (wave filter), 204
pick_number function, 436–437, 449
pictures. *See* images
pinpoint light filter effect, 206–211
pipe symbol (|). *See* vertical bar (|)
Play method (transition filter), 211
plug-ins, 5
positioning HTML elements (cross-browser)
    cross-browser compatibility issues, 384–386
    dynamically using CSS1 positioning,
        404–408
    moving elements to shopping cart, 439–443
    presentation page components, 399–401
positioning HTML elements (IE), 151–177
    absolute positioning, 155
    animating elements, 171–173
    clip property, 158–159
    combining relative and absolute
        positioning, 157–158
    containers for elements, 153–154
    CSS1 positioning properties, 154–161
    dynamically changing positions, 167–170
    example, 152, 174–176
    interactive drag-and-drop example,
        224–230
    layering elements along z-axis, 161–167
    overflow property, 159
    overview, 8, 151–153
    relative positioning, 155–156
    style object positioning properties, 170
    style sheets for, 156–157
    switching style sheets, 167–169
    visibility property, 159–161
    z-index property, 163–167
positioning HTML elements (Navigator),
        287–319
    absolute positioning, 290
    animating the menu bar, 312–314
    animating using layers, 307–311
    clip property, 294–295
    combining relative and absolute
        positioning, 292–293
    containers for elements, 289–290
    CSS1 positioning properties, 290–298
    dynamically changing positions, 304–307
    example, 287–289, 314–318
    HTML elements supporting CSSP
        positioning, 296
    interactive drag-and-drop example,
        357–365
    layering elements, 298–304, 341–342
        (continued)

positioning HTML elements (Navigator),
    (continued)
  overflow property, 296
  overview, 8, 287
  relative positioning, 291
  style sheets for, 292, 306–307
  visibility property, 296–298
  z-index property, 300–304
Positive parameter (drop shadow filter), 197
post_load function
  cross-browser, 500–501, 504
  IE, 486–487, 491
  Navigator, 472, 473, 479, 481
pound sign (#) in CSS1 syntax, 21
presentation, interactive. *See* interactive
    presentation (cross-browser)
prev_page function, 435
PrivilegeManager object (Navigator), 283–284
privileges, console mode, 283–284
procedural-level variables (VBScript), 76
procedures (VBScript), 86–87
progressive documents (cross-browser),
    457–509
  article and page buttons (cross-browser),
    503–508
  article and page buttons (IE), 484–494
  article and page buttons (Navigator),
    467–477
  combining Navigator and IE approaches,
    499–508
  common elements, 459–462
  defined, 458
  e-zines, 457–458
  IE-specific application, 481–499
  layout (cross-browser), 499–500
  layout (IE), 482–484
  layout (Navigator), 462–467
  Navigator-specific application, 462–481
  Remember button (cross-browser), 500–503
  Remember button (IE), 497–499
  Remember button (Navigator), 479–481
  screen_resolution object, 460
  style sheets, 459–460
  TOC button (cross-browser), 500–503
  TOC button (IE), 495–497
  TOC button (Navigator), 477–479
  tools for, 458–459
properties
  background properties (CSS1), 37–40,
    181–182, 514
  background properties (CSS1), 181–182
  block-level properties (JASS), 332–336
  box properties (CSS1), 23–31, 511–513

CSS1 positioning properties (IE), 154–161
CSS1 positioning properties (Navigator),
    290–298
CSS1 properties, 17
document object properties (IE), 111–112,
    519–520
document object properties (Navigator),
    253–254, 536
event object properties (IE), 92–93, 135,
    220–221, 529
event object properties (Navigator), 65, 265,
    540
filter properties (IE), 193–214
font properties (CSS1), 31–34, 182, 513
font properties (JASS), 325–328
history object properties (IE), 116, 521–522
history object properties (Navigator), 258,
    537–538
inheritance from containing parent, 187
inheritance of CSS1 style sheet properties,
    46, 47
JASS style properties, 325–339
layer object properties (Navigator),
    271–272, 542–543
list properties (CSS1), 40–42, 515
location object properties (IE), 116, 521–522
location object properties (Navigator), 258,
    537–538
miscellaneous JASS properties, 336–339
navigator object properties (IE), 116,
    521–522
navigator object properties (Navigator),
    258, 537–538
screen object properties (IE), 126, 526
screen object properties (Navigator), 265,
    542
ShowModalDialog method properties, 97–98,
    518–519
style object positioning properties (IE), 170
style object properties (IE), 120–123,
    523–526
text properties (CSS1), 34–37, 182, 514–515
text properties (JASS), 328–332
TextRange object (IE), 527
window object properties (IE), 107–108, 516
window object properties (Navigator), 72,
    246–247, 531–532
window properties (VBScript), 96–97
pt, measurement unit, 21
px, measurement unit, 21

Q

query methods, 113

R

Radio object (Navigator), 261
rect function, 388
relative positioning (IE)
    absolute positioning combined with,
        157–158
    overview, 155–156
relative positioning (Navigator)
    absolute positioning combined with, 292–293
    overview, 291
reload function, 507
Remember button
    cross-browser, 500–503
    IE, 497–499
    Navigator, 479–481
remember function
    IE, 497
    Navigator, 479
removing
    constructive versus destructive changes, 462
    filters, 194
Reset object (Navigator), 261
resize events, 502, 508
resolution
    testing (Navigator), 468–469
    testing color depth and resolution (cross-
        browser), 460
    testing color depth and resolution (IE),
        126–128
    testing color depth and resolution
        (Navigator), 265–266
returnValue property of event object (IE), 228,
    231
revealTrans method (transition filter), 211
reverse_cycle function, 407
RGB values for colors, 22, 23
ridge border style value, 30
rollover effect, 182–183, 355–357
rows collection, 143–146
    with data binding, 145
    example, 143–145, 146
    overview, 143

S

scalar data types
    JavaScript, 53–55
    VBScript, 77–80

screen object (IE), 126–128
    overview, 126
    properties, 126, 526
    testing color depth and resolution, 126–128,
        265–266, 460
    testing resolution, 468–469
screen object (Navigator), 265–266
    overview, 265
    properties, 265, 542
    testing color depth and resolution, 265–266
screen_resolution object, 460
script signing, 281–286
    activate codebase principals, 281–282
    certificates for, 281–282, 286
    console mode, 282–285
    overview, 246, 249, 281
scripting
    cross-browser compatibility issues, 9, 384–386
    ECMA standard, 10
    IE 4.0 and, 9
    interactivity scripting techniques, 419–421
    object models versus, 6, 75
    See also JavaScript; VBScript
script-level variables (VBScript), 76, 77
scripts collection, 148
security
    console mode, 281–285
    signed scripting, 246, 249, 281–286
Select Case statement (VBScript), 83–84
Select object (Navigator), 261
selection object (IE), 136
semicolon (;) in style definitions, 20
set_articles function
    IE, 486
    Navigator, 469–470
set_cookie function
    IE, 114
    Navigator, 254–255
    progressive document example, 461, 476,
        479, 500
set_current_article function
    IE, 498
    Navigator, 480, 481
setInterval function
    JavaScript, 68–70
    VBScript, 93, 95–96
set_menu function
    cross-browser, 504
    IE, 487–488
setTimeout function
    JavaScript, 68
    in make_move function, 441
    VBScript, 93–95

shadow filter
  described, 196
  emulating in Netscape, 345–347
  example, 197–198
  parameters, 197
  syntax, 196
shadows
  blur filter effect, 203–206
  drop shadow filter effect, 196–198
  shadow filter effect, 196–198
shareable methods (Navigator), 252–253,
    534–535
Shift key, testing for, 228
show_article function
  cross-browser, 504, 505, 506–507
  IE, 489–490
  Navigator, 472–473
show_highlight function, 356
show_me function, 388–391
ShowModalDialog method
  opening window using, 96, 98–100
  properties, 97–98, 518–519
Siegal, David, 5, 151
signed scripting, 281–286
  activate codebase principals, 281–282
  certificates for, 281–282, 286
  console mode, 282–285
  overview, 246, 249, 281
sizing
  fonts using font-size property, 31, 32
  fonts using JASS, 325
  shrinking images with clip property, 294–295
slide show effect, 191–193
solid border style value, 30
spacing
  letter-spacing property (CSS1), 35, 36
  margin properties (CSS1), 24–26, 512
  margin properties (JASS), 323–324, 333,
    334
  padding properties (CSS1), 26–28, 513
  padding properties (JASS), 333, 334–335
  word-spacing property (CSS1), 35, 36
<SPAN> tag, grouping and positioning elements
    with, 154
srcElement property of event object (IE), 134,
    187
start_number function, 443–444
start_rotate function, 405
startX parameter (alpha filter), 195
startY parameter (alpha filter), 195
static HTML, limitations of, 4
stop method (Navigator), 252
Strength parameter

blur filter, 204
wave filter, 204
stub hypertext links, event capturing with,
    353–354, 363, 420, 421–425
<STYLE> tags
  style sheet rule declarations, 19–20
  TYPE attribute, 19
style object (IE), 118–126
  Click event example, 124
  mouseover event examples, 124–125
  overview, 118
  positioning properties, 170
  presentation-style Web page example,
    118–120
  properties, 120–123, 523–526
style parameter (alpha filter), 195
style sheets. See Cascading Style Sheets (CSS1);
    JavaScript Accessible Style Sheets
    (JASS)
styleSheets collection, 141, 148–149
sub keyword value (vertical-align property), 36
Submit object (Navigator), 261
subroutines (VBScript), 86–87
super keyword value (vertical-align
    property), 36
switch statement (JavaScript), 59

T

tables
  cells collection, 143–146
  positioning with, 6, 151, 153–154
  rows collection, 143–146
tagName property (IE)
  accessing elements with, 188
  printing all on page, 141–143
tags specifier (JASS), 322–323
testing
  for browser type and version, 116–118,
    258–259, 385, 444, 463
  for color depth and resolution, 126–128,
    265–266, 460
  DHTML equalizer objects, 391–394
  for resolution, 468–469
  for Shift or Ctrl key, 228
text
  changing with mouse movement, 182–184
  displaying on load event, 231
  hiding and showing with mouse movement,
    190–191, 232–237, 368–371, 374–378
  JASS properties, 328–332
  shrinking with clip property, 295
Text object (Navigator), 261

text properties (CSS1), 34-37
  defined, 35
  for script references, 182
  syntax, 35-36, 514-515
text-align property (CSS1)
  defined, 35
  syntax, 35
textAlign property (JASS), 330-331
Textarea object (Navigator), 261
text-bottom keyword value (vertical-align
    property), 36
text-decoration property (CSS1)
  adding underlines and overlines, 35
  blink value, 37
  syntax, 36
textDecoration property (JASS), 329-330
text-indent property (CSS1), 35
textIndent property (JASS), 331
TextRange object (IE), 128-132
  creating, 128-129
  methods, 130-132, 527-528
  overview, 127
  properties, 527
text-top keyword value (vertical-align
    property), 36
text-transform property (CSS1), 35, 36
textTransform property (JASS), 331
theend function, 410, 411-412
tic-tac-toe example
  IE, 132-134
  Navigator, 277-280
timer functions
  JavaScript, 68-70
  VBScript, 93-96
tips windows
  Microsoft example, 232-237
  Netscape example, 367-371
TOC button
  cross-browser, 500-503
  IE, 495-497
  Navigator, 477-479
toc_page function
  Internet Explorer, 496, 497
  Navigator, 478-479
top keyword value (vertical-align property), 36
transition filter, 211-214
  applying to entire page, 214
  effects, 212
  example, 212-213
  methods, 211
  overview, 211-212
transparency effects with filters (IE), 194-196
transparent GIFs, one-pixel image, 5, 151

U
update_menu function
  cross-browser, 507
  IE, 491-492
  Navigator, 473-474, 476

V
variables
  assigning filters to, 194
  effect variable, 402
  JavaScript, 52-53
  VBScript, 76-77
  See also arrays
VBScript, 75-101
  arrays, 80-81
  capturing user events, 88-93
  collections, 140-149
  conditional statements, 82-84
  creating variables, 76, 77
  JavaScript versus, 110
  JavaScript with, 142
  looping statements, 84-86
  multiple windows, working with, 96-100
  naming variables, 76-77
  procedures, 86-87
  scalar data types, 77-80
  timer functions, 93-96
  See also JavaScript; scripting
vertical bar (|)
  Boolean "or" (||), 58
  in CSS1 syntax, 20
vertical-align property (CSS1), 35, 36
verticalAlign property (JASS), 330-331
visibility property
  button highlight example (Navigator),
    371-373
  creating "base" objects to hide
    implementation details, 386-388
  creating DHTML equalizer objects (IE),
    388-390, 391-396
  creating DHTML equalizer objects
    (Navigator), 390-394, 396-399
  display property versus, 188-191, 234
  emulating HTML change (cross-browser),
    408-412
  help tips example (IE), 232-237
  hiding and showing images (IE), 223-224
  hiding and showing images (Navigator),
    355-357
  (continued)

visibility property *(continued)*
    hiding and showing page contents
        (cross-browser), 401–403
    hiding and showing text (IE), 190, 237–240
    hiding and showing text (Navigator),
        367–371, 374–379
    kid's entry page components, 433–434
    overview, 159–161, 296–298
    slide show effect (IE), 191–193
    using layers (Navigator), 341–345
visual filters. *See* filter properties (IE)

W

W3C. *See* World Wide Web Consortium (W3C)
warning messages. *See* messages to user
warping, wave filter effect, 203–206
wave filter
    described, 203
    example, 204–206
    parameters, 204
    syntax, 203
Web browsers
    finding display size, 226–227
    opening browser window (IE), 517–518
    opening browser window (Navigator),
        535–536
    testing for browser type and version,
        116–118, 258–259, 385, 444, 463
    See also Internet Explorer; Netscape
        Navigator
Web pages
    content prior to dynamic HTML, 4–7
    creating cross-browser Web page object,
        384–389
    CSS1 style sheets in, 43–45
    kid's Web page, 428–455
    presentation-style page example, 118–120
    prior to dynamic HTML, 4–6
    for testing DHTML equalizer objects,
        391–394
    See also interactive pages (cross-browser);
        interactive presentation (cross-browser);
        kid's Web page; progressive documents
        (cross-browser)
while statement (JavaScript), 60
whiteSpace property (JASS), 337, 339
width property (JASS), 333, 336

window attributes (Navigator), 249–250
window keyword, 107
window object (IE), 107–111
    example, 109–111
    methods, 109
    overview, 107
    properties, 107–108, 516
window object (Navigator), 246–253
    example, 247–248
    methods, 250–253, 533–535
    overview, 70–71, 246
    properties, 72, 246–247, 531–532
    window attributes, 249–250
window status, button for, 110–111
window-level event capturing (JavaScript),
    66–68
windows, multiple
    JavaScript with, 70–72
    VBScript with, 96–100
word-spacing property (CSS1), 35, 36
World Wide Web Consortium (W3C)
    CSS1 standard, 7, 152
    Document Object Model (DOM) working
        group, 9

X

x-ray filter
    described, 201
    example, 201–203
    syntax, 201

Z

z-axis, layering elements along (IE), 161–167
z-index property (IE)
    drag-and-drop example, 224, 227–228
    menu bar example, 164–167
    overview, 163
z-index property (Navigator)
    drag-and-drop example, 358, 362–363, 364
    menu bar example, 301–304
    overview, 300–301
    progressive document example, 482
z-order value for shopping cart, 442

IDG Books Worldwide, Inc. End-User License Agreement

READ THIS. You should carefully read these terms and conditions before opening the software packet(s) included with this book ("Book"). This is a license agreement ("Agreement") between you and IDG Books Worldwide, Inc. ("IDGB"). By opening the accompanying software packet(s), you acknowledge that you have read and accept the following terms and conditions. If you do not agree and do not want to be bound by such terms and conditions, promptly return the Book and the unopened software packet(s) to the place you obtained them for a full refund.

1. **License Grant.** IDGB grants to you (either an individual or entity) a nonexclusive license to use one copy of the enclosed software program(s) (collectively, the "Software") solely for your own personal or business purposes on a single computer (whether a standard computer or a workstation component of a multiuser network). The Software is in use on a computer when it is loaded into temporary memory (RAM) or installed into permanent memory (hard disk, CD-ROM, or other storage device). IDGB reserves all rights not expressly granted herein.

2. **Ownership.** IDGB is the owner of all right, title, and interest, including copyright, in and to the compilation of the Software recorded on the disk(s) or CD-ROM ("Software Media"). Copyright to the individual programs recorded on the Software Media is owned by the author or other authorized copyright owner of each program. Ownership of the Software and all proprietary rights relating thereto remain with IDGB and its licensers.

3. **Restrictions on Use and Transfer.**

(a) You may only (i) make one copy of the Software for backup or archival purposes, or (ii) transfer the Software to a single hard disk, provided that you keep the original for backup or archival purposes. You may not (i) rent or lease the Software, (ii) copy or reproduce the Software through a LAN or other network system or through any computer subscriber system or bulletin-board system, or (iii) modify, adapt, or create derivative works based on the Software.

(b) You may not reverse engineer, decompile, or disassemble the Software. You may transfer the Software and user documentation on a permanent basis, provided that the transferee agrees to accept the terms and conditions of this Agreement and you retain no copies. If the Software is an update or has been updated, any transfer must include the most recent update and all prior versions.

4. **Restrictions on Use of Individual Programs.** You must follow the individual requirements and restrictions detailed for each individual program in Appendix B, "What's On the CD-ROM," of this Book. These limitations are also contained in the individual license agreements recorded on the Software Media. These limitations may include a requirement that after using the program for a specified period of time, the user must pay a registration fee or discontinue use. By opening the Software packet(s), you will be agreeing to abide by the licenses and restrictions for these individual programs that are detailed in Appendix B, "What's On the CD-ROM," and on the Software Media. None of the material on this Software Media or listed in this Book may ever be redistributed, in original or modified form, for commercial purposes.

5. **Limited Warranty.**

(a) IDGB warrants that the Software and Software Media are free from defects in materials and workmanship under normal use for a period of sixty (60) days from the date of purchase of this Book. If IDGB receives notification within the warranty period of defects in materials or workmanship, IDGB will replace the defective Software Media.

(b) IDGB AND THE AUTHOR OF THE BOOK DISCLAIM ALL OTHER WARRANTIES, EXPRESS OR IMPLIED, INCLUDING WITHOUT LIMITATION IMPLIED WARRANTIES OF MERCHANTABILITY AND FITNESS FOR A PARTICULAR PURPOSE, WITH RESPECT TO THE SOFTWARE, THE PROGRAMS, THE SOURCE CODE CONTAINED THEREIN, AND/OR THE TECHNIQUES DESCRIBED IN THIS BOOK. IDGB DOES NOT WARRANT THAT THE FUNCTIONS CONTAINED IN THE SOFTWARE WILL MEET YOUR REQUIREMENTS OR THAT THE OPERATION OF THE SOFTWARE WILL BE ERROR FREE.

(c) This limited warranty gives you specific legal rights, and you may have other rights that vary from jurisdiction to jurisdiction.

6. Remedies.

(a) IDGB's entire liability and your exclusive remedy for defects in materials and workmanship shall be limited to replacement of the Software Media, which may be returned to IDGB with a copy of your receipt at the following address: Software Media Fulfillment Department, Attn.: *Dynamic HTML*, IDG Books Worldwide, Inc., 7260 Shadeland Station, Ste. 100, Indianapolis, IN 46256, or call 1-800-762-2974. Please allow three to four weeks for delivery. This Limited Warranty is void if failure of the Software Media has resulted from accident, abuse, or misapplication. Any replacement Software Media will be warranted for the remainder of the original warranty period or thirty (30) days, whichever is longer.

(b) In no event shall IDGB or the author be liable for any damages whatsoever (including without limitation damages for loss of business profits, business interruption, loss of business information, or any other pecuniary loss) arising from the use of or inability to use the Book or the Software, even if IDGB has been advised of the possibility of such damages.

(c) Because some jurisdictions do not allow the exclusion or limitation of liability for consequential or incidental damages, the above limitation or exclusion may not apply to you.

7. U.S. Government Restricted Rights.
Use, duplication, or disclosure of the Software by the U.S. Government is subject to restrictions stated in paragraph (c)(1)(ii) of the Rights in Technical Data and Computer Software clause of DFARS 252.227-7013, and in subparagraphs (a) through (d) of the Commercial Computer – Restricted Rights clause at FAR 52.227-19, and in similar clauses in the NASA FAR supplement, when applicable.

8. General.
This Agreement constitutes the entire understanding of the parties and revokes and supersedes all prior agreements, oral or written, between them and may not be modified or amended except in a writing signed by both parties hereto that specifically refers to this Agreement. This Agreement shall take precedence over any other documents that may be in conflict herewith. If any one or more provisions contained in this Agreement are held by any court or tribunal to be invalid, illegal, or otherwise unenforceable, each and every other provision shall remain in full force and effect.